THOMAS CARLYLE

Thomas Carlyle

John Morrow

hambledon
continuum

Hambledon Continuum, a Continuum imprint
The Tower Building, 11 York Road, London SE1 7NX, UK
80 Maiden Lane, Suite 704, New York, NY 10038, USA

First Published 2006

ISBN 1 85285 318 2

A description of this book is available from the
British Library and from the Library of Congress.

Typeset by Egan-Reid Ltd, Auckland, New Zealand.
Printed in Great Britain by MPG Books Ltd, Cornwall.

Distributed in the United States and Canada
exclusively by Palgrave Macmillan,
a division of St Martin's Press.

Contents

Illustrations

For Di
With my love and thanks

Preface

Long recognised as one of the most powerful and widely-read figures in the Victorian intellectual landscape, the formative stages of Thomas Carlyle's life and career were, in fact, pre-Victorian. Carlyle's formal education was completed before the end of the Napoleonic War and his identification of a distinctive literary mission took place before British society had come to grips with the impact of the conclusion of that war. Having first begun to make his mark in the 1820s as an essayist and translator, by the late 1830s Carlyle had laid the basis for a reputation that grew steadily over the next three decades. His writings were directed originally to the educated middle and upper classes, but their appeal spread far more widely, facilitated by the cheap, 'popular' editions of his works that were published in the 1870s. These books continued to sell strongly after his death in 1881, and were augmented by volumes containing previously unpublished writings on autobiographical, historical, literary and political themes. Odd volumes and broken sets of these nineteenth-century editions that languish on the least accessible shelves of modern second-hand bookshops provide mute testimony to Carlyle's popularity throughout the Victorian period.

Although Carlyle professed weariness and disgust at the prospect of being the object of biographers, his own performances in this role (most notably as a strongly interventionist editor of Oliver Cromwell's letters and speeches, and as author of a massive study of the life of Frederick the Great of Prussia) and his contemporary readers' readiness to see associations between cultural significance, intellect, moral insight and spiritual sensibility, made it inevitable that he would suffer this fate. The burst of biographical activity that occurred in the decades after his death has persisted into the twenty-first century. Carlyle's life, and particularly his complex and at times intensely difficult relationship with his wife, Jane Welsh Carlyle, remain of sufficient general interest to warrant large-scale biographical studies and the occasional article in the literary press. A few of his books have been included in series such as the Oxford World's Classics and he has recently, if belatedly, joined a number of his contemporaries – Matthew Arnold, Lord Byron, Samuel Taylor Coleridge, Charles Dickens and John Stuart Mill – in being granted the accolade of a collected edition produced in accordance with the standards of modern scholarship. This project is in its infancy but a definitive edition of the Carlyles' *Collected Letters* covering the period to September 1856 fills thirty-one handsome volumes. In common with other students of Carlyle I am greatly indebted to Professors K. J. Fielding and Ian Campbell and their colleagues for their ongoing work on this edition and have drawn extensively on it. When quoting from these volumes and from manuscript sources I have expanded contractions and given abbreviated words in full. It is a matter for regret that the *festschrift* for Professor Fielding, *The Carlyles at Home and Abroad*, came into my hands after this book had gone to press. This collection, edited by David R. Sorensen and Rodger L. Tarr, includes essays on a range of topics relevant to themes addressed in the present study.

In this book I have drawn on the *Collected Letters* and other primary and secondary sources to establish the context for a study of Carlyle's ideas that focuses on what both he and many of his nineteenth-century readers took to be a distinctive mission. This mission directed the choice of subjects on which Carlyle wrote and the genres which he used. His historical and biographical studies, for example, dealt with the relationships between the intellectual and moral character traits of significant historical actors, the particular requirements of the times in which they lived, and the aspirations and capacities of their contemporaries. In common with his other works, these studies were meant to advance Carlyle's mission to his contemporaries.

The very idea of a mission presupposed a sense of profound dissatisfaction with prevailing views on the aspirations and needs of individuals, their relationship with one another and the structures of ideas and institutions that were necessary to give form and effect to them. In Carlyle's case, this dissatisfaction was apparent in the strongly critical cast of his writings and in an increasingly marked tendency to upbraid his contemporaries for their myopia, self-indulgence and capacity for self-delusion. It was apparent also in the markedly radical stance he took, both to ideas and practices inherited from the past and to a wide range of alternatives offered to them by writers from across the political, religious and social spectrum. Although Carlyle's personal outlook and writings were tinged with despair, he offered his readers a pathway to deliverance that they were keen to follow. Because the implications of Carlyle's mission could be understood in a variety of ways, his writings found an extensive, attentive and admiring readership throughout the Victorian period. The idea of a mission, however, points to a highly prescriptive view of literature that was quite different from that of later periods and is quite foreign to our world. For this reason, and also because Carlyle promoted ideas on such themes as democracy, race and liberalism that clash with modern sensibilities, the popularity of his writings has not outlived the particular sense of crisis that prompted them.

The substantive chapters of this book trace the various stages of Carlyle's mission, focusing on the ideas on religion, personal and social morality, and politics that were central to it. This approach reflects the position taken by one of Carlyle's contemporary critics when evaluating the Library Edition published in 1870. On that occasion John Morley, editor of the *Fortnightly Review*, a Liberal MP who later obtained Cabinet rank, wrote that with Carlyle 'History and literature have been ... what they will always be with wise and understanding minds of creative and even of the higher critical faculty – only embodiments, illustrations, experiments, for ideas about religion, conduct, society, history, government, and all the other great heads and departments of a complete social doctrine.'

Acknowledgements

In the course of writing this book I have drawn on the Carlyle papers held in the National Library of Scotland and on its printed holdings. I am most grateful to the Trustees of the Library for permission to quote from these papers and to reading room staff for their efficient and courteous assistance. The material from the Norman and Charlotte Strouce Collection in note 86 page 248 is quoted with permission of Special Collections, University Library UC Santa Cruz. I must acknowledge my gratitude to librarians at the University of Auckland Library, the Bodleian Library, the Cambridge University Library, Edinburgh University Library and the Victoria University of Wellington Library. Linda Skippings, the curator, was most welcoming and helpful when I visited Carlyle's house in Chelsea in August 2001. The author and publishers are grateful to Columbia University for permission to reproduce plates 7 and 9, and to the National Trust for permission to reproduce plates 3 and 8.

Victoria University granted me a period of study leave in 2001 to work on this book and funded my travel to Edinburgh to consult material in the National Library of Scotland. I am most grateful for this support. My stay in Edinburgh was enriched by an attachment to the Institute for Advanced Studies in the Humanities. I acknowledge with gratitude financial support provided by the University of Auckland which enabled me to travel to the United Kingdom in 2003 to consult material held in libraries in Cambridge and Oxford.

I have benefited greatly from a range of responses to early versions of the chapters which follow. In October 2001 Professor Gareth Stedman-Jones invited me to give a paper to the history of political ideas seminar that he chairs at Cambridge; a few days later I presented this paper at a seminar in the Institute for Advanced Studies in the Humanities at the University of Edinburgh. Professor Jonathan Scott of the University of Pittsburgh has commented extensively on a number of chapters, as has Professor Miles Taylor of the University of York. Professor Miles Fairburn of the University of Canterbury, Dr Patrick Maloney of Victoria University and Dr Duncan Kelley of the University of Sheffield have made valuable suggestions on particular sections of the book. Professor Mark Francis of the University of Canterbury, Professor J. A. W. Gunn of Queen's University, Ontario, Emeritus Professor Carole Keene of Southern Illinois University, Professor John Pratt of Victoria University, Associate Professors Ruth Barton and Frederick Voit of Auckland University, Susan Grogan of Victoria University and Derek Dow of Auckland have responded most helpfully to particular inquiries. Jocelyn Gamble of the Faculty of Arts at The University of Auckland has provided valuable clerical assistance in the latter stages of this project. In thanking these people for their generous assistance I of course remain responsible for the shortcoming of this study. My wife Diana Morrow has read drafts of the whole book in a number of stages of completeness, and has made invaluable suggestions for improvement. I dedicate this work to her in very partial recognition of her ongoing help and encouragement.

Abbreviations

The following abbreviations are used in the notes. Unless otherwise indicated all references to works by Thomas Carlyle are the edition of the *Works of Thomas Carlyle* identified in the Bibliography, p. 274.

Chartism	Thomas Carlyle, *Chartism*, *CME*, vi.
CL	*Collected Letters of Thomas and Jane Welsh Carlyle*, ed. Charles Richard Sanders, K. J. Fielding, Ian Campbell et al. (Edinburgh and Durham, North Carolina, 1970–).
CME	Thomas Carlyle, *Critical and Miscellaneous Essays*.
CN	*Carlyle Newsletter*.
CSA	*Carlyle Studies Annual*.
FG	Thomas Carlyle, *History of Friedrich II of Prussia, called Frederick the Great*.
FR	Thomas Carlyle, *The French Revolution: A History*.
Froude, *EL*	*Thomas Carlyle: A History of the First Forty Years of His Life, 1795–1835*, new edition, 2 vols (1896).
Froude, *LL*	*Thomas Carlyle: A History of His Life in London, 1834–1881*, new edition, 2 vols (1897).
HHW	Thomas Carlyle, *On Heroes, Hero-Worship and The Heroic in History*.
John Sterling	Thomas Carlyle, *The Life of John Sterling*.
LDP	Thomas Carlyle, *Latter-Day Pamphlets*.
LHR	Thomas Carlyle, *Lectures on the History of Literature*, second edition (1892).
Life of Schiller	Thomas Carlyle, *Friedrich Schiller: Comprehending An Examination of His Works*.
Marrs	*The Letters of Thomas Carlyle to his Brother Alexander With Related Family Letters*, ed. Edwin W. Marrs, Jr. (Cambridge, Massachusetts, 1968).
NLS	National Library of Scotland.
OC	Thomas Carlyle, *Oliver Cromwell's Letter and Speeches With Elucidations*.
Past and Present	Thomas Carlyle, *Past and Present*.

Reminiscences	Thomas Carlyle, *Reminiscences*, ed. K. J. Fielding and Ian Campbell (Oxford, 1997).
Rescued Essays	*Rescued Essays of Thomas Carlyle*, ed. Percy Newberry (1892).
SR	*Sartor Resartus: The Life and Opinions of Herr Teufeldröckh.*
Two Notebooks	*Two Notebooks of Thomas Carlyle*, ed. Charles E. Norton (1898).
Two Reminiscences	*Two Reminiscences of Thomas Carlyle*, ed. John Clubbe (Durham, North Carolina, 1974).
Wilhelm Meister	Thomas Carlyle, *Wilhelm Meister's Apprenticeship And Travels.*

Beginnings

On 10 February 1881 a procession of five carriages made its way from the railway station at Ecclefechan, a village in south Dumfrieshire less than ten miles from the border between Scotland and England, to the parish burial ground. The leading carriage carried the body of Thomas Carlyle; among the mourners in the other carriages were his youngest and only surviving brother James and his niece Mary Aitken Carlyle. Three distinguished members of the Victorian intelligentsia were also there: James Anthony Froude, a noted historian whose public career had begun with a controversial statement doubting the truth of Christianity and was to conclude in a welter of criticism over his role as Carlyle's biographer; William Lecky, another historian; and John Tyndall, FRS, a leading figure in the scientific establishment. Carlyle's last illness and death attracted national and international attention. Queen Victoria sent a messenger to his home in Chelsea to enquire after his condition, while admirers at home and abroad were kept informed by press reports. Carlyle's burial beside his parents in the bleak mid winter landscape of Dumfrieshire was, however, a local, and largely private affair. No public notice was given of the funeral, and, except for a handful of family members and friends, and a few journalists, it was attended only by local people. School children looked on from outside the cemetery gate and a hundred or so young farm workers stood in the graveyard itself. The interment took place without ceremony, prayer or a word of commendation, according to the custom of the Scottish Calvinist churches.[1]

An outpouring of public memorialising followed the mute privacy of Carlyle's funeral. Dean Stanley, thwarted in his attempt to have his friend buried in Westminster Abbey, overlooked Carlyle's hostility to the Church of England and his dislike of gothic architecture, and preached at a memorial service in the Abbey. In the weeks that followed, numerous obituaries and weighty articles of appreciation were published in international, national, provincial newspapers and periodicals. One of the earliest of these notices, appearing in the *Times* two days after Carlyle's death, recorded the close of a 'well-ordered, full, stately, and complete life.'[2] These responses to Carlyle's death reflected his distinctive standing both in Victorian literary culture, and among a far broader range of people who looked to men of letters to provide assurance in the face of religious perplexities, enlightenment, inspiration and moral guidance.

Although in the course of his career Carlyle became increasingly frustrated at his contemporaries' failure to grasp fully the significance of what he had to say, the responses to his death indicated that readers shared his view that his writings were key elements in a transformative mission. Carlyle saw literature as a vehicle by means of which he might encourage his contemporaries to respond productively to the challenges posed by the far reaching economic, political and social changes taking place in western societies. He regarded these challenges as being particularly daunting because it was becoming increasingly clear that conventional Christianity could no longer provide the focus of intellect and belief. Carlyle's mission was sustained for four decades in a wide range of critical essays, in *Sartor Resartus* (an experimental prose essay on the modern condition), a series of historical studies of the French Revolution, English puritanism, medieval faith and authority, a monumental biography of Frederick the Great and a series of works of literary, social and political criticism.

From the early part of his career Carlyle was known to the reading public as an ardent admirer of Goethe. His respect for this writer was, however, matched by that he felt for Shakespeare. His letters and published works abound with more or less direct allusions to Shakespeare's plays. Carlyle was particularly struck by Prospero's expression of what he regarded as a profound truth about the cosmic significance of individual lives:

> We are such stuff
> As dreams are made on, and our little life
> Is rounded with a sleep. (*Tempest*, Act IV, Scene 1)

In Carlyle's case, the journey began where it ended, in Ecclefechan.

Thomas Carlyle was born in a modest house in the village on 4 December 1795. He was the eldest son of James and Margaret Carlyle (neé Aitkin) who married in the year of his birth, a little over two years after the death of James's first wife. Carlyle was deeply attached to his parents. James was commemorated in reflections written immediately after his death in 1832 but published posthumously in *Reminiscences of Thomas Carlyle*. Margaret Carlyle makes fleeting appearances in some of these essays, and is a significant presence in Carlyle's letters.

Carlyle's correspondence with his mother is marked by intense warmth and frequent expressions of affection and mutual consideration. James Carlyle's austere, direct and unforgiving manner endowed the relationship between father and son with a very different tone, but Carlyle nevertheless saw him as an exemplar of a range of traits that formed the basis of his own system of personal morality. Deep, unspoken tenderness expressed in the grasp of a handshake co-existed with what Carlyle described as 'dread' at his father's controlled wrath: 'passion never mastered him, or maddened him; it rather inspired him with new vehemence of insight, and more piercing emphasis of wisdom'. His son claimed that James

Carlyle's life demonstrated the value of unstintingly honest industry, remorseless veracity, an insistence on personal independence, indifference to mere rank and wealth, and 'wisely generous' economy.[3]

James Carlyle began his working life as a child-labourer on farms and then learned the mason's trade, using his expertise to set himself up as a partner in a building business. He pursued this occupation with considerable success, improving the economic position of his family and leaving numerous testaments to his commitment to honest work in the built environment of the Ecclefechan area. In 1815 James returned to agricultural work, this time as an independent tenant farmer at Mainhall, a few miles to the north west of Ecclefechan. According to local informants interviewed for a biographical essay published in 1877, the young James and his brothers ('the fighting masons of Ecclefechan') were renowned for their effective resort to unarmed violence in some of their dealings with those who offended their sense of right.[4] In his mature years, however, James's righteous pugnacity was called into the service of moral values derived from the perspective of the 'New Light Burgher Church'.

In his reminiscence of James Carlyle his son stressed the significance of his father's decision to join the Burgher Church: 'from this time ... may be dated his spiritual majority; his earthly Life was now enlightened and overcanopied by a heavenly: he was henceforth a Man'.[5] The 'Burgher Seceders', a sectarian offshoot of an offshoot of the established Church of Scotland, were noted for their hostility to elite control of clerical appointments, for stressing individual independence in religious matters, and for the importance they placed on the obligation to apply God's precepts directly to everyday life. This God, a stern manifestation of Calvinistic religious imagination, took a direct interest in human life and was unyieldingly severe on sinners and on those who mistook lip-service for true faith. The practice of the church focused on preaching the word of God in ways that imprinted these values in the hearts and minds of members of the congregation so that they became the consistent basis of all aspects of human life.

The impact of the faith and practice of this Church pervades Carlyle's account of his father, being reflected in his frequent use of direct quotations from the Scriptures when explaining the significance of James's life and death. The sectarian implications of attachment to the Burgher Church also left their mark on the social outlook of the Carlyles. They were proud and clannish, a stance that they thought was justified by the feeling that members of the family had, as Carlyle put it in a letter to one of his brothers, 'something original in our formation, and find, therefore less than common sympathy with others'.[6] They were also fiercely independent, self-sufficient, and utterly unyielding in the face of what they saw as unworthy social power. Independence and self-sufficiency were demonstrated in the family's preference for modesty and mutual self-support, its abhorrence of luxury and dependence, and its willingness to judge others while remaining indifferent to their judgements. Even after he forswore the use of his fists, James Carlyle had a reputation for direct, public condemnation of those who failed to measure up to his exacting standards. Neither social superiors, such as General Sharpe, an MP and a rich landlord, nor hapless farm labourers were spared from the lash of his withering, scornful, sarcastic, and at times, whimsical tongue.[7]

Not surprisingly, perhaps, given the close and self-sufficient character of his family circle, its outlook marked Carlyle's style of personal engagement and was apparent also in many of his writings on literature, history, society and politics. These works were marked by an absence of deference, by bold forthrightness and a willingness to pass judgement. At times they also exhibited a tendency to exaggeration, a penchant for harsh ridicule and, from the late 1840s, an upbraiding tone. But while there are many records of Carlyle's heated exchanges with those with whom he disagreed, he generally refrained from importing the blunt manners of rural Scotland into the drawing rooms of Edinburgh and London. He also possessed a tendency to geniality and a consideration for others that was not prominent in his father's character. The impatient intolerance of perceived shortcomings and the apparent lack of generosity that marked many private evaluations of friends, acquaintances and other contemporaries were tempered when Carlyle looked back on their lives. His obituary comments invariably mingled expressions of pity for human weakness with praise for specific achievements and for perceived virtues of character and action. The difference in tone between Carlyle's judgements on the quick and the dead might be attributed to an underlying strain of jealousy in his character. It probably owed something, however, to the complex feelings engendered by his view that questions about human immortality were among the unknown multitude of things beyond the scope of human reason. It might also have reflected his understanding of the implications of his commitment to truth, and the belief that, in summing up a life that had come to an end, due weight should be given to all the qualities exhibited in the course of it.

After the birth of her eldest son, Carlyle's mother had eight more children, three boys and five girls. His eldest sister, Jean, died in infancy in 1799; Margaret, born in 1803, died from cancer in 1830. Thomas's recollection of her – 'a comely, quiet, intelligent, affectionate and altogether mildly-lucent creature (tho' strong in heart and mind)' – typified the close, appreciative and affectionate relationships that he had with his brothers and sisters.[8] Both in later life and earlier, when his own material circumstances were far from prosperous, he provided financial support to other members of his family and took a keen and sympathetic interest in their affairs. He was particularly attached to Alexander ('Alick', born in 1797) and to John Carlyle ('Jack' born in 1801). After Alick's capital had been eroded significantly by a series of unsuccessful investments in farming, rural brokering and retailing, he emigrated (in 1843) to Canada.[9] Once clear of a situation where intense competition between small farmers encouraged landlords to charge rents that imposed very high risks on their tenants, Alick flourished. He farmed successfully in southern Ontario and brought up a large family. One of his sons visited Carlyle in old age and eventually married his niece, edited some of his letters and posthumous writings and led the family charge against Froude. Even when separated by the Atlantic Ocean, Alick's relationship with his older brother remained close, and was sustained by an extensive correspondence that was kept up until Alick's death in 1876. His last words, 'Is Tom coming from Edinburgh the morn?' and Carlyle's comment on them, testify to the strength of the bonds that bound them together: 'Poor Alick, my ever-faithful Brother come back across wide oceans and long decades of time to the scenes of brotherly companionship with me; and going out of the world, as it were, with his hand in mine. Many times he conveyed me to meet the Dumfries coach or to bring me home from it.'[10]

Carlyle took John under his wing when the latter followed him to attend the University of Edinburgh. They shared lodgings, and Carlyle gave John money and helped him secure bits and pieces of translating work to eke out support from family sources. After his brother graduated in medicine, Carlyle fretted about his prospects and wrung his hands over what he took to be his lack of focus and drive. 'Jack, poor Jack, I feel convinced is going to make a figure yet: he inherits a good head and an honest heart from his parents; and no bad habit of any kind has perverted these invaluable gifts. His only faults at present are his inexperience, and the very excess of his good qualities.'[11] As things turned out, John secured a lucrative post as a private physician and quite quickly accumulated sufficient capital to secure financial independence. His intellectual interests were not confined to medical science. He published a successful translation of Dante and was awarded the honorary degree of doctor of letters by his alma mater. It is common for Carlyle's biographers to dismiss John as dogged, self-willed and a little dull. These judgements are unduly harsh. It would have been hard to outshine Thomas Carlyle, and much of John's apparent doggedness may be attributed to his understandable reluctance to be consumed by the force of his elder brother's personality. John was prepared to offer Thomas independent and sensible advice on medical and financial matters, and tried to mitigate the air of hypochondria that pervaded his elder brother's household. He offered sharp critical comments on some of his writings from the late 1840s and early 1850s, and sometimes acted for Thomas in transactions with editors and publishers.[12] In later life, John Carlyle assumed a more significant role in his brother's affairs, overseeing renovations to his property, managing his bank accounts and investments, and chiding him for his unwillingness to come to grips with the details of his financial situation: 'I think that you cannot fail to understand the sense of the whole if you will only look at it steadily for a few minutes.'[13]

The area in which the Carlyle family lived was relatively prosperous, producing grain well in excess of the needs of the local population and being self-sufficient in potatoes, the staple of the poorer sections of the community.[14] The infant mortality rate in the Carlyle household was low by contemporary standards. This achievement no doubt owed something to genetic good luck, but says much about Margaret Carlyle's skills as a mother and housekeeper. It also reflects, however, the social and economic status of the family. When Carlyle's father died in 1832 he left £600 (about three times his son's annual income at this time) and property that was rented for £28p.a.[15] Although never remotely well-to-do, the Carlyles were by no means poorly off by the standards of the time and place, and were able to provide adequate, if somewhat austere, provision for their children. All the Carlyle children were better educated than their parents. James was a competent reader and writer, but Margaret never advanced beyond a very minimal level of written literacy, acquired late in life so that she might correspond directly with her much loved oldest child. While the financial, social and pedagogical tradition of the Scottish universities meant that they were far more open and democratic than their English counterparts, industry, frugality and good management by James and Margaret was crucial to the family's capacity to forego the youthful earnings of two of its sons, and to contribute in cash and in kind to the costs of a prolonged course of secondary and tertiary education.

Carlyle's early skill in reading, and his ready grasp of mathematics and rudi-mentary Latin, prompted the teacher in the elementary school at Ecclefechan to pay him special attention. When his progress in Latin had taken him beyond the competence of this teacher, arrangements were made for advanced tuition from a local clergyman. After three years' elementary schooling, Carlyle was sent in 1806 to attend the Annan Academy, five miles away as the crow flies. Judging from passages in *Sartor Resartus* and remarks on education in his unpublished papers, Carlyle found this move difficult. He exchanged a privileged position in a warm and supportive family for lodgings in a local Annan household. He also faced the challenge of adjusting from being a favoured pupil in a village school to being a stranger in the far more hostile environment of a secondary school for boys.

Although he did not enjoy his time at the Academy, Carlyle received a fairly good education there. He studied French, Geography, the Greek alphabet and Latin, and did well at these subjects. His attention was engaged most closely, however, with Mathematics, and through private reading rather than directed study, with a wide range of works of fiction and non-fiction, establishing thereby a habit that persisted throughout life. Even in the 1870s he continued to read widely, revisiting favourite works and taking up fashionable, recently published ones such as W. H. Mallock's *New Republic*, a 'wildly miserable burlesque of present opinions and speculations ... which I strode through not without some amusement as through a wild Atlantic of seething nonsense'.[16] When he entered the University of Edinburgh, in November 1809, Carlyle's taste for reading could be indulged more widely by drawing on the poorly housed but extensive collection in the university library. His diet at this time included the forty five volumes of Chambers' *British Essayists*, read through, according to one of his fellow students, without interruption.[17] In later life, Carlyle regarded access to the Library as one of the few positive boons of his University career. With characteristic exaggeration, he speculated that the growth of universities in early medieval Europe was directly attributable to the scarcity of books before the advent of printing.[18]

In the early nineteenth century, the Scottish universities catered to a far broader section of society than those in England. Classes were large, tuition fees were relatively low (two or three guineas a year) and living costs could be reduced to a minimum. Rather than residing in expensive colleges, Edinburgh undergraduates might lodge in cheap boarding houses in the picturesque but decaying quarters of the 'old town'. When Thomas Carlyle occupied such accommodation his family worried about its effect on his health and encouraged him to take preventative measures. Alick, for example, applauded his elder brother's practice of taking regular exercise, reporting that the family 'are satisfied not a little to hear that you make a point of walking before eating your porridge, it is certainly a line of conduct which every lank jaw't son of study ought to vouchsafe to follow, especially when situate in so unwholesome a climate as the old town of Edinburgh'.[19] In Carlyle's case, as in that of the many other university students from humble rural backgrounds, the cost of living in the city was reduced by relying on the family for basic foodstuffs and laundry services. His early correspondence is full of references to the arrangements necessary to secure supplies of food and clean clothes without recourse to the expensive and dubious products of Edinburgh shopkeepers and the services of local washerwomen. These habits died hard. When established in his own household in London, Carlyle continued to receive basic supplies (oats, butter, hams, and potatoes) from his family, including, on one occasion, a keg of illicit whiskey on which English duties had not been paid.[20]

Despite the scope for economising (something that came naturally enough to the Carlyles) the cost of providing a university education for two children made significant inroads into the family's very modest resources. Thomas Carlyle spent about £20 a year while a student, a fifth of the family's cash income.[21] Sacrifice on this scale was not, however, uncommon in early nineteenth-century Scotland. In the Carlyles' case, as in that of their peers, it was made in the expectation that clever sons would proceed from their undergraduate studies to specialised training for a profession. The most common options were the Church, the Law and Medicine. Carlyle's parents hoped that he would enter the first of these professions, not, as one might expect, as a minister in the Secession Church, but in the established Church of Scotland on which they had so resolutely turned their backs. This choice, which ran counter to the laws of supply and demand as well as to the recent tradition of the family, seems to have been based on prudence rather than principle. While it was easier for qualified candidates to find a parish in the Secession Church than in the Church of Scotland, Burgher ministers were required to be scholars of Hebrew as well as Greek and Latin.[22] Since Carlyle had concluded his secondary education as a highly competent Latinist, only an elementary Grecian, and with no knowledge of Hebrew, the family and its advisors may well have decided that their son should set his sights on the least linguistically demanding option.

The academic programme in Scotland at this time was divided into annual sessions, running from October through to May. This arrangement made it possible for students to return home to assist on farms during the harvest season. Carlyle pursued studies as an Arts student for four sessions, beginning in early November of 1809 and concluding with the session that terminated in the spring of 1813. Between sessions he lived at home with his family, studying privately and reading widely in general literature. His initial university programme focused primarily on Greek and mathematics, but he also undertook formal studies in natural and in moral philosophy and, in the first session at least, in Latin. In his second session, he attended classes in logic. This subject was regarded as the basis of the Edinburgh curriculum but Carlyle found it arid and repellent. He was equally unimpressed with the lectures on moral philosophy given by an up-and-coming professor, Thomas Brown. Carlyle, who was at this time notably rough-hewn in his manners and speech, dismissed Brown – 'the immaculate Dr Brown (a really pure, high if rather shrill and wire-drawing kind of man)' – as an academic dandy, clothing abstract and mechanical distinctions between different human faculties in showy garments stitched together from remnants of literature and poetry.[23] He was far more impressed with John Leslie, Professor of Mathematics and a noted writer on natural science, who fired his imagination on this subject and on its place in broader fields of metaphysical speculation. When combined with insights derived from natural philosophy, these studies pointed the way to a deeper understanding of the world than that which could be gained either from 'logic choppers' or moral philosophers of Brown's stamp.[24]

Carlyle's tendency to refer to his career as an arts student at Edinburgh as an experience endured rather than enjoyed, does not wholly accord with what is known about this period in his life. There were few material comforts, but then he never set great store on such things. The university, inadequately housed and struggling with the aesthetic and practical deprivations of a stalled rebuilding programme, was far from being an oasis of beauty, order and tranquillity, and, as a whole, the professoriate was not inspiring. At the same time, however, Carlyle benefited greatly from Leslie's teaching and support, and was able to contribute in a modest way to his scholarly work, receiving acknowledgement in one of his books for an original geometric solution. The fact that Carlyle later relied on a number of professors to provide references in support of applications for employment suggests that his relationships with his university teachers were not as distant and unfruitful as he sometimes suggested.

Indeed, some of his experiences at the university were of central importance for the career that followed. Carlyle owed to his early teachers an interest in intellectual developments in continental Europe that played a key role in his literary career.[25] This interest focused originally on French contributions to mathematics and natural philosophy. From 1819 the desire to keep abreast of scientific work written in German was the impetus for commencing studies of that language. The early stages of this programme can be seen on an unused side of a letter dated 16 February 1819 which Carlyle filled with exercises and notes on German vocabulary.[26] He progressed to a mastery of German language with great rapidity, a feat he later repeated with Italian and Spanish. In this way he became prepared to broaden the focus of his interest in the intellectual life of modern German so as to embrace the work of poets, dramatists and philosophers. Goethe played a critical role in Carlyle's mission. He admired Goethe's works, promoting them through translations and in review essays published in the 1820s and early 1830s. From June 1824 until Goethe's death in 1832, the relationship had a strong personal dimension. Carlyle sent him a copy of his translation of *Wilhelm Meister's Apprenticeship*, the first move in a correspondence that involved the exchange of books, portraits and other mementos. It culminated in a presentation medal that Carlyle arranged on behalf of other British admirers to mark Goethe's eighty first birthday in August 1831.[27]

Carlyle's social life in Edinburgh was not as bleak and isolated as his later comments indicated. Thomas Murray recalled that, even at the beginning of his second year at the university, Carlyle was a striking character, exhibiting 'sarcasm, irony, extravagance of sentiment, and a strong tendency to under value others, combined, however, with great kindness of heart and great simplicity of manner'.[28] Letters dating from 1813–14 provide glimpses of him in a small circle of college friends who admired his intellectual talent and were generous in their praise of him. These friends drank his health when he was absent from Edinburgh in the early summer of 1814 and wrote to him.[29] Carlyle corresponded with three of them (James Johnston, Robert Mitchell and Thomas Murray) for a number of years and exchanged news of others. They may also have been responsible for introducing Carlyle to Dr David Brewster, a leading figure on the local literary scene, who later commissioned him to write a number of biographical essays for his *Edinburgh Encyclopaedia*.[30] Although Carlyle outgrew some of these relationships, they certainly meant something to him at the time. He recalled James Johnston with affection and respect in his reminiscence of Francis Jeffrey.[31]

When Carlyle concluded his studies in the Arts programme in the spring of 1813 he did not take the MA degree, but, as was common for people in his situation, used his studies for it to gain entry to the programme in Divinity Hall that would qualify him for the ministry. From November 1813 until March 1814 he studied in Edinburgh, thereafter pursuing self-directed studies away from the university, periodically re-enrolling in Divinity Hall and presenting himself from time to time to deliver trial sermons. In May 1814 he returned to Annan Academy as a teacher of mathematics, remaining there until November 1816 when he was offered the post of master at a school in Kirkcaldy. Although this seaside town was only ten miles to the north of Edinburgh across the Firth of Forth and in sight of the city, it was a great deal further removed from it in terms of cultural and intellectual advantages.

Carlyle did not have happy memories of his time as a pupil at Annan Academy and his experience as a teacher there was hardly more inspiring. He felt socially and intellectually isolated, disliked dealing with poorly motivated pupils and was uncertain about his future plans and prospects. The move to Kirkcaldy allevi- ated some of these difficulties because Edward Irving was master of a school in the town. Carlyle's first meeting with Irving at the end of 1815 was marred by displays of mutual suspicion and one-upmanship, but over the summer of 1816 they became increasingly friendly. Carlyle and Irving were close companions in Kirkcaldy. Carlyle recalled that Irving's 'wide just sympathies, his native sagacities, honest-heartedness and good-humour, made him the most delightful of companions. Such colloquies, and rich rovings about, in bright scenes, in talk or in silences, I have never had since.'[32] He made use of Irving's library and attended his trial sermons in the local church. The two men took walks on the coast, engaging in earnest discussion of their plans for the future and of religious issues.

Irving, who had been Carlyle's predecessor at the Annan Academy, was destined for the church. He had enjoyed some celebrity as a student, and was already regarded as someone who was likely to go far. His reputation as an overly enthusiastic flogger of recalcitrant pupils prompted some of the citizens of Kirkcaldy to appoint Carlyle to run a rival school, but it did not impede Irving's rise to national prominence. He was soon to be assistant to the Reverend Dr Thomas Chalmers of Glasgow, a leading figure in the Church of Scotland. Irving moved from this post in 1822 to become a spectacularly successful minister in London. He drew large and fashionable congregations to his sermons and secured sufficient support from followers to build a large and impressive church in Regent Square. Irving's fame spread beyond the capital and in 1828 he made a triumphant return to Scotland on a preaching tour. From thenceforth, however, he began to experience a series of reversals that blighted his career. By 1832 the millenarian enthusiasms of sections of his congregation had become a source of acute embarrassment to friends such as Carlyle and to more sober members of the Presbyterian communion. When Irving refused to curb those who had taken to 'talking in tongues', he was ejected from his church. His followers formed themselves into the 'Holy Catholic Apostolic Church' and took their place among the many sects of the capital. In 1833 Irving's published views on the incarnation were judged heretical and he was deprived of his clerical status. His death in 1834 was attributed to physical and spiritual exhaustion and demoralisation.

While he never doubted Irving's sincerity and fundamental goodness, Carlyle was regretfully critical of his friend's commitment to expressions of religious faith that sapped his moral and intellectual fibre. In the early spring of 1832 Carlyle tried to remonstrate with Irving. The terms of this admonishment reflected Carlyle's views on the demands placed on thinking men in the contemporary world. He claimed that Irving's intellect-denying biblical literalism (in this case focused on the references to prophecy and talking in tongues in *Corinthians* 1.13) privileged 'a little text of *writing* in an ancient book' over 'all human science and experience'. He went on gently to chastise Irving in terms that recalled implicitly the earlier stages of their relationship, when Irving had seemed to Carlyle to be one of those on whom he could rely to help him and his contemporaries come to terms with the modern world. 'It did not beseem him, Edward Irving, to be hanging on the rearward of mankind, struggling still to chain them to old notions not now well tenable; but to be foremost in the van, leading on by the light of the eternal stars, across this hideous delirious wilderness where we all were, towards Promised Lands that lay ahead.'[33]

When Irving left Kirkcaldy in mid 1818 to become Chalmers's assistant, any attractions that the place held for Carlyle vanished. He resigned his post in the autumn of 1818 and returned to Edinburgh. This move was preceded by the termination of Carlyle's preparation for the ministry. In the spring of 1817 he waited on one of the divinity professors to renew his registration. Finding that he was not at home, Carlyle left the city without obtaining the signature necessary to maintain his enrolment. In so doing he effectively abandoned the path that had been mapped out by his parents and which he had followed dutifully, if not enthusiastically. A variety of considerations had a bearing on this decision. He was not impressed with the teaching staff of Divinity Hall, dismissing the institution as 'one of the most melancholy and unprofitable corporations'.[34] It seems very likely that Carlyle found the academic study of something that was a stern, unyielding faith to him and his family radically unsatisfactory, perhaps even impious.[35] Moreover, although Carlyle was preparing for the ministry of the Church of Scotland, he never reconciled himself to the role that lay patrons played in appointing ministers, and he resented what he saw as the worldly, non-intellectual tone of clerical society. 'These persons desire, not to understand Newton's philosophy but to obtain a well "plenished manse".'[36] Although Carlyle's studies for the ministry have left remarkably few traces in his correspondence and journals, the decision to terminate them was highly significant. James and Margaret Carlyle did not remonstrate with their favoured son over this momentous decision, but he was acutely aware of the pain that it caused them. The sense of guilt engendered by disappointing his parents' long-cherished expectations was almost certainly sharpened over the months that followed when Carlyle's mother suffered a severe illness that seems to have involved a mental breakdown.

The apparently casual way in which Carlyle discontinued his studies for the church was symptomatic of the highly unsettled state of his spirits, but it did not, of itself, imply anything about his attachment to Christianity.[37] There are indications, however, that fundamental questions about his commitment to orthodox religious views were raised in conversations with Irving in Kirkcaldy and Glasgow. Carlyle's later concerns at the turn taken by Irving's religious enthusiasm were matched by Irving's regret at his friend's move away from Christianity: 'Oh that God would give rest to his mind, and instruct him in his truth. I mediate a work upon the alienation of clever men from their Maker'.[38] In February 1818 Carlyle found that when he read Edward Gibbon's *Decline and Fall of the Roman Empire* his doubts became more deeply entrenched.[39] From this time, he increasingly saw both Presbyterian orthodoxy, and the more radical ideas being developed by Irving, as intellectually unconvincing and inadequate to the requirements of modern humanity. When combined with financial uncertainties, status anxieties, emotional turmoil and poor health, these doubts contributed to a prolonged sense of crisis and depression that was both highly personal and more generally significant. Tortured with doubts about his own faith and the point of life, Carlyle regarded these difficulties as manifestations of an overwhelming malaise that afflicted contemporary European civilisation.

The years between 1818 and 1824 were particularly difficult ones for Carlyle. While he was certain that he did not wish to be either a clergyman or a school-teacher, he did not settle on anything more suitable or congenial. In the autumn of 1819 he attended lectures in Scottish Law at the University of Edinburgh but he soon found this field of study unappealing and abandoned it. Later, the law and the legal profession became one of his *bêtes noires*, representing to him materialism, supreme social complacency, an intellectual standpoint that paid blind and exaggerated respect to 'forms' rather than to substantive matters of truth and justice, and a practice that gave precedence to forensic oratory. The tenacity of these prejudices was demonstrated in Carlyle's last major work, *Frederick the Great*, where he treated the King's contempt for the Prussian judiciary as a sign of his grasp of reality.[40] Carlyle's passing interest in the law was followed by an even briefer examination of what the engineering profession might have to offer.

Even if these professional options had proved congenial, however, they would not have provided a solution to the problem of how Carlyle was to support himself during his studies, and for the indeterminate period that it would take to become established as a practitioner. His response to this situation was twofold. He undertook a range of paid literary activity, most of which was no more than hack work.[41] At the same time, he deployed the skills that he had developed in his career as a schoolmaster in the marginally less irksome role of a private tutor. Having taken a few private pupils in Edinburgh in late 1818 and 1819, he was offered (in October 1820) a lucrative residential tutorship in Yorkshire teaching a child who was retarded in his intellectual and physical development. Carlyle did not find this prospect appealing. In any case, he sensed that he would be treated as an inferior member of the household and was not prepared to tolerate this.[42] A year and a half later, however, a recommendation by Irving helped him to secure appointment as tutor to the two sons of Mr and Mrs Charles Buller, members of a well-to-do Cornish family who had recently returned to England with their fortunes enhanced by a period of official life in India.

Carlyle tutored the Bullers' sons in Edinburgh while they studied at the university, went into residence with them when the family took a house in Perthshire in spring of 1823, and followed them to London in the summer of 1824. This engagement provided Carlyle with a number of introductions to London society. It also laid the basis for an ongoing friendship with the elder boy, Charles, who became a significant figure in parliamentary politics. To these advantages were added those that came from an escape from the hand-to-mouth financial existence that Carlyle had lived since he quit school teaching. His remuneration, '£200 a-year with superior accommodation', far exceeded anything he had yet earned.[43] Moreover, he enjoyed this boon without suffering any damage to his self-respect, and enduring the minimum possible intrusion on his other interests. The Bullers were very accommodating employers who allowed him considerable leeway. Carlyle nevertheless chaffed under the constraints placed upon him and felt a great sense of relief when he left the family's employ in July of 1824.

When Carlyle went to Perthshire with the Bullers they provided him with separate accommodation in a cottage adjacent to the main house where they stayed. This arrangement was welcomed by Carlyle because it provided a safeguard against disturbances that threatened his sense of mental and physical wellbeing. From late 1818 he had began to suffer from a range of ailments – more or less severe digestive disorders (generally referred to as 'dyspepsia'), insomnia, non-specific nervous agitation and depression – that were to plague him to a greater or lesser extent for the rest of his life, but were particularly trying for the next five or six years. These ills, compounded by the usual round of colds, sore throats and influenza, became a common (and at times a relentless) theme in Carlyle's correspondence, giving rise at particularly gloomy moments to wildly inaccurate expectations of pending mortality. Significantly, he related his various physical ills and their psychological effects to a far more general, deep-seated and dehabilitating sense of malaise:

> Such disorders ... are the heaviest calamity, the very heaviest, that the lot of life has in store for mortals. The bodily pain is nothing, or next to nothing; but alas for the dignity of man! The evil does not stop here. No strength of soul can avail you; this malady will turn that very strength against yourself; it banishes all thought from your head, all love from your heart – and doubles your wretchedness by making you discern it. O! the long, solitary, sleepless nights that I have passed – with no employment but to count the pulses of my own sick heart – till the gloom of external things seemed to extend itself to the very centre of the mind, till I could remember nothing, observe nothing! All this magnificent nature appeared as if blotted out, and a grey, dirty, dismal vapour filled the immensity of space; I stood alone in the universe – alone, and as it were a circle of burning iron enveloped the soul – excluding from it every feeling but a stony-hearted, dead obduracy, more befitting a demon in its place of woe than a man in the land of the living![44]

Ill-health had a particularly damaging impact on Carlyle because it compounded a sense of alienation and futility resulting from his loss of personal faith in the certainties of conventional Christianity. In early 1822, Margaret Carlyle urged her son to 'live in a humble dependence on providence and walk in the ways of virtue.'[45] Try as he might, however, he could not at this time find a morally and intellectually satisfying way of framing these admirable objectives.[46] While modern humanity had found that there seemed nothing that was worth believing in, it had not shaken off, indeed could not shake off, the feeling that human beings must believe in something and that this need could only be supplied by objects of belief that they regarded as 'true'. Since neither the religious faith of the past, nor the secular ideas that were offered as alternatives to it, were capable of satisfying these requirements, those who were clear-sighted and honest wandered in a moral and spiritual wasteland whose wretchedness was accentuated by the ancient and modern delusions that littered it.

This state of desperate anxiety was exacerbated by the impact of illness and depression on Carlyle's capacity to work. He came to regard immersion in his work as the only remotely effective antidote to spirit-sapping depression, seeing illness as but one dimension of a cosmic challenge, 'another element in the Chaos of materials out of which the intellect and the will (if any) are to create a glorious and manly history'.[47] When his stamina was undermined by sleeplessness and stress, however, work itself became a source of frustration and despair, one that was compounded by the hand-to-mouth existence of a struggling writer. In order to save himself from slipping into this downward spiral, Carlyle sought to manage his affairs so as to minimise threats to his physical and psychological wellbeing. He made a point of his preference for being visited rather than visiting, and, although he went out in London quite regularly, when he admitted to enjoying himself the admission was invariably qualified by comments on the moral and intellectual triviality of parties and soirees. Dinner engagements were treated with particular suspicion, partly out of puritan principle, but also because Carlyle found that exotic food and fashionable hours exacted a toll on his digestion and his sleep patterns that far outweighed any pleasure to be gained from them. When he could be persuaded to stay in other people's homes, Carlyle was an exacting guest, making numerous demands on his hosts and complaining to his wife when arrangements were not up to snuff. A visit by Carlyle in August 1847 prompted W. E. Forster to reflect on the 'salutary discipline of having a man in the house whose way is constantly consulted before my own; partly because he will have it, and partly because I prefer giving it to him.'[48] Both at home and abroad, the fear of sleeplessness exacerbated Carlyle's aversion to unwanted environmental noises, making him an inveterate enemy of the keepers of cockerels and those who were inconsiderate enough to build railway lines within earshot of houses where he stayed. As he grew older, Carlyle's acoustic phobia became more pronounced and extended beyond his concern to secure a decent night's sleep. He resented the sound of his neighbours' piano and the calls of street vendors and organ grinders. These intrusions prevented him hearing the inner voice of literary inspiration and led him to arrange the construction of a sound-proof study in the attic of his house.

Carlyle's apparently overwrought reactions to bouts of ill health no doubt owe something to the privileged position that he occupied in his family and in his own household. But while modern readers may be inclined to nod in agreement when they read Frederic Harrison's response to the publication of material detailing Carlyle's accounts of his health – 'we are not raised or purified by it' – they should perhaps pause before passing hasty judgements about hypochondria and self-indulgence.[49] The Carlyles were at the centre of one of the most extensive, well preserved and widely circulated networks of nineteenth-century correspondence. They devoted scarce resources to paying relatively costly postal charges and invested considerable time and ingenuity in finding alternatives to it, including the use of carriers, parliamentary franks provided by Francis Jeffrey, and messages written (in contravention of the law) on newspapers which were carried through the post at no charge. The extent of Carlyle's surviving correspondence means that, while many of his complaints about his health have survived to face the unsympathetic scrutiny of modern readers, it is not possible to tell whether he was more obsessed about this issue than others whose expressions of concern were not recorded for posterity.

In any case, reactions to Carlyle's complaints about his health need to take account of the grim realities of nineteenth-century medical practice. Carlyle and his contemporaries lacked access to such basic comforts and cures of modern medicine as aspirins and antibiotics. They were also subject to treatment regimes that were not based on reliable evidence and involved frequent and excessive resort to medications (alcohol, mercury and opiates) that were positively harmful.

Real, exaggerated, or merely just imagined, Carlyle's bouts of ill health played a significant role during a prolonged personal crisis that lasted from 1818 to 1826. The depressing effect of ill-health was compounded by ongoing financial uncertainty. Employment by the Bullers provided a temporary solution, but the security gained thereby would last only so long as Carlyle was prepared to place himself at the direct service of others. One clear advantage of this arrangement was that it provided a steady source of income while he tried to establish himself on the lower, very precarious, slopes of the literary landscape in England and Scotland. When he quit the Bullers' employ in mid 1824 Carlyle hoped that he no longer needed this safety net, but, although he managed to survive without it, he was often hard pressed for, and worried about, money. It was not until the latter years of the 1830s that the success of *The French Revolution* and the resurrection of *Sartor Resartus* banished the spectre of financial uncertainty from his life.

Long before this however, the worst of Carlyle's problems had found some sort of resolution. *Sartor Resartus* not only drew on his experience of the alienation, dislocation and pain resulting from a prolonged period of unnaturally suspended belief, it also showed how immobilizing doubt might be overcome by individuals affirming a belief in their role in the world and charting a course of action that would give ongoing effect to it. Carlyle identified the beginning of this process with a moment of revelation experienced (in 1821 or 1822) on Leith Walk, a thoroughfare leading from the city of Edinburgh to the seaport and beach at Leith where he frequently refreshed himself physically and mentally by bathing in the bracing waters of the Firth of Forth. The hero of *Sartor* undergoes this experience in Paris on the Rue Saint-Thomas de l'Enfer and moves to a productive and reassuring but by no means soothing understanding of his role in relation to human destiny: 'The situation that has not its Duty, its Ideal, was never yet occupied by man. Yes here, in this poor, miserable, hampered, despicable Actual, wherein thou even now standest, here or nowhere is thy Ideal: work it out therefrom; and working, believe, live, be free.'[50] In the years following the experience on Leith Walk, Carlyle's state of mind and spirit underwent a steady improvement. His condition remained volatile, however, and he continued to be prone to anxiety about his health and to bouts of chronic insomnia and depression. At times his temper was very uncertain, prompting outbursts of exaggerated speech and verbal aggression.

Carlyle's recovery from the most tenacious manifestations of his personal crisis coincided with the stabilisation of his relationship with a young woman called Jane Welsh. Thomas was introduced to Jane by Edward Irving, her former tutor and admirer, in 1821. The early stages of their relationship aggravated his difficulties rather than soothing them. Jane was the only child of Dr John Welsh, a highly respected physician who had laid the basis for a thriving practice in the small town of Haddington, some fifteen or so miles to the east of Edinburgh. Dr Welsh died in 1820 before his investment in this practice had yielded much fruit. His widow and daughter were left with a substantial house in Haddington, a small estate ('Craigenputtock') in the wilds of Dumfrieshire, very little money and a strong attachment to the ethos of professional gentility. Mrs Welsh's relationship with her daughter was sometimes stormy, but Jane's sense of duty dictated that she should pay close attention to her mother's views on important questions and should not conceal correspondence with Carlyle. Mrs Welsh seems to have had no intellectual interests and she probably regarded Carlyle's poetic intensity with disdainful alarm. His very uncertain financial prospects and the social distance that separated the Carlyles from the Welshs, was almost bound to be a source of difficulty, even if Jane and Thomas had been of one mind. This was very far from being the case in the early years of their friendship. Jane was very attractive and personable and had a number of well-heeled admirers. It took some time before she began to reciprocate the sense of warm attachment that Thomas demonstrated very soon after their first meeting. By early 1825, however, a relationship that was initially seen by Jane to involve intellectual mentoring developed into 'love for' Thomas reflecting 'simple, honest, serene affection, made up of admiration and sympathy', if not the blind passion which she associated with being '*in love*'.[51] Shortly thereafter the couple entered into a commitment to marriage.

Jane and Thomas were married in October 1826 and lived initially in Comely Bank, on the outskirts of Edinburgh. Carlyle later developed an aversion to aspects of Edinburgh society, but at this time both he and Jane relished the social opportunities that were opened to them. They made acquaintances and friends among the literati of the capital and entertained on a modest scale in their small home. It was during this period that Carlyle established a close relationship with Francis Jeffrey, the editor of the *Edinburgh Review*, one of the two most important periodicals of the time. Jeffrey, a leading figure in Scottish legal circles, was later a member of Lord Grey's government. Carlyle also became acquainted with John Gibson Lockhart, another Edinburgh advocate who in 1825 had assumed the editorship of the *Edinburgh*'s main rival, the *Quarterly Review*. While the *Edinburgh* was identified with cautiously progressive forces of political Whiggism, the *Quarterly* was aligned with those in the Tory party who sought to defend the political, social and ecclesiastical status quo. It led the charge against moves that threatened to undermine the constitutional position of the Church of England and opposed measures to enfranchise the middle classes. It also published essays by Robert Southey and other Tory critics of liberal economic and social policy and elite attitudes that compromised traditional paternalism.

In the early summer of 1828 the Carlyles left Edinburgh and took up residence at Craigenputtock, left to Jane in her father's will. At Carlyle's suggestion,
her mother was given a life interest in this property so that her daughter and
son-in-law were her tenants. Thomas and Jane lived in a house on the property,
while Alick ran the farm on his own account. The removal to Craigenputtock
was largely motivated by financial considerations. Although the house required
substantial renovation to make it comfortable, Carlyle reckoned that he and Jane
could live more economically in the country than in the city. The advertisement
that Carlyle drew up in 1834 when the house was let, gives some idea of it:

> It has Dining-room, Drawing-room, Library, 4 Bed-rooms, small Dressing-room,
> Servants' apartment, Kitchen, with all appurtances; and, for Offices, in an enclosed court,
> Fuel-house, gig-house, Mangle-room, Stable of 4 stalls: the whole new, sufficient, and
> in perfect repair.[52]

There was, however, a cost to pay for enjoying accommodation on such a scale
on the Carlyles' slender income. Craigenputtock was removed from the social
and intellectual life of Edinburgh, and was generally remote and inaccessible,
particularly in winter. In order to pay the quarterly rent to her mother, Jane had to
ride sixteen miles to the bank at Dumfries, another sixteen miles to her mother's
house at Templand and then sixteen miles back to Craigenputtock. Jane felt the
accumulative effects of self-imposed banishment particularly severely. A witty,
vivacious and attractive woman, she had enjoyed life in Edinburgh and found
the compensations of rural life completely inadequate. Shortly before they left to
move to London in 1834 Jane referred to the 'almost fearful silence' of the place,
and Thomas himself likened the move to being liberated from the Bastille.[53]

Carlyle sought to lessen their isolation by arranging visits from friends. A
reluctant, complaining, although frequent traveller, he made light of the tortuous
journey from Edinburgh, and from places even further away. Francis Jeffrey and
Ralph Waldo Emerson were among the visitors. Others, including J. S. Mill, were
urged to come but did not do so. Thomas and Jane escaped to London on two
occasions, staying there over the autumn and spring of 1831–32 and for four
months in the winter and early spring of 1833. By this time it had become clear,
even to Carlyle, that the economic benefits of living at Craigenputtock and the
opportunities it provided to work without distractions, were far outweighed by
the material, social and psychological effects of prolonged isolation. Both Thomas
and Jane found London an exciting place, and while they had many complaints
about the environment and bemoaned the moral failings of native Londoners,
Carlyle's early verdict summed up their response to life in the capital: London was
'an almost terrific place, never a dull one'.[54] In early 1834 the decision was made
to settle there. Thomas went on ahead to find a house, leaving Jane to manage
the removal of their furniture and household effects. By early summer the couple

were settling into a cheap, well-appointed, soundly-built, recently decorated and bug-free house in Cheyne Row, Chelsea. The house was a stone's throw from the unembanked river side of the Thames and close, at times uncomfortably close, to the chaotic household of Leigh Hunt, his hard drinking, slatternly but artistically talented wife Marianne and their numerous, casually-raised, offspring.

The Carlyles' life in London followed a routine that was prescribed by Thomas's work, his need to relax when staging posts in large projects were reached, by financial necessity and then by self-imposed economy, and by concerns about his health and that of Jane. He sometimes visited friends who lived out of London and frequently escaped the heat and dust of the city during the summer months for the relative solitude of Scotland and the company of his family there. Initially these journeys were made by stage coach and on coastal sailing vessels but Carlyle then became an early user of the rapidly expanding network of railways. He was both appalled and exhilarated by the experience, recalling a journey through the English Midlands as a 'yelling flight through some detestable smoky chaos, and midnight witch-dance of base-looking nameless dirty towns'.[55] Anthony Trollope, who wrote much of the Barchester Chronicles on train journeys, reported that Carlyle did not even approve of people reading on trains. They should, he proclaimed, '"sit still and label [their] thoughts"'.[56]

Despite pressing invitations from Ralph Waldo Emerson and other admirers in the United States, Carlyle's foreign travels were restricted to Europe and Ireland. He made fleeting visits to Paris and the Netherlands and more prolonged tours to parts of German and central Europe in 1852 and 1858 in connection with his researches on *Frederick the Great*. In 1846 he visited Dublin and its environs. Three years later he returned to Ireland for a more extensive tour of the country, accompanied for some of the time by Charles Gavan Duffy, a Young Irelander, editor of The *Nation* and later premier of Victoria in Australia.

Even by the norms of Victorian households, Carlyle made heavy demands on his wife's time and patience. True to an understanding reached when they decided to marry, Jane played her role admirably. She ensured that daily household routines and large-scale renovation and refurbishment projects did not upset her husband's equilibrium. On one occasion, when Thomas had fled from the noise of builders and the smell of paint, Jane slept with a pistol by her bed so she could confront burglars who had taken advantage of the painter's scaffolding and gaping window frames to gain entry to the Carlyles's house.[57] She also rose to a formidable challenge from the tax authorities, taking on the Commissioners of Inland Revenue on her husband's behalf, and making a spirited appearance before them in November 1855. She managed to reduce the tax assessed on his literary income by half, upbraiding a Commissioner who strayed beyond the matter under discussion: 'I am not here to explain what Mr Carlyle *has to live on*; only to declare his income from Literature during the last three years.'[58] But while she devoted herself to her husband's career and wellbeing, Jane's deep affection for him, and her equally strong sense of duty, did not induce her to suffer in silence. She teased Carlyle about his domestic expectations with varying degrees of sharpness, and in moments of frustration made barbed references to them in letters to her friends.

Carlyle's tastes, health and initially at least, his income, dictated that the domestic economy of Cheyne Row was modest. There were never more than two female servants and Jane played an active role in the management of the household. She often struck up close relationships with her maids and was hurt (as well as being inconvenienced) when they left precipitously or had to be dismissed. Some servants could not cook, others drank to excess; one gave birth to an illegitimate child in the kitchen, concealing both the pregnancy and the birth from Thomas and Jane. In the interests of economy and to avoid the poor quality wares of London suppliers Carlyle arranged for home produced, or locally purchased hams, bacon, beef-ham, butter, potatoes, oats and whiskey to be shipped from Scotland. These foodstuffs were the staples of a diet that was supplemented by a limited range of goods purchased in London: eggs, bread, cheese, mutton chops and steak, turnips, beans mignonette, gooseberries, strawberries and seasonal vegetables grown in their tiny garden.[59] The Carlyles drank tea and coffee, brandy (in milk) and 'grog' made from contraband Scottish whiskey, probably mixed with hot water, lemon juice and sugar. They also bought madeira, beer (mostly for the servants who expected this as part of their conditions of employment) and table wines.

Carlyle made much of the plain and frugal fare served in his home, but while he and his wife's diet was far from lavish by contemporary middle-class standards, it was not always as constrained as his remarks might suggest. Thus while Leigh Hunt eagerly joined Carlyle for his evening ration of porridge with milk in the late 1830s, William Brookfield was an unexpected and well satisfied guest at a dinner on Christmas Day in 1852 that consisted of soup, mutton, woodcocks, nut brown, with port, sherry, madeira. Brookfield remarked that Carlyle was a 'kind, unaffected host, genial and spontaneous.'[60]

Leigh Hunt was one of the earliest of a long succession of friends whom the Carlyles entertained in their home on a regular and informal basis. These visits spared Thomas from the perils of visiting others and provided one of his few forms of relaxation from studying and writing. They often ended with Carlyle accompanying his guests on long walks through the streets of London and its inner suburbs, one of his strategies for purchasing sleep and keeping ill health at bay. He seems to have been an impulsive reckless pedestrian, plunging into what he called the 'Niagara of cabs' on London streets, using his walking stick to poke horses' heads when it became necessary.[61] Riding was regarded very much in the same light as walking, something to be done for the sake of health and relaxation from the strain of work. For a number of years he rode out in the afternoons to the countryside to the south of the city, travelling 30,000 miles in late afternoon and early evening rides in search of relief from the burden of writing *Frederick the Great*.[62] Carlyle's other recreations were very limited. He sometimes took advantage of complimentary theatre tickets provided by William Macready but rarely went to operas or orchestral concerts. He preferred to listen to Jane's homely rendition of Scottish folk songs on the piano at home, upholding this form of musical entertainment as preferable to anything offered by modern composers.[63]

The success of *The French Revolution: A History* in 1837, and the belated appearance of the British edition of *Sartor Resartus* in 1838, marked the beginning of the end of the financial worries that had dogged the Carlyles in the early years of their marriage. Thereafter, Jane's taste and capacity for good domestic management helped sustain a life of modest comfort and tranquillity, disturbed from time to time by unreliable servants, inconsiderate neighbours and raucous street vendors. More serious causes for concern arose in the late 1840s when Jane's health deteriorated and Thomas's absorption in his literary work made him neglectful of her needs and prompted expressions of bitter resentment. In late 1855 she complained that this pattern had become established during the years of almost penal servitude at Craigenputtock.[64] Jane's account was coloured by present concerns to some degree, but it was true that, partly for financial reasons, partly because of the challenges that Thomas set himself, and partly also because he saw his literary mission as a duty, the demands of his work dominated his life and that of his wife.

Carlyle's books cost him a great deal of effort and he complained constantly about the burdens of authorship. Francis Jeffrey thought he made far too much of this: 'I cannot but smile at the picture you draw of your idle misery – and your working misery – I know you are not so miserable as your words might imply – and that, if you would only task yourself and your fellow creatures a little less highly, you would both be more contented.'[65] Carlyle, however, did not share Jeffrey's faith in the moral value of 'contentment' and, in any case, he did not find it easy to write for publication. He agonised over his compositions, subjecting his work to painstaking revision and enhancement, in much the same way as a painter might work up a picture with much 'over painting'. A practice that seemed to be a necessity was elevated into a general virtue. Carlyle's contempt for 'easy composition' was one of the themes of an essay on the author of *Waverley*.[66] He was highly critical of Sir Walter Scott's apparently effortless fluidity, his genius for what was condescendingly dismissed as 'ready-writing': 'It is a valuable faculty this of ready-writing; nay farther, for Scott's purpose it was clearly the only good mode. By much labour he could not have added one guinea to his copyright; nor could the reader on the sofa have lain a whit more at ease.'[67] Earlier in the same essay, Carlyle contrasted the staggering quantity of Scott's literary output with its predominately commonplace quality. He went on to evoke Shakespeare, Milton, Goethe and Schiller to support the maxim that 'in the way of writing, no great thing was ever, or will ever be done with ease, but with great difficulty'.[68]

Although Carlyle was not as fluid or productive as some of his contemporaries, his output was nevertheless impressive. Between 1835 and 1865 he wrote a three-volume history of the French Revolution, collected, edited and heavily annotated three volumes of Oliver Cromwell's letters and speeches, and wrote his mammoth six-volume biography of Frederick the Great. He also produced three volumes of social and political criticism (*Chartism*, 1839; *Past and Present*, 1841 and *Latter-Day Pamphlets*, 1850) and a biography of his friend John Sterling (1851). He gave three series of public lectures between 1837 and 1839, one of which provided the basis of the widely read *On Heroes, Hero-Worship and the Heroic in History* (1839). Carlyle's lectures generated much needed income, and, since they were reported in the national press, they helped to introduce him to a wider public. These gains were not sufficient to prompt Carlyle to prolong the experiment. He found the whole experience exceedingly stressful, suffering agonies of nervousness before and during each lecture; it was, he recalled, the 'vilest welter of confusions, horrors and repugnancies.'[69] When he felt that he was coming to terms with the demands of public speaking he began to worry that he might turn into an orator, an adept in the oral equivalent of 'ready-writing'.

From the time when Carlyle had been the Bullers' tutor, he had enjoyed a steadily increasing acquaintance among the literati and its patrons in the upper middle and upper classes. Residence in Edinburgh at the start of his married life, visits to London and his relocation there widened this circle, as did his growing reputation as a highly significant figure *in*, if not precisely *of*, the literary world. Thomas and Jane went out in society and they also received a stream of visitors in the evenings at their house in Cheyne Row. Although Carlyle acquired a reputation as a formidable and sometimes overbearing and overwrought conversationalist, a wide range of his contemporaries were eager to seek his company. On meeting him in 1832 Henry Crabb Robinson thought he had the manner of a religious zealot and clearly found this distasteful. To others, however, Carlyle's presence and speech were striking and attractive. For example, Caroline Fox described him in 1842 as a

Tall, robust-looking man; rugged simplicity and indomitable strength are in his face, and such a glow of genius in it ... His manner is very quiet, but he speaks like one tremendously convinced of what he utters, and who has much – very much – in him that was quite unutterable, quite unfit to be uttered to the uninitiated ear.[70]

As with other people, Carlyle's relationships with acquaintances and friends ebbed and flowed. His impact on them was also affected by his prevailing state of mind. After a visit in the mid 1840s Harriet Martineau told Jane that 'I have seen all manner of good things in him before, but what he was in good spirits I never had witnessed – nor imagined. Oh! He was so light and gay.'[71] At one time or another, Carlyle was on reasonably familiar, and in some cases very close, terms with many of the leading literary figures of the late Georgian, and mid Victorian period: Francis Jeffrey, Leigh Hunt, J. S. Mill, Erasmus Darwin, Charles Dickens and his biographer John Forster, George Eliot, G. H. Lewes, Edward Fitzgerald, Thomas Arnold, Harriet Martineau, W. M. Thackeray, the Brownings, Tennyson, John Ruskin, Fitzjames Stephen and Leslie Stephen. He also formed close relationships with a number of leading political figures, including Charles Buller, Sir Arthur Helps, Lord Ashburton, the conservative minister, Viscount Goderich, a Liberal politician and Richard Monckton Milnes, an MP who was associated with Benjamin Disraeli's 'Young England' faction in the House of Commons. In addition to these relationships with British figures of note, Carlyle's friendships extended across the English Channel, to the far side of the Atlantic and out into the empire.

In the 1820s Carlyle had applied unsuccessfully for a number of professorships in mathematics and moral philosophy, and at times in the 1840s he seems to have given some thought to embarking on an official career as a member of the recently created Board of Education. He may also have been interested in playing a role in framing poor law policy in the late 1840s.[72] Later invitations to serve on the 'permanent committee' of the Public Health Section of the Council of the Social Science Association (a body dedicated to providing information to influence government policy making), and (less plausibly, perhaps) to join William Macready and John Ruskin on a 'Committee on Taste' to advise the Shakespeare Memorial Committee in Victoria, Australia, do not seem to have been accepted.[73] Carlyle's non-literary public services were fairly restricted. He accepted a position as one of the vice presidents of the Poor Law Reform Association but seems to have played no active part in this organisation. He also served on a committee charged with identifying fit subjects for the National Portrait Gallery, a role that fitted in well with his published views on the importance of historical portraiture to a community's sense of collective identity.[74] Carlyle gave evidence in 1849 to the Royal Commission enquiring into the library in the British Museum, reflecting on his experience of undertaking historical research there. He also played an active role in a campaign to secure adequate copyright protection for authors, composing a submission to Parliament on this theme in April 1839: 'the Petition of Thomas Carlyle, a Writer of Books ... being incited thereto by various innocent or laudable considerations, chiefly by the thought that said books might in the end be found to be worth something.'[75] Carlyle's prominent role on a committee established in 1865 to defend Edward James Eyre, the former Governor of Jamaica, seems less innocent or laudable. This committee sought to defend Eyre against charges that he was responsible for the misconduct of military officers who had used excessive, unwarranted, illegal and deadly force in suppressing riots by blacks on the island.

At least some of those who recoiled from Carlyle's defence of Eyre had been warm supporters of what might perhaps be regarded as his most significant act of public service during these years, the establishment of the London Library. This project was close to Carlyle's heart, with his interest in it reflecting one of the many drawbacks of life in Craigenputtock: the difficulty in securing access to books needed to continue his studies and to write articles for the reviews. Even when he lived in London and had regular access to the British Museum, Carlyle found that work on serious historical projects was impeded by the requirement that readers must put up with working in public reading rooms. Beginning in earnest in early 1839, he played a prominent role in a campaign to establish a well-stocked library in London that allowed its members to borrow books. He canvassed support for the project, assisted in drawing up a prospectus, and went to some trouble to ensure it was circulated widely. In mid 1839 copies of this document were handed out at the door during one his lecture series. Carlyle wrote what he called a 'fierce blast' in support of the proposal for the *Examiner*. The *Times* was also persuaded to publish a piece that generalised from Carlyle's uncomfortable experiences in the British Museum:

> To all readers the buzz and bustle of a public room is an importunate distraction; to this waste of facility add waste of time in coming and going; waste of patience in waiting; add discomfort, perturbation, headache, waste of health; and, we may fairly calculate that, for any book requiring study, one night in a man's own room might be worth a week in the other situation.[76]

He worked with others to establish a committee of distinguished lords and commoners to organise a well-attended public meeting at the Freemason's Tavern in London on 28 June 1840. Carlyle was also active in the search for a librarian. When the appointment was made in late January 1841, he remained on the management committee but restricted his involvement to offering advice on book purchases, presumably applying the criteria advanced at an earlier stage of London Library campaign: 'popular, entertaining, what people will read, and *continue to read*'.[77]

During the decade that ended in 1865, Carlyle was absorbed, perhaps buried is a more appropriate term, in writing what turned out to be a six volume study of the life and times of Frederick the Great. Shortly after the last volume of this work was published, Carlyle agreed to be a candidate for the office of Rector of the University of Edinburgh. In the autumn of 1865 the student body elected him by a vote of two to one to succeed J. S. Mill in this role. The defeated candidate was Benjamin Disraeli, for long the unconscious target of Carlyle's sharpest and most distasteful barbs. Rectors were obliged to give an inaugural address and to appoint an 'assessor' who would attend the University Court on their behalf. But while the role might be largely ceremonial, at least some of those who were active in university politics in Edinburgh thought it had more practical possibilities. Carlyle seemed to share this view, and, for a brief period, lasting from late 1865 until the middle of the following year, was poised to take a relatively active role in the affairs of the university. When his candidature was being canvassed, J. S. Blackie, Professor of Classics and a powerful figure in the political life of the university, questioned John Carlyle on his brother's capacity for business. John replied that Thomas had 'plenty of talent for *practical* business if once fairly tackled to it'. He was 'not a rash man' but had 'resolution enough when it is called for'.[78] Carlyle and his younger brother discussed university matters, including the appointment of an assessor, considering carefully the personal qualities and capacities of likely candidates, their knowledge of both the University and of education in Scotland. The Rector and his assessor's roles on this body were potentially significant as a counterweight to the parochial and conservative influences exerted by members nominated by the city council. Carlyle's concerns were related to a reform agenda, having to do with overhauling the faculties and raising the national standing of Edinburgh degrees, an issue which had long been of interest to him.[79] Any plans he may have to play an active role in these or other causes connected with the university ended with his wife's unexpected death shortly after his triumphant installation in office on 2 April 1866.

Jane's life, like that of her husband's, has been laid bare to posterity through the survival of correspondence and other first hand records. She was intelligent, very quick-witted and observant, and when in good health and spirits wrote letters that are a delight to read. Jane was given to occasional bouts of petulance and jealousy, the latter being particularly marked in her reaction to her husband's innocent but irritatingly gallant relationship with Lady Harriet Baring, later Lady Ashburton.[80] The first wife of a prominent Conservative politician who also became a close friend of Carlyle, Lady Ashburton was the centre of a circle of public and literary figures who met at her houses in London and the country. The language of Thomas's letters to Lady Ashburton dating from the mid 1850s makes Jane's response to the relationship understandable. Within an hour of the end of a visit by Lady Ashburton to Cheyne Row, probably in early 1857, he wrote to tell her that she was 'the Queen of women! Magnanimous, patient, gentle, brave and beautiful, beyond the Daughters of Eve. Oh, if I could fly away into Heaven with you – would I! – The thought of you gilds all darkness in my existence; makes wretched London fog itself into clouds of red and gold.'[81]

Jane's tongue could be very sharp. She deployed it in alliance with her husband against others, but also in alliance with others (often women friends) against him. In 1833 she quoted Thomas as having observed that 'Man is a mass of contradictions' and then went on to proclaim on the 'quantity of wisdom new and old [that] falls from his lips in the course of one solar day! ... On the crumbs that fall from *his* table I might positively set up a respectable little breadshop of my own.'[82] Ten year later when Carlyle laboured to complete *Oliver Cromwell* she described him as 'all fidgety and flurrying ... like a hen in the distraction of laying its first egg ... writing down every word as with his heart's blood.'[83] Lord Ashburton remarried after Harriet died in 1857 and in an odd twist Jane became closely attached to the second Lady Ashburton, adopting an effusive tone in her letters. These letters contain numerous slightly subversive references to 'Mr. C' and his doings, including an account of preparations for travel to Edinburgh in the spring of 1866 to present the Rectorial address. 'Mr. C', Jane wrote, 'is in the agonies of making up his mind and "gathering himself together" for the flight to Scotland! For Mr. C every journey is a *Flight* – from present evils and difficulties to evils and difficulties as certain, tho' in the future tense!'[84] It is very telling that 'Mr. C' also appears in the opening paragraphs of Jane's *The Simple Story of My Own First Love*, written in 1852 in response to the couple's discussions of the treatment of love in Thackeray's *Henry Esmond*. In this tale, unpublished during the Carlyles's lifetime, Thomas is referred to as '"the greatest Philosopher of our day"' before being subjected to some not particularly gentle satire for his views on the 'beggarly futility' of the focus on love in a 'Heroic Age'.[85]

Admiration for Jane's style and wit was not universal. She did not get on well with most of Thomas's family and retailed unfavourable accounts of them to correspondents. There were tensions with Alick at Craigenputtock and complaints about his drinking. Later she clashed with John Carlyle over his refusal to accept at face value her statements of the perilous condition of her health.[86] Blanche Smith, Arthur Clough's fiancée, described her manner as 'sharp' and 'flighty' and thought her disregard for convention smacked of the wilfulness of a spoiled child.[87] Jane's intolerant dismissals of the Church of England in particular, and religion in general, upset some visitors. Even those who were generally well dispossessed noted her sharp, sarcastic turn of speech.[88] In other quarters, however, there was widespread appreciation of her charm, enthusiasm and personal warmth, with many visitors to Cheyne Row reacting in much the way that Charles Duffy did in 1845. He noted that while Jane was no longer handsome, she was 'full of intellect and kindness blended gracefully, lovingly together'.[89]

As with judgements about Thomas's reaction to the state of his health, discussions of the Carlyles' marriage are bedevilled by the alluringly comprehensive documentation. There is a lot of material but it is far from complete or evenly balanced. Froude's lack of perspective in handling Jane's criticisms of her husband's conduct towards her exacerbates this difficulty, as do Thomas's responses to reading some of this material shortly after her death. His state of mind at this time is perhaps best illustrated by the intensity of his expressions of guilt at having not stumped up a few shillings for a cab to spare his wife's feet from the mud of a London street: 'Painful at this moment is the recollection ... Shame on me!' The incident referred to had occurred more than twenty years before.[90]

Even allowing for the skewed evidence, however, a number of points about the Carlyles' relationship seem clear. The first is that their correspondence bears touching testimony to their love for one another. Thus while the couple were not always on good terms, and sometimes quarrelled bitterly, their relationship was never cool or distant. Expressions of anger and disappointment are far outweighed by those indicating warm regard. Moreover, Thomas's commitment to his literary career was endorsed by his wife and formed an important part of their relationship, rather than being something that intruded on it. Jane read his work, commented on it and was generous in her praise of, and pride in, his achievements. At the same time, however, Thomas's domestic requirements were demanding and Jane sometimes chaffed at having to devote her life to meeting them. Until the late 1830s, the Carlyles's financial position was precarious and this, not surprisingly, injected additional stress into their lives.

Jane did not have any children but there is no firsthand evidence of her response to this, or that of her husband. After Thomas' death rumours of impotence and an unconsummated marriage were in circulation but these claims lacked any documented support. The fact of the matter is that the surviving material does not provide conclusive evidence on the Carlyles's sexual relationship. There are some indirect grounds for thinking that Jane may have suffered a miscarriage in the late summer of 1831 and it is at least plausible to read signs of mutual physical warmth into some of their correspondence. More compelling, perhaps, is a remark in Thomas's reminiscence of his father, written in 1832: 'Let me not mourn for my Father; let me do worthily of him: so shall he leave, even Here, in me; and his worth plant itself honourably forth into new generations.'[91] If the last part of this plea alludes to Thomas's hope that he and Jane might have children (rather than to his literary work) then claims of impotence and an unconsummated marriage seem highly implausible. Carlyle set great store on honesty and practised this virtue with great consistency. To have wilfully deluded himself in a reminiscence of his father would have been seen as showing a shocking lack of respect to the memory of a man who shared his commitment to truth.

Carlyle's works cost him a great amount of labour and he gave frequent vent to frustration on this theme, on the uncertainty of how they would be received, on their lack of impact and so on. All this, one imagines, was the experience of hosts of people who lacked a private or professional income and sought to live by their pens. At times, Jane's frustrations were sharpened by feelings of neglect, either as a result of her husband's liking for the Ashburtons's company, or when he was struggling with various writing projects. This particular cause for resentment was acute in the late 1850s and through until 1865 when Carlyle battled obsessively to complete his multi-volume biography of Frederick the Great while Jane suffered from a more or less continual series of physical and psychological illnesses. Resort to opiates and alcohol-based medications further undermined her physical and mental health, reducing her capacity to cope with the difficult and unsatisfactory aspects of her married life.

There were, in any case, causes for resentment on both sides. One intimate of the household in Cheyne Row noted Jane's determination not to be excluded from her husband's conversations with visitors and her use of anecdotes on his inconsistent practical recognition of the virtue of silence to put him in his place. Andrew Symington, writing immediately after Carlyle's death and before the publication of his reminiscences, claimed that for all her charms, Jane sometimes harboured resentments that her husband could not understand and that left him feeling 'bewildered, wet-blanketed, and very miserable.'[92]

As work on *Frederick the Great* finally reached a conclusion, one senses a lightening of the gloomy atmosphere that pervaded the house in Cheyne Row for much, but never for all, of the previous decade. By this time, however, it was almost too late. Shortly after Thomas had given an acclaimed speech at his installation as Rector of the University of Edinburgh, and before his return to London, Jane died. In the course of a recreational drive through Hyde Park on 21 April 1866, she was found lying dead in the cab by the driver, most probably the victim of a heart attack. Within a few weeks of her death Carlyle set about memoralising her in the longest and most poignant of his reminiscences. In a letter to Jane written shortly before their marriage, Thomas prayed that 'the heart thou has believed in so nobly may prove no refuge of lies!' declaring that 'I swear it will break my heart if I make you unhappy.'[93] The 'Reminiscence of Jane Welsh Carlyle' recalled both of these pleas. It was informed by harrowing insights into Jane's feelings derived from reading her private record of the trials of the last ten years, and was suffused with Carlyle's guilt at having been so blind to her needs. But while this work is a testament to his commitment to truth and to his deep affection for his wife, it is hardly a balanced assessment of their relationship, or of his treatment of her.

After Jane's death, the pace of Thomas's life began to slow down markedly. Initially, he was stunned by grief, but this did not prevent him writing the reminiscence of his wife and then moving on to those on Irving, Francis Jeffrey, Robert Southey and Wordsworth. Age and inclination formed increasingly solid and daunting barriers to literary activity, and, as discussed in more detail below, by this time Carlyle thought that he had completed his mission to his contemporaries.[94] This mission, Carlyle's perception of it and its role in a wide range of biographical, critical, historical, literary and political writings is the subject of the chapters that follow.

2

Literature as Mission

During the early stages of his literary career, a period that began in 1818 and lasted until the early 1830s, Carlyle sought to establish his identity as a distinctive voice by persuading his contemporaries of the importance of his 'mission'. He regarded the state of anguish and alienation that had dogged him since 1816 as a particular and personal manifestation of a more general malaise. It was his special role in life to help his contemporaries confront their collective inner demons and make the most of the opportunities for individual and collective endeavour present in the modern world. His mission addressed a range of questions concerning humanity's commitment to moral goodness and its uncompromising rejection of evil, the relationship between the inner and outer worlds, and the limitations of perspectives that were appropriate only to the latter. These were familiar concerns for committed Christians. For Carlyle, however, they were particularly pressing and problematic because he believed the intellectual and cultural frameworks that had sustained Christianity were no longer tenable. Whether contemporaries clung to traditional forms of Protestantism or Roman Catholicism, or adopted less orthodox positions, they nevertheless found themselves in a welter of confusion and moral and intellectual insincerity.

Views such as these were not compatible with a career in the Church of Scotland, but in deciding to apply himself to literature, Carlyle was embracing a profession which he saw as the modern successor of the priesthood. The moral and rhetorical impulses that might have been deployed in the pulpit were now called up in the service of literature. While this change of focus is a biographical commonplace, its implications were profound. It completely transformed the scope of Carlyle's mission – as the seventeenth-century Presbyterian divine Richard Baxter had put it, 'Why is it not as good to Preach by the Press to many thousands, and for many years after I am dead, as to Preach to a Parlour full for a few hours?' – and it also affected the manner in which it was pursued.[1] Upright and zealous preachers were expected to be concerned with the spiritual welfare of their congregations, not with making them feel comfortable and self-satisfied. Chastisement, rebuke and a certain roughness or even violence of expression were not at all untoward in this context; indeed, complaints at such treatment were often seen as a sign that severity was justified. In this respect, Carlyle's approach to his mission mirrored that of John Knox, the promoter of Calvinistic Reformation in both England and Scotland and the object of Carlyle's admiration in some of his later writings.[2]

In preparing himself for the role to which he had decided to devote his life, Carlyle struggled in private to define the nature of his mission and to persuade himself that literature was the medium through which it should be pursued. He also mapped out the personal and ideological basis of this quest, adopting an uncompromisingly radical stance on religious and political issues and eschewing any identification with what he came to see as the redundant nostrums of conventional piety and political practice. He stressed the importance of moral and intellectual rather than material values, and of the need to adopt a perspective on life that placed a premium on personal independence. In formulating these positions, Carlyle built upon the psychological and cultural legacy of his family. He looked farther afield however, in his search for artistic and intellectual inspiration, finding it, and a distinctive voice, in his promotion of ideas identified with Goethe and some of his German contemporaries.

Although Carlyle did not have a job when he moved back to Edinburgh in October 1818, he had accumulated savings of about £100 (equivalent to perhaps a year's salary), and no dependants to support. He also retained the option of retiring to the family home if his situation in Edinburgh became intolerable. Even so, the abandonment of a relatively secure teaching post exposed him to the deprivations and uncertainties that faced many of the impecunious products of the Scottish universities in an overstocked and competitive professional employment market.[3] It also raised questions about a new choice of career that were not answered by brief and unsatisfactory experiments with engineering and law. The effect of these frustrations was exacerbated by the strain imposed by his family's growing awareness that he no longer shared their understanding of Christianity, by the onset of the digestive disorders that afflicted him in varying degree for the rest of his life, and the emotional, intellectual and psychological strains arising from his sharpening sense of the moral incoherence of the human condition.

The last of these difficulties provided the focus of Carlyle's first original book-length publication, *Sartor Resartus*, written in the late 1820s.[4] *Sartor* cannot be read simply as autobiography, although much of it relates directly to the intellectual and moral confusion and alienation that blighted Carlyle's life from about 1816 until 1826. This condition was marked by a growing dissatisfaction with traditional accounts of the destiny of humanity, scepticism towards alternatives to these accounts, and a desperate sense of lost opportunities. These doubts and anxieties were doubly painful because they were experienced by one who felt the need for faith and hope: 'Doubt had darkened into Unbelief ... shade after shade goes grimly over your soul, till you have the fixed, starless Tartarean black'.[5]

Carlyle had never shown much enthusiasm for teaching but after giving up plans to enter the church he could no longer countenance it even as a stop-gap. By the end of his stay in Kirkcaldy the profession had become intolerably 'irksome'. Significantly, this objection had less to do with the day-to-day duties of the profession than with the ambivalent social status of its members. Carlyle found himself 'enveloped in a dense repulsive atmosphere' which he traced to 'the undefined station I have hitherto occupied in society'. He feared that prolonged exposure to this atmosphere would turn him into a withdrawn and embittered misanthrope.[6] Status anxieties (which persisted after the termination of Carlyle's teaching career) no doubt exacerbated the feelings of alienation and spiritual unease that had seeped into his soul, and encouraged him to escape from them by moving to Edinburgh. This move may also have been sparked by the early stirrings of an ambition that came to dominate Carlyle's thoughts over the next two decades, and provided the driving force of life, the spur of literary activity.

Although Carlyle had earlier fantasised about attaining 'intellectual greatness' and 'literary fame,'[7] and been encouraged by some of his university friends to think that this aspiration was attainable, he seems to have arrived in Edinburgh without any clearly formulated literary plans beyond the vague prospect of contributing to a projected 'Monthly Review', or perhaps to Dr David Brewster's *Edinburgh Encyclopaedia*.[8] At one level, at least, Carlyle's attitude towards literature as a career option was ambivalent. He referred to writing as a way of supporting himself while preparing for a profession: the law, and engineering were fleeting possibilities, and academic employment seemed a relatively attractive prospect for a number of years. He also tacitly endorsed Irving's view that literary success demonstrating force and originality would make him known, and open doors to employment that would enable him to make significant contributions to human knowledge.[9] But what may at first have been seen, or presented to an anxious family back in Annandale, as a means to an end, increasingly became an end in itself. The early stages of this shift cannot be recovered fully from extant correspondence, though it seems to have advanced a fair way by the middle of 1820 when Carlyle complained that neither the radical utilitarian Jeremy Bentham, the reformist Whig Thomas Malthus, nor the Tory Poet Laureate Robert Southey were providing the public with the guidance it needed to make its way through the economic and political difficulties of the post-war period. While there 'seems at present a general fermentation of minds, an indeterminate longing after something new, and a heartfelt nausea of the ancient nostrums which have so long delighted us ... so few writers or speakers of eminence have yet appeared to regulate or awaken the current of public thought'.[10]

The ideological even-handedness of this swipe at the 'unhappy herd' of contemporary luminaries, and the assumption that guidance could not be found in the past, were characteristic of positions that became cornerstones of his mature thought. Although Carlyle was still virtually unknown in the literary world he felt no need to defer to well-established figures; on the contrary he already saw himself as a powerful rival to them. Sensing an aspiration for a new cultural authority among the educated classes in England, he sought both to articulate this aspiration and to satisfy it. Between 1816 and 1818 William Hazlitt's penetrating satirical reviews of Coleridge's poetry, intellectual autobiography and lay sermons sparked a clash between an ethos steeped in a libertarian expression of Enlightenment values that appealed to the potentially democratic court of 'public opinion', and what Hazlitt represented as the intensely conservative, even reactionary position of Coleridge and his associates. Hazlitt argued that Coleridge's claim to cultural authority on behalf of a small band of those who saw themselves as imbued with poetic genius, really privileged the subjective will of these figures – coloured by a range of prejudices serving to mask various forms of self interest (emotional, psychological, material and political) – over the sense of the community.[11] At this stage, Carlyle (who later plumped for a radicalised version of the elitist position while tacitly endorsing Hazlitt's criticisms of entrenched literary influences) was a silent spectator of this public struggle for cultural authority. By the early 1820s, however, he had committed himself to engaging in it on his own account. He saw himself as being in the grip of a life-long thraldom to literature – 'if a man taste the magic cup of literature, he must drink of it forever, tho' bitter ingredients be mixed with the liquor' – and had already embarked upon a long search for the subject of a book-length study to promote his claim to influence in the field.[12] Over the course of his literary career Carlyle was forced to choke down many unpalatable draughts – chronic financial insecurity, the irksome company of mercenary and inept authors, the sheer labour and frustration of research and writing and the abuse of critics and the misunderstandings of admirers – but his sense of duty, principled indifference to happiness as an object worthy of human striving, and an unshakeable belief in his own moral rectitude and in the importance of what he had to say, helped him to do so.

The quest for a significant subject was of great importance. As David Masson later pointed out, Carlyle was not content to write *about* literature or literary people; rather, he wanted to use literature to make statements about the human condition that would fulfil a deeply felt contemporary need.[13] Literature without a sense of mission vitiated the most successful of careers: as Carlyle later noted of T. B. Macaulay, he 'feels not the want of any force belonging to himself, wherewith he might *do* somewhat; has yet attained no *belief*, and apparently is not wretched for not having any'.[14] When explaining his aspirations to his mother, Carlyle stressed that writers might serve the 'good old cause' to which they were both, in their different ways, committed. This formulation was tailored to Mrs Carlyle's pious sensibilities, but the idea that literature was, or could be, a mission, was a strong and consistent motivation for pursuing the most precarious of careers. The idea, later developed into an account of modern men of letters as a new priesthood, provided a focal point for Carlyle's ambition and his sense of self-worth in the mid 1820s. In late 1824 he confessed to Jane Welsh that 'In hours of happy musing,

I figure myself as the interpreter of truth and manly integrity and imaginative beauty to thousands of my fellow men'.[15] By the time he was writing *Sartor Resartus* in the late 1820s, Carlyle thought that the products of successful literary endeavour were of immense significance for both writers and their audiences.

> Wondrous indeed is the virtue of a true Book ... like a spiritual tree ... it stands from year to year, and from age to age ... and yearly comes its new produce of leaves (Commentaries, Deductions, Philosophical, Political Systems; or were it only Sermons, Pamphlets, Journalistic Essays), every one of which is talismanic and thaumaturgic, for it can persuade men. O thou who art able to write a Book, which once in the two centuries or oftener there is a man gifted to do ... art a Conqueror and Victor; but of the true sort, namely over the Devil: thou too hast built what will outlast all marble and metal, and be a wonder-bringing City of the Mind, a Temple, and Seminary and Prophetic Mount, whereto all kindreds of the Earth will pilgrim.[16]

The instincts which Carlyle brought to bear on this mission were radical and independent.[17] Even before abandoning a career in the Church of Scotland, his principled objections to established churches placed him on the progressive side in contemporary debates on church and state. Indeed, in the immediate post-war years, when British politics was marked by turmoil and a polarisation of views, Carlyle's political attitudes were decidedly radical. For example, he was highly critical of the hysterical, reactionary tone of the Tory press, much preferring the elegant iconoclasm of Leigh Hunt's *Liberal* to the jeremiads of the Tory *Quarterly Review*. He complained that the latter was 'getting into a very rotten frothy vein' and vilified Robert Southey, a leading contributor to this periodical, as a 'most unblushing character'.[18] Southey's sympathies were at this time buried under his grim, but in some senses, complacent forebodings at the imminent collapse of public order, and he was unapologetic in support of the repressive legal measures adopted by the government. In common with the Tory administrations of the post-war period, Southey's obsessive fears for the safety of the prevailing social order blinded him to what Carlyle termed the 'well-founded complaints of poverty' coming from the urban working classes and from small tenant farmers, a segment of the population whose struggles were particularly familiar to his family.[19] He was contemptuous of the 'zeal and foolish terror and fury' of 'gentry people's' response to an upsurge of working-class radicalism in Glasgow in 1819, noting with apparent approval the hostility shown by bystanders to a detachment of yeomanry leaving Edinburgh for duty in that city. When a lawyer of his acquaintance urged Carlyle to take up a musket and join a drill session of 'Gentleman Volunteers', he was met with the reply 'Mm, yes; but I haven't yet quite settled on which side!'[20]

Like Hazlitt before him, Carlyle launched a deep-seated cultural critique, rather than restricting himself to the machinations of parties and politicians. Thus in addition to condemning the political stance of the Tory press, Carlyle attacked the snobbish and supine demeanour of the entire 'polite' literary establishment. He objected strongly to the appeal to 'people of quality' as the adjudicators of literary and philosophical worth, complaining that such misplaced deference perverted critical judgements of widely different figures such as Samuel Johnson, Goethe and his German contemporaries. In support of this position, Carlyle sought to correct the impression left by J. W. Croker's apparatus to his edition of Boswell's *Life of Johnson*. Croker, a professional politician, holder of a string of subaltern but lucrative offices, and a leading contributor to the *Quarterly Review*, patronised Johnson and sneered at his biographer. Carlyle reacted particularly sharply to Croker's treatment of Boswell's foibles. Unlike Macaulay, who paid Boswell the back handed compliment of attributing the genius of his *Life* to his failings as a human being – 'If he had not been a great fool, he would never have been a great writer' – Carlyle commended Boswell for having resisted the temptation (which must have been very strong in a man of his character) to place himself at the feet of the fashionable and powerful. He had shown that he possessed the insight to discern the true worth of a superficially unattractive, even vulgar, figure and to respond lovingly and nobly to him.[21] Boswell's conduct stood in stark contract to his modern detractor and served to allow Carlyle to make a general point about contemporary Britain. He thought that Croker's edition of Boswell's *Life of Johnson*, a work disfigured by name-dropping and toadyism towards the great and powerful, exemplified the spirit of dependence and servility that prevailed in modern literary culture.[22]

Carlyle's progressive and radical inclinations were underwritten by a steely determination to retain his personal independence. While still committed formally to a clerical career, he railed against the steps necessary to secure a livelihood in this least worldly of professions. Carlyle had particularly strong reservations about the need for clergymen to rely upon demeaning patronage, to 'flatter and wheedle' the 'piques and prejudices' of 'some pitiful country squire'.[23] This statement is a personally-focused formulation of one of the key issues at stake in the dispute that resulted in the creation of Burgher Secession Church from the Church of Scotland, namely the role of lay patrons in clerical appointments. Given his unwillingness to submit to the scrutiny of others, it is unlikely that Carlyle would have been any happier to rely on the good opinions of a congregation than on those of a patron. In any case, by abandoning both the church and the teaching profession, Carlyle sought to insulate himself from the irksome control of others and resolved to retain his independence at virtually any cost. This determination was apparent when he decided to supplement the meagre returns from reviewing by private tutoring. Given the precariousness of Carlyle's financial position and the lowly social status of tutors, the line that he took in negotiations with potential employers was startlingly imperious. Thus a central issue in considering a lucrative offer of employment from a family in Yorkshire was whether 'an inferior shall ever, in the company of this Gentleman, be enabled to forget ... the barriers which discriminate the different ranks of society, and to speak with him as man to man'. This offer was not taken up, and Carlyle later found far more congenial employment with the Bullers. Even though the family treated him with great forbearance and consideration, Carlyle never reconciled himself completely to his role, eventually withdrawing from its service after many irritated private comments on the family's failure to accommodate his desire to settle down in one place.[24]

Carlyle's privileged position in his own family confirmed his sense that he would not place himself under the direction of others. Indeed, on one occasion, Carlyle showed signs of wishing to override his father's views on where the family should live. He was usually satisfied, however, if his freedom of action was not constrained.[25] Home visits were always made on his own terms; he came and went as he pleased, expected domestic management to correspond to his requirements, and never seems to have been required to lend a hand with work on the farm.[26] Carlyle insisted that this pattern was to continue when he and Jane were married. In a letter to Jane Welsh in 1826 on the eve of their marriage, Carlyle wrote that while he was prepared to accept unconditional gifts from his mother-in-law, he would not entertain cost-sharing measures that introduced Mrs Welsh into 'his' household. Such arrangements were unwelcome because Carlyle doubted whether Jane and Mrs Welsh could live together harmoniously; later experience suggested that these misgivings were well founded. At the time, however, Carlyle had no qualms at resisting this proposal on the grounds that it would prevent him replicating the position of dominance that he exercised in his own family. As he explained to his fiancé, the Carlyles 'simply admit that I am [master of the house], and act upon this conviction. Here there is no grumbling about my habitudes and whims ... .'[27] Once married, Carlyle looked to his wife to provide an emotional and physical setting that was conducive to the single-minded pursuit of his literary goals.

Carlyle's jealous concern for his independence reflected a perception of the challenges to recognition and respect posed by his humble birth, straightened financial circumstances and uncertain prospects. As a student, these anxieties might be passed off with a jest. In a letter to one his University friends, Carlyle juxtaposed the 'coronets and crowns, and principalities and purses, and pudding and power' which fortune bestowed on the 'great and noble and fat ones of the earth', with the 'heart of independence' necessary for 'literary fame'. As an awareness of the difficulties of making one's way in the world sharpened in the early 1820s, Carlyle's hypersensitivity concerning his social position and smouldering resentment that his talents were not recognised by the Edinburgh literati, goaded him into displays of verbal aggression that exacerbated the situation.[28] Carlyle heeded Irving's advice that he curb these tendencies and pay more attention to those he wished to attract, later recognised the unappealing figure that he cut at this time: 'so proud, shy, poor, at once so insignificant-looking and so grim and sorrowful.'[29] He nevertheless continued to regard personal independence as a prerequisite for a literary mission and as a key feature of an idealised republic of letters. It was a

> free and independent scene of effort, where no low artifice, no pitiful humiliation of the mind can be of any use, where all that is worthiest in our nature finds ample scope, where success is in our own hands, and each addition to our knowledge, each improvement of our sentiments is a genuine treasure which the world can neither give nor take away.[30]

Literature would only realise this ideal if its devotees assumed a heavy burden of responsibility. In early essays on two working-class heroes of contemporary literature, Robert Burns and Ebenezer Elliott, the 'Corn-Law Rhymer', Carlyle claimed that, although writers from humble origins had to contend with financial hardships, they enjoyed an advantage over those who came from the comfortable classes, being spared the more permanently damaging exposure to false standards of taste that reflected social rather than artistic or intellectual considerations. Elsewhere, in remarks that have special force given his own circumstances, Carlyle pointed to two problems facing those who wished to make literature a noble mission rather than a mercenary and mechanical trade. Aspirants had to find a way of keeping themselves alive by 'speaking forth the *Truth* ... and speaking it *truly* ...'.[31]

Veracity was a key value for Carlyle and in his later writings the idea that contemporaries wilfully ignored the obligation to seek truth reached the level of an obsession. From the first, this idea had an important bearing on Carlyle's strongly positive attitude towards political reform and on the form that it should take. This point emerges with eloquent and sympathetic force in an obituary comment on Charles Buller's political progressivism: 'His luminous sincere intellect laid bare to him in all its abject incoherency the thing that was untrue, which henceforth became for him a thing that was not tenable, that it was perilous and scandalous to attempt maintaining'.[32] Buller's sincerity withstood prolonged immersion in what Carlyle termed the 'dreary, weltering lake of parliamentary confusion'.[33] Authors faced their own distinctive but equally formidable array of challenges, some originating in their emotional and psychological needs, others deriving more directly from the social and economic environment in which they worked.

In *Sartor Resartus* Carlyle dwelt at length on the 'dandy', a figure represented, but by no means exhausted by, slaves to sartorial elegance. For Carlyle, the dandy of the fashionable world was a trope for theatrical figures whose anxiety about their personality reflected a conviction that existence depended upon recognition by others. As a consequence of this alienating fiction, dandies sought to confirm their reality by displaying themselves to the astonishment and wonder of the world. Dandyism was a telling symptom of contemporary society's failure to come to terms with the dislocating uncertainties confronting it, one that parodied a far more widespread tendency to confuse outward 'forms' with the fundamental values that found necessary but transient expression in them. In *Sartor Resartus* the long-suffering editor is faced with the task of presenting the 'philosophy of clothes' to a bemused reading public and demonstrating its importance to them: 'in this one pregnant subject of CLOTHES, rightly understood, is included all that men have thought, dreamed, done, and been: the whole External Universe and what it holds is but Clothing; and the essence of all Science lies in the PHILOSOPHY OF CLOTHES'.[34] Carlyle's exploration of the relationship between 'forms' and 'realities' was prominent in the sympathetic accounts of the anti-formalism of English Puritanism that he produced in the 1830s and 1840s. It also underwrote his insistence that human law was only of value if it embodied the underlying realities of immutable 'natural laws' that governed the universe.[35] Opportunities for display and for ostentatious externalisation of self-consciousness made the field of literature prone to dandyism, a particularly dangerous temptation in light of Carlyle's exalted expectations about its role in the modern world. In so far as his own career was concerned, Carlyle went to considerable lengths to insulate himself from influences that might subvert his mission. The formulation of this mission in heroic terms, and his determination to set his face against unfavourable criticism, all contributed to Carlyle's sense of independence and helped to ensure that his personality, his work and his relationship with his audience, were not reliant upon recognition by others.[36] To the contrary, his role, like that of all genuine writers, was to convey truths to his more or less imperfectly perceptive readers. While Carlyle did not assign a purely passive role to his audience, he assumed that he was endowed with powers they lacked.

Carlyle was particularly concerned at the threat posed to authorial independence and veracity by those whose economic or political influence was deployed to support social, as opposed to intellectual and moral, standards of judgement. His views on this issue reflected his family's disinclination to defer to the claims of social status and wealth when these were not accompanied by what they perceived as more significant virtues. At Mainhill this stance had given rise to a prolonged dispute with General Sharpe, a powerful local landlord and member of parliament, that was still recalled with relish by his neighbours long after his death.[37] When translated onto the literary stage, a concern for threats to independence and moral veracity focused on the dangers posed by unwarranted deference to 'polite' opinion and the economic influence of the booksellers and publishers who wished to avoid alienating it.

In an essay on Boswell's *Life of Johnson*, Carlyle set these threats in the context of the emergence of a modern literary culture. He located Johnson's career at the point where aristocratic patronage was being displaced by an emerging market for literature that enabled some authors to live on the proceeds of sales of their works. When patronage was underwritten by mutual recognition of worth, it supported authors without compromising their commitment to appropriate intellectual, moral and literary values. By Johnson's time, however, the support of talented writers by disinterested aristocratic patrons had begun to be undermined by expectations and relationships that encouraged sycophancy and threatened to choke literary progress. Johnson's revulsion against such dangerous support was expressed most forcefully in his scathing rejection of Lord Chesterfield's offer of patronage, one that was made only when his struggles to produce the *Dictionary* had come to an end.

> Seven years, my Lord, have now past, since I waited in your outward rooms, or was repulsed from your door; during which time I have been pushing on my Work, through difficulties, of which it was useless to complain, and have brought it to the verge of publication, without one act of assistance, one word of encouragement, or one smile of favour ... I hope, it is no very cynical asperity, not to confess obligations where no benefit has been received; or to be unwilling that the public should consider me as owing that to a patron which Providence has enabled me to do for myself.[38]

Carlyle, who was highly critical of the toadying tone of Chesterfield's *Advice to his Son*, used this episode to signal that the degree of independence necessary to make significant contributions to the world of letters was incompatible with reliance on an aristocratic patron. But while the market provided authors with an alternative to the corrupting influence of aristocratic patronage, it exposed them to a new range of threats from greedy and ignorant booksellers.[39] Here, as elsewhere, Carlyle assumed that there was sufficient taste among the reading public to support sound literature, provided that authors overcame the thickets of obstruction and the temptations created by publishers and booksellers and produced works that educated public taste and morals. This process was already underway in Germany. England, however, presented the alarming spectacle of its candidates for membership of the new 'church' being harried by internal and external demands which threatened to compromise the practice of their calling.[40]

Carlyle's correspondence with Edward Irving in the 1820s indicated that even at this stage he realised that his ambition to attain a leading role in contemporary literature would sooner or later require him to leave Scotland and move to London.[41] He first visited the capital in 1824–25 and returned in 1831–32 before finally settling there in 1834. The first of these visits was very successful. Carlyle was greatly impressed by at least some of the scenes of London and its suburbs, and recorded a striking first impression of St Paul's Cathedral that later played a role in *Sartor Resartus*.

> I was hurrying along Cheapside into Newgate-street amid a thousand bustling pigmies, and the innumerable jinglings and rollings and crashings of many coloured labour, when all at once ... I looked up from the boiling throng, thro' a little opening at the corner of the street – and there stood Paul's – with its columns and friezes and massy wings of bleached yet unworn stone; with its statues and its graves around; with its solemn dome four hundred feet above me, and its gilded ball and cross gleaming in the evening sun, piercing up into the heavens thro' the vapours of our earthly home![42]

Irving and other Scots provided him with a range of introductions and he quickly established contact with a number of appreciative people. His second visit in 1831–32 was marred by the frustrations of trying to secure a publisher for *Sartor Resartus*. It did, however, provide him with the opportunity of adding Leigh Hunt and J. S. Mill to a growing circle of literary friends and associates. After Carlyle returned to Scotland, Mill urged him to settle in London, emphasising the regard in which he was held by what he termed 'true believers', and presenting London as focal point for those most likely to be sympathetic to Carlyle's way of thinking and to share his faith that 'all is not hollow and empty'.[43] Although Carlyle's later comments on London often emphasised its less attractive features, likening it to a large begrimed and impersonal machine, he thought that life there nevertheless provided compensatory opportunities for independence that were lacking in his native land. The lure of peace and quiet prompted Carlyle to make frequent escapes to Scotland, but while the refreshing effect of these holidays usually repaid the discomfort and expense of the journey, they tended to revive his aversion to the dogmatic and narrow ethos he identified with his homeland.[44] From this perspective, the benefits of London life far outweighed the disadvantages produced by city noise, dubious food, unreliable servants and the irritations of 'cockneyism'. Geographical advantages were not, however, sufficient on their own so while Carlyle benefited from the stimulation of what he saw as a more open and liberal literary culture than the one he had left behind, he was at pains to maintain a psychological distance from it. The criticisms of the liberal intelligentsia in the *Reminiscences* may be read in this light.[45] Thus while Carlyle and his wife attended Harriet Martineau's 'frequent and crowded' soirees to seek out 'notabilities and notorieties', he claimed that they gradually acquired a true perspective on what were commonly regarded as the peaks of literary society, learning how 'insignificant such notabilities nearly all were'.[46]

Carlyle believed that a self-consciously cultivated inner strength, and a capacity to distinguish 'literary greatness' from popular acclaim or personal enrichment, was necessary to take advantage of the opportunities opened up by residence in the capital. This issue had been a theme in discussions with his university friends – as one of them noted with reference to Dr Johnson, the status of a 'man of genius' was infinitely higher than that of a rich 'man of the world' – and it also conditioned his reflections on the contemporary literary scene in the 1820s.[47] Both Edinburgh and London provided a series of important object lessons in the form of individual examples of cultural stereotypes. Robert Burns's passing lionisation in Edinburgh literary circles exposed him to self-destructive feelings of 'jealous indignant fear of social degradation'. Fecklessness blighted the lives and careers of William Hazlitt and Leigh Hunt, while a very different vice – demeaning materialism – compromised expatriate Scots who lacked the strength of character to overcome the alienating pressures of metropolitan life.[48] Carlyle's anxieties at the precarious nature of his condition and the difficulty of sustaining his independence, reached a peak during the closing stages of the French Revolution project in 1837:

> In bright days, I say: It is *impossible* but I must by and by strike into something! In dark days, I say: And suppose, nothing? My sentiment is a kind of sacred defiance of the whole matter ... In this humour, I write my Book; without hope of it, except of being *done with it*: properly beginning to be as good as feel the Literature has *gone* mad in this country, and will not yield food to any honest cultivator of it ... The longer I live "fame" seems by me a more wretched *Kimmera*; really and truly a thing to shied if it came.[49]

Overwork, anxiety and pressing economic insecurity goaded Carlyle into torturing himself with overwrought assessments of his future prospects. He sought reassurance against failure by looking for forms of distinction that were not measured by the standards of the vulgar.[50] This strategy was reflected in Carlyle's standoffish attitude towards the periodical press. Although he launched his own literary career as a critic writing essays for the literary journals, he was highly disdainful of criticism as a profession. He believed that those committed to the pursuit of popularity were reliant on the dubious taste and moral judgement of critics and sought to avoid this threat to his independence by resisting the temptation that fostered it. Unlike Bulwer Lytton, a contemporary writer who disdained critics while being deeply wounded by adverse reviews and by critical neglect, Carlyle managed to maintain a degree of indifference from the plaudits and censure of those whose judgement he did not value.[51]

As in other cases, Carlyle's personal experiences served as a launching pad for social criticism. He thus coined the terms 'gigmanism' and 'gigmanity' to refer to those who were obsessed with attaining the degree of 'respectable' material prosperity symbolised by keeping a gig. By making 'anti-gigmanism' his 'creed', Carlyle sought to retain a critical distance from the demands of this way of looking at life.[52] What had begun as a principle born out of necessity became a preferred way of life; even in the 1870s when royalties from the popular editions of his works helped to push his annual income to more than £1000,

Carlyle continued to live at a level that could have been sustained without these windfalls.[53] Such modesty made a favourable impression on contemporaries. Visitors to Cheyne Row commented on the homely comfort and elegance of the Carlyles's household. Froude, for example, thought that Carlyle's attitude to material wealth heightened his appeal among the young and earnest. Edward Fitzgerald (by no means an unqualified admirer) remarked on the heroic features of Carlyle's independence, even if it sometimes took the form of bloody-minded-ness, while the author of an obituary noted that Carlyle's modest style of life meant that he was able to 'choose for himself in dignified seclusion the subjects of his indefatigable literary labours'.[54]

Early in his career, when Carlyle was often hard pressed financially, he exerted his independence against what he saw as the literary and monetary impositions of periodical editors, booksellers and publishers. Despite the widely accepted convention that editors had the final say over what appeared in their periodicals, Carlyle resisted editorial interference even when it came from well-intentioned and well-disposed editors. He thus adopted a brusque, dismissive tone when responding to suggestions from Francis Jeffrey, and gave way with very bad grace to John Cochrane's sharply worded 'request' for cuts to an essay on Diderot to eliminate introductory material that 'will apply quite as well to twenty other subjects'.[55] When introducing himself to Macvey Napier, Jeffrey's successor, Carlyle referred to difficulties they had experienced in 'adjusting the respective prerogatives of author and editor' and made it clear that he would resist 'light editorial hacking'.[56] He also took the high ground in negotiating terms with publishers. In his unsuccessful dealings with John Murray over the publication of *Sartor Resartus* in the summer of 1831, Carlyle was unmoved by references to a slump in book sales. He was indignant at suggestions that a work of this kind would be a difficult financial proposition under any conditions, offering Murray the less than comforting advice that the depressed state of the market was not surprising given the quality of publications generally served up to the public. Carlyle flatly refused to give Lord Byron's publisher the right to anything other than one edition of his work and haggled vigorously over other terms.[57]

In March of the following year, he adopted an equally uncompromising stance in 'negotiating' with James Fraser of *Fraser's Magazine*:

> It were in the highest degree unreasonable did I object ... to the rules that you have laid down for paying your Magazine Contributions ... On the other hand, it were extremely unwise, if I too had not rules for my guidance, and did not walk by them. Allow me with all clearness, as one plain-spoken man to another, to explain in a few words my position towards you.
>
> Besides your Magazine there are *four* other Publications, of perfect respectability, from which I have at this time applications for Contributions: the *lowest* offer any of these makes is the one I have proposed to you: two of them ... are between a fourth and a

fifth part *higher*. To your Magazine I have no particular attraction; it is much like others to me; much of its *spirit* I can approve of, much of its tone and execution and practical speculation I must disapprove of: on the other hand *your* personal character (allow me to say this, with the same sincerity) being, as I think, that of a thoroughly punctual, honest and even religious-principled man (almost a Phoenix in your Trade, I fear!) is of that sort which I should decidedly *wish* to do business. So that on the whole *Fraser's Magazine* ... is a vehicle I should as soon select as one of the others.[58]

Carlyle was not ambitious to emulate the triumphs of the Irish literary celebrity Thomas Moore who's *Lalla Rooku* (1817) secured the staggering advance of £3000, nor was he concerned with personal enrichment.[59] Rather, his dealings with publishers and his attitude to the trade were determined by his views on the need for those who took literature seriously to retain a sense of appropriate authorial independence. He was equally uncompromising in his reaction to the responses of readers. After failing to secure a publisher for *Sartor Resartus* Carlyle reluctantly published it in a 'slit condition' as a series of articles in *Fraser's*. He later reported a hostile reception from subscribers – '"What wretched unintelligible nonsense! ... If you publish any more ... I shall be obliged to give up my Magazine!" and so forth' – but declared triumphantly that this had not induced him to revise the work.[60]

Carlyle's reaction was surprising in some ways because his association with *Fraser's* was very valuable financially and artistically. It gave him opportunities to experiment with unconventional literary styles and also provided an outlet through which he could participate in a literary sub culture that challenged the tradition of 'gentlemanly authors' from whom he wished to distinguish himself. The tone of *Fraser's* was both highly intellectual and outrageously (sometimes brutally) humorous, with 'Literary dandies', fashionable novelists such as Bulwer Lytton, as favourite targets.[61] These advantages notwithstanding, Carlyle freed himself from what he saw as the compromising drudgery of reviewing as soon as his financial position allowed it, and declined to capitalise on his growing attractiveness to the editors and proprietors of literary periodicals.[62] Thereafter, in his private negotiations with publishers, and in his public support for an effective regime of copyright protection, he sought to ensure that he and other authors could insulate themselves as far as possible from the direct and indirect control of booksellers and publishers.

In the early stages of his literary career, Carlyle's expectations about the strongly positive role that literature might play in refashioning contemporary culture was tempered by awareness that writers might merely compound the difficulties that beset those who stood on the verge of a new, challenging but chronically unsettling era. He responded to this perceived danger by insisting on a sharp distinction between writers who were worthy of attention and respect, and those who were not. He warned his readers that one of the consequences of the fragile state of the modern mind was that this distinction was either ignored or perverted. Given the prominence of these themes in Carlyle's early writings, and the tendency for him to become increasingly impatient at what he saw as the dangerous absurdities of mid Victorian literary culture, it is ironic that John Stuart Mill would later associate Carlyle's stress on the importance of literature with the pretensions of what he termed the 'feeble and poor minded set of people' who dominated contemporary letters.[63] It is doubly so given Carlyle's discussions of German literature in the 1820s. These essays formed a central component in his strategy of discriminating between worthy and worthless writing and in identifying himself as a leading figure in contemporary literary culture.

Carlyle's approach to the world of English letters reflected attitudes that were characteristic of his family, and were epitomised by its preference for the Burgher Secession Church over the Church of Scotland. The family was intensely clannish and was imbued with an unselfconscious sense of its superiority which resulted in an attitude to the rest of the world that was tinged with censorship and pity. In Carlyle's case, the early recognition of his scholastic abilities reinforced a familial disposition to stand apart from, and feel superior to, others in his intellectual and social milieu. Even in the early intriguing glimpses of Carlyle as a lively member of a student social set in Edinburgh, he stands out as a quite distinctive character and struck his friends that way. The fact that Carlyle later saw himself as a marginal figure in English and Scottish literary culture – one who 'comported' himself 'wholly like an alien' – explains why he looked outside Britain for personal inspiration and for something important and distinctive to offer to his contemporaries and why he made so much of his German points of reference.[64]

Since Carlyle's earliest contributions to published works were translations of French material that he undertook while still a student, his later interest in German literature might be seen as part of a long running engagement with European thought.[65] Nevertheless, the earliest surviving references to Carlyle's sense of literature as a mission correspond very closely with his absorption in modern German writings and with his increasing confidence in that language. In June 1820, he commended Fichte, Goethe and Schiller to Irving as writers who 'have some muscle in their frames'. Shortly afterwards, he claimed that even a very slight study of their works revealed the promise of a 'new Heaven and new Earth'.[66] Carlyle's tendency to exaggerate the distinctiveness of the role that he had assumed as a promoter of German literature, implicitly dismissing the claims of Byron, Coleridge and Hazlitt to cultural authority, was consistent with this way of confronting the world. Although presenting himself as a pioneer in the study of modern German literature in Britain, he was, in fact, really attempting to redirect and invigorate pre-existing expertise and interest identified with

Coleridge, Walter Scott and a wider body of now obscure figures.[67] During the course of the 1820s, the immediate objective of his mission was to reveal at least some of the promise of German writing to British readers. This message was expected to deliver a sharp, salutary jolt to a literary culture that prided itself on being witness to a memorable era in modern letters.[68] In pursuit of this objective, Carlyle produced a steady stream of translations and critical essays on aspects of German literature and a brief, single-volume appreciation of Schiller's life and work.

Although he often complained that reviewing and translating were irksome and financially unrewarding, these supposedly inferior activities brought Carlyle to the attention of literary circles in Edinburgh and London. For example, Barry Proctor introduced Carlyle to William Fraser of the *Foreign Review* in September 1827 as a writer who had been 'enlightening the world as to the merits of German and other exotic writers'.[69] His early work also won him flattering and much-needed expressions of support from Goethe and lesser lights in the German literary firmament. Since his compatriots often dismissed the German writers whom Carlyle admired as 'mystics' or uncouth fantasists, his highly favourable accounts of their work provided a vehicle for identifying and then rectifying some of the deficiencies of the English mind and spirit. In contrast to the ordinary run of critics who pandered to the insularity and self-conceit of their readers by portraying the literary terrain of foreign countries as 'cloud mountains, and *fatamorgana* cities', Carlyle promised to serve as a 'priest of Literature and Philosophy ... as a faithful preacher, teaching [the common man] to understand what is adapted for his understanding, to reverence what is adapted for higher understandings than his'.[70]

The recent history of German literature provided a number of models that highlighted the superiority of German culture. While Carlyle commended Schiller (whose struggles against obscurity and poverty parallel Carlyle's early career) for his 'sincerity of heart and mind' and 'patient long continuing, earnest devotedness', he dismissed Voltaire, a supposedly towering figure in European culture, as 'a great *Persifleur*; a man for whom life, and all that pertains to it, has, at best, but a despicable meaning; who meets its difficulties not with earnest force, but with gay agility; and is found always at the top, less by power in swimming, than by lightness in floating'.[71] By stressing the earnest sincerity of German writers, a virtue that he later associated with English Puritanism, Carlyle drew attention to qualities that accorded with his specifications for moral and intel-lectual greatness, and with his own experiences. Thus in early essays on Jean-Paul Richter and Henreich Heine, he dwelt on the significance of a personal battle for knowledge undertaken by those who sprang from humble backgrounds. Richter's career also demonstrated the possibility of giving an authentic account of religious experience that departed from current orthodoxy. Richter was far from being an infidel. To the contrary, his ideas conveyed a true sense of religion by demonstrating a 'not a self-interested fear, but a noble reverence for the spirit of all goodness'.[72]

When considering the social origins of leading German authors, Carlyle emphasised the need to adopt standards of judgement and taste that were based on appropriate intellectual and moral criteria. Unlike their English contemporaries, the higher class of German writers was not tempted to become devotees of the 'spirit of mammon'. The wide scope for public employment in art galleries, libraries, museums and universities, and the respect with which aristocratic patrons treated their protégés, made German writers less reliant on, and hence less exposed to, the risks of the market for literature. Carlyle presented the situation of German writers in this respect as being markedly better than that of their English contemporaries. In England 'the literary man, once so dangerous to the quiescence of society, has now become perfectly in noxious, so that a look will quail him, and he can be tied hand and foot by a spinster's thread'.[73] English snobbery – apparent in the widespread tendency to look down on German writers merely because they were poor and socially obscure – had much to do with producing and sustaining this sorry state of affairs. Because English literary culture lacked a commitment to aesthetic egalitarianism, readers were predisposed to overlook the benefits that they might derive from the work of German writers. By implication at least, these conditions also made it difficult for newcomers like Carlyle to make their mark without compromising their principles. The English literary establishment, and its offshoots in Scotland, conspired to undermine the republic of letters and obscure the true source of taste and veracity. Carlyle resisted these tendencies, insisting that literature, like true religion, was blind to distinctions based on birth, rank or wealth: 'The charms of Nature, the majesty of Man, the infinite loveliness of Truth and Virtue, are not hidden from the eye of the poor; but from the eye of the vain, the corrupted and self-seeking, be he poor or rich.'[74]

The comparisons that Carlyle made between the literary cultures of Germany and England reflected a wider concern with the hollowness and falsity of English life in the early nineteenth century. He sought to lay bare the flaws in British culture while at the same time holding out the prospect that these might be made good. These flaws were revealed in the penchant for puffing and show and the avoidance of honest endeavour that intruded itself into the most basic productive activities and commercial transactions. In the privacy of a posthumous reminiscence, Carlyle presented his father's dedication as a stern rebuke to these pitiful practices: 'nothing he undertook ... but he did it faithfully and like a true man'.[75] But while this comparison highlighted his father's personal qualities, its real point was far more wide-reaching. Behind the characteristic business practices of the day lay a culture of moral, political and social falsity that needed to be brought forth into the light, confronted and discredited. Those like Carlyle who sought to guide their contemporaries would need to consider 'how far ... man's Want is supplied by true ware, how far by the mere Appearance of true Ware: – in other words, To what extent, by what methods, with what effects ... Deception takes the place of wages of Performance.'[76]

Germany provided a compelling illustration of the virtues of an independent literary culture. Freed from the cloying sycophancy of gentlemanly conceptions of the authorial role, relieved from the burden of pressing want and the temptations arising from an overvaluation of personal affluence, German writers were able to treat literature as a mission. Consequently, their works provided inspiration and guidance rather than being mere playthings that momentarily satisfied the desire for diversion and vicarious sensual stimulation. Even in Germany, however, only *some* writers measured up to Carlyle's ideal. At an early stage of his study of German literature, he distinguished writers of real value from a range of popular dramatists (Heinse, Miller, Vest, Weber the Younger, and, above all, Kotzebue) whose overwrought productions at best formed the froth, and at worst the scum, on a deep vat of substantive literary sustenance.[77] Later, Carlyle refined his classification of recent German authors, distinguishing between a small group of really significant figures and a larger group (whose contribution mirrored that of Byron in England) dubbed the '*Kraftmänner*' or 'powermen'. These writers' achievements were arrested developments in a process that had reached its apogeé in the career of Goethe and was manifest to varying degrees in those of Schiller, Novalis, the Schlegels and Richter.

Carlyle considered that the frequency with which the charge of 'mysticism' was levelled at German writers was indicative of the blinkers imposed on the English mind by enlightenment conceptions of the understanding. As with Mephistopheles in Goethe's *Faust*, the 'ridiculous, the unsuitable, the bad' was readily apparent to the 'lynx vision' of the enlightened intellect; at the same time, however, it was blind to 'the solemn, the noble, the worthy'.[78] This point was most sharply delineated in the blank incomprehension that greeted the work of Novalis in England. In reaction to this response, Carlyle sought to show his compatriots that Novalis was a serious thinker whose ideas were of direct relevance to them. He identified Novalis with 'transcendentalism', a stage in thought ascending beyond the senses, positing a conception of 'reason' that was distinct from the mechanical 'understanding' which reigned unchallenged in the enlightenment scheme of things. Novalis had grasped that reason is 'the pure ultimate light of our nature; wherein ... lies the foundation of all Poetry, Virtue, Religion' and had used this insight to show that these qualities are 'the everlasting basis of the Universe'.[79] Since poetry deals with the invisible rather than the visible, it can only be discussed adequately by new modes of explanation, hence the charges of jargon-ridden mysticism that had been levelled at Novalis and his contemporaries.

While making a strong case for the importance of Novalis's work, however, Carlyle confessed that he was not in a position to explain more fully a way of thinking that defied straightforward exposition. Carlyle's reticence on this point may perhaps have been due to his awareness of his tentative grasp of the history of recent German philosophy.[80] He was far less inhibited in his approach to Fichte and Goethe since he had extensive firsthand knowledge of their work. Carlyle remarked that whatever the shortcomings of Fichte's metaphysics, he should be credited with identifying the 'literary man's' duty to grasp the 'Divine Idea' and present images of it to his readers. As Carlyle later put it, Fichte showed him that only the literary hero was able to see the significance of the ideal of active humanity and convince his contemporaries of it.[81] But while Carlyle was struck with the 'sublime stoicism' of Fichte's sentiments, he credited Goethe with demonstrating the full significance of his thesis. Unlike the typical *Kraftmänner*, whom he had at one time resembled, dealers in 'sceptical lamentations, mysterious enthusiasm, frenzy and suicide'[82], the mature Goethe brought the force of his intellect to bear upon his emotions rather than merely yielding them up to his readers. He thus rose above the bifurcation of human faculties implied by the Enlightenment and the *Kraftmänner's* responses to it. Goethe's corpus provided an artistically and intellectually powerful means of inspiring his contemporaries to embark on the long journey of self and cultural understanding. Goethe had grasped the features of the recent intellectual and spiritual history of European culture that were necessary to understand the modern predicament. He had exposed the limitations of the materialism that blighted the intellectual culture of England and France, and in its place set up two ideas that were central to Carlyle's literary mission: the claim that work or action was a fundamental human response to the world; and the demand that this should be approached in a spirit of 'renunciation'. At the same time, however, Goethe showed that the challenge confronting humanity could be taken up in a spirit of hopeful expectation rather than grim foreboding: 'that *chaos*, into which the eighteenth century with its wild wars of hypocrites and sceptics had reduced the Past, begins ... to be once more a *world*. ... There is in them a New Time, the prophecy and beginning of a New Time'. Goethe had once been gripped by the despair experienced by the hero of *Sartor Resartus*. Having once overcome this, he encouraged his readers to see that the world was 'not tolerable only, but full of solemnity and loveliness'.[83]

Some contemporary critics, as well as later scholars, have noted significance differences between Carlyle's idea of 'renunciation' and the Goethean notion of *Enstagen* with which Carlyle associated it. Goethe's ideal was one of personal harmony that necessitated the appropriate ordering and subordination of elements that would otherwise produce a jarring cacophony.[84] For Carlyle, however, renunciation required the suppression of impulses that were derived from what he took to be shallow and unworthy conceptions of humanity and its destiny: 'it is not what we *receive*, but what we are made to *give*, that chiefly contents and profits us'.[85] As will become apparent in later chapters, these impulses were associated with hedonistic utilitarianism, with conventional egotism, as well as with ideas that were seen to rest on self-inflicted delusions concerning the tractability of notions of right and wrong and related attempts to mould the moral, social and political world so that it would satisfy commonplace ideals of comfort and convenience. When Carlyle promoted renunciation as a necessary feature of aspiration and action, he extolled earnestness, self-abnegation and sincerity and set these virtues in a context framed by concerns for social morality and engagement, rather than by the aesthetic considerations which motivated Goethe. Despite these differences, Carlyle nevertheless presented Goethe's stance as the source that inspired his search for a model that would place optimistic earnestness at the service of beauty and truth, thus providing scope for human fulfilment, and the only viable solution to the challenges facing his contemporaries. This aspiration was forged in the 1820s but it remained with Carlyle throughout his life. More than forty years later at the conclusion of his Rectorial address to the student body at Edinburgh, he urged his enthusiastic listeners to ignore the

> gloomy, austere, ascetic people, who have gone about as if this world were all a dismal prison-house! It has indeed got all the ugly things in it which I have been alluding to; but there is an eternal sky over it; and the blessed sunshine, the green of prophetic spring, and rich *harvests* coming; – all this is in it too.[86]

A long line of critics, including Henry Crabb Robinson, J. S. Mill and Matthew Arnold, has drawn attention to the exaggerated, even idolatrous, features of Carlyle's treatment of Goethe. At times Carlyle himself expressed reservations about Goethe's apparent willingness to subsume other values, including those most closely connected with social and political issues, into aesthetic categories. He kept these reservations to himself and usually refused to be drawn on the question.[87] There is, however, little doubt that his deep sense of gratitude to Goethe was completely sincere. When Ralph Waldo Emerson, who also had reservations about Carlyle's unqualified praise of Goethe, questioned him on the influence of Goethe's 'velvet life' on his morals, Carlyle responded by stressing his great personal debt to the poet and statesman of Weimar. Goethe 'proclaimed to me (convincingly, for I saw it *done*): "Behold, even in this scandalous sceptico-Epicurean generation, when all is gone but hunger and cant, it is still possible that Man be a Man"'.[88] If Carlyle's public worship of Goethe was sincere, it was also quite deliberate and strategic. While he was far from being the first British writer to promote German literature, his relationship with Goethe gave him some claim to having attained a distinctive position in the field. Carlyle's views on this matter can be discerned in his delight at the warmth of his correspondence with Goethe, and the tokens of mutual esteem signified by the exchange of books, engravings and personal presents. These signs of intimacy distinguished him from other British admirers of Goethe, a number of whom collaborated with Carlyle in the public gesture of subscribing to a presentation medal to mark Goethe's eighty first birthday in 1831. As the mediator of Goethe's reputation in Britain, Carlyle hoped to establish his own claim to the sort of cultural authority that he attributed to his German predecessor.[89]

In the case of his presentation of Goethe's views, as in that of other German writers, it must be recognised that conventional literary judgements were not Carlyle's primary concern. He used German literature as a quarry for new ideas. His engagement with it also provided a testing-ground for ideas that he had arrived at independently and which he found stated with particular force and elegance in contemporary German literature. For example, his remarks on the context of Novalis's writings should be seen as a stalking horse for materialism and utilitarian-ism, rather than as scholarly judgements on the history of German philosophy. Similarly, statements about the importance of work in Carlyle's correspondence predate his interest in German literature, while notions of renunciation (with a strongly religious and social rather than aesthetic focus) were prominent in the particular Christian atmosphere in which Carlyle was raised. In a more general sense, the attempt to extol the virtues of German literary culture reflected a wish to identify a distinctive basis for his literary mission, one that encouraged Carlyle's readers to think anew about the challenges that confronted them. At the same time, however, the reading of Goethe and his contemporaries that Carlyle offered his readers meant that he could see himself as an independent actor on the literary scene, drawing on them but establishing his own distinctive claim to be heard.[90]

3

Facing the Modern World

Between 1829 and 1831 Carlyle published two important essays in the *Edinburgh Review* that focused on pressing manifestations of universal problems in his own society. These essays ('Signs of the Times' and 'Characteristics') were written at the invitation of Francis Jeffrey and his successor in the editor's chair, Macvey Napier. Carlyle also produced a polished, but not a final, version of *Sartor Resartus*, a book-length account of the anxieties felt by modern humanity and how they might be confronted. These works presented a distinctive perspective on the condition of the modern world, one that related features of an unsettled outward condition to failings of inner strength, discernment and moral understanding. Carlyle was sharply critical of ideas and practices that demonstrated his contemporaries' failure to come to terms with the fact that the nostrums and ways of the past could not serve the modern age. These criticisms focused on the popular religious, moral and political beliefs of the educated classes. Carlyle always saw it as his duty to challenge orthodox views. Indeed, he thought that literary figures who failed to do so were unsound, and in a sense dishonest, a charge he later levelled against Robert Browning. Browning was 'clever but not truthful ... He accepts conventional values'.[1] At the same time, however, Carlyle was also deeply sceptical of heterodox ideas advanced by putative luminaries of the worlds of literature, high culture and philosophy who were rivals in the struggle for intellectual and moral leadership. He thought they did not understand the problems of the modern age or promote adequate responses to them.

The invitations to write 'Signs of the Times' and 'Characteristics' for the *Edinburgh Review* confirmed Carlyle's growing reputation as a writer with interesting things to say about the challenges facing contemporary British society. Having previously published 'literary' pieces in the *Edinburgh* on John-Paul Richter (1827) and Robert Burns (1828), these essays were his first (and as it turned out, his last) ventures in the field of social and political philosophy under its colours. Since the essays were critical of Benthamite utilitarianism and of the mechanical caste of the modern mind, they were not out of place in a periodical that was the scourge (through the agency of T. B. Macaulay) of James Mill. The founders of the *Edinburgh* were also at one time associated closely with Dugald Stewart, a thinker whom Carlyle credited with having given 'sufficient and final answer' to 'all possible forms of materialism'.[2]

These articles were prepared against a background marked by highly vocal expressions of anxiety at recent and expected developments in the political world. When 'Signs of the Times' appeared, public life was dominated by intense debate of proposals to repeal the Test and Corporation Acts. These measures, dating from the seventeenth century, entrenched the privileged position of the Church of England by discriminating against Protestant Dissenters and Roman Catholics. Those who saw themselves as the true friends of the Established Church resisted repeal on the grounds that it would undermine the Anglican establishment and the traditional social and political order with which it was closely identified. Seen from this perspective, one that was adopted by Tory 'ultras' in Parliament, promoted by influential journals such as the *Quarterly Review*, and endorsed by the King and other members of the royal family, repeal was a significant, even critical, battle in a campaign against the Church of England being waged by an unholy alliance of liberals, Roman Catholics, Protestant Dissenters and closet atheists. For their part, proponents of repeal stressed the illiberal and discriminatory character of measures that had once been justified only because of threats to the constitution. They argued that the Church weakened its credibility by relying on such unjust measures for protection, and advanced principled objections to using the power of the state to support particular Christian denominations. Depending on one's perspective, the repeal of the Test and Corporation Acts and the emancipation of Roman Catholics from a range of civil disabilities might thus be seen as heralding either a new and enlightened era, or the reckless overthrow of an established and beneficial social and political order.[3]

The circumstances in which 'Characteristics' was written were even more highly charged than those in which 'Signs of the Times' had been conceived. During 1831 public debate was dominated by the prospect of 'parliamentary reform', a process that raised questions about the distribution of parliamentary seats, the representation of growing urban centres, and changes to voting qualifications that would enfranchise a greater proportion of the population. Parliamentary reform dominated political debate in parliament and the press and spurred extensive extra-parliamentary agitation. Some demonstrations developed into full-scale riots, the most serious of which occurred at Bristol in October and November 1831. The city was gripped by a prolonged breakdown in public order during the course of which many buildings were burned and a large number of people were killed or seriously injured. The atmosphere of crisis produced by reform agitations was heightened by incidents of rick burning and machine breaking in country districts in reaction to hardship attributed to the introduction of agricultural machinery, and by the outbreak of cholera in cities in the north of England. In some quarters, these events aroused deep public and private apprehension of impending collapse in the economic, social and political orders. Robert Southey, who had fought a ferocious rearguard action against Roman Catholic Emancipation, claimed that the language and demeanour of those attending a radical reform meeting in 1831 epitomised the danger that faced the country. The occasion was marked by displays of 'revolting ribaldry ... nefandous impiety ... daring and rabid blasphemies'. In late 1832 when parliamentary reform had become a fact, the Tory politician J. W. Croker and Bishop Philpott of Exeter warned their countrymen that Britain was 'entering on that calamitous career which our ancestors ran between 1640 and 1660.'[4] Carlyle had wished originally to include Robert Southey's *Colloquies* in his 'Signs of the Times' as an example of the futility of attempting to solve the problems of the present by escaping in to the past, but was thwarted because T. B. Macaulay had already been signed up to review this book.

Although 'Characteristics' was published two years after 'Signs of the Times', Carlyle regarded it as a sequel to the earlier piece. His correspondence and journals show that he was pursuing themes that were incorporated in the article long before Napier's invitation was issued in the early autumn of 1831. 'Signs of the Times' provided a critical analysis of the ideas that dominated contemporary life and thought. 'Characteristics' drew on German literature to outline a perspective on the human condition that pointed the way forward from the disjointed and chaotic present. These essays were related closely to *Sartor Resartus*. Carlyle began serious work on this book in October 1830 and completed it by July of the next year. He told a correspondent that 'Characteristics' was not only a second 'Signs of the Times', it was also distinctly 'Teufelsdröckhish'; that is, it was stamped with the idiosyncrasies of thought and style that characterised the writings of 'Herr Professor Diogenes Teufelsdröckh', the putative hero of *Sartor Resartus*, and author of the profound but obscure philosophical system presented in *Clothes, their Origin and Influence*.[5] In all three of these works, Carlyle sought to present his contemporaries with insights into their condition that no other British author could offer.

The prevailing atmosphere of debate and crisis stimulated Carlyle's interest in social and political issues, particularly during his visit to London in the summer of 1831.[6] Its role in framing the lines of argument that he advanced in 'Signs of the Times', 'Characteristics' and *Sartor Resartus* was, however, oblique, rather than direct. On one level at least, the fierce, highly wrought debates on the justice and wisdom of eliminating religious tests left Carlyle unmoved. His relative detachment was apparent in the wry response to Southey's attempt to stoke the fires of anti-Catholic alarmism in the pages of the *Quarterly Review* in 1829: 'What a strange thing that Quarterly Review! How insular, how lawn-sleeved'. This anti-Episcopalian jibe at bishops' attire epitomised Carlyle's long-standing contempt for Tory jeremiads.[7] In *Sartor Resartus*, Carlyle developed an elaborate metaphor of 'church clothes' to convey the idea of a radical lack of fit between the requirements of present and future generations and the outward symbols of religious faith that had satisfied early ages. Elsewhere, he adopted an architectural image, picturing the Church of England as a partly ruined and wholly incommodious structure. He resisted any suggestions that it might be spiritually and intellectually restored. The church had become a 'deserted edifice' that 'people may leave … alone till a grove of natural wood grow round it; and no eye but that of an adventurous antiquarian may know of its existence'. If it obstructed the way, however, it should be pulled down.[8]

The biography of John Sterling that was published in 1851 provided a warm and loving appreciation of its subject but contained much harsh criticism of the Church of England and of those who deluded themselves into seeing it as the vehicle of national salvation. As time went on, Carlyle's exasperation with the Church of England prompted him to even more intemperate condemnations of the Anglican clergy. In 1857, for example, he accused them of 'solemnly, and in the face of God and man, professing their steadfast faith and belief in that which they know they do not steadfastly believe in'.[9] He was equally critical of High Church Anglicans, Roman Catholics, and of what he regarded as the materialistic turn of contemporary nonconformity. Carlyle's dislike of theological speculation and self-conscious religiosity, and his suspicion of all forms of organised religious practice, played a role in these criticisms. Reluctant to commit himself to any elaborate statement on the significance or meaning of Christianity, Carlyle gave only the briefest glimpses of his views on these issues. For example, in a series of lectures that he gave on the history of literature in London in 1838 (but not published until after his death), he described Christianity as being based on the belief that a 'gift of the Creator' was responsible for the 'dignification of man's life and nature'. This belief should be accompanied by humility, not by pride, and by an acute awareness that humanity's special status was quite as likely to be a source of sorrow as of pleasure. Christianity revealed 'eternity existing in the middle time of man'. It meant that

> Every man may with truth say that he waited for a whole eternity to be born, and that he has now a whole eternity waiting to see what he will do now he is born. It is this which gives to his little period of life, so contemptible when weighed against eternity, a significance it never had without it. It is thus an infinite arena, where infinite interests are played out; not an action of man but will have its truth realised and will go on for ever. His most insignificant action, for some are more so than others, carries its print of this endless duration.[10]

While Carlyle was thus reluctant to dwell upon what he regarded as fruitless theological speculation, he was adamant about the value of religious faith in relation to human action, and passionate in his desire to bring this critical truth home to his contemporaries. Religion endowed human beings with an indelible sense of right and wrong that provided the basis of their duties to one another, and with a faith that justice would sooner or later be done. In the past, these beliefs were 'clothed' in elaborate systems of religious observance, the viability of which had been destroyed by the spread of science and enlightenment. Religion now rested on direct communication between God and humanity, and on an understanding of that relationship that emphasised humanity's responsibility for its fate. The cause of truth was impeded by those who, like Anglican bishops, paraded 'between men's eyes, and the eternal light of Heaven'.[11]

Although Carlyle summed up the condition of the country in 1831 in dire terms – 'nothing on all hands but broken heads, broken hearts, woe, want, wickedness and madness over the whole world' – it is significant that even in this climate of crisis, he scorned the millennial fantasies that gripped some sections of the population. In 'Signs of the Times' he reviewed a work by his old friend Edward Irving, treating it as representative of the perspective of a number of contemporary sects that saw recent events as the closing sequences of a series of signs that the world was to undergo an apocalyptic transformation.[12] There was, he coolly observed, a 'common persuasion among serious ill-informed persons that the *end of the world* is at hand'.[13] Carlyle rejected this way of thinking emphatically, warning his contemporaries that no direct help could be expected from God. Periods of crisis posed challenges to humanity rather than foreshadowing divine intervention in human affairs. They presented opportunities for human beings to save themselves, rather than serving as signs that human agency was at an end.

At various places in Carlyle's early work, and in a chapter dedicated to the theme in *Sartor Resartus*, he evoked the image of a phoenix arising from the ashes to signal his understanding of the meaning of the sense of chronic dislocation that gripped contemporary society. This image has significant implications for Carlyle's perspective on the conflagrations and explosions that periodically confounded attempts to manage widespread social and political reconstruction through incremental change, controlled burn-offs, and carefully executed demolition. Thus while he regarded traumas such as the French Revolution as having been necessary for the emergence of modern society from the thralls of the past, he did not see them, as Irving and his followers were inclined to do, as parts of a sequence that was independent of human agency. Teufeldröckh's English editor pretends to deplore his subject's 'philosophical fatalism' only to make it clear that this stance is compatible with an ethos of active engagement. Human beings are capable of contributing to processes of reformation that give meaning to their lives because they transcend the limits of their temporal existence.[14] The image of the phoenix is critical to Carlyle's presentation of this position. It precludes nostalgic, immobilising reaction, and complacent, easily disillusioned and destabilised utopianism. The phoenix heralds a golden age in the future, not in the past, and conveys the hopeful expectation that, by contending with the travails of the present, human beings are partaking in a process of salvation. Society's fiery destruction is but the beginning of its 'long travail-throes of Newbirth'.[15]

While the focus of political debate made it seem as if the current crisis was caused by attempts to transform political and social structures, Carlyle saw the outward derangement of human life as the product of a deep-seated, inward, spiritual and intellectual malaise. His work was closely related to current political debates and to exchanges in the periodical press, but he saw himself as offering a far more deep-seated and fundamental explanation than those of other literary and political figures.[16] Ironically, given his later reputation as a prophet of doom, 'Signs of the Times' linked the vogue for prophecy, apparent both in millenarianism and in the secular optimism of the 'Millites' of all denominations, with the external and the internal dimensions of these distempers. In 'Characteristics' he was equally critical of what he saw as his contemporaries' morbid penchant for self-conscious reflection, reminding them of the proverb, 'the healthy know not of their health, but only the sick'.[17] The hero of *Sartor Resartus* was famous for his coffee house and tavern disquisitions, but it is noted that while his performances were spell binding, Teufeldröckh's delivery was marked by an uncanny lack of self-consciousness. The most memorable utterances pour forth from a head

> apparently not more interested in [his audience], not more conscious of them, than is the sculptured stone head of some public fountain, which through its brass mouth-tube emits water to the worthy and the unworthy; careless whether it be for cooking victuals or quenching conflagrations; indeed, maintains the same earnest assiduous look, whether water be flowing or not.[18]

By contrast, the obsessive, fretfully self-conscious displays of the putative saviours of contemporary Britain are symptomatic of the problems faced by their society, not diagnoses or healing prescriptions for it.

In *Sartor Resartus* Carlyle presented a highly personalised account of the process through which such an understanding might come about, one that took the form of a spiritual and intellectual biography with strongly autobiographical overtones. This story was framed, however, by accounts of Teufelsdröckh's philosophical views that incorporated the more broadly focused historical and social perspectives which characterised Carlyle's contributions to the *Edinburgh Review*. The 'signs of the times' must be understood historically, not contingently. They were particular manifestations of a recurring problem that faced human beings: how they could come to terms *productively* with the world, and with their place within it. Carlyle did not think that the resolution of this problem required an accurate or complete understanding of the universe. This ambition, the hallmark of the putatively 'enlightened' mind of eighteenth-century European high culture and of its antique precursors, could never be realised. As far as human understanding was concerned, the universe would always remain a 'great deep sacred infinitude of Nescience'.[19] To think otherwise was to fall victim to what Carlyle saw as a typically confused combination of species self-abnegation and hubris. Total understanding was to be the product of a conception of the progress of science that would destroy 'Wonder and in its stead substitute Mensuration and Numeration'.[20] Carlyle did not think that this objective could be achieved because neither the human nor the natural worlds could be reduced to these terms. He warned, however, that the pursuit of this mirage exacerbated greatly the difficulties that faced his contemporaries in coming to terms with the challenges of charting a course from the old world to the new.

Carlyle thought that the extreme hopes and fears that gripped secular reformers ('Millites') and religious enthusiasts ('Millenarians') were indicative of a more fundamental public and private malaise. Those who wished to arrive at an accurate understanding of the nature and cause of current disenchantment would have to look beyond these manifestations of a distempered condition and examine the characteristic beliefs of modern humankind. In 'Signs of the Times', Carlyle claimed that the emphasis that his contemporaries placed upon 'mechanical genius' and their lack of understanding of, or appreciation for, the 'dynamic', were telling indications of the flawed character of their belief systems, and of the fundamental causes of the troubled condition of individuals and society. In the modern world, the dynamic forces had been overwhelmed by the 'mechanical' ones, the reliance upon which was, in its turn, a response to panic engendered by a perception that the world seemed to have ceased to make any sense because it had ceased to be organic.[21] Consequently, movements for social and political regeneration actually exacerbated the ills of humanity by fostering misplaced hopes of social and personal salvation while promoting a perspective upon human life that systematically undermined the basis of these expectations.

The term 'dynamic' was used by Carlyle to characterise ways of thinking that took account of the fundamental nature and value of things and ideas. The 'science of dynamics' gives primacy to the question 'what is it?' not 'how is it?' It relies on 'direct vision' into things, rather than on the superficial account of their relationships that is produced by conventional logical analysis. Dynamics denoted a mode of thinking, a way of looking at the world, that both reflected and addressed the 'primary, unmodified energies of man ... all of which have a truly vital and *infinite* character'.[22] A sense of infinitude anchors humanity in a complex, organic, universe, providing the basis for feelings of shared identity which make social life viable: 'only in looking heavenward, take it in what sense you may, not in looking earthward, does what we call Union, mutual Love, Society, begin to be possible'.[23] Carlyle never explains systematically what is implied in 'deep vision', but he identifies it with the values expressed in art, music, philosophy and, above all, with religion. When treated in ways that give due consideration to humanity's distinctive status, these forms of experience engage the fullest possible range of human faculties. But while ordinary people can respond to accounts or expressions of 'deep vision', they are not able, individually or collectively, to exercise it to any high degree. This responsibility falls on people of genius, particularly, in the modern era at least, on men of letters.

In 'Signs of the Times' the requirements of a perspective that recognises humanity's dynamic qualities is juxtaposed with one that views human life, thought and spirituality through the lens of the 'science of mechanics'. The unstated but specific target of this theme in Carlyle's essay was William Alexander MacKinnon's *The Rise, Progress, and Present State of Public Opinion in Great Britain and Other Parts of the World* (1828).[24] MacKinnon thought that the mechanisation of production, distribution and communication provided the conditions for creating a powerful body of public opinion capable of stimulating economy, intellect, literature, morals and taste, and regulating the exercise of political power. This view of public opinion was not a popularist one; rather, it was seen, in a way that echoed the position that James Mill advanced in his *Essay on Government*, as the collective and exclusive province of a prosperous middle class.[25] Carlyle's assault on the aspirations of the 'Millites' was designed to discredit the pretensions of this class by demonstrating the inadequacy of the basis on which its claims to superiority rested. Far from being the holders of a key that would sooth the present by unlocking the treasures of the future, those to whom MacKinnon looked were wedded to a dangerously inadequate perception of the human and natural world. Human beings were endowed with qualities that were quite literally beyond the ken of the exclusively 'mechanical' conception of human thought and experience that had increasingly dominated religion, philosophy and ordinary life since the seventeenth century.

Carlyle allowed that in some significant respects 'mechanical genius' – the capacity to relate cause to effect in the material world, and to use this knowledge to expand the physical capacities of humankind – made important contributions to human welfare, and to humanity's capacity to reduce parts of the natural world to a more orderly and beneficial condition. He insisted, however, that attempts to apply mechanical ingenuity to all aspects of life were characteristic errors of the modern age: 'Not the external and physical alone is now managed by machinery, but the internal and spiritual also. Everything has its cunningly devised implements, its pre-established apparatus; it is not done by hand, but by machinery.'[26] The key issue was not that the mechanical capacities of humanity played an increasingly important role in the modern world, but that the mechanical cast of mind had attempted to usurp the province of the dynamic by being applied to aspects of human life and thought that should be guided by aesthetic, moral and religious values.

In post-war England this line of argument was associated with Coleridge's and Southey's conservative romanticism, and before that it had been expressed in more ideologically ambivalent aphorisms penned by Novalis.[27] But while these writers saw a mechanistic worldview as a danger to be avoided, Carlyle claimed that it had already become the dominant mode of modern society and the guiding principle of social action. Carlyle's demonstration of this point was prominent throughout 'Signs of the Times'. He claimed that the mechanical frame of mind was so deep-seated and pervasive that the present time might best be characterised as the 'mechanical' age'. This was most obviously true of communications and production, but it applied also to areas of human thought and endeavour where the misapplication of the 'science of mechanics' demeaned human life and gave rise to deep personal unhappiness and social dislocation. Thus mechanical genius attempted to address the non-material needs of humanity by devising institutions for combining effort, focusing activity, fostering efficiency and for generally minimising the reliance on individual initiative.

Giving free rein to his penchant for making serious points through absurd exaggeration, Carlyle underlined the insidiousness of the mechanical spirit by a remorseless exemplification of this misplaced principle in diverse and surprising areas of life.[28] He accused contemporaries of adopting mechanical solutions to educational problems, treating the cultivation of the human mind as an objective that could be pursued through refining systems of mass instruction. London clubs, just coming into vogue in the 1820s, were manifestations of the same tendency: 'the principle of sociability being quite gone, that of gregariousness is there in full action'.[29] These institutions, along with societies formed to disseminate the Christian faith and to promote the work of artists, scholars and writers, sought to combine and organise human capacities and interactions in the same way that machines harness, concentrate and regulate the energy put into them. Christianity was to be spread by funding, printing and distributing Bibles and religious tracts as efficiently as possible. In philosophy, art and literature, reliance on the solitary thinker or artist was implicitly rejected and preference was given to mechanically contrived structures dominated by magazines and learned societies.[30] These institutions stimulated the products of artistic and scientific endeavour and harnessed and controlled the outcomes resulting from it. Even the art of composition was reduced to mechanical terms, with authors such as the German biographer of Heine 'writing by pattern':

> this species of writing comes to resemble power-loom weaving; it is not the mind that is at work, but some scholastic machinery which the mind of old constructed, and is from afar observing. Shot follows shot from the unwearied shuttle; and so the web is woven, ultimately and properly, indeed, by the wit of man, yet immediately and in the mean while by the mere aid of time and speed.[31]

Similarly, contemporaries saw political regeneration wholly in terms of the overhaul of electoral, administrative and legal machinery, ignoring the spirit of political actors and the moral assumptions that they brought to their work.

Carlyle deployed these caricatures to draw attention to what he saw as a fundamental characteristic of modern humanity. 'Men', he wrote, 'are grown mechanical in head and in heart, as well as in hand. They have lost faith in individual endeavour, and in natural force of any kind … Their whole efforts, attachments, opinions, turn on mechanism, and are of mechanical character.'[32] This line of argument was not to be construed as a general critique of organised social effort, or taken to imply that Carlyle saw no role for it in the modern world. To the contrary, he regarded solidarity and sociability as one of the fundamental fruits of humanity's godlike status. He insisted, however, that mechanical collective endeavour could not compensate for the 'spiritual impotency' that afflicted his contemporaries.[33] Carlyle's critical observations on his contemporaries' reliance on mechanics reflected the organic cast of his own thinking. His organicism was, however, 'relational' not 'holistic'; that is, he believed that organic structures, including societies, were a product of the interaction of discrete units rather being a self-subsistent entity with subordinate elements. This way of viewing society was concerned particularly with the relationship between classes, and with individuals' capacity and willingness to engage with their fellows and take responsibility for performing within the social whole.

The practical reliance on the science of mechanics was underwritten by an assumption that morals and religion were explicable in similar terms. In promoting public opinion, MacKinnon was placing his faith in a mechanical device, one utilising the stimulating effect of approbation and the repressive effect of disapprobation, as the sole source of moral notions and as the regulator of conduct. In so doing, he demonstrated his faith in 'greater perfection of police', rather than 'greater love of virtue'.[34] Carlyle claimed that this faith also lay at the heart of modern notions of religiosity, contrasting this woeful state of affairs with the authentic expression of humanity's religious sense in the medieval world:

> Religion … is no longer what it was, and should be, – a thousand-voiced psalm from the heart of Man to his invisible Father, the fountain of all Goodness, Beauty, Truth, and revealed in every revelation of these; but for the most part, a wise prudential feeling grounded on mere calculation; a matter, as all others now are, of Expediency and utility; whereby some small quantum of earthly enjoyment may be exchanged for a far larger quantum of celestial enjoyment.[35]

The illustrations drawn from literature and religion reinforce a point (implied by the choice of MacKinnon as the focus of his critique of this characteristic delusion) that emerges from the array of instances of mechanical genius that Carlyle educes in 'Signs of the Times'. Although MacKinnon stood for the 'Millites', he was, in fact, a much more mainstream figure than this association may suggest. Far from being a philosophical radical, he was not even numbered among the less ideologically pure followers of Bentham, and in 1830 secured election to the House of Commons as a Tory Member.[36] In focusing on MacKinnon Carlyle was demonstrating that the mechanical spirit was not the exclusive preserve of vulgar Utilitarians and other over-rationalists. Rather, he sought to show that it pervaded contemporary life, finding its way into the arts, literature, education and religion.

Despite its apparent vigour, however, the attempt to apply mechanical genius in these areas was bound to fail. Literature, the fine arts, and religion were manifestations of the dynamic forces to which human beings were inextricably tied, forces that were beyond the reach of what Carlyle termed 'common school logic.' When considering these aspects of human existence, it was necessary, as Teuflesdröckh demonstrated, to proceed by 'large Intuition over whole systematic groups and kingdoms; whereby, we might say, a noble complexity, almost like that of Nature, reigns in his Philosophy, or spiritual Picture of Nature: a mighty maze, yet, as faith whispers, not without a plan.'[37] By attempting to substitute mechanical understanding for 'large intuition', modern thinkers either struggled vainly to reduce the dynamic to mechanical terms, or ignored those aspects of human life that were incompatible with their principles. As Novalis had remarked of the eighteenth-century science of optics, a concentration on the mechanical, refractory qualities of light blinded people to the 'magical play' of its colours.[38] Rather than expanding the field for human endeavour, as the Enlightenment had promised, the reliance on machinery depreciated individual human effort, reduced the scope for moral freedom and deprived society of the inspiring contribution of genius.

The critical consciousness of the Enlightenment had played an important and necessary role in exposing the inadequacy of earlier modes of thought and the forms and institutions that sprang from them. It had also, however, created the conditions in which an increasingly unbridled mechanical intellect could be set to work. As a result, it left humans bereft of ideas that could satisfy their needs as infinite beings. But while the mechanical understanding could displace dynamic forces, it could not erase them from the human consciousness. To the contrary, when it was misapplied it gave rise to states of mind and social relationships and prescriptions for organising the life of the community, which clashed with fundamental facets of human nature, and could never provide the basis for a stable, sustainable social order, or for a general sense of human wellbeing. The necessarily frustrating outcomes of the misapplication of the science of mechanics were apparent in what Carlyle took to be the distinctive symptoms of the ills that afflicted his contemporaries, including particularly their morbidly heightened sense of self-consciousness.

In 'Characteristics', Carlyle claimed that an excess of self-consciousness, most obviously manifested in speculation about human nature and the current condition of humanity, was a symptom of individual and social ill-health:

Unconsciousness belongs to pure unmixed life; Consciousness to a diseased mixture and conflict of life and death: Unconsciousness is the sign of creation; Consciousness, at best, that of manufacture. So deep, in this existence of ours, is the significance of mystery.[39]

The idea that the unconscious signifies an awareness of, and a reconciliation with the mysterious dimensions of human existence, is related to Carlyle's intense suspicion (expressed with increasing vehemence as time went on) of those who relied on the power of the spoken word and his closely related claims concerning the significance of silence: 'Experience often repeated, and perhaps a certain instinct of something far deeper that lies under such experiences, has taught men ... that the loud is generally the insignificant, the empty.'[40] Boastful contemporary references to the 'march of intellect', weighty tomes on 'man', and the sheer volume of contemporary enquiries into theology, politics and philosophy, were signs of a heightened, and Carlyle thought, a fervid self-consciousness, that had developed in response to a growing uncertainty about the purpose of human existence and the present direction of humanity:

Our whole relations to the Universe and to our fellow-men have become an Inquiry, a Doubt; nothing will go on of its own accord, and do its function quietly; but all things must be probed into, the whole working of man's world be anatomically studied.[41]

These expressions of rampant self-consciousness were symptoms of a radically unsettled condition; they also represented tragically unsuccessful attempts to find solutions to it. In his later writings, and particularly in the 'Latter-Day Pamphlets' of 1850, Carlyle often gave the impression that he thought his contemporaries had given up the struggle. This was not the issue in the 1820s and 1830s. To the contrary, these decades were marked by strenuous attempts to address a range of social, political and spiritual difficulties facing English society. Some of these attempts, directed at the misery that seemed to be becoming more prevalent among the lower classes, were responses to the paradox of unprecedented wealth and productivity in the midst of deprivation.[42] Carlyle was far from being indifferent to the material hardships suffered by the poor. He nevertheless insisted that an exclusive concentration upon them was indicative of a lack of understanding of the true nature of the crisis facing humanity. Even responses that focused on humanity's intellectual, moral and spiritual condition reinforced the conditions of mind to which the crisis could be traced.

This tendency could be seen in the strenuous religious controversies over the 'evidences of Christianity' and the way in which these proofs should be propagated. Christianity, or any other authentic expression of human infinitude, could not be addressed in legal-scientific terms, and was, in fact, not in need of support from these sources. Literature and philosophy manifest different, but related, shortcomings. Modern letters were increasingly dominated by the bloated self-consciousness of authors and critics, a tendency that Carlyle (ironically given the focus of his early career) thought was epitomised by the importance placed on reviews and reviewers. Guidance could not be expected from these sources, or from philosophical products of the 'sceptical inquisitory' art of modern metaphysics.[43] Carlyle regarded metaphysics as a largely negative discipline, one that sometimes exposed the weaknesses of outmoded ways of thinking and cleared the way for human progression. While it might thus have a role to play in certain circumstances, it could not make a positive contribution to an intellectual, moral and spiritual condition marked by dehabilitating doubts about the purpose of human life. Conviction was not a product of negation; it required a positive affirmation of what Carlyle, in a central chapter in *Sartor Resartus*, characterised as the 'Everlasting Yea'.

Those who struggled honestly, if ineffectually, to replace the outmoded expressions of traditional faith with materialism and commonplace ideas of happiness, were absolved of the moral weakness that Carlyle identified with Coleridge's attempt to defend the Church of England even when he must have known it to be a chimera. They were also free of the tragic delusions that destroyed Edward Irving. Carlyle's attitude towards these two tendencies in modern thought is apparent in the tone he adopted in discussing them. When considering defenders of outmoded religious ideas and institutions he was pitying, yet dismissive. By contrast, he treated those who were seeking to provide supposedly progressive alternatives to these relics of the past as serious antagonists and subjected them to the full blast of his withering criticisms. The claim that reliance upon mechanical aspirations and ideas gave rise to suggestions for solving the difficulties of the age that were not only nugatory, but also counterproductive, was central to Carlyle's critique. Ideas derived from such a source could not satisfy infinite beings, nor could they inspire them to act morally. To the contrary, the products of mechanical genius ignored the dynamic requirements of humanity and made human life seem senseless. They could not offer any convincing moral and spiritual recompense for the unavoidable hardships of the human condition. Carlyle insisted that the fact that there could be no delusions on this score had the effect of sharpening the sense of alienation that gripped modern humanity: 'the sum of man's misery is even this, that he feels himself crushed under the Juggernaut wheels, and knows that Juggernaut is not a divinity, but a dead mechanical idol'.[44]

The deadening effects of extreme materialism were demonstrated in what Carlyle dubbed the 'last work and testament' of Thomas Hope, author of *Origins and Prospects of Man*, and one of the characteristic voices in the 'stunning hubbub' of modern demonstrations of doubt-ridden self-consciousness. Carlyle described Hope's work as the 'apotheosis' of the creative powers of materialism; it was 'scarcely intelligible' and 'wholly unreadable'. Other voices include those of Byron – 'rushing madly into the dance of meteoric lights that hover on the mad Maelstrom' and going 'down among its eddies'; Shelley – 'like the infinite, inarticulate grief and weeping of forsaken infants'; Hazlitt – wrestling 'among endless Sophisms, doing desperate battle as with spectre-hosts'.[45] The work of Frederick Schlegel, whose *Philosophical Lectures* from 1829 was one of the putative subjects of 'Characteristics', was more promising. Although Schlegel and his countrymen remained trapped in the vortex of metaphysical speculation, they had at least shown that science and religion were not incompatible. But while their work held out the prospect of a 'new revelation of the Godlike', it provided a hopeful symptom of a change in the condition of the European mind rather than furnishing evidence that a cure had been found for its ills.[46]

Carlyle's account of Schlegel's work was brief and sketchy, really no more than a convenient peg on which to hang his own ideas than the subject of a serious review. His references to it did, however, provide an opportunity to reiterate earlier claims about the relative superiority of German literary culture and the failings of that of England. He warned however, that the struggle to fulfil the promise signalled by Goethe and his contemporaries would be protracted:

> The doom of the Old has long been pronounced, and irrevocable; the Old has passed away: but, alas, the New appears not in its stead; the time is still in pangs of travail with the New. Man has walked by the light of conflagrations, and amid the sound of falling cities; and now there is darkness, and long watching, till it be morning.[47]

But although the watch would be long – Carlyle seems to have thought in terms of generations rather than years – humanity need not be filled with a gloomy sense of foreboding. The origin of the contemporary sense of dislocation itself provided grounds for hope: 'our spiritual maladies are but of Opinion; we are but fettered by chains of our own forging, and which ourselves also can render asunder. This deep, paralysed subjection to physical objects comes not from Nature, but from our own unwise mode of *viewing* nature'.[48] The dynamic forces connecting human beings to the invisible world had not been eradicated from humanity's consciousness. Indeed, Carlyle regarded the sufferings of his contemporaries as proof of their persistent impact on humanity. These sufferings would only be alleviated when human thought and action gave due recognition to an intrinsic aspects of human nature. This task made it necessary for Carlyle's countrymen to accept the light offered by Goethe and his contemporaries, and to give up the futile and dangerous attempts to lay bare the mysteries of the infinite. Only when this was done would modern societies be able to address effectively the external requirements of humanity.[49]

This critique of the mechanical cast of the modern mind did not mean that Carlyle saw himself as being engaged in a battle against modern science; to the contrary. Like some of his predecessors among the German romantics, Carlyle had a long-standing interest in current developments in experimental science, having been attracted to professors at Edinburgh with interests in geology, mathematics and physics.[50] He later impressed John Tyndall, the eminent scientist, with his ready and sympathetic grasp of recent developments in scientific thinking, and with his willingness of take account of evolutionary thinking.[51] In this case, as in his earlier reaction against the pervasive influence of the science of mechanics, the real issue concerned the misapplication of modes of analysis that might well be appropriate and beneficial in other contexts. In 'Signs of the Times', Carlyle appealed to his contemporaries to 'coordinate' the application of mechanics and dynamics, thus avoiding the delusions and fanaticism resulting from an undue reliance on the latter, and the obliteration of morality that resulted from dependence on the former.[52] Because the balance between these two modes of understanding had tilted so far to the mechanical side, however, Carlyle concentrated his energies on encouraging his contemporaries to recover values that he thought were critical to any attempt to forge an emotionally and spiritually satisfying pathway to the future.

The science of dynamics expressed and secured the faith that gave meaning to human life; it also attached the present generation to past and future generations that shared it. Despite his insistence that his contemporaries could not rely on the ideas, institutions and practices of the past, Carlyle nevertheless believed that a sense of belonging in time, identification with former manifestations of timeless values, and the expectation that they might be realised in the present, were inescapable features of the human mind. The importance of such a faith was amply, if negatively, demonstrated by the crushing impact of uncertainty upon the contemporary human spirit, and its disastrous effect on social and political life. The age, as he later put it, was 'at once destitute of faith and terrified at scepticism'.[53] The fact that human beings were unable to endure a felt lack of faith, pointed obliquely to the inescapable importance of the dynamic requirements of human existence.

These requirements formed the basis of a true conception of morality that gave priority to humanity's obligation to play a creative and ordering role in the world. This role was the focal point of Carlyle's doctrine of 'work'.[54] He applied this term to all worthwhile forms of human endeavor, using it to signify all the practical, intellectual and moral activities that were necessary to human well being.[55] The chaotic, unfathomed and unformed reaches of the universe provided opportunities for human beings to secure the sense of self-worth and satisfaction that Carlyle regarded as personal, social and cosmic necessities. As he put it in *Sartor Resartus*,

> a certain inarticulate Self-consciousness dwells dimly in us; which only our Works can render articulate and decisively discernible. Our Works are the mirror wherein the

spirit first sees its natural lineaments. Hence, too, the folly of that impossible precept, *Know thyself*; till it be translated into this partially possible one, *Know what thou canst work at.*[56]

Carlyle urged his contemporaries to conduct their lives by this rule, and he sought to show them that honest commitment to the 'gospel of labour' was their only safeguard against the corrosive demoralisation caused by the gnawing doubt that currently blighted their lives. At the same time, however, he thought it necessary to warn against a range of ideas that insulated them from this truth or deflected them from adhering rigorously to it. For this reason, he insisted that the satisfaction available to humanity should not be confused with the conventional notions of 'happiness' assumed in moral thinking and moral practice in the modern world. Stated most forcefully in the works of the utilitarian philosopher Jeremy Bentham and his followers, the assumptions that underlay philo- sophical utilitarianism had, in fact, become unquestioned axioms of popular morality.

In *Sartor Resartus*, Carlyle made grim sport with the conceit of progressive novelty that permeated English statements of the doctrine of utility, casting himself as an advanced figure while castigating his contemporaries for being wedded to tired commonplaces derived from Locke, Hartley and Helevetius. This system had already run its course in France and Germany, and the ongoing English attachment to it was a mark of the outmoded condition of the intellectual and moral culture of that country. Those who preened themselves as 'advanced' thinkers were, in fact, merely echoing what had become a widespread popular belief. Utilitarianism was thus well on the way to sinking into an unreflective tradi- tion rather than being in the vanguard of the march of mind.[57] This outcome was particularly ironic since, unlike some the traditional expressions of human understanding that it challenged, utilitarianism lacked any capacity to express dynamic values. Hedonistically framed desires for ease and contentment took no account of the dynamic requirements of human life, completely ignored the implications of the limits of human understanding, and evaded the challenge posed by the protean condition of the universe. As infinite beings, humans could not expect to be satisfied by finite values and would suffer grievously as long as they continued to believe that they would. In any case, those who made the pursuit of happiness the supreme object of human life ignored what Carlyle took to be the incontrovertible fact that humanity inhabited a world in which suffering, contradiction and error were inescapable. His views on this issue, as unequivocal as those of the tradition of Christian moralism from which he sprang, meant that evil was humanity's constant, indeed necessary, companion.

> Evil, what we call evil, must ever exist while man exists: Evil, in the widest sense we can
> give it, is precisely the dark, disordered material out of which man's Freewill has to create

an edifice of order and Good. Ever must Pain urge us to Labour; and only in free Effort can any blessedness be imagined for us.[58]

Consistent with this sobering view of the human condition, Carlyle set his face against all consolatory conceptions of religion, whether they came from conventional Christians, or from far less orthodox figures such as J. S. Mill. He later dismissed Mill's statements on religion as the 'last mews of a drowning kitten', complaining of the widespread tendency for people to speak 'as if "comfort" were the only thing; as if Divine Providence had not intended a man to go through many things and learn much thereby, by labour and self-denial and even misery'.[59] Rather than regarding this inescapable feature of human life as a cause for displays of self-pitying lamentation or myopic denial, Carlyle saw it as the source of a divinely-ordained challenge to humanity. It provided humans with an unending series of opportunities to demonstrate their practical commitment to an ideal of goodness by seeking to combat evil and striving to fulfil their duty in the face of it. Those who failed to seize these opportunities and either added to the sum of evil, or railed weakly against humanity's lot, deprived themselves of any chance of making sense of the world, or feeling at home in it.

Carlyle regarded the underlying implications of the science of dynamics as universal. They underwrote historically specific expressions of intellect and spirituality, and, as far as the bulk of the population was concerned, provided a largely unconscious and non-self reflective basis for their lives, underpinning morality and prompting ordinary human beings to fulfil their obligation to labour. At the same time, however, the way in which these ubiquitous features of human existence were conceptualised reflected distinctive aspects of particular societies. For long periods of human history, most recently in the middle ages, societies had possessed, and individuals had largely been possessed by, a unifying 'Idea' or set of integrated conceptions that provided the substance and focus of popular faith. In order to serve this role, however, 'Ideas' had to address the dynamic aspects of human life, particularly those that gave rise to religion. Every 'Idea' 'has in it something of a religious, paramount, quite infinite character; it is properly the Soul of the State, its Life; mysterious as other forms of Life, and like these working secretly, and in a depth beyond that of consciousness'.[60] All 'Ideas' contain particular expressions of underlying truths about the human condition, and while these truths do not change – they are, as Carlyle put it, 'realities' – both the 'Ideas' in which they are expressed at given periods in human history, and the 'forms' in which these ideas are clothed, do, indeed must, change.

In *Sartor Resartus*, Carlyle used the metaphor of 'clothing', drawn supposedly from Teufeldröckh's 'philosophy of clothes', to convey the relationship between 'forms' and 'realities'. Starting with the trope of the dandy's reliance on garments as the substance of personality, the history of clothes is represented as an account of the different ways in which human beings express, signal and confirm their, and their society's, perception of universal truths that underlie human existence. Garments give distinctive shape, colour and form to the bodies they clothe, shielding humanity not only from climatic rigours but, more significantly, from a condition of nakedness that Carlyle presented both as primitive, unformed, 'Adamite', and as the goal of some forms of revolutionary enthusiasm. In the first case, humanity – a 'forked biped' – has not yet achieved any of the dignity of which it is capable; in the second, the very basis of ordered human existence is jeopardised.[61] By playing thus on the dandyesque dictum 'clothes maketh the man', Carlyle points the significance of what he takes to be the profound truth that human beings need to find ways to express their understanding of the cosmos, and their role in it, in ideas, institutions and practices that have meaning for them. Such conceptualisations are historically specific, a point that Carlyle underlined in a preliminary exposition of Teufeldröckh's philosophy dealing with the 'history of clothes'.

In this account, changing modes of dress were presented in relation to a far broader treatment of the development of modern European society. The analogy of changing tastes making out of fashion dress seem sad and ridiculous, the empty and lifeless inhabitants of the twilight world of the second-hand market, was applied to the changes that occur in philosophical and religious expressions of the human condition, and in the institutions that give effect to them. Finally, items of clothing are unpicked and rewoven, a process that symbolises the constant remaking of human institutions during the course of social evolution.[62]

The early stages of processes of change are often not clear to those involved in them. Eventually, however, the disjuncture between realities, 'Ideas' and forms becomes quite apparent to many participants in the events and movements produced by it. The Protestant Reformation, the English Revolution of the seventeenth century, the Enlightenment, the French Revolution, and the early signs of the emergence of industrial society, were all-important moments in the transformation of European society. They indicated with a relentless, and increasingly unequivocal series of signs, that the expressions of faith and purpose that had structured medieval life were redundant. By the early nineteenth century, the break with medieval culture was irrevocable and the journey to the new world of modernity was well advanced. Carlyle wished to encourage his contemporaries to advance boldly into the future, but to do so in the realisation that their personal sense of spiritual wellbeing depended upon their conduct on the voyage, not upon any salvation that might await them at their destination. Like Goethe, he insisted that 'here or nowhere is America' but like Goethe too, Carlyle wished to assure his contemporaries that if the voyage was unavoidable, and the destination unknown, it was nevertheless worthwhile.[63]

The first task was to arrive at as clear an understanding as possible of the fundamental nature of the difficulties that afflicted the contemporary spirit. Carlyle addressed this issue in his 'biography' of Teufeldröckh. In the early chapter of *Sartus Resartus* Teufeldröckh is portrayed as being afflicted by a sense of hopeless, spiritually immobilising alienation. Since he cannot shake off the implications of infinitude, he cannot accept proposed resolutions that fail to reflect this distinctive feature of the human condition. 'Doubt', a condition that implies (paradoxically) a continued commitment to truth and faith, gives way to 'unbelief', and to the onset of spiritual and practical paralysis: 'a feeble unit in the middle of a threatening Infinitude, I seemed to have nothing given me but eyes, whereby to discern my own wretchedness'.[64] This condition is overcome as the result of a three-stage process, the first of which involves the paradox of defiant self-affirming negation through what Carlyle calls the 'Everlasting No':

> 'What *art* thou afraid of ? ... [W]hat is the sum-total of the worst that lies before thee? Death? Well death; and say the pangs of Trophet too, and all that the Devil and Man may, will or can do against thee! Hast thou not a heart; canst thou not suffer whatsoever it be; and, as a Child of Freedom, thou outcast, trample Trophet itself under thy feet, while it consumes thee? Let it come, then; I will meet it and defy it!' And as I so thought, there rushed like a stream of fire over my whole soul; and I shook base Fear away from me forever. I was strong, of unknown strength; a spirit, almost a god. Ever from that time the temper of my misery was changed: not Fear or whining Sorrow was it, but Indignation and grim fire-eyed Defiance.[65]

Having secured his selfhood by defying the satanic power of the fear of unbelief, and determining to courageously 'front' the world by defying it, Teufelsdröckh moves towards the 'centre of indifference', a condition in which selfhood is confirmed by indifference to the world, a lack of regard for it, and a lack of engaged commitment to it. This stage provides the basis for the re-emergence of a self that is capable of facing the world and engaging productively with it. Infinitude is reaffirmed through the 'Everlasting Yea', the acceptance of 'the God-given mandate, *Work thou in Welldoing*', and the dedication of life to it. The experiences that flow from this commitment transform humans' view of the world – 'the Universe is not dead and demoniacal, a charnel-house with spectres, but godlike and my Father's' – and soften and reinvigorate social feelings.[66] From henceforth, life is to be approached in the spirit of 'renunciation': commonplace notions of happiness and self-worship must be replaced by a clear conception of duty and a stern adherence to its requirements:

> there is in man a HIGHER than Love of Happiness: he can do without Happiness, and instead thereof find Blessedness! Was it not to preach-forth this same HIGHER that sages and martyrs, the Poet and the Priest, in all times, have spoken and suffered; bearing testimony, through life and through death, of the Godlike that is in Man, and how in the Godlike only has he Strength and Freedom?[67]

Teufeldröckh's journey mirrors in some respect the process of alienation, despair and regeneration that Carlyle experienced between 1818 and 1824. His account of it ends with a declaration that was related closely to Carlyle's understanding of his mission. He claimed that by embracing renunciation as a rule of life his contemporaries would make the transition in moral sensibility that distinguished Goethe from Byron. At times, Carlyle treated Byron as an English 'powerman', an agonised and self-consciously overwrought railer against the world; at others, he admired his courageous refusal to compromise with the ethos of Regency society. In this instance, however, Byron is portrayed as 'a huge sulky dandy' incapable of self-effacement or renunciation. Carlyle therefore urged the reader to 'Close thy *Byron*; open thy *Goethe*'.[68] This demand implicitly elevates Carlyle above Byron because he is identified with Goethe and calls him to centre stage in place of Byron. Byronism exemplifies aspects of the problems confronting modern humanity; Goethe (and Carlyle) have understood the source of these problems and can show how they are to be addressed.

Carlyle's perception of his mission, and the way in which he pursued it, was influenced both by assumptions about the needs of his audience, and his expectations about the role that they should play if they were to respond appropriately to what he had to tell them. As already noted, Carlyle's promotion of German literature was set in the context of sharp criticisms of the moral and intellectual shortcomings of the reading public. These failings were significant because Carlyle believed that the process of reform required the active participation of his readers. As with the religious views espoused by his family, salvation had to be achieved through the efforts of individuals, rather than being bestowed upon them through the efforts of others. For this reason, high demands were placed on those to whom his message was addressed. The distinctive character of the challenge that Carlyle threw out to his readers, and the role that that challenge played in his mission, are related closely to the stylistic and compositional idiosyncrasies of *Sartor Resartus*.

Sartor is presented as the work of an editor who is laying the works of a hitherto unknown writer before the public. This technique was commonly used by the 'Fraserians' with whom Carlyle was to some degree associated, but he carried it to extreme lengths. To take one example: Teufelsdröckh's 'English' editor felt that Teufelsdröckh's philosophy of clothes could only be understood if it was set in the context of the author's life. In pursuit of this elusive quest, the long-suffering editor seeks to make sense of fragments of manuscript that are distributed randomly among six paper bags marked only by the signs of the zodiac, and other fragmentary material relating to Teufelsdröckh's education and to issues that were of interest to him.[69] He engages in a correspondence with a 'German editor' who is reputed to have information on the author of these scraps and reports on their exchanges to his readers. The editor's labours give rise to a text made up purportedly of translations of Teufeldröckh's autobiographical writings and editorial interpolations. Some of these interjections subject the putative creator of the philosophy of clothes to expressions of disbelief, ridicule and wonder. Others juxtapose Germanic flights of fancy with examples of staunch British common sense.

Although Carlyle handled all this with great flair and with much characteristically abrasive humour, the serial publication of the book in *Fraser's Magazine* aroused hostility from at least some of the journal's subscribers and made Fraser unwilling to risk publishing the work in book form.[70] These rebuffs only served to confirm Carlyle's views on the deficiencies in modern taste, intellect and moral tone, and stiffened his resolve to correct them. There was, however, another reason why he was unapologetic about what some critics regarded as the self-indulgent stylistic and structural oddities of *Sartor*. While Carlyle was quite capable of providing succinct statements of his understanding of the human condition, the complexities of *Sartor* signalled the limitations inherent in attempts to give written expression to an impenetrable infinite. At the same time, readers of this work were inducted into a process in which they underwent their own version of Teufelsdröckh's journey. Like the editor, the readers of *Sartor* have to make sense of the various fragments that are presented within it.[71] That is, rather than merely offering an account of this journey of cultural and self discovery, Carlyle invited readers to embark upon it and prepared them for it.[72]

One important aspect of this preparation was designed to encourage Carlyle's readers to distinguish the 'real' from the 'sham'. Carlyle ascribed the afflictions of his contemporaries to their failure to replace outmoded ideas and practices with ones that would express the realities of the modern condition in appropriate forms. They either clung desperately to what would no longer serve them, or relied on novelties that were radically inadequate because they were unworthy of their status as 'infinite' beings. Although Carlyle insisted that ordinary human beings needed the help of men of genius to see them through these difficulties, he did not think that they could simply be presented with the truth. Rather, he seemed to believe that, like true believers of Christ, they needed to be active participants in the processes necessary to secure their salvation. As a result, he did not think that it was appropriate to present *Sartor* as a simple didactic text, or even as a conventionally straightforward one. To the contrary, it was constructed in such a way as to ensure that readers were obliged to grapple with a multi-layed, irony-laden text that developed their capacity to distinguish the plausible from the true.[73]

It has been observed that, although the experience offered to the reader in Carlyle's account of Teufeldröckh's life follows the cycle of scepticism-despair-regeneration found in ritualised Puritan struggles, it is historically specific rather than being timeless and generic. It concerns the fate of humanity in early nineteenth-century Europe and is designed both to provide his readers with an understanding of the distinctive features of their condition and to encourage them to come to an understanding of how they can resolve it.[74] This approach is consistent with one of the central themes of the book – the call to work or action – and it is offered in a way that suggests that independence is a universal human value, not one that is important only for genuine men of letters. Independence is a requirement of freedom, and this in turn is necessary for morality: human action is of earth-making significance because it results from voluntary determinations of the will. Carlyle does not identify this requirement with the view of liberty defended by J. S. Mill, nor did he think that it necessitated political or social equality.[75] To the contrary, his views on social and political authority were anti-democratic and strongly hierarchical. At the same time, however, he stressed the universal importance of human action and emphasised this by ascribing an active role to the readers of *Sartor*. They were not passive recipients of the fruits of authorial authority but were obliged to engage with the problems with which the putative author grapples. This approach is important for true authors as well as for their readers. But for the fact that Carlyle seeks to engage his readers and promote them to act rather than to display his own talent, the apparent extravagance of *Sartor* might be thought of as a form of authorial dandyism. The techniques that he deployed in the work, especially the role he ascribed to 'the Editor' should be seen in response to this threat. By adopting the personae of 'the Editor' Carlyle sought to remove the author from the centre of the stage, to avoid self-conscious display and court obscurity.[76]

In correspondence and other private papers dating from the late 1820s and early 1830s, Carlyle warned of the danger of expecting relief from either parliamentary reform, or through the realisation of any of the utopian fantasies that had currency in this period. In both his essays for the *Edinburgh Review*, and in *Sartor*, however, it is possible to discern a growing interest in the social and political dimensions of what is clearly seen as a crisis of personal existence.[77] At this stage, however, this development may be set in the context of Carlyle's evolving engagement with, and utilisation of themes that he identified with Goethe and with other inspirational figures from recent German literature. At the very time that Carlyle had succeeded in staking his claim as an English-language authority on Goethe's writings, he began to express private reservations on their capacity to provide his countrymen with the sort of guidance that they required if they were to rise to the challenges that faced them.[78] These reservations reflected Carlyle's concern about the ability of English readers to respond to a body of work framed in terms of the aesthetic authority of its creator in ways that would prompt the transformation of both their ethical outlook and the social and political practices that sprang from it. While Carlyle's ongoing utilisation of his own formulations of Goethean themes showed that such a move was possible, and while he continued to celebrate Goethe's importance in a series of essays published in the 1830s, he seems to have been increasingly doubtful whether his contemporaries were able to make it. He raised the issue in a rhetorical reflection made while he was writing *Sartor Resartus*: are 'men's minds … yet shut to art, and openly only at best for oratory? not fit for a *Meister, but only for a better and better Teufelsdröckh?*' He also extolled the moral point of view over the aesthetic one in his essay on Boswell's life, privileging the sense of engagement that he identified with Johnson over the stance of contemplative withdrawal that he associated with 'art'.[79]

Carlyle's subsequent career showed that he answered this question in the affirmative. Over the next two decades, the critic of vaticination claimed the attention of an increasingly wide circle of readers because they saw him as a prophetic figure. His increasingly elaborate prose was forged in a crucible that was raised to white heat, and the fervent desire to instruct was displaced at times by an equally fierce urge to chastise. Carlyle insisted, however, that his oratory was superior to that of contending voices because it was grounded in truth and was directed towards encouraging his readers to become the active authors of their own salvation. As noted above, the idea of engagement was central to both the form and content of *Sartor Resartus*. It was inherent in the gospel of labour, in the challenges posed by the structure of the work, and the techniques that Carlyle deployed in it. Salvation was not to be achieved by withdrawing from the world and cultivating the inner self; rather, it required active commitment to meeting the challenges posed by the transformations of consciousness, intellect, economy, society and polity that had occurred in Europe since the middle ages.

Over the next two decades, Carlyle focused increasingly on the social and political implications of these developments, addressing these in a series of highly topical tracts that developed lines of argument that had been signalled in his earlier writings and applying them to issues that formed the staple of contemporary political argument. One of the major challenges here was to treat pressing political and social concerns in ways that provided a viable alternative to the mechanically framed perspectives that vitiated other responses to what Carlyle was to label as 'the condition of England question'. These tracts were produced in parallel with a number of large-scale historical works that were linked thematically and conceptually with them. The chapters that follow first consider Carlyle's direct contributions to Victorian social and political criticism and then look in detail at the way that the key themes in these writings are related to his widely read historical works.

4

The Condition of England

Carlyle's major contributions to social and political criticism, *Chartism* (1839), and *Past and Present* (1843), appeared in the wake of the upsurge of interest in his work that was prompted by *The French Revolution: A History* (1837), and by the belated, but triumphant, appearance of an English edition of *Sartor Resartus* in 1838. While most of his works addressed the 'condition of England question' in one way or the other, the use of this term in relation to these particular works highlighted dimensions of the contemporary crisis that had direct implications for conceptions of the state and its role, for the relationship between classes, and the moral ideas that underpinned them.[1] These matters received some attention in Carlyle's earlier writings, cropped up in his correspondence, and provided common ground in his exchanges with the Saint Simonians.[2] In *Chartism* and *Past and Present*, however, they became central themes and were dealt with in a way that reflected Carlyle's growing sense of urgency about the condition of contemporary society. As he put it in a letter to John Stuart Mill in the spring of 1833: 'in these days, all light Sportfulness, and melodious Art, has fled away from us, far away; not in Poetry, but only ... in stern Old-Hebrew Denunciation, can one speak of the accursed Realities that now, and for generations lie around us, and weigh heavily on us!' The issue that particularly concerned Carlyle at this time was widespread underemployment throughout Great Britain and a perception that significant sections of the lower classes were becoming pauperised.[3] Articles on these and related themes had been a regular feature of *Fraser's Magazine* since its establishment in 1830 and had also been canvassed by Thomas Arnold (who very much approved of *Chartism*).[4]

Carlyle's condition of England writings incorporated perspectives on the modern condition from his earlier work, advancing a trenchant critique of the political and social implications of his contemporaries' fascination with 'mechanical philosophy'. This critique was generalised rather than tightly specific; that is, it did not engage directly with published statements of the positions against which it was directed, and it operated at two levels. The first and declared target was a perspective or widespread state of mind rather than a unified body of thought, one that embraced utilitarianism in both its secular and Christian forms, and classical political economy. It also extended to a less clearly defined body of thought and practice (referred to by Carlyle as '*laissez-faire*') that favoured market driven solutions to social and economic problems and deprecated the desirability in principle, or the practical effectiveness, of either an active state or a paternalistic elite. But when directing his critical attention at these impediments to human well being and human well doing, Carlyle was at pains to demonstrate the failings of responses to the condition of England problem that were, in their own ways, equally hostile to mechanical philosophy. He thus made it clear that he differed sharply from those (such as Samuel Taylor Coleridge and Robert Southey) who placed their trust in the prospects of a revival of the Church of England, or in a traditional aristocracy. Moreover, while Carlyle looked to active government and to responsible and engaged social and political elites to lead Britain beyond her present troubled state, his views on their roles and responsibilities differed from those of other prominent proponents of pater- nalism, such as the Tory MPs Henry Drummond and Michael Sadler. Finally, though Carlyle was disturbed at outbreaks of public disorder and held views on humans' differing intellectual and personal capacities which made political and social hierarchy necessary and popular government impossible, his 'condition of England' writings were free of expressions of outrage at the reckless presumption of trades unionists and working-class political activists (typified by Blackwood's reference to their 'detestable and criminal objects') that were commonplace across the spectrum of conventional political opinion.[5] In his social and political writings, as in his earlier criticisms of the moral and spiritual shortcomings of the modern mind, Carlyle thus sought to place a distinctive mark on a territory that had already been mapped in some detail by a number of cartographers who had adopted a range of quite different projections.

Carlyle's early thoughts on the 'condition of England' question were published in 'Characteristics'. He argued that the fact that there were few signs that much- boasted increases in the productive capacity of society had produced any real benefit for the working classes was an important matter that his contemporaries would need to address.[6] This theme received a fair amount of attention in Sartor Resartus. In a chapter titled 'Helotage', dealing with Malthusianism and its implications for the conditions of the lower orders, Carlyle suggested that society was becoming polarised around two equally inhuman material extremes, the 'dandiacal' and 'poor-slave'.[7]

These comments appeared in works written in the 1820s when Carlyle was determined to avoid entanglement in day-to-day political controversy and tended in his published works to adopt the stance of a social and political spectator. From the early 1830s, however, while continuing to emphasise the distance separating him from the political mainstream, he became more obviously interested in contemporary political discussions. This development, originally sparked by the excitement of the crisis over parliamentary reform in 1831, seems to have been stimulated further by his relationship with John Stuart Mill. Although Carlyle was sometimes prompted in the course of this correspondence to comment on day-to-day affairs, his perspective on politics remained distinctive and unconventional. Thus while he shared Mill's contempt for the government led by Lord Grey, he focused on the moral failings of the Whigs rather than on weaknesses in their legislative programme:

> Unbelieving mediocrity, barren, dead and death-giving speaks forth more and more in all they do and dream. The true atheist in these days is the Whig: he worships and can worship nothing but respectability ... The Tory is an idolater: the Radical a wild heathen iconoclast: yet neither of them strictly are 'without God in the world': the one has *infinite* hope, the other an infinite remembrance.[8]

In the mid 1830s Carlyle widened the scope of this criticism to include the 'philosophical radicals' with whom Mill was associated. While he had no sympathy for William Cobbett's promotion of radical measures of electoral reform, Carlyle spoke warmly of his admirably human and sympathetic understanding of the plight of the poor, drawing on his current work on the French Revolution to point unflattering parallels between Mill's allies in British politics and the ill-fated and contemptible Girodin faction in the French National Assembly in 1793–94: 'There is the same cold clean-washed patronising talk about "the masses" (a word, expressive of a thing, which I greatly hate); the same formalism, hidebound pedantry, superficiality, narrowness, barrenness'.[9] Widespread popular distress needed to be 'articulated', or explained in terms of its fundamental causes: this was not a task that could be left to those beset by 'bloodless formalism, self-conceit and pusillanimity'.[10]

These remarks focused in part on the *tone* of philosophical radicalism, and reflect a view, endorsed by the Chartists themselves, that the middle classes had singularly failed to use their newly won political influence to alleviate the hardships and injustices inflicted on the working classes through the misuse of political power. Rather than taking on the aristocracy, the middle classes seemed to have entered into a tacit coalition with them to use state power unjustly.[11] As Carlyle's response to the condition of England question unfolded, other grounds for his dismissive attitude to philosophical radicalism became apparent. This group was identified with the promotion of a range of ideas and policy positions that Carlyle thought had contributed significantly to the dangerously unsettled state of the British and Irish working classes: the science of political economy; the doctrine of *laissez-faire*, and a consequent suspicion of active government; the misguided belief that reform of constitutional machinery, and particularly extensions to the franchise, were the key to national salvation. The gulf that had begun to separate Carlyle and the philosophical radicals, and his exploitation of it to give a sharp critical edge to his condition of England writings, had a significant bearing on the pre-publishing history of his essay on Chartism.

Chartism was conceived originally as a controversial essay intended for journal publication, with Mill's *Westminster Review* as a likely venue. But although Carlyle was still on reasonably friendly terms with Mill in the late 1830s, he was irritated by his initial response, complaining that Mill wanted him to conclude his account by recognising that the material position of the lower classes was improving gradually.[12] John Lockhart, the editor of the Tory *Quarterly Review*, was more sympathetic, but in the end reluctantly declined to publish the essay. He was worried that it was far too radically critical of the upper classes to suit the tastes of his readers. In any case, Lockhart was offered another essay dealing with Chartism by J. W. Croker, and considered himself obliged to accept it because of a long-standing agreement to publish one of Croker's pieces in every number of the journal.[13] By late 1839 the *Westminster* was floundering, and Mill was keen to publish Carlyle's essay as a parting salvo. With encouragement from his wife and brother, however, Carlyle believed the piece too important to go down with the struggling *Westminster*. He now took comfort from the thought that the financial failure of the *Westminster* was an indictment of its bankrupt radicalism, and saw *Chartism* as a means of determining 'whether there be not a believing radicalism possible'.[14] This experiment was vindicated by the sales of the work – it went through three editions within a year – and by its impact upon a rising generation who, like the young J. A. Froude, regarded it as the basis for a new social and political faith. It also seems likely that after the increase in public attention accorded to Carlyle as a result of the *French Revolution*, *Chartism* found an audience among a wider, more general public than the restricted literary readership he had addressed in his early essays.[15]

Past and Present was even more successful than *Chartism*. Written while Carlyle was wrestling with a larger project on Oliver Cromwell, this book was framed dramatically, if not literally, by the sight of paupers at St Ives, Huntingdonshire, during a visit to Cromwell's native county. Often regarded as the most attractive of Carlyle's social and political writings, *Past and Present* was widely and favourably reviewed and made a lasting impression on nineteenth century readers. Francis Jeffrey, never a convert to Carlyle's views, admired this work and thought it was the most effective of Carlyle's writings to date, the one that was most likely to get his message across to his readers.[16] Years after it was first published, Frederick Harrison, who was far from being an unqualified admirer of Carlyle's writings, recalled the work as 'a happy and true thought, full of originality, worked out with art and power', and providing the basis of all 'worthwhile thought on social problems'.[17] It was also praised by those who were active in radical politics in continental Europe. Frederick Engels drew the book to the attention of German readers, applauding Carlyle's independence of spirit and the vigour and accuracy of his account of the impact of capitalism on the lives of the working classes. Giovanni Ruffini, active in Young Italy, credited the book with reminding readers that they still had souls.[18]

Carlyle was in no doubt about the close connection between *Past and Present* and *Chartism*, suggesting that the pre-publication announcements of the former should describe it as '*A Chartism*, Part Second'.[19] But while this characterisation might be true of the main political and social themes of the two works, they were markedly different in other respects. *Chartism* was a straightforward collection of short essays each of which dealt with a different dimension of the condition of England question. By contrast, *Past and Present* was a highly wrought literary production that focused ostensibly on a recently published account of a monastic order in thirteenth-century Bury St Edmunds. Carlyle incorporated this material into an elaborate overarching structure that was framed by the juxtapositioning of what he took to be representative institutions of the medieval and modern worlds: the monastery and the workhouse. This approach, already employed by Robert Southey in *Colloquies of Society: Sir Thomas Moore* (1829), and pictorially by A.W. Pugin in his *Contrasts* (1836), was mirrored in the details of the work, perhaps most notably in the comparisons between the 'practical devotion' of the effective, heroic, largely silent leader of the community, Abbot Samson, and the verbose inaction of modern political elites. These contrasts highlighted concerns with the relationship between widespread deprivation and failures of political leadership, key themes in both *Chartism* and *Past and Present*.

By adopting 'Chartism' as the ostensible theme of his first major contribution to social and political criticism (the title seems to have been chosen very late in the day), Carlyle capitalised on what was widely seen as an important and threatening feature of the contemporary political landscape. The Chartists' immediate objective was to secure parliamentary endorsement of the 'People's Charter'. This proclamation spelled out the six key points of the political aspects of the Chartist programme: 'universal' (that is, manhood) suffrage; annual parliaments; voting by ballot; equal electoral districts; abolition of property qualifications for MPs; and payment of MPs. Some Chartists were also committed to socialist doctrines that were hostile to conventional political economy and sought to realise an ideal of 'economic justice' reflecting a belief that labour was the source of all value.[20]

Having first emerged in the early 1830s following the very limited extensions of the franchise that resulted from the 1832 Reform Act, Chartism became a national movement by 1838. Towards the end of that year it was announced that a massive petition in favour of the Charter would be presented to Parliament during the course of a National Convention that was scheduled for early 1839. In the event, the convention met in London in February 1839, moving to Birmingham, a Chartist stronghold, on 13 May. After violent clashes between the police and some Chartists, the petition was returned to London and presented to the House of Commons on 12 July. The House's rejection of the petition prompted calls for a national strike, and when an attenuated version of this demonstration took place in August 1839, a number of Chartist leaders were arrested. There had been debates throughout the year in some Chartist circles on the desirability of direct action by the Chartists themselves, as opposed to appeals to established authority to recognise the justice of their claims, and, on 3–4 November seven thousand workers marched on Newport to release a leader from jail and then to set up a people's republic. The 'Newport Rising' was put down by armed troops and a series of arrests followed.

Carlyle watched these developments closely and set them in a broader socio-economic context. Following a visit to the north of England and Scotland in the early autumn of 1838, he commented on the hardship prevalent in these parts of the country, making it quite clear, however, that he believed that the effect of material hardship on the working classes was compounded by a more generalised indifference to their humanity:

> whether we pay them ill or well, we treat them equally as mere machines for providing us with selfish indulgences … [W]e have utterly neglected and abandoned all duties towards them, till they have sunk into a brutalised state which is becoming quite intolerable to them.[21]

Carlyle's direct exposure to Chartist activity seems to have been restricted to seeing a peaceful meeting in his native Ecclefechan during a visit there in late July.[22] He was, however, a careful (although characteristically sceptical) reader of the daily and weekly press, and it is significant that his work on *Chartism* during the autumn of 1839 coincided with trials of some of those arrested earlier, and with the attempt by the workers of Newport to take matters into their own hands. These alarming developments are alluded to in the opening pages of the work and provide the basis for two of its themes, namely, the futility of attempting to put Chartism down by force, and the reality of the threat that the movement posed to internal order and security.

Although Chartism appeared to have suffered a serious reverse in the latter part of 1839, the campaign for a convention and petition began again in September of 1841. A new convention met in Birmingham in April 1842, and on 1 May the House of Commons rejected a second petition with three million signatures. In July and August of that year, Chartists became involved in a series of strikes in the Midlands and North of England sparked by unemployment, wage reductions and high food prices. These events formed part of the context of *Past and Present*. During the autumn and winter that followed, Carlyle frequently referred in his correspondence to the wretched state of the industrial poor in England and Scotland, comparing their conditions unfavourably with those of black slaves. He described the working classes of Paisley, thrown out of work by a collapse in the local textile trade, as victims of the 'accursed laws of egoism and mammonism'. These laws, the ethical basis of the much-vaunted 'science' of political economy, rather than any concern for the environment, put a temporary stop to industrial pollution in Manchester in May 1842. When some mills were closed because of a collapse of demand for cotton goods and others reduced to short-time work, Carlyle reported that the atmosphere over the city was 'dreadfully *clear of smoke*'.[23] During the summer of 1842, a series of responses to this state of affairs (the 'Plug Plot' crisis) culminated in a confrontation between the working classes and the authorities that had all the hallmarks of the early stages in an outright insurrection. The 'Plot' involved a series of concerted attempts by cotton workers to support a strike against a reduction in wages by disabling the boilers that drove factory machinery, thereby preventing non-union 'scab' labour from replacing them. After seeming likely to result in a pitch battle, a tense confrontation between the strikers and troops was defused by strike leaders. Although Chartists were not the prime movers behind these developments, their involvement in them provided government with grounds for a wave of arrests in September of 1842; many of the trials that followed resulted in harsh sentences of imprisonment and transportation.

In light of the events of 1842, it is particularly significant that Carlyle's explanation of Chartism stressed the continuity of the political aspects of the Chartist programme with the apparently distinctive objectives of other contemporary working class movements. Thus, while the events of 1838–39 inspired the title of his pamphlet, Carlyle regarded Chartism itself merely as one of a number of manifestations of spiritual, social and political crises that faced his countrymen and were felt in a variety of different ways across Europe. When he used the term 'Chartism' he referred not only to the organised and disorganised pursuit of political rights by the working classes, but also to conspiratorial and open trade unionism, rural incendiarism and urban rioting. All these expressions of extreme working-class disaffection could be traced to 'the bitter discontent grown fierce and mad, the wrong condition therefore or the wrong disposition, of the Working Classes of England'.[24]

Even when his writings dealt *with* the condition of the working classes, Carlyle did not address himself *to* them. His works were neither uplifting homilies of the kind produced by Harriet Martineau, nor were they contributions to a culture of working-class self-determination fostered by some Chartists. To the contrary, Carlyle's mission focused on the middle and upper classes. It was meant to alert them to the dangers that threatened society and to stimulate them to acquire the level of self and cultural awareness necessary to understand the challenges facing modern humanity and to set about addressing the difficulties that confronted it. An earlier and much briefer statement of this position had been advanced by Carlyle in 1832. In his essay on the 'Corn Law Rhymer', he had described this poet's works as 'an authentic message from the hearts of poor men' to those members of the upper classes who still retained a sense of their responsibilities to the working classes.[25] His initial discussions with Lockhart envisaged a similar appeal; it was to be an exercise in 'pleading and protesting to the upper classes on behalf of the under'. By late October 1839, however, Carlyle thought this approach was no longer viable.[26] The time had now come to speak to the upper classes in a far more direct way, one that was meant to both instruct and to upbraid them.

Carlyle made it clear that Chartism needed to be understood at a number of different levels. In the most obvious sense, it was symptomatic of the inability of a numerically significant section of the working classes to secure the basic material prerequisites of human existence, an issue that was frequently the subject of comment in Carlyle's correspondence in the 1830s and 1840s. In addition to registering absolute deprivation, however, Chartism reflected the dislocating effect of wild fluctuations in the demand for labour that seemed endemic to industrial capitalism. Such fluctuations damaged even those whose rates of pay were adequate to meet their needs when they were in work. Carlyle also stressed the psychological hardships imposed on the working classes by the transition to a new economic and social order. These developments meant that the world seemed to be a strange and unwelcoming place, 'no home, but a dingy prison-house, of reckless unthrift, rebellion, rancour, indignation against themselves and against all men'.[27] Finally, and fundamentally, he claimed that the impact of deprivation and alienation was compounded by the working class's well-grounded sense that it had suffered prolonged and systematic injustice at the hands of its social and political superiors. Such treatment was incompatible with an ideal of right conduct that Carlyle thought was essential to beneficial social order: 'An ideal of right does dwell in all men, in all arrangements, pactions and procedures of men: it is to this ideal of right more and more approximated to, that human society forever tends and struggles'.[28]

The intractability of Carlyle's conception of right order meant that 'mights' and 'rights' were synonymous: 'the rights of man … are little worth ascertaining in comparison to the *mights* of man – to that portion of his rights he has any chance of being able to make good'.[29] Some contemporaries and later commentators were alarmed at this claim because it seemed to be a prescription for deducing moral norms from physical capacity. This was very far from Carlyle's intention. Rather, the issue at stake concerned the relationship between spiritual power and secular authority, one that particularly concerned Carlyle in the 1830s and 1840s because he thought that Britain lacked figures like Cromwell and his associates, who brought these qualities together.[30] He maintained that, in the long term at least, only that which is right will flourish: its rightness will ensure that it acquires the strength to sustain itself in the world. By contrast, that which does not embody right, or embodies it in an incomplete form, will not survive. As Carlyle noted in later comments clarifying his views of this issue: 'no man who is not in the *right*, were he even a Napoleon I at the head of armed Europe, has any real *might* whatever ... Abolition and erosion awaits all "doings" of his, except just what part of them *was right* ... Right is the eternal symbol of might.'[31]

These comments demonstrate that for Carlyle material deprivation was only one of a number of causes of popular distress and the discontent generated by it. Indeed, deprivation of this kind was really only significant if it was considered in relation to fundamental moral issues about humanity's role in the world and its relationship with the forces that underwrote it. In *Sartor Resartus* this theme was explored largely, but not exclusively, in terms of the career of an anguished spirit whose education had elevated him above the general run of the ordinary population. Even here, however, Carlyle recognised the wider social ramifications of his hero's afflictions. In *Chartism* and *Past and Present* the field of analysis was extended to include a detailed consideration of the impact of alienation and deprivation on the working classes. The sense of dislocation that afflicted the artist and the man of letters was now presented as endemic in modern society, and as symptomatic of a general disruption of the cosmic order. In his condition of England writings, Carlyle became more interested in promoting a concerted 'cultural re – adjustment' than he had in his earlier works, and gave rather less emphasis to 'collective *self*-adjustment'.[32] As in these writings, however, he related these tendencies to the intellectual, moral and spiritual shortcomings of the educated classes, focusing particularly on those who were perceived as rivals for intellectual and moral leadership.

In 'Signs of the Times' Carlyle claimed that his contemporaries were in the grip of intellectual misconceptions that induced them to see life in mechanical terms. Any improvements of the human condition were thought to depend upon refining cultural, educational, political and religious machinery and applying it to more and more areas of life. In a comment made in 1852, Carlyle provided a succinct formulation of what he took to be the fallacy of relying on 'reform associations'. The problem lay in the assumption that such bodies could act on society as if it were a machine in need of extra power. In fact, the root of the problem was a lack of social cohesion, self-understanding and honesty of character in members of society, deficiencies that could not be made good by external agencies.[33] This line of argument reflected more general concerns about ways of thinking that were inadequate because they were not grounded on a full, well-rounded understanding of the complexities of human nature. Since they were incapable of addressing the human condition, these perspectives prompted responses to the condition of England question that exacerbated the evils they were meant to cure.

For Carlyle, as for a number of his contemporaries, these moral, intellectual and practical shortcomings tended to coalesce in the growing reputation enjoyed by the increasingly self-confident science of political economy. This science, emerging from the Scottish Enlightenment's engagement with 'commercial society', was promoted in a broader context in the pages of the *Edinburgh Review* and was taken up in other periodicals, including the *Westminster Review*, the organ of philosophical radicalism. In recent years, articles on political economy in this journal were marked by a particularly narrow and dogmatic tone.[34] Other contemporary proponents of the new science included evangelical Tories associated with the 'liberal' wing of the party, authors of cautionary homilies directed at the working classes, one of the most prominent of whom was Harriet Martineau, and a far more diffuse body of pro-free trade figures whose efforts at this time were focused on abolishing the 'Corn Laws', tariff measures designed to protect English wheat growers from foreign competition.[35] The traffic was, however, by no means all one way. Some Chartists and socialist writers developed rival theories of political economy that included a general theory of economic depression. They linked false values stimulated by an exclusive concern with profit with the misdirection of productive activity, and advanced a theory of exploitation that rested on a labour theory of value.[36] Other more ideologically ambiguous figures such as the radical journalist and MP William Cobbett, Richard Oastler, the factory reformer and 'people's friend', and a host of traditionally-minded paternalistic Tories, opposed the application of the 'laws' of political economy to issues such as master-servant relationships and the conditions governing the public provision of relief through the 'poor law' system.[37] Carlyle was probably most familiar with the critique of the mechanical and narrowly materialistic basis of political economy developed by Coleridge and Southey in England, and by figures associated with the romantic movement in late eighteenth- and early nineteenth-century Germany.[38] In terms of arguments advanced in his condition of England writings, however, he was perhaps more directly indebted to the writings of Jean Charles Léonard Simonde de Sismondi, a Swiss political economist who wrote in French. Sismondi's work was well known to Carlyle since early in 1819. In 1820 he sought Dr David Brewster's advice on translating it, and while Brewster was not initially encouraging, having already commissioned an essay from Sismondi for his *Edinburgh Encyclopaedia*, he later engaged Carlyle to translate this piece for him.[39]

Three distinctively Sismondian themes are prominent in Carlyle's social and political criticism. First, Sismondi provided an account of the status of political economy that reinforced, and in some ways clarified, the assumptions underlying English and German romantic views on this issue. Sismondi insisted that economics was of no value if it treated its subject matter in isolation from other aspects of human experience, explaining that the analysis of economic phenomena must take account of the distinctive character of human beings in given social and historical contexts, rather than attempting to impose mechanical prescriptions upon them. Secondly, and related to this general perspective, he stressed that the object of economic analysis was to promote the moral and physical well being of *all* classes in the community. As Sismondi put it, 'any theory that does not on the last analysis result in the increase of the happiness of mankind does not belong to the science [of political economy] at all'.[40] Thirdly, Sismondi questioned claims made by other political economists about the self-correcting capacities of free markets.

In the teeth of strenuous objections from 'classical' political economists such as David Riccardo, Sismondi maintained that free markets may give rise to a *general* glut of commodities. The orthodox view was that while partial and shifting gluts in *particular* commodities may occur, the market would clear itself before they became general. Sismondi's unorthodox position raised important questions concerning the impact of economic development on the short- to medium-term prospects of the working classes. For example, he argued that while intense competition lowered labour costs, this was not an unmixed blessing: 'When the low price of labour arose from the poverty of the day-labourers ... though commerce may profit by the circumstance, it is nothing better than a national calamity'.[41] This dire state of affairs would only be averted if governments protected the labouring population from the worst effects of the periodic bouts of overproduction to which modern economies seemed to be prone, and took measures to ensure that at least some of the benefits of economic development were available to them. Sismondi did not question the rights of the rich to enjoy their wealth; rather, he wanted to prevent their often inadvertent spoliation of the poor.[42]

Carlyle's condition of England writings take a perspective on the nature and scope of political economy that is very similar to Sismondi's. He thus accused economists of attempting to usurp the role previously performed by political philosophers, while restricting the focus of political discourses to exclude aspects of human experience that were not accessible to political economy. This mode of enquiry was contrasted with a romantically conceived form of political philosophy as the source of the 'scientific revelation of the whole secret mechanism whereby men cohere together in society'. Carlyle saw political economy as a subaltern discipline that produced material for scientific reflection; its practitioners were the 'hodmen of the intellectual edifice'. Unfortunately, these fetchers and carriers had begun to elbow the masons off the scaffold, interfering with more skilled tradesmen while failing to attend to their own role of unearthing and transmitting accurate factual information.[43]

Although this characterisation was highly unflattering, it at least showed that Carlyle did not entirely discount methodical, statistically-based examinations of the condition of the working classes. But while allowing somewhat grudgingly that these investigations might 'yield results worth something', he insisted that they must be set in a broader interpretative framework that took account of the full range of human aspirations and interests.[44] It also needed to be recognised that some of the factors having a crucial bearing on the working classes' sense of well-being – the constancy and certainly of employment, the quality of the network of social relationships in which they lived and worked, feelings of hope, levels of humane enlightenment, and the sense that they were being justly dealt with – were not reducible to statistical formulations. The condition of England question could be understood only by 'utterances of *principles*, grounded on facts that all may see'.[45]

This remark was perhaps an unconscious echo of a phrase from Coleridge's first Lay Sermon of 1816, but Carlyle's analysis of political economy also included more specific criticisms.[46] For example, aspects of his general perspective on contemporary views on statistically-based social and moral science mirrored, and were clearly influenced by, a criticism of the London Statistical Society that was published in the *London and Westminster Review* in June 1839. The author of this article ridiculed the society's ambition to exclude all 'opinions' from its investigations, observing that if this objective could be realised, it would deprive their work of any direction or point. The society treated facts as toads with jewels in their heads but then retained the toads and set aside the jewels.[47] Carlyle adopted the methodological points advanced by this critic to develop a characteristically romantic critique of prevailing attitudes towards social investigation, one that was far more sophisticated than those deployed by earlier English writers such as Coleridge and Southey, or by Carlyle's German models. For example, Carlyle warned that correlations between rising levels of deposits in savings banks and working class-thrift might well prove to be spurious because they ignored informal investment devices that were used by the working classes before savings banks became widespread. Elsewhere, he pointed out that an increasing demand for skilled labour in an economy that systematically deskills most of the population provided no grounds for optimism about opportunities for employment for the bulk of the working classes.[48]

These criticisms of contemporary attitudes towards political economy were consistent with Carlyle's general views on the role of scientific enquiry. That is, he claimed that they misapplied scientific ideas, not that these ideas were false and of no value.[49] Carlyle thought that his contemporaries' reliance on naïve empiricism – a view that lay behind the position that Mill encouraged him to take on the condition of the working classes – exemplified the overwhelmingly mechanical cast of the modern mind. It was assumed, for example, that aggregate data relating annual wages to the price of staple commodities provided an index of working-class wellbeing. Carlyle pointed out, however, that this approach ignored the fact that open signs of discontent were more common among the better-off workers than among their more materially disadvantaged fellows. The more general point lying behind this observation was that those who wished to understand 'Chartism' should look beyond the simple fact of gross income and consider the full range of economic and other factors that had a bearing on the quality of life possible for members of the working classes. Stability of employment and regularity of income needed to be taken into account since they affected attitudes towards continuity of material independence and incentives to thrift. The nature of the relationship between classes was also important because it determined the psychological quality of social life that could be enjoyed by *all* members of the community.[50]

The fact that Carlyle approached the condition of England question through a critique of contemporary uses of statistics was particularly important because of the assumptions that lay behind much social investigation and policy promotion. By lending support to claims of economic progression and increasing prosperity, statistical demonstrations deflected criticisms from government and from the economic and social system.[51] This strategy made it seem more plausible to blame social unrest and political agitation on the feckless and vicious tendencies of the working classes and those from other classes who sought to mobilise them to further their own ends. Even when such investigations were used to make cases for reform in areas such as education and public health, these measures were thought to be necessary to secure working-class acquiescence to ethical and social ideas that provided the basis for a morally progressive, economically buoyant and politically stable order.[52] Both these approaches focused exclusively on what were seen as the intellectual and moral shortcomings of the working classes, and on the need to eliminate these by ensuring that they inculcated the values of the 'respectable' world. For Carlyle, however, these values were themselves deeply suspect. Indeed, they were largely responsible for producing the alarming state of affairs to which they were proffered as a solution. In this respect, as well as in relation to a wide range of issues that concerned the conduct of governmental and social elites, the condition of England question had at least as much to do with the attitudes and behaviour of the middle and upper classes as it did with the intellectual and moral flaws of their social inferiors.

This perspective was consistent with the approach taken in earlier essays, and as we shall see, it followed necessarily from the emphasis Carlyle placed on social and political leadership. In *Chartism* and *Past and Present* he pursued the line, first taken in 'Signs of the Times', that elite responsibility would not be fulfilled by merely adopting one or a number of devices – systems for education, church extension, and so on – and applying them to the lower classes. To the contrary, the faith placed in these panaceas was indicative of a fundamental misunderstanding of the roles of mechanical and dynamic forces in human life.

This misunderstanding lay behind the promotion of statistically based social investigations in the 1830s; it also played a role in promoting morally flawed attitudes to poverty that had given rise to the Poor Law Amendment Act of 1834.[53]

Carlyle was highly critical of the perception of the working classes that was implicit in the new poor law system and in the language of those who defended it. He did not, however, endorse the view (common among some working-class radicals and Tory paternalists) that the Poor Law Commissioners were inhuman monsters. Nor did he promote a return to the old, unreformed poor relief system.[54] Indeed, Carlyle acknowledged that, to the extent that the new act reflected the important truth that idleness was insupportable, it marked a clear advance on the old system. It erred, however, in assuming that idleness afflicted only the working class and in ignoring its alarming prevalence among the better-off sections of the population. Partly as a result of this class bias, the provisions of the new system of poor relief were premised on the false assumption that pauperism could be eliminated merely by increasing the penalties imposed on those who became destitute. In *Sartor Resartus* Carlyle joked grimly that there was little to choose between modern views of how to deal with 'surplus population' and those that led the Spartans to hunt their helots when they became too numerous.[55] In *Chartism* he objected to arguments in favour of the new system that assumed that the poor could be viewed in the same light as vermin. This parallel prompted disturbing insights into the public mind: 'to believe practically that the poor and luckless are here only as a nuisance to be abraded and abated, and in some permissible manner made away with, and swept out of sight, is not an amiable faith'.[56]

Contemporary ways of thinking about pauperism provided another example of the misapplication of a mechanical approach to human problems: workhouses were devices for segregating paupers and conditioning the rest of the working population. They were products of an intellectual and moral universe that lacked any coherent view of beneficial social order, and relied instead on competitive mechanisms that condemned those who failed to get the better of their fellows to forfeit their humanity. As Carlyle noted when the new poor law was being framed, the 'Commission stands on the *rich* side of the question, and looks at the poor as *things*, who nevertheless are men too'.[57] The new system's indifference to human considerations meant that Carlyle was unlikely to have been impressed with Edwin Chadwick's account of the miraculous transformation undergone by dissolute labourers who had been subjected to the astringent influences of the new poor law.[58] Changes of this kind were merely triumphs of mechanical application that failed to embody what Carlyle saw as a fundamental truth: 'human things cannot stand on selfishness, mechanical utilities, economics, and law-courts'.[59]

The conceptual and practical failings of the new system of poor relief were particularly important for Carlyle because they had a direct bearing upon opportunities for, and attitudes towards, labour, a crucial component of human well being. During the 1830s and 1840s he thought that the threats posed by an alienated and increasingly unruly working class were the direct result of the elite's failure to understand the significance of work for the rest of the population. At most, this issue was seen in material terms, and hence as something that could be dealt with through physical sanctions and incentives, stimuli that would be called into play by the market provided that it was not undermined by distortions like those produced by the old poor law system. For Carlyle, however, work was a moral and spiritual necessity. Consequently, the disorderly behaviour of the working classes could not be seen merely as bread riots to be put down by main force. This line of argument was central to *Chartism*, but it found its most forceful and clearly articulated statement in *Past and Present*.

One of the central themes of *Past and Present* was that the spell that made workers into stunned paupers had been cast over the whole of society, producing a series of paradoxical bipolarities that confused the human mind and immobilised its will. A Midas-like enchantment chained the radically different classes of 'master workers' and 'master unworkers' together; it produced a general tendency to 'luxury alternating with mean scarcity and inability' in place of 'noble thrift and plenty'; it combined material prosperity and worldly success with feelings of chronic insecurity and with actual life-sapping deprivation: 'in the midst of plethoric plenty, the people perish; with gold walls, and full barns, no man feels himself safe or satisfied'. Finally, the Midas touch induced moral and social paralysis in an environment marked by hectic movement: 'Workers, Master Workers, Unworkers, all men come to pause; stand fixed cannot further'.[60] In this setting, physical suffering was less damaging to humanity than the pain suffered by the devotee-victims of the gospel of Mammon:

> The haggard despair of Cotton-factory, Coal-mine operatives, Chandos Farm-labourers, in these days, is painful to behold; but not so painful, hideous to the inner sense, as that brutish god forgetting Profit-and-Loss Philosophy and Life-theory, which we hear jangled on all hands of us, in senate-houses, sporting clubs, leading articles, pulpits and platforms, everywhere as the ultimate gospel and plain-English of Man's Life, from the throats and pens and thoughts of all-but all men![61]

The new poor law added the workhouse-idleness paradox to other outcomes of the gospel of mammon, and did nothing to positively assist the working classes in their struggle to avoid idleness and dependence. Unlike other critics who stressed the poor's right to subsistence, Carlyle focused on their right to be gainfully and, as he thought, humanly, employed.[62] In *Chartism*, he described men in a state of involuntary idleness as 'perhaps the saddest sight that Fortune's inequality exhibits under this sun'.[63] Unlike many of his contemporaries, he placed little emphasis on the working classes's alleged proclivities to court reliance on private charity or public relief. This point is made with great power and sympathy in the essay on the works of the 'Corn Law Rhymer'. In the Rhymer's 'drama of life' the working classes are haunted by a fear of the workhouse and by a spectre of demeaning dependence that would not be banished merely by abolishing outdoor relief.

> Mournful enough that a white European Man must pray wistfully for what the horse he drives is sure of ... that the strain of his whole faculties may not fail to earn him food and lodging. Mournful that a gallant manly spirit, with an eye to discern the world, a heart to reverence it, a hand cunning and willing to labour in it, must be haunted with such a fear. The grim end of it all, Beggary! A soul loathing, what true souls ever loath, Dependence, help from the unworthy to help; yet sucked into the world-whirlpool – able to do no other: the highest in man's heart struggling vainly against the lowest in man's destiny![64]

Passages like this reflect the deeply ingrained ethos of Carlyle's family. In his *Reminiscences*, Carlyle recalled his father's account of impoverished labourers whose sense of self-respect led them to conceal from their employer the fact that they had nothing to eat in the midday break from work.[65] Carlyle's approach to his personal affairs evinced a similar spirit. He was loath to accept assistance from anyone outside his family, and husbanded his resources to spare his brothers and sisters from this indignity.

The stress that Carlyle laid on finding labour for the working class, and his sympathetic insights into the toll exacted on those who were unable to sustain themselves through their own efforts, goes some way towards explaining his appeal to sections of the working classes over the course of the nineteenth century.[66] In the late 1830s and early 1840s, however, these ideas were part of a project that was meant to enlighten and invigorate the educated classes. In particular, Carlyle sought to convince them that the deprivations endured by the working classes were the immediate cause of their demoralised condition and their apparently reckless and socially destabilising behaviour. At the same time he made it clear that responses to this state of affairs based upon perspectives that were incompatible with the moral status and potentials of human beings, were not only futile but had done much to bring it about. In *Chartism* and *Past and Present* Carlyle framed this line of criticism by reference to the contrast between dynamics and mechanics that had been advanced in his earlier writings, but he now gave it a distinctly political point of reference.

In his essays from the 1820s Carlyle used the term 'mechanical' to refer to a cast of mind that combined some characteristics of Enlightenment thinking with images reflecting recent developments in productive technology.[67] This idea underwent development in his later writings. By the late 1830s he claimed that the expansion of international capitalism meant that humanity was at the mercy of a vast mechanical force that careered unpredictably through the world like a monstrous runaway steam locomotive. A

> huge demon ... smokes and thunders, panting at his great task, in all of English land; changing his *shape* like a very *Proteus*; and infallibly, at every change of shape, *oversetting* whole multitudes of workmen, and as if with the waving of his shadow from afar, hurling them asunder, this way and that, in their crowded march and course of work or traffic; so that the wisest no longer knows his whereabouts.[68]

The vacuum in the slipstream of this juggernaut expelled forethought and determined activism from social life and encouraged reliance on the blind forces of the market. In contemporary political argument this state of affairs was explained by reference to the fashionable doctrine of '*laissez-faire*'.

Sismondi's writings probably played a role in forging Carlyle's critical views on the implications and prevalence of this doctrine. His attitude towards it may have been hardened by exposure to Harriet Martineau, a frequent visitor to Cheyne Row in the late 1830s, author of the periodical publication *Illustrations of Political Economy* which sold more than ten thousand copies a month at the height of its popularity.[69] J. S. Mill (who later described *laissez-faire* as a sound general rule to which exceptions may be made on the grounds of the public interest) insisted that Miss Martineau's version of the doctrine did not provide a fair test of its usefulness. As he wrote to Carlyle in 1833, Harriet Martineau 'reduces the *laissez-faire* system to absurdity by merely carrying it out in all its consequences'.[70] Carlyle, however, did not choose to recognise the point lying behind Mill's comment, namely that the term '*laissez-faire*' was applied to a range of differing accounts of legitimate state action. Rather, he concentrated on what he saw as a general characteristic of this way of thinking about the role of the state.

Carlyle thought that *laissez-faire* reflected a mechanical conception of the state and of human agency in general. That is, it was assumed that society and the economy were largely self-regulating devices that worked best when not interfered with by authoritative agencies. Carlyle reacted strongly against this idea, arguing that *laissez-faire* was inconsistent with the very idea of government. It was particularly damaging at the present time because of the fluid state of society and the stresses created by the turbulent passage from the old world. When *laissez-faire* was championed by putative elites (whether drawn from the aristocracy or from commerce and industry), it undermined their claim to political power, social influence and respect. It also made it hard to justify their wealth and other privileges. *Laissez-faire* entailed 'an abdication on the part of governors'; it was an 'admission that they are henceforth incompetent to govern, that they are not there to govern at all, but to do – one knows not what!'[71]

Carlyle's critique of *laissez-faire* was linked in a number of ways to his consistent appeals for self-reformation. This attitude towards the state was underwritten by a mechanical ethos that ignored the dynamic aspects of human nature. Moreover, it was deployed to give a veneer of scientific credibility to the conduct of individuals and classes who either failed to see, or refused to acknowledge, their responsibilities to other members of the community. Seen from this perspective, the doctrine of *laissez-faire* was part of a system of dishonesty and delusion that prevented Carlyle's contemporaries from coming to terms with the modern world. Finally, he looked on moralised individuals to provide social and political leadership that would take account of humanity's dynamic qualities. Without such leadership, an active state would merely replicate on a large scale the mechanical tendencies that Carlyle discerned in the flawed collective endeavours of his contemporaries.

Laissez-faire loomed large in Carlyle's consideration of the condition of England question because he thought that Chartism and other manifestations of working-class disaffection were a response to an absence of social, spiritual and political leadership. Attitudes to this doctrine were thus a litmus test of the sagacity and sincerity of current elites and of those who sought to displace them. The fact that such an ideology had become influential among the middle and upper classes was an alarming sign of the lack of elite understanding of the requirements of the modern age. At one time, Carlyle thought that philosophical radicalism seemed to offer an invigorating, if only partially satisfactory, alternative to bankrupt Whiggism. By the late 1830s, however, the failure of the parliamentary representatives of this movement to propose plausible responses to the condition of England problem, and their attachment to *laissez-faire*, put their pursuit of political power in a very different light. While scrambling desperately to get the levers of power in their hands, they denied that state action was an appropriate response to the problems facing modern society. Radicalism had become 'paralytic' and no progress would be made until it was banished from the political stage: 'the public highways ought not to be occupied by people demonstrating that motion is impossible'.[72]

Carlyle's account of the relationship between Chartism and *laissez-faire* rested on his belief in the omnipotence of 'right' in human affairs. In the case of the modern working classes, this idea was expressed as a demand that the 'rights of man' should be recognised. Insofar as this claim represented a potent moral force, it referred to the 'real rights of man' not to the formal claims to liberty and property that dominated seventeenth and eighteenth-century political thought. Carlyle's detailed prescriptions for meeting the claims of the working classes indicated that he thought that there was a degree of overlap between the implications of the 'real rights of man' and the ideas of economic justice promoted by some Chartists. In *Past and Present* he reiterated one of the slogans of the 'Plug Plot' crisis of 1842, 'a fair-days-wages for a fair-day's-work', and lamented that 'time was when the mere *hand*worker needed not announce his claim to the world by Manchester Insurrections'.[73] The practical denial of this claim was one of the many unsettling paradoxes of a dislocated age. Although obsessed with productivity and the maximisation of wealth, the governing classes left questions concerning work and wages that were fundamental to human wellbeing to be determined by the impersonal and mechanical outcomes of the market.[74]

But while Carlyle was sympathetic to at least some of the Chartists' demands, and seems to have grasped the point (overlooked by many later historians of Chartism) that they saw political power as the key to preventing the systematic injustices to which the old and new ruling classes had subjected them, he emphatically denied that universal political rights were among the 'real' rights of man.[75] To the contrary, he insisted that the most important right of the working classes was the right to be well governed. This idea was a commonplace of conventional paternalism, but in more orthodox hands than Carlyle's it was often accompanied by expressions of deep resentment at the presumption of Chartists' attempts to take control of their own destiny by overcoming the propertied classes' domination of parliament. By contrast, Carlyle added a distinctive dimension to this position by attributing Chartism to the working classes' unconscious grasp of the requirements of justice and to their attempts to articulate their claim to them. At the heart of Chartism and other working-class movements lay a demand for effective leadership: '[A]ll popular commotions ... from Peterloo to the Place-de-Grève ... are inarticulate prayers: "Guide me, govern me! I am mad and miserable, and cannot guide myself"'.[76] Carlyle thought that the fact that this plea was couched as a demand for democracy confirmed his interpretation of Chartism by showing that in the absence of elite leadership the working classes had been forced to take the reins of government into their own hands.

Chartism, like its fearsome French precursor 'Sansculottism', meant something important; those holding positions of political and social responsibility needed to understand its meaning and frame appropriate responses to it. For this reason, Carlyle's treatment of Chartism was not peppered with conventional expressions of moral outrage at the sinister presumption of working-class leaders and their debased followers. The bogey of corrupt self-serving manipulators of the working classes (the darkly clad gentleman on the white horse beloved of government spies in the late eighteenth century) was not a feature of Carlyle's account of Chartism. For this very reason, however, he thought the movement was far more dangerous for the working classes and the rest of society than even its most rabid critics imagined. Government in the true sense of the term existed only where the less able were placed under the careful superintendence of the more able. Democracy, 'government by the people' was, in fact, the consummation of non-government since it left the less able to their own devices. While popular government was necessarily anarchic and was thus emphatically not an answer to the challenges facing modern society, the demand for it was highly significant. It signalled the end of the formulae and practices of the old order; if its meaning was misread or ignored, the working classes' demands for justice would be transmuted into 'Sansculottism.'

Parallels between contemporary developments and those that took place in late eighteenth-century France, played an important role in Carlyle's condition of England writings. French elites had faced a challenge that was similar in many respects to that confronting their counterparts in nineteenth century Britain and to which they had singularly failed to respond. As the author of an important recent study of the Revolution, Carlyle was in a unique position to utilise its exemplary potential, and his countrymen were receptive to seeing their position in these terms. In November 1841, a time when the Complete Suffrage Union sought to forge an alliance between the middle and working classes on a democratic and anti-protectionist platform, the *Manchester Times* reprinted extracts from *The French Revolution* and issued them as a pamphlet.[77] Earlier, before Carlyle had started work on *Chartism*, elements within the Chartist movement and their critics in parliament had made extensive references to events in France during the 1790s. For some Chartists, the Revolution provided a source of inspiration: thus in late 1838 and 1839 leading figures in the Chartist London Democratic Society adopted Jacobin language to promote violent confrontation with the guardians of the status quo and referred to episodes in the French Revolution to support claims about the viability of working-class insurrection. Parallels of this kind were a source of acute discomfort to other sections of the community and provided the basis for hostile responses to Chartism from within parliament and in the respectable periodicals.[78]

While Carlyle was as eager as any conservative MP to avert revolution in Britain, his understanding of recent French history meant that the lessons to be derived from it were far more complex and radical than his contemporaries imagined. The Revolution represented the 'open violent rebellion, and victory, of disimprisoned anarchy against corrupt worn-out authority'.[79] Terrible as this experience was, it marked the triumph of a destructive truth and cleared the ground for the construction of what Carlyle called a '*formed* regulated world' that would represent humanity's grasp of truth, rather than its entanglement in a web of decaying falsehoods.[80] When this perspective was applied to Chartism, it emphasised the requirements of justice rather than the alleged depravity, greed and insubordination of the working classes, and it showed what happened if their demands were ignored. Chartism signalled the working classes' determination to assume collective political responsibility for their own fate; the fact that such a desperate remedy was being self-prescribed, demonstrated their deep sense of injustice and their lack of faith in any of the palliatives offered to them. Working class radical activism, itself a symptom of a society out of joint, contributed to a heightened sense of general unease, exacerbating the effect of the general dislocation of the human spirit. While the working classes were gripped by 'a sullen, revengeful humour of revolt', those responsible for the injustice suffered by them were fearful of their physical safety, racked by an obsession with material culture, and immobilised by scepticism and the diversionary attitudes associated with dilettantism.

Carlyle's explanation of Chartism was framed in such a way as to show that neither reliance on the corrective forces of the market, nor the palliative measures promoted by his contemporaries were viable responses to the condition of England problem. He also insisted that a resort to coercion would be ineffective in anything more than the very short term. Because Chartism was an unavoidable consequence of ignoring the just claims of the working classes, hopes that it might be 'put down' by measures such as the arrest of leading members of the movement were groundless. Even when the Chartists seemed completely overwhelmed by the forces pitted against them in 1848, Carlyle warned that 'Chartism' would reappear until measures were taken to address effectively the miseries of the people.[81]

Justice, the recognition of right, is a requirement of the natural laws that govern the universe and is upheld by unwitting human agents of the inscrutable powers that underwrite them. When injustice is widespread and persistent, these agents inflict upon humanity the apparently capricious cruelties attributed to the Furies in Aeschylean drama. Carlyle thought that there were a number of indications that the Furies had already begun to stalk contemporary Britain. Chartism, violent conspiratorial trade unionism, fenianism, and incendiary activity in the English countryside, were political and social manifestations of their appearance. Carlyle was also deeply struck by incidents of deprivation-driven infanticide reported in the press – 'the stern Hebrew imagination could conceive no blacker gulf of wretchedness; that was the ultimatum of degraded god-punished man' – and by what he took to be the perverse and deadly reminder of human interdependence implicit in the devastation wrought by epidemics.[82] Fatal diseases such as cholera appeared first in poor quarters, but their rapid transmission to members of the upper classes was a consequence of a shared vulnerability that symbolised the intractability of human interdependence.

Carlyle's account of the Irish dimensions of the condition of England question provides a particularly elaborate example of his understanding of the relationship between injustice and retribution. Carlyle's personal integrity, his independence of the political or church establishment in England, and his expertise as a historian of revolutions, predisposed some leading Irish nationalists towards him. When Charles Gavan Duffy and other members of 'Young Ireland' visited the Carlyles in Chelsea in April 1845 however, they remonstrated with him over his treatment of their countrymen.[83] In common with later readers of *Chartism*, Duffy and his colleagues were offended at Carlyle's statements on Irish degradation and his claims that the Irish working classes ('sanspotato') were 'immethodic, headlong, violent, mendacious' and lacking in any regard for truth or honesty.[84] Indeed, Carlyle claimed that they were so degraded that they had lost the will to resist. Their only recourses were hopeless, bestial indulgence or emigration. These harsh judgements were not based upon any first-hand knowledge of Irish conditions, or informed accounts of them. *Chartism* merely retailed vivid reformulations of ethnic stereotypes that were common in contemporary English accounts of the Irish.[85] It should be noted, however, that Carlyle's references to the Irish were not completely unsympathetic and nor were they likely to give much comfort to the English. Despite his prejudices on this issue, Carlyle prefaced his comments on Irish affairs with a powerful statement of universal human solidarity:

> All men ... were made by God, and have immortal souls in them. The Sanspotato is one of the selfsame stuff as the superfinest Lord Lieutenant. Not an individual Sanspotato human scarecrow but had a Life given him out of Heaven, with Eternities depending on it; for once and no second time. With Immensities in him, over him and round him; with feelings which a Shakespeare's speech would not utter; with desires illimitable as the Autocrat's of all the Russia's![86]

That beings with these potentialities could sink so far as to be no more than the bearers of the notorious 'wild Milesian features, looking false ingenuity, restlessness, unreason, misery and mockery', was a consequence of the complete failure of English political elites to ensure the recognition of even the most rudimentary requirements of justice.[87]

As in France, systematic injustice prompted retribution, but in this case it took an indirect form. The influx of desperate Irish countrymen into England and Scotland drove down the price of labour, impoverished the British working classes (including, Carlyle noted, during a visit to Annandale, labourers in agricultural districts) and spurred them to revolt rather than to accept work on Irish terms and conditions. In this way England 'reaps, at last, in full measure, the fruit of fifteen generations of wrong-doing.'[88] The interrelationship between English injustice to Ireland and the unjust treatment of the lower classes in England by their putative superiors meant that the condition of England question could not be resolved until the ills of the Irish were addressed. As in the case of the carriers of cholera, injustice had generated a characteristically perverse community of interest between apparently antagonistic interests.

While Carlyle did not downplay the degree of transformation that society must undergo in order to fit itself for the modern world, he continued to view these changes in a positive light. He insisted, however, that the recent history of France provided a series of salutary lessons on the costs that would be paid if his contemporaries failed to grasp both the need for change, and to manage the process in ways that reflected a properly informed understanding of the realities of their situation. Carlyle hoped that, with the help of insights furnished by himself and others who understood the first-order requirements of the situation, the English might negotiate a peaceful process that was at least as revolutionary as that experienced by the French: 'we, with better methods [than the French], may be able to transact it by argument alone'.[89]

Although echoes of the French Revolution reverberated through *Past and Present*, the tone of the work was generally encouraging and hopeful. Carlyle's response to the conclusion of the 'Plug Plot' crisis was particularly interesting from this point of view. By stepping back from the brink, the 'Manchester insurrectionists' had shown that there were some grounds for hoping that Britain may yet avoid the horrors of violent revolution. In making this point, Carlyle drew attention to the as yet unrecognised qualities exhibited by the despised leaders of the working classes in Manchester:

> A deep unspoken sense lies in these strong men ... Amid all violent stupidity of speech, a right noble instinct of what is doable and what is not doable never forsakes them ... Governors and governing classes that *can* articulate and utter, in any measure, what the law of Fact and Justice is, may calculate that here is a Governed Class that will listen.[90]

This observation encapsulated the key and distinctive aspects of Carlyle's understanding of the significance of Chartism. It focused on the shortcomings of the upper classes, seeing the destructive tendencies of working-class activism as a response to these failings that was true in the sense that it reflected legitimate claims of prolonged and systematic injustice. But while endorsing the Chartists' appeal for justice, Carlyle rejected emphatically both the specific goals of the movement and its ideal of working-class self-direction.[91] Given this stance, it is scarcely surprising that *Chartism* was not well received by Chartists themselves; Carlyle, however, would not have been unduly concerned by this response. The target audience for *Chartism* was a middle and upper class whose failure to provide leadership lay at the heart of the condition of England question. The same was true of *Past and Present*, a work that Carlyle described as a study of '*these* times and aristocracies'.[92]

The lessons learned from the failures of pre-revolutionary France and the message inherent in the unconscious plea for guidance that Carlyle attributed to Chartism, had important implications for putative members of the elite, for perceptions of social life, for prescribing the structure of the state and the ethos that guided it. Carlyle had begun to address some of these issues in the early stages of his mission in the late 1820s and early 1830s. In works from this period, the need for self-knowledge on the part of the middle and upper classes was a central concern, a point that Carlyle emphasised when he insisted that the 'condition of England question' needed to be understood systemically and by reference to its fundamental causes.

As a starting point, he urged his contemporaries to recognise the malign relationship between their personal failings and the destructive forces that threatened to overwhelm modern society: 'cease to be a hollow sounding-shell of hearsay, egoisms, purblind dilettanisms; and become, were it on the infinitely small scale, a faithful discerning soul'. He appealed to what he took to be the truly religious instincts of his readers, urging them to eschew the fashionable but false conceptions that played such an important role in modern culture. 'Religion' was not a quack remedy, a 'Morrison's pill' concocted and applied through external agencies, but a 'reawakening of thy own self from within'.[93] Although Saint Simonianism, Puseyism and the evangelical revivalist movements with which Edward Irving was associated expressed deeply-felt and authentic concerns, they addressed them in the language of delusion, not the language of truth. As such, they were manifestations of one of the determining delusions of the age: 'It is not according to the laws of Fact that ye have lived and guided yourselves, but according to the laws of Delusion, Imposture and wilful and unwilful *Mistake* of fact'.[94]

These errors blighted people's moral and religious consciousness and they also reduced political and social discourse and action to a tissue of 'unveraci-ties'. Carlyle's analysis of the condition of England question, and his critical treatment of a range of contemporary responses to it, were designed to expose these impediments to effective thought and action. Shortcomings in moral understanding were almost universal, afflicting the vast majority of the popula-tion. Carlyle's account of the real meaning of Chartism made it clear, however, that the failure of elite leadership, indeed the practical denial that such a thing was desirable or possible, was the crucial issue in understanding the ills of the present and determining the way forward. He claimed that the history of the last two centuries demonstrated a growing incompatibility between traditional ideas of political, social and spiritual leadership, the actual conduct of putative elites and the requirements of the community. By the middle of the nineteenth century traditional ideas about clerical and secular authority, and the structures through which they were put into effect, had lost all contact with truth and reality. Influential sections of the aristocracy supported measures such as the Corn Laws that favoured the landed interest at the expense of working classes, who were thus forced to pay a premium for their dietary staple; these laws symbolised the cause – elite neglect and self-interest – of which Chartism was the consequence.

At the same time, however, they appealed to the principles of the free market when opposing legislation to regulate conditions and hours of work in factories and mines, or in support of the rigorous application of the new poor law regime. These diverse stances, imbued with a spirit that was completely at odds with Carlyle's ideal of self-sacrifice – 'In a valiant suffering for others, not in a slothful making others suffer for us, did nobleness ever lie' – demonstrated an indifference to ideas of leadership that was as marked as that of the most unabashed devotees of Mammon.[95]

Carlyle's views on the upper classes' dereliction of duty was shared by traditionally minded Tories such as Benjamin Disraeli and 'Young England' and those, among whom Michael Sadler was prominent, who were highly critical of the new regime of poor relief. Lockhart's initial interest in *Chartism* reflected the plausibility of these parallels, but his response to the completed draft of the essay was a telling indication of their limitations. Although Carlyle evoked the language of chivalry when upbraiding the upper classes, this was a response to their spiritual impoverishment, not an expression of nostalgia for the medieval ideals that captivated Lord John Manners' and other Young England figures. Indeed, he challenged Young England to 'fling its shovel-hat into the lumber room, much more cast is purple stockings to the nettles, and honestly recognising what was dead ... address itself frankly to the magnificent but as yet chaotic and appalling future, in the *spirit* of the Past and Present'.[96]

It has been observed that Tory paternalists' primary concern seemed to be to protect the working classes rather than to improve them.[97] Sadler, for example, opposed the new poor law because it ignored the working classes' 'right' to relief. This claim, one that was derived from a 'natural' right in a stock of common property upon which subsistence depended, guaranteed relief on non-punitive terms. Since public relief sustained the purchasing power of recipients, this right could be recognised without harming the economy. As a consequence of these views, Sadler rejected state sponsored emigration schemes on the grounds that they encouraged the community to evade giving due recognition to the rightful claims of some of its members.[98] This position differed markedly from that of Carlyle. He condemned the new poor law as inhumane because of the perspective on human nature that was implied by it and because it failed to give effective recognition to the fundamental right to work. This stance rested on an understanding of the importance of self-directed action that had more in common with the perspective of John Stuart Mill than that of conventional Tory paternalism. Mill characterised the latter as proponents of the view that 'The rich should be *in loco parentis* to the poor, guiding and restraining them like children. Of spontaneous action on their part there should be no need'.[99] Carlyle's ideal of active humanity was as removed from this position as Mill's, but he wished to use the state to lay the foundations for it. In *Chartism*, popular education and emigration were identified as key areas where an active state might have an immediate and positive effect on the condition of the working classes.

Carlyle promoted a system of state-supported education as a means for developing the intellectual capacities of the entire population, not merely as an instrument for reconciling the lower classes with their lot, or facilitating social control. 'The spiritual kingdom' was closed to those who were denied an education; their lives were devoid of meaning: it was as if they had 'never lived'.[100] These remarks suggest that Carlyle's conception of popular education, and his promotion of an active role for the state in providing it, was the product of a humanistic, and, in this sense, classless and egalitarian, perspective, not one that was dictated by concerns for material prosperity or public order. In common with those with whom he was associated on *Fraser's Magazine*, Carlyle sought to forge a distinctive perspective on an issue of current importance that challenged those offered by philosophical radicals and political economists.[101] The moral and intellectual opportunities opened up through universal education were to be complimented by opportunities for labour resulting from state-organised emigration, a way of supplementing the efforts of those who promoted productive labour by 'home colonisation' (involving the cultivation of 'waste' lands in England and Ireland) and through a more effective organisation of labour in the industrial arena. The stress on education and emigration in Carlyle's condition of England writings demonstrated the progressive character of his paternalism: the power of the state and the influence of elites should be used to stimulate the population rather than make them passive recipients of care and attention.

While emphasising the need for the state to take an active role and condemning views that militated against this, Carlyle did not provide a developed account of its responsibilities, brushing aside claims about the vagueness of his prescriptions with the retort that it was his mission to identify the fundamental causes of the condition of England problem, to persuade his contemporaries what *should* be done, not *how* it can be done.[102] For the most part, Carlyle fulfilled this role through his publications, but at times he also took part in concerted attempts to promote reforms in areas in which he was particularly interested. In 1835, for example, he encouraged associations promoting national education and the establishment of 'normal schools' to provide trained teachers for them; and for a brief period in the 1840s, he gave some thought to using Charles Buller's influence to secure a position on the National Education Board. In the mid 1850s education formed one of the themes of Carlyle's correspondence, and presumably also of his conversations, with Lord Ashburton.[103] He was also involved in initiatives to reform aspects of poor law administration and wrote encouraging letters of support to working men's institutes in Edinburgh and Manchester. In the latter case he commended efforts to 'provide working people with a place of reunion, where they might enjoy books, perhaps music, recreation, instruction; and at all events, what is general to all men, the society and sight of one another'.[104]

Some flesh was added to Carlyle's reform suggestions by his friend Sir Arthur Helps, an experienced public servant who published detailed blue prints for a range of social reforms. Carlyle's influence was particularly marked in Helps's *Claims of Labour* (1844), where he emphasised that the mere pursuit of wealth was unworthy of human beings' distinctive status in the universe. This work was imbued with an ethos depreciating narrowly focussed self-striving and extolling commitment to public objectives in a spirit of renunciation.[105] While making it clear that he was not a devotee of the contemporary cult of things feudal, Helps nevertheless thought that in the modern world there was still as much need for 'protection and countenance on the one side, and for reverence and attachment on the other' as there had been in a feudal order.[106] Helps's detailed treatment of the responsibilities of elites embraced education, training, living and working conditions, and schemes for beautifying urban environments.[107] In 1848 in an open letter on practical responses to Chartism, Helps urged government to act on health, education, emigration and the regulation of both labour markets and ventures such as railway speculations.[108] At the same time, however, he continued to stress the ongoing responsibility of those who employed labour. This theme was prominent in the *Claims of Labour* and also in Helps' biography of Thomas Brassey, a contractor responsible for large-scale railway projects in England, her colonies, the Crimea and the Argentine. He portrayed Brassey in a heroic light, and frequently echoed Carlyle's expectations of 'captains of industry' in a reformed social and political order presided over by a new aristocracy.[109]

This body might include members of the landed classes who staked their claim to political influence on their capacity to address the challenges facing modern society, rather than relying on traditionally-based criteria. Carlyle made it clear, however, that commercial and industrial capitalists would have prominent leadership roles in the future because they controlled resources that determined the working prospects of an increasingly large proportion of the population. Although highly critical of 'Millocracy's' subscription to the tenets of 'Mammon worship', Carlyle noted that the adoration of wealth was not peculiar to it. Moreover, although tainted strongly by materialism, the industrialists' responses to this gospel were far more promising for the future prospects of society than that of many of the landed classes. On this point, at least, Carlyle's analysis relied on a distinction between productive and parasitic classes that was central to Chartism.[110] The 'unworking aristocracy' were disdainful of what Carlyle ironically referred to as 'ignoble manufacturing individuals', but shamelessly exploited its wealth and political influence so as to enhance its capacity for idleness and dissipation. Industrialists – whose hostility to legislative protection was applied consistently – were at least working earnest devotees of the gospel of Mammon whose commitment and energy might be redirected into more worthwhile channels. While Carlyle thus warned that the world 'will have much to say, reproachfully, reprovingly, admonishingly' to the working aristocracy 'steeped too deep in mere ignoble Mammonism, and as yet all unconscious of its noble destinies, as yet but an irrational or semi-rational giant, struggling to awake some soul in itself', he likened the idle, 'grouse-shooting' aristocracy to unregenerate sinners for whom there was no hope: the verdict passed on them would be unremittingly painful.[111]

Carlyle's understanding of the role of the 'working aristocracy' is closely related to the idea that work is a universal value, and to his expectations concerning the almost infinite scope for labour in an industrial age. When economic striving became human and rational (and effectively ceased to be Mammonism at all), industrialists would see that the pursuit of wealth must be integrated with the realisation of other values, including a just estimation of the character of labour and the claims of labourers. In *Past and Present* Carlyle identified a number of practical implications of this perspective. For example, industrialists would have to abandon their obsession with underselling their competitors, something that Sismondi had seen as being characteristic of English capitalism. They must also take steps to ensure that gains in productive capacity were matched by mechanisms for ensuring a fair distribution of the outcomes of production. These measures might include the creation of jointly-owned enterprises that gave workers and their employers a permanent focus for their shared interests.[112] The state was to promote emigration, encourage the cultivation of wastelands, particularly in Ireland, and set standards in conducting its own affairs that would provide an exemplary benchmark for other employers of labour.

If the 'Millocracy' renounced the gospel of Mammon, its members might become 'captains of industry', that is, permanent leaders of their workers rather than casual exploiters of a commodity that was seen as barely human. The leadership role that Carlyle envisaged for the captains of industry was economic and social rather than political. That is, while he shared the Saint Simonians' ideas on the distinctly industrial character of the coming age, he did not see the state as the preserve of a technocracy. Indeed, state action and care would be necessary to support captains of industry. Carlyle shared the anti-Corn Law campaigners' view that the Corn Laws and other measures of protection threatened the economic viability of English manufacturers by imposing additional costs upon this sector of the economy. He therefore urged the political and social elite to eliminate fiscal burdens upon the manufacturing interest so that it would be possible for its members to balance the claims of labour with the economic imperatives to which they were subjected. In addition to these essentially negative measures, political elites would also need to foster an ethos that was appropriate for the new order. The governing classes would have to teach industrialists 'by noble precept and law-precept, by noble example most of all, that Mammonism was not the essence of his or any other station in God's Universe'.[113]

At the core of Carlyle's idea of 'captains of industry' was the hope that morality might be imposed on market operations by acts of heroic will exercised by employers with the active support of other elites.[114] He seemed to have thought that this goal was feasible if capitalists focused on their proper social and economic roles rather than pursuing the abstract and damaging goal of profit in disregard of these considerations. An interesting sidelight is thrown on this position by Carlyle's personal finances. As a shareholder in the Caledonian Railway Company in the 1870s he allowed his proxy to be given in support of a move to rein in the directors on the grounds that it was their business to run an effective railway service, not pursue speculative chimera that would detract them from this objective: they should 'stand to their real business' and give up 'their other strategic & ambitious operations'.[115]

In *Past and Present* the ideal of heroic government was explored through an analysis of Abbot Samson's role as governor of the monks and retainers of St Edmundsbury. Samson was able to transform a nearly bankrupt and ramshackle abbey into a solvent, revitalised and well-regulated community because he possessed what Carlyle described as an 'internal model of government', a 'heart-abhorrence of whatever is incoherent, pusillanimous, unvaracious – that is to say, chaotic, *ungoverned*; of the Devil, not of God'.[116] But while Carlyle emphasised Samson's personal qualities, he also claimed that effective leadership could only be exercised over those who were themselves heroic to some significant degree. The monks of St Edmundsbury may have seemed merely dull, limited, blind devotees to 'unreformed' religion. At the same time, however, by selecting Samson as their abbot and willingly following his directions, these 'superstitious blockheads' demonstrated 'reverence for Worth, abhorrence of Unworthy'.[117] They thus exhibited characteristically heroic qualities that ensured that leaders could interact effectively with those they governed. The lesson of twelfth century St Edmundsbury was held up to highlight the need for heroic leadership to be set in the context of a heroic society. The ruling classes and the captains of industry should promote a 'chivalry of labour' that incorporated both masters and men and gave practical effect to 'noble humanity and practical diviness of labour' on this earth'.[118]

These prescriptions played an important role in other aspects of Carlyle's social and political criticism, with the idea that an appropriate relationship needed to be forged between heroic leaders and moralised followers being discussed at greater length in a distinctly political setting in the 'Latter-Day Pamphlets' of 1850. Writing from the late 1840s also developed themes concerning the relationship between labour and empire that had first been explored in Carlyle's condition of England writings.

5

Work, Race and Empire

In *Sartor Resartus* Carlyle urged his contemporaries to set their sights on an ideal of stoic self-fulfilment in which a commitment to action was informed by an ethic of renunciation. This requirement made 'labour' or 'work' a fundamental human preoccupation, and the need to commit one's life to it one of the clearest and most positive lessons that Carlyle offered his contemporaries.[1] It played a prominent role in both his public and private lives, forming an enduring theme in his published writings and in his correspondence. In letters to his family, Carlyle rhetorically fortified himself against temptations to idleness, and sought to convince his correspondents of the moral, physical and psychological benefits of labour. 'The unhappiness of a man lies around him as so much work to do, so many devils to be subdued, and order and beauty to be created out of it.'[2] Work was a blessing disguised as a curse: 'In labour lies health of body and of mind; in suffering and difficulty is the soil of all virtue and all wisdom.' In a more directly personal reflection, Carlyle stressed the therapeutic qualities of work: 'So long as I can work, it is all well with me ... The only thing I have to struggle against is idleness and falsehood – two Devil's emissaries'.[3]

As noted in an earlier chapter, Carlyle thought that the role ascribed to action, and the identification of action with labour, was one of the most important insights that Goethe had vouchsafed to his contemporaries. This insight was especially likely to appeal to someone like Carlyle who was brought up in an environment where necessity and popular theology set earnest endeavour and personal austerity at a premium.[4] James Carlyle's commitment to these values had enhanced the social standing of the family and ensured a margin of disposable income sufficient to allow his two most gifted sons to attend university. It also reinforced a strong pre-existing sense of familial independence and moral rectitude. The lessons taken from Goethe and the experiences of everyday life confirmed the message of *Genesis* 2:15: 'And the Lord God took the man, and put him in the Garden of Eden to dress it and to keep it'. These diverse sources provided the basis for the overwhelmingly positive view of labour that underwrote Carlyle's responses to the 'condition of England question'. His faith in its benefits was also central to his understanding of the significance of Britain's imperial role. Carlyle was primarily concerned with 'white' settler colonies, seeing them as providing his countrymen with an almost infinitely varied range of opportunities for worthwhile work. His most controversial claims about work and empire, however, concerned non-whites who were perceived as subjects of empire rather than participants in the imperial mission of 'England'. In this case, the fate of the 'gospel of labour' depended on how Europeans responded to the challenges posed by what were claimed to be the racially determined capacities of non-whites to commit to it. This theme, explored originally with respect to British colonies in the West Indies, also played an important role in Carlyle's response to moves to eradicate slavery in the United States.

Carlyle's most developed statements of the 'gospel of labour' appeared in *Past and Present*. This work bore the formidable Goethean motto '*Ernst ist das Leben*' (life is a serious matter) and reiterated the medieval exhortation, '*Laborare est Orare*', (to work is to pray). Carlyle used the term 'labour' to encompass a wide range of activities. Literature, prophetic religious leadership, military command, statesmanship and positions of social and intellectual responsibility all provided opportunities for worthwhile human endeavour. When these opportunities were seized by extraordinary characters who understood the implications of the laws of nature for their own time and place, they gave rise to universal exemplars of heroic leadership. The elevating effects of labour were not restricted, however, to world historical figures: 'even in the meanest sorts of Labour, the whole soul of man is composed into a kind of real harmony, the instant he sets himself to work!'[5] The universal obligation to labour, and the positive role of all forms of authentic human effort in relation to the progressive development of human society, pointed to a fundamental moral equality of all those who labour conscientiously.

Work was the means by which human beings fulfil their obligation to reduce chaotic nature to the condition of beneficent order that is immanent within it. Carlyle seemed to hold the view (found also in the works of a diverse range of contemporary thinkers including the political economist James McCulloch and the far more congenial Thomas Arnold) that God's creation was deliberately incomplete and that it was his intention that humans should fulfil themselves by striving to perfect it. The challenges posed by a chaotic but orderable world were tasks that destiny had contrived to foster the cultivation of the human spirit, and to give expression to humanity's status as infinite. For this reason, Carlyle insisted that work should be undertaken in a spirit of personal renunciation; it should not be seen as an instrument for gratifying material aspirations or promoting conceptions of well being that depended upon consumption. Since the efforts of *homo operarius* were a reflection of the God-like capacity of humanity to turn the chaotic and hellish into the beneficial and orderly, they should not be associated with these banal and unworthy conceptions of human endeavour. Labour is life, but it is life as 'worship' – as active, positive, affirmative engagement with the divinely created order of the universe. True work 'cannot be carried on without religion. You have not work otherwise; you have eye-service, greedy grasping of wages, swift and ever swifter manufacture of semblances to get hold of wages'.[6] Carlyle endowed labour with moral characteristics that assumed the priorities that Schiller had urged on the artist: 'Let him look upwards to his dignity and his mission, not downwards to his happiness and his wants'. Unlike Schiller, however, who regarded work as necessary but demoralising, and looked to fine art to restore harmony to human existence, Carlyle argued that labour was an unqualified good for all members of the community.[7] The only adequate reward for labour was to be found in 'Heaven', not in the prospect of a life of pomp (a dandyesque illusion), ease (an affront to Carlyle's conception of human dignity), or conventional notions of plenty (more or less sophisticated expressions of animalistic materialism).

Labour played a crucial role in human development, providing a range of experiences that generate self-knowledge and knowledge of the world. Carlyle treated a commitment to effective work as the touchstone of human veracity. Since moral worth hinged on human beings' capacity to act in correspondence with the laws of the universe, work provided an irrefutable and lasting testament of the quality of the worker: 'Whatsoever of morality and of intelligence; what of patience, perseverance, faithfulness, of method, insight, ingenuity, energy; in a word, whatsoever of Strength the man had in him will lie written in the Work he does'.[8] When human beings respond to the challenges posed in the natural and social world, they are moulded by the experience. This process generates self-knowledge and knowledge of the world, stimulating such virtues as 'Patience, Courage, Perseverance, Openness to light'.[9]

Carlyle saw work as the key value in a secularised metaphysics that addressed the fundamental religious instincts that could not be presented to modern humanity through the medium of Christian doctrine: work was quite literally, a 'gospel', or 'God's message'. In some respects, however, he saw the gospel of labour as an alternative to all metaphysical speculation: 'We shall never know "what we are"; on the other hand, we can always partly know, what beautiful or noble things we are fit to do, and that is the grand inquiry for us'.[10] Three sets of parallel ideas stand at the centre of this new gospel: those concerning salvation and consolation; ideas of voluntary commitment that mirror some conceptions of Christian liberty; and a notion of immortality.

The idea that work was the basis of personal salvation and the sole source of lasting consolation was a central theme in *Sartor Resartus*. Carlyle adopted the motto 'Work and despair not!' for his mission to his contemporaries, constantly reiterating it in a variety of formulations. 'Let us stand to our work, and see that it is honest: there is no other remedy; and that, under Heaven's goodness, is remedy enough'.[11] Carlyle would not countenance what he took to be John

Stuart Mill's abstract and dogmatic promotion of liberty because he thought it privileged the whims of even the most ignorant individuals over substantive outcomes.[12] He nevertheless valued personal independence because it meant that individuals could subscribe voluntarily to the requirements of morality, including in this case, those focused in the gospel of labour. As he put it in 1872, 'work by compulsion is little good. You must carry a man's volition along with you if you are to command any good'.[13] But since liberty was conditioned by the requirements of a given end, it could not be claimed by those who were indifferent to the end in question. Carlyle's views on this issue resembled those taken by seventeenth century Protestant proponents of 'Christian liberty'. Like the recalcitrant 'ungodly' members of a Christian commonwealth, those who would not voluntarily endorse the gospel of labour should be compelled to subscribe to its external requirements. This possibility might impose a range of demands on individuals holding positions of political and social responsibility, including, Carlyle at times suggested, obligations to coerce the idle so as to ensure that they did not hinder humanity's fulfilment of its obligations. In 1852, for example, he argued that, if the relationship between workers and employers was to be reformed, a sharp distinction would need to be drawn between those willing to work and habitual, wilful paupers. The latter lived off the earnings of their industrious fellows, disrupted labour markets and tainted the moral tone of the working class as a whole.[14]

But while some of the implications of Carlyle's position were harsh and authoritarian, others pointed in a different direction. His preference for free commitment to the gospel of labour thus had important implications for his views on the conditions under which labour should be carried out. Drudgery debased labour by making it a matter of material necessity rather than voluntary commitment; it allowed for no rest or reflection and, since it was driven by selfishness and Mammon worship, it was morally degrading.[15] So too was work undertaken in conditions like those that Carlyle witnessed during a visit to the industrial areas of South Wales in the summer of 1850. He described Merthyr Tydfil as 'a vision of *Hell* … those poor creatures broiling all in sweat and dirt, amid their furnaces, pits and rolling-mills … 50,000 grimy mortals, black and clammy … screwing out a living for themselves'.[16] In a later recollection of this scene Carlyle described Merthyr as the '*Non-plus-ultra* of Industrialism wholly mammonish … presided over by sooty Darkness physical and spiritual, by Beer, Methodism and the Devil'.[17]

Carlyle's claim that work was a supreme duty imposed on humanity by God, has superficial similarities with the position propagated by contemporary proponents of theologically grounded forms of political economy such as William Paley, Thomas Malthus, Frederick Copleston, Richard Whately and Thomas Chalmers. These writers regarded poverty as a divine contrivance for stimulating human effort and they argued that true happiness and material success were positively related in the tradition of protestant practice. They saw competition as a divinely ordained way of turning human frailty to good ends and condemned social and political intervention in the economy as an unwarranted interference with Divine design.[18] These writers placed a premium on individual effort, but in other respects their views were quite foreign to Carlyle's conception of labour. They rested ultimately on mechanical attitudes towards production that treated human action as a response to rewards and sanctions rather than being a self-directed answer to the call of duty.

Although he had no faith in orthodox Christian notions of an afterlife, Carlyle thought that labour made it possible for human beings to participate in some sort of immortality, hence his insistence that the rewards of labour would be found only in 'Heaven'. Workers left permanent memorials of their labours and these relics became objects of remembrance (or of contempt) to succeeding generations.

> Behold, the day is passing swiftly over, our life is passing swiftly over; and the night cometh, wherein no man can work. The night once come, our happiness, our unhappiness – it is all abolished; vanished, clean gone; a thing that has been ... But our work – behold that is not abolished, that has not vanished: our work behold, it remains, or the want of it remains – for endless times and eternities remains.[19]

The expectation that future generations would admire the fruits of their predecessors' labour provided the only sure source of consolation for the toils of the honest and true: 'all speech and rumour is short lived, foolish, untrue. Genuine WORK alone, what thou workest faithfully, that is eternal, as the Almighty Founder and World-builder himself'.[20] For the most part, these achievements represented the accumulated efforts of countless legions of individual workers who had slipped silently into oblivion. In some cases, however, the past yields up chance glimpses of emblematic worker-heroes that serve to assure and fortify the current generation:

> Look up, my wearied brother; see thy fellow Workmen there, in God's Eternity; surviving there, they alone surviving; Sacred band of the immortals, celestial Bodyguard of the Empire of Mankind. Even in the weak Human Memory they survive so long, as saints, as heroes, as gods; they alone surviving; peopling, they alone, the unmeasured solitudes of Time! To thee Heaven, though severe, is *not* unkind.[21]

In *Past and Present* Carlyle presented his readers with inspiring examples drawn from a medieval monastic community. In this setting, the link between work and worship was singularly direct, but he thought that the same principles underlay *all* worthwhile human existence. The contemplation of truthful work in a single lifetime, or between generations, aided individuals as they traversed their brief shaft of daylight. Thus, in the private intensity of his reminiscence of James Carlyle, Carlyle took comfort from the surviving products of his father's labours as a mason in Annandale:

> their works follow them: the Force that had been lent my father he honourably expended in manful well-doing: a portion of this Planet bears beneficent traces of his strong Hand and strong Head; nothing that he undertook to do but he did it faithfully and like a true man ... no one that comes after him will ever say, Here was the finger of a hollow Eye-servant.

In a less charged but still significant aside, Carlyle recalled M'Corkindale, the foreman printer for Ballantynes of Edinburgh. This working-class hero, 'a gigantic man, with patient anxious eyes', was 'still memorable' to Carlyle after the passage of more than forty years.[22]

While labour played a crucial role in the lives of individuals, it was also the constitutive force of organic societies and, when embedded in the distinctive laws, *mores* and literary and material culture of particular historical communities, it was the source of their collective consciousness. This position represented a distinctive variation on accounts of historical communal consciousness associated with romantic conceptions of national identity that were current in the late eighteenth and early nineteenth centuries. For Carlyle, national identity was forged through labour and sustained by reflection upon its merits. As with the other deeds of humankind, communities that survived the test of time did so because they successfully accommodated themselves to the divinely ordained laws of the Universe; their collective labour was central to this process. In both *Chartism* and *Past and Present* Carlyle expounded this theme by reference to the self-knowledge of the 'English', a term that embraced the post-Celtic inhabitants of Scotland and Wales as well as those of England. 'This English land ... is the summary of what was found of wise, and noble, and accordant with God's Truth, in all the generations of English men'.[23] These works focus exclusively on the English past, but elsewhere Carlyle made it clear that this country's experience was by no means unique. Thus in the course of a visit to the Netherlands he noted a similar achievement embodied in the civic and ecclesiastical architecture of Bruges: 'Honour to the long-forgotten generations; they have done *something* in their time: this city, nay this country is a work of theirs'. Significantly, Carlyle concluded this account with a reprimand to Coleridge for his 'poor sneer' that the soil of the Netherlands was the work of man not God: 'All the more credit to man, Mr Samuel Taylor!'[24]

For Carlyle, as for a number of contemporary thinkers, the history of the nation was the primary objective of historical reflection, but for him this focused on a broad notion of human activity encapsulated in the idea of 'labour'.[25] The fighting warlords and bickering political factions that dominated conventional literature were peripheral to real history since they had not played a positive role in the emergence of the English as a significant force in universal history. Carlyle's account of this process emphasised a number of distinctive highlights that included the arrival of the Saxons, the absorption of the native Celts into a more vigorous culture, the centuries-long creation of the material culture of the community, the release of the practical and spiritual energies of the population through the impact of Puritanism, and the celebration of a self-conscious national community in the works of Shakespeare and Milton.[26]

By understanding these earlier 'eras of England', the English would come to grasp what is entailed in the current stage of their mission, one that saw the intelligence and moral energies of the population applied to the development of England's industrial capacity: 'Nature alone knows thee, acknowledges the bulk and strength of thee: thy Epic, unsung in words, is written in huge characters on the face of this Planet – sea-moles, cotton-trades, railways, fleets and cities'.[27] Carlyle warned of the dislocating effect of industrialisation if responses to it were not framed and organised in ways that took account of the distinctive 'god-like' status of humanity, and, as noted above, he was aware that it often debased the experience of labour and devastated the environment. Nevertheless, he thought that the industrial revolution had greatly enhanced humans' capacity to develop and order both the natural world and their collective interaction with it, and adopted a far more positive view than older contemporaries such as Robert Southey. The industrial revolution was not a stage in the process of a national decline into materialism; to the contrary, it projected a shaft of bright clear light onto a landscape that had long been sunk in gloom and confusion. It was, Carlyle wrote, 'the one God's Voice we have heard in these two atheistic centuries', a period during which the English had turned their backs on all the other implications of the values that had invigorated their intellectual, moral and political life when Puritanism shaped the national ethos.[28]

Labour made its immediate impress upon a *national* community by creating a second order natural environment that framed its life. At the same time, however, these efforts may be endowed with a far wider and more direct universal significance. In the present case, the labouring triumphs of the English since the late seventeenth century were the prelude to a global mission pursued within the framework of Britain's empire.

England's imperial mission was in some sense merely a geographical expansion of its domestic one. Empire was a 'mighty conquest over chaos' embracing two related tasks, the 'industrial' one of making the planet useful for humanity, and the 'constitutional' one of ensuring that the fruits of conquest were shared by all.[29] These tasks called for heroic commitment of a highly practical kind. Carlyle was contemptuous of what he saw as the pointless heroics of exploration, declining to share popular alarm over the fate of Sir John Franklin in the Arctic and dismissing David Livingston, the missionary and explorer of parts of eastern Africa, as a 'meandering ass'.[30] While Carlyle thought that the industrial part of England's mission was well advanced, however, he complained that its constitutional dimensions – raising political problems of how to convert staggering gains in productivity into general benefits – had been only fitfully and unsuccessfully pursued in both Britain and in her colonies.

Much of what Carlyle had to say on England's imperial mission was framed implicitly by a view of empire in which settler colonies were a predominant concern. One of his rare references to India expressed the hope that the subcontinent might provide scope for colonisation and would benefit from it.[31] This expectation reflected a marked tendency to consider colonies from the point of settlers rather than of the indigenous populations. Thus while Carlyle displayed a sympathetic interest in the fate of the Māori in pre-annexation New Zealand, and urged European settlers to protect them, this appeal was not supported by any reference to the rights or interests of the original inhabitants of the lands that colonists were urged to reduce to order and productivity.[32] When issues of land use and occupation were at stake, indigenous people were either assumed to have a tenuous, nomadic and essentially wasteful relationship to the lands they nominally occupied, or they were ignored completely. Like the Celts, these people were to be displaced by those who proved able to put the land to 'better' use. This assumption might also have been accompanied by the expectation – promoted by Carlyle's former pupil Charles Buller, now an MP and important figure in pro-colonial circles – that indigenous populations would be absorbed by the more numerous and vigorous descendants of colonisers.[33] Certainly, Carlyle's account of the emergence of 'England' as a distinctive, unified entity suggested that this model would be appealing to him.

Carlyle's 'condition of England' writings added his voice to those promoting emigration as a means of providing the human resources necessary to develop the Empire and ensure that the entire population of Britain and Ireland had opportunities for gainful employment.[34] He accepted the fact of overpopulation in Western Europe and was dismissive of anti-Malthusians (a group that included radicals such as William Cobbett and conservative figures such as Coleridge, Michael Sadler and Robert Southey) who closed their eyes to this fact and quoted the Bible in justification of their wilful myopia.[35] At the same time, however, he was highly critical of those who placed their faith in sexual abstinence prompted by the working class's desire to enhance its standard of living. This position was unrealistic; it was also morally unacceptable because it flew in the face of nature and relied on a mechanical reflex to stimuli grounded in the primacy

1. The earliest picture of Thomas Carlyle, drawn by Daniel Maclise when Carlyle was thirty-six-years old, and published in *Fraser's Magazine* in June 1833 as part of a series of literary notables. The drawing gives Carlyle an uncharacteristically dandyish air.

2. Edward Irving's close relationship with Carlyle between 1816 and 1822 was critical for his intellectual and literary development. Irving's later millenarian inclinations were treated by Carlyle as highly indicative 'signs of the times'.

3. Jane Welsh Carlyle, aged thirty-seven, a crayon drawing by Samuel Lawrence made at a time (*c.* 1838) when the Carlyles' prospects seemed at their brightest. The success of *The French Revolution* and *Sartor Resartus* had confirmed Thomas's position as a major figure and Jane's state of health was relatively good. (*National Trust*)

4. Carlyle's birthplace in Ecclefechan; the house was designed and built by his father, James Carlyle, and his uncle; the brothers were partners in a building business.

5. Craigenputtock, the Carlyles' home from 1828 to 1833. Thomas composed many of his early works in this country retreat but the isolation and bitter winter weather made frequent escapes to Edinburgh and London imperative.

6. Thomas and Jane's house in Cheyne Row, Chelsea, their home from June 1833; a 'right old strong roomy brick-house, built near 150 years ago, and likely to see *three* races of their modern fashionables fall before it comes down'.

7. Carlyle at work in July 1857; the lack of clutter on the table suggests that he was correcting proofs of recently completed volumes *Fredrick the Great*, or the latest edition of his works, rather than writing the next stage of his daunting *magnum opus*. This picture was probably taken in the garden of Cheyne Row, where Carlyle sometimes worked under an awning.

(*Columbia University*)

8. A carbon photograph of Carlyle by Elliot & Fry, taken in 1865 when Carlyle was approaching seventy. (*National Trust*)

9. Past, Present and Future: Carlyle with Emerson's grandson, Edward Emerson Forbes (1873–1969), taken around 1878. The subjects in this photograph link Craigenputtock in 1833, when Carlyle and Emerson first met, with high Victorian London and with twentieth-century Boston. Edward Emerson Forbes became a distinguished art historian and curator at Harvard University. (*Columbia University*)

of materialism. In any case, so long as colonies offered such a promising range of opportunities for labour to the 'surplus' population of Britain and Ireland, Carlyle regarded population growth in a positive light:

> in a world where Canadian Forests stand unfelled, boundless Plains and Prairies un-
> broken with the plough; on the west and on the east green desert spaces never yet made
> white with corn; and to the overcrowded little western nook of Europe, our Terrestrial
> Planet, nine-tenths of it yet vacant or tenanted by nomads, is still crying, Come and till
> me, come and reap me! And in an England with wealth, and means for moving, such as
> no nation ever before had.[36]

Carlyle's views on the immediate beneficiaries of colonial settlement echoed those of Edward Gibbon Wakefield, the promoter of 'systematic' settlement in New Zealand and South Australia whose efforts he had encouraged. Colonial expansion opened up opportunities for members of the working classes and for possessors of small capitals and agricultural skills like Carlyle's family and their hard-pressed, land hungry neighbours. It also improved the prospects of the under-occupied members of professions – another echo of Carlyle's experiences on the overstocked professional labour market in Scotland in the 1820s – and of half-pay military and naval officers.[37] Military and naval men who sought to provide heroic leadership in the incomplete epic of England would, however, need to utilise steam engines and ploughshares rather than battle-axes and other instruments of destruction.[38]

These ideas, first formulated in the 1830s and early 1840s, remained central to Carlyle's thinking thereafter. As an avid (though complaining) reader of news-papers and periodicals, he was exposed to a torrent of information, commentary and promotional literature on imperial affairs. These sources were supplemented by correspondence (and infrequent meetings in Chelsea) with admirers who were actively engaged in colonial administration and politics. Charles Duffy became Premier of Victoria, and Henry Parkes held the same office in New South Wales; James Anthony Froude had a close interest in South Africa.[39] Even when he had ceased to make public pronouncements on colonisation, Carlyle gave private support to Sir George Grey's campaign in the late 1860s to resist those who argued that Britain should shed her colonies. Grey, a former governor of South Australia, New Zealand and the Cape Colony, wished to cement the ties between Britain and her rapidly maturing colonies by a system of imperial federation. He described state-sponsored immigration as the 'handmaiden to federation'.[40] In 1869 Carlyle roused himself from apolitical lethargy to sign a petition in favour of emigration organised by a working men's association.

Although many of the details of Carlyle's statements on empire were common-places of pro-colonisation sentiment, his handling of them was distinctive. In the first place, his conception of colonisation was heroic, eschewing, for example, the more prosaic expectations of its advantages extolled in a contemporary essay in *Fraser's Magazine*: 'relief from pressure by such as abide at home, wider and more genial dwelling-places by such as go abroad, and an extension of its own power and influence by the government which promotes emigration'.[41] The idea that colonies would provide opportunities for applying and developing the fruits of industrialisation was not considered primarily in relation to the material enrichment of either the colonists or the 'mother' country in Carlyle's accounts, while his remarks on the significance of technological advances rested on a view of development that was not driven by profit maximisation imperatives. In 1857 he bewailed the fact that colonisation seemed to have become 'all heaving of wood and drawing of water; nothing nobler or better'. He showed no interest in promoting colonisation as a means of providing markets for British manufactured goods, or for under-employed capital.[42] Rather than seeing Britain as the 'workshop of the world', an image beloved of free trade parliamentary radicals in the 1830s and 1840s, he urged the English to transform the world into a workshop.[43] Imperialism was the latest stage in a cosmic mission imposed on the English by God, one that was challenged by developments such as the mid century gold rushes that exemplified a debased spirit devoted to the earth-grubbing pursuit of mammon.[44] This view mirrored those of some missionary lobbies in Britain, but in Carlyle's case any evangelical aspirations were framed in terms of the gospel of labour not that of Christ.[45]

Furthermore, although Carlyle often used language that conjured up images of conquest, territorial acquisition and the extension of political control, he did not admire those who placed their trust in armed force, nor was he wedded to any distinctive conception of the Empire as a political unit.[46] Contrary to the impression given by superficial readings of *Frederick the Great*, Carlyle's views tended towards pacifism rather than militarism. Thus when he scoffed at Richard Cobden's 1848 campaign to pursue a triple-headed strategy involving retrenchment in military spending, the extension of free trade and the promotion of international disarmament (dismissing it as 'Cobden's calico millennium'), he did so out of ingrained scepticism of schemes that promised to make the world a bed of roses and suspicion of mechanical solutions to human problems, in this case one that relied on the self-interested responses of actors in a free trade environment.[47] Neither of these sets of reservations implied an endorsement of militarism or admiration of those who placed their trust in armed force. *Sartor Resartus* contains some striking passages on the savagery and futility of war, and when Carlyle wrote in praise of military figures he made it abundantly clear that their achievements on the battlefield were of value because they exemplified earnestness, sincerity and a grasp of the underlying realities of the universe.[48] This perspective is apparent in his unqualified approval of Oliver Cromwell and his far more guarded assessments of both Frederick the Great and Napoleon.[49]

In other cases – for example, pirates, warlike American Indians and the warring dynasties of eighteenth century Europe – he spoke contemptuously of a reliance on force of arms, claimed that no military cause since the English Civil war was worth dying for, or even spending money on. He dismissed peacetime armies as monuments to idleness and useless expense, 'perpetual solecism[s] dressed in scarlet'.[50] He was equally scathing in his condemnation of Palmerstonian 'gun boat diplomacy', rejected the bellicose anti-Russian strategy that drew Britain into a war in the 1850s and threatened to do so again in the 1870s as an ally of the Turks, and regretted that British policy in South Africa had given rise to armed conflict with the Zulus. These attitudes were noted by Carlyle's admirers, some of whom appealed to him to make a public stand in support of pacifism.[51]

In the imperial context Carlyle used the term 'conquest' as part of a metaphor referring to humanity's (and more specifically to England's) obligation to reduce a supposedly unformed world to a condition of order by 'conquering' chaos. This task called for courage, a point that Carlyle emphasised in a phrase in *Past and Present* – 'the valiant all-conquering sons of toil' – but the valor required differed from that of the battlefield.[52] The heroes of the most recent stage of England's mission were Thomas Brindley, the canal builder, James Watt, the engineer, and Thomas Arkwright, the inventor of textile machinery, rather than military or naval figures. The future would depend upon those who were capable of undertaking the 'constitutional' requirements of England's mission: 'the future work of human wisdom and human heroism is … not of fighting with, and beating to death one's poor fellow-creatures in other countries, but of regimenting into blessed activity more and more one's poor fellow-creatures in one's own country, for their and all people's profit'.[53]

For Carlyle the 'empire' was significant because it provided a range of opportunities for continuing England's 'industrial' mission, not as a theatre for grandiose geopolitical demonstrations. As a result, he was only alarmed by the development of independent political institutions in the colonies when they threatened to replicate features of British political culture that undermined effective government, or when support for them was merely a manifestation of the British government's attempts to evade its responsibilities. Carlyle was largely indifferent to arguments that hinged on the desirability of maintaining the empire as a hegemonic political entity, and when he supported Sir George Grey's campaign, he did so because he thought any weakening of Britain's ties with her colonies would encourage those who wished to dissolve the union between Britain and Ireland.[54] In addition, however, it was necessary for Britain to retain her colonies so that she could fulfil her obligations to her subjects: 'England will not readily admit that her own children are worth nothing but to be flung out of doors!'[55] Thus, while Carlyle's strongly positive attitude towards emigration was part of a widespread reaction (attributed in part to the advocacy of Edward Gibbon Wakefield) against Malthusian ideas that colonies were useful safety values for venting surplus and dangerous inhabitants of Britain, he emphasised its ethical significance and anchored this firmly to his own distinctive gospel of labour.[56]

Carlyle's attitude to the United States brings his conception of the politics of empire into sharp relief. Although dismissive of American democracy and materialism, Carlyle did not think that the country's political independence destroyed its significance for England's mission. He thought that the Americans had been quite right to eliminate the British government's role in their affairs, and, unlike his disciple J. A. Froude, did not regard British emigration to that country as a threat to the Empire. The United States was 'a country of our brothers', a 'piece of England'; like Canada, it was to be valued because it provided a range of valuable opportunities for the English to pursue their mission in the world.[57] As in his treatment of economic activity in general and industrialisation in particular, Carlyle tended to focus upon the cosmic significance of colonialism and on the moral benefits that it might secure to the colonists themselves, rather than on the economic, political or strategic interests of the metropolitan country.[58]

Carlyle wished to persuade his contemporaries that labour was the sole remaining source of value left to them, the only means through which they could express fundamental values in a world that was otherwise devoid of veracity.[59] If work was to play this role, however, it needed to be preserved from ideas and practices that undermined its moral significance. Carlyle identified a range of threats to the gospel of labour emerging from within the economic sphere itself (consumerism, careless workmanship, a mercenary labour force and 'promoterism') and a more general one resulting from the doctrine of *laissez-faire*.

The perversity of his contemporaries' views on labour was a recurrent theme in Carlyle's correspondence and published writings. He complained not only of the quality of workmanship but also of the obsessive determination to secure as many of the inferior products of modern labour as possible. The fact that this bizarre worship of falsity was becoming endemic was a final, fateful reflection of the crisis that gripped the contemporary world. The debasement of labour, and its displacement by a culture where appearances were given precedence over reality, was epitomised for Carlyle by gimmicks such as the seven-foot hat paraded around the streets of London to advertise the indifferent products of a hatter.[60] The moral status of labour was compromised fatally when it was placed at the service of a materialistic and hedonistic ethos that was radically at odds with the divine spark in humanity, and completely contrary to the requirements of the doctrine of renunciation.

In *Chartism* and particularly in *Past and Present*, Carlyle was relatively optimistic that 'captains of industry' and members of the working classes would respond positively to the gospel of labour. Later, however, as he saw new challenges arising to threaten these expectations, he became far less sanguine on this score. In 'Shooting Niagara: And After?' (1867), and in posthumously published fragments, he was highly critical of what he saw as the narrow, unworthy instrumentalism of the increasingly active forces of 'organised labour'. This idea, used by Carlyle in the late 1840s and early 1850s to refer to elite leadership of the working classes in their response to the challenges to the gospel of labour, seemed to have been utterly perverted in subsequent campaigns to decrease the length of the working day, to increase wages, and to accord legal recognition to trades unions. Carlyle's comments on these questions were not part of an argument in favour of ill-paid drudgery but one that was directed against those who neglected the moral significance of labour. His view was apparent in the highly unfavourable comparisons that he drew between modern trades unions and medieval guilds. Like the overarching contrast between the monastery and the workhouse that framed *Past and Present*, these contrasting ethos were representative features of their respective periods.

> *Guilds* were for quickening the conscience of workmen, teaching Every workman that it was not permitted him to think of doing His work ill; that the *honour of a workman* and all his Brethren, consisted in faithful, skilful, and excellent doing of work, and in never by any temptation debasing himself to work like a thief and knave. Trades-Unions ... are avowedly for increase of wages alone; of thievery, knavery, botchery ... no account is had, or, if any, rather a preference shown for these such qualities! Guilds, therefore, we define as tending towards Heavenward for all parties ... Trades-Unions are tending Hellward.[61]

This image haunted Carlyle to the end of his life. In a letter written in late 1880 to Sir James Whitworth, a captain of industry who had made a fortune in engineering, Carlyle praised Whitworth's treatment of his workers and repeated his earlier laments on what he took to be the attitude towards labour prevailing among the working classes. Even a hundred years ago

> All England awoke to its work with an invocation to the Eternal Maker to bless them in their day's labour and help them do it well. Now, all England – shopkeepers, workmen, all manner of competing labourers – awaken as if with an unspoken but heartfelt prayer to Beelzebub – 'Oh, help us, thou great lord of shoddy, adulteration, and malfeasance, to do our work with the maximum of slimness, swiftness, profit, and mendacity, for the devil's sake. Amen'.[62]

It is important to note that these criticisms were not part of a general endorsement of the conduct or ideas of contemporary business. To the contrary, Carlyle was sharply critical of one-sided treatments of disputes between workers and employers, and continued to insist that the latter must shoulder the responsibilities that their control of labour imposed upon them.[63]

By the late 1860s the blind pursuit of wealth had become even more prevalent than before, giving rise to the nightmare images of Merthyr Tydfil that signified appalling human drudgery and the degradation of the natural environment. The last of these issues was raised in 'Shooting Niagara' where Carlyle asked whether the liberty of 'free industry' extended to the spoliation of an environment 'created by Heaven herself?' This question, which echoed concerns being voiced by Carlyle's admirer John Ruskin, was prompted by the belief that human beings should interact beneficially with the natural world, rather than exert their god-like capacities to degrade it.[64] The misapplication of human effort that gave rise to these outcomes was driven by a blind and reckless commitment to the pursuit of wealth that threatened to subvert the gospel of labour entirely.

This threat had already materialised in the growing tendency for qualitative productive values to be sacrificed in the causes of profit and cheap consumer gratification. In the early 1870s, however, Carlyle identified an even more insidious manifestation of it in the rise of what he termed 'promoterism', a state of mind that lay at the heart of a virulent contemporary culture of speculative capitalism. This culture provided the theme for a number of fictional works that were published throughout the Victorian period, including Anthony Trollope's The Way We Live Now, a very successful novel that was more or less contemporary with an unpublished essay that Carlyle wrote on the subject.[65] The timing of this essay, and references in it to 'South American aqueducts' and 'Patagonian railways', make it likely that it was prompted by a scandal that broke out in the second half of 1872 concerning loans dating back to the late 1860s. The fact that these loans were raised on behalf of Central and South American governments (Honduras, Santo Domingo, Costa Rica and Paraguay), to consolidate existing debts and raise capital for infrastructural development, set this form of speculation in direct opposition to the ethos that underwrote Carlyle's ideas on both work and empire.

The collapse of the Honduran Loan stock on the London markets in June and July 1872 was the primary subject of a Select Committee of the House of Commons that reported at the end of July 1875. The report (which surveyed a range of loans) revealed a welter of sharp practices (some involving brazenly unrepentant MPs) in the floatation and manipulation of the stock, the security offered for loans and the management of them. For example, the Committee noted that the transaction costs of the Honduran Loan were out of all proportion to the substantive developments funded by it and that the original debt of one million pounds had swollen to six and a half million pounds by 1875 to finance a fifty three mile stretch of now abandoned 'ship-bearing' railway track.[66] These figures illustrated the damaging implications of 'promoterism' for the gospel of labour: the putative objective of speculation – the aqueduct or railway – was merely a decoy to further the true object, that is, the ill-deserved accumulation of wealth by the promoters playing on cupidity of the general public. By using fantasies of production to generate wealth for themselves, promoters and their accomplices denigrated the ideal of commercial and industrial leadership and debased the gospel of labour. Promoterism meant 'the conversion of Human Commerce and Enterprise which is Heaven's Eternal mandate, into ardent gambling which is the Devil's mandate'.[67]

While the excesses of speculative capitalism that were of particular concern to Carlyle in the 1870s added a new challenge to the gospel of labour, there was a sense in which this creed had always been threatened by contemporary values. As noted already, Carlyle thought that pauperism owed much to elite subscription to *laissez-faire*.[68] Under the influence of this malign doctrine the provision of opportunities to work, and the conditions under which it was undertaken, were treated as functions of the market, and labour was reduced to a commodity that was only related to the rest of society through the 'cash-nexus'. In a world where work was worship, the assumptions upon which *laissez-faire* rested flew in the face of fundamental human and cosmic values: neither worship nor the relationship between worshippers should be seen in materialistic terms. The social and political implications of *laissez-faire* were equally damaging to the gospel of labour because it was evoked to justify a general avoidance of governmental and elite responsibility to the lower classes. These responsibilities were wide-ranging but the most important of them required that personal, social and state power should be used to enhance opportunities for labour.

Carlyle's views on this issue played a role in his initial response to the 1848 Revolution in France. He thought that the various work creation schemes (the 'national workshops') set up by the fledgling republic provided a rare example of an issue on which the English might take a positive lesson from the French.[69] These initiatives emphasised the inadequacies of the Poor Law Amendment Act of 1834, a measure that punished unemployed members of the lower classes but did nothing to create opportunities for effective labour for them. Carlyle looked to state action to ward off the pauperisation of large sections of the working classes, not to the mechanical combination of *laissez-faire* and the poor law.[70] Ideologically driven inactivity in domestic affairs was matched by the refusal of successive governments to become active and effective partners in promoting emigration to the colonies. Their failure to take up what Carlyle saw as one of the key functions of a revitalised active state imperilled England's imperial mission, blighting the material and moral prospects of the lower classes throughout the kingdom. While these failures of elite vision and leadership had a profound impact in England and Scotland, they were felt most sharply in Ireland.

In 1849, ten years after he had pronounced on Ireland in *Chartism*, Carlyle
finally gained some detailed and relatively extensive first-hand knowledge of the
country. In the course of a five-week tour in late summer, he visited a number of
rural counties in both the northern and southern parts of the country, and spent
a little time in Dublin and most of the main provincial cities. Although he told
Charles Duffy that he expected to learn very little from the tour – 'Ireland is', he
commented complacently, 'pretty satisfactorily intelligible to me' – Carlyle prepared for it by reading works on the history of Ireland and its current condition,
studying maps of the country and securing advice on who and what he should
see. On his return he affirmed that while his views had not really changed, 'the
empty theorems' were now clothed with a 'flesh-and-blood Body'; the experience
was 'painfully impressive and oppressive'.[71] In *Chartism* Carlyle treated the issue
of English injustice towards Ireland in relation to its immediate implications for
the 'condition of England' question. Even when he focused more sharply on the
particulars of the Irish situation, he still viewed it in a broader context. Ireland
epitomised an advanced, indeed, an almost terminal, state of material and moral
degradation: '*Universal* IMPOSTURE (its own, and ours, and all the world's) ...
is fallen there into palpable downbreak, into flat bankruptcy ... and lies now
the most detestably sordid mass of foetid ruin eyes ever saw, or thoughts ever
dreamed of '.[72]

In Dublin at the start of his tour Carlyle avoided taking up the Viceroy's (Lord
Clarendon) offer of letters of introduction and carefully evaded his invitation to
dine at Dublin Castle. These precautions were wise since Clarendon's welcoming
gestures were motivated by a sense of political self-interest not by admiration
for Carlyle. The proffered letters of introduction to 'safe' people were meant to
offset the impact of the far more critical constituency to which Duffy was likely
to expose him, and to head off the prospect of 'that double-barrelled coxcomb
perambulating the provinces collecting abuses'.[73] That the Viceroy felt such
precautions were necessary was a testament to his perception of the importance
of Carlyle's links with the political establishment in London and of the likely
impact of any publications that arose from his experiences in Ireland.

One positive result of Carlyle's visit was that he developed a more nuanced
perspective on the Irish people than was apparent in his earlier published comments. In a characteristically frank farewell note to Lord Clarendon, Carlyle
commented favourably on the rising generation of socially responsible members
of the professional and upper class upon whom he thought the fate of the country
rested. He had 'found *more* good men of all descriptions, busy in their plans, and
more germs of hope and benefit ... in this waste scene of human distractions and
delusions than I had dared to anticipate'.[74] At the same time, however, he noted
that the warm welcome given to him as a stranger and a guest was set against a
dark background of bitter inter-communal distrust:

I have seen an immensity of *kinds* of people; find them distinguished by two qualities: generous warmth of hospitality, welcoming the stranger of whatever colour with open arms; and secondly by mutual animosity, each class bitterly accusing every other, and in fact blaming and accusing all things, except its own self the one accusable thing.[75]

While personal experience modified some of Carlyle's earlier prejudices on the private and personal qualities of individual Irish people, it served primarily to confirm the spectral nightmare conjured up by a country in which failures of governmental and non-governmental elites made the gospel of work a dead letter.

Although Carlyle was not indifferent to the charms of pristine nature, he tended to see pleasing landscapes as joint ventures between God and men. In many parts of Ireland, the human contribution to this partnership was notable by its absence: 'Ireland is one of the barest, raggedest countries now known; far too ragged a country, with patches of beautiful park and fine cultivation, like shreds of bright scarlet on a beggar's clouted coat – a country that stands decidedly in need of shelter, shade, and ornamental fringing'.[76] This image was used in an essay (published in Duffy's *The Nation*) prompted by a campaign to encourage supporters of Duffy's cause to plant 'trees of liberty' in imitation of earlier French and American practice. Carlyle sought to deflect the revolutionary symbolism of the campaign into an appeal for concerted programmes of reforestation as a first step in restoring the battered landscape of the country. These programmes would give real meaning to the idea of 'trees of liberty' being bandied about in nationalist circles by marking the beginning of the end of elite irresponsibility and enforced popular idleness that blighted Irish life.

At present there were too few signs of progress on this or any other work of environmental or human reclamation. Underemployment and deprivation was well nigh universal and in some parts of the country the condition of the people was utterly hopeless. For example, Carlyle's informants told him that in Westport, Co. Mayo close to 60 per cent of the population was dependent upon poor relief, only a small fraction of which could be raised through the local poor rate.[77] As in his earlier accounts of the 'condition of England question', Carlyle associated the breakdown of social order and the dehumanisation of social relationships with the currency of *laissez-faire*. Thus the lesson that he drew from these 'insolvent' poor law unions of the west of Ireland and from the general prevalence of beggary, hunger and idleness was that '"indolent *Laissez-faire* plus a *Poor Rate*" is not, by any manner of means, the Solution of Human Society'.[78] The gloom produced by this negation of the idea of government was only occasionally dispelled by beacons of hope that shone bravely but fitfully on scenes of economic and spiritual desolation. Some national school masters ('practical missionaries of good order and wise husbandry ... *anti*chaos missionaries'),[79] and a few landlords, agents and local government officials provided a model of the conduct that would have to become widespread if both the upper and lower classes were to dispel 'cants, cowardices, Godforgettings and Devil-worshippings' from Ireland.[80]

With what seemed at best extreme and perverse insensitivity and at worst heartless cruelty, Carlyle regaled his Irish hosts and his English correspondents with the idea that a continued failure of the potato crop would prove a blessing to Ireland by destroying any remaining illusions about the economic and moral viability of an economy that tried to support both an extensive rural population and an expensive, irresponsible and largely absentee elite on such a precarious and sub-subsistence footing.[81] Shortly after Carlyle left Ireland, Duffy wrote to tell him that the potato crop was again showing unmistakable and widespread signs of blight, and to remark (with understandable bitterness) that his wishes had thus been granted. Duffy took this opportunity to make an appeal to Carlyle and to throw out a challenge to him:

> Now that the crisis has come I trust you will insist upon such a permanent settlement of the land question as will save us from eternal new famines ... If you threw your weight into the scale, justice will be done the unfortunate people we saw deformed into locusts in the South and West.[82]

Carlyle's response to this appeal was almost certainly less helpful than Duffy must have hoped, largely, one suspects, because he was more interested in questions about the provision of opportunities for work than in those concerning owner-ship and tenure. This perspective gave priority to the role of elites rather than to ideas of peasant proprietorship; it almost certainly reflected an assumption that this was not a viable model in a very populous country. Carlyle's experience of Scottish conditions may well have prompted this conclusion and his views on the degraded condition of the Irish tenantry would have confirmed it. For whatever reason, Carlyle restricted himself to giving private support in principle to the reform of Irish land law, urging Duffy to research the subject carefully by refer-ring to experience elsewhere in the United Kingdom.[83] He did not write on the issue for publication, preferring to reiterate his view that government and elites must mobilise resources to convert the wastelands of Ireland into productive fields capable of absorbing some of the desperately underemployed workforce. If this objective was to be achieved, those in positions of political and social power would need to adopt the ethos previously applied to the far less worthy objective of turning Irish countrymen into model soldiers.[84] Carlyle's military references were appropriate since his writings on Irish affairs placed increasing emphasis on the need to organise, control and 'regiment' the pauper population of the country. However, the connotations of coercion that attach to military discipline, and which Carlyle sometimes presented as preferable to continued idleness, should not necessarily be read into what are, in part at least, typically exaggerative Carlylean figures of speech. When addressing the need for the English and Irish lower classes to be set to work, Carlyle stressed the responsibilities of governmental and non-governmental elites, and assumed that enlistment in 'regiments of labour' would be voluntary. Later, in discussing Frederick the Great's domestic policy, Carlyle noted the distinction he drew between the 'willing' and 'unwilling' poor and applauded Frederick's just and considerate treatment of the latter.[85] Significantly, Duffy shared these views. When commenting on the itinerary for Carlyle's Irish visit, he stressed the importance of meeting 'practical men', engineers and railway contractors who had contrived 'to marshal the people into battalions of labour'. He believed that the population of Ireland needed to be organised and disciplined to become an effective workforce by receiving an adequate education; elite leadership was essential to the future wellbeing of Ireland. Similar views were expressed by Lord George Hill, an improving, socially conscious landlord whom Carlyle admired.[86]

Since Carlyle thought that the expansion of the Empire and the commitment of resources to emigration would supplement the efforts of responsible elites and 'working governors', Irish salvation was closely tied up with England's imperial mission. At the same time, however, Carlyle's understanding of the conditions prevailing in Ireland, and the chain of events that had given rise to it, provided an important reference point for his views on the prospects of 'white' settler colonies such as Australia, Canada, and New Zealand, and for his treatment of those parts of the Empire that were not suitable for mass immigration from Britain and Ireland. Carlyle's thoughts on the last of these issues were framed by reference to Britain's West Indian colonies, and presented to the public in an essay, the 'Occasional Discourse on the Negro Question', that appeared in *Fraser's Magazine* in December 1849. This essay was revised and reissued as a pamphlet in 1853 with a quite deliberately provocative change to the title: it had now become the notorious *Occasional Discourse on the Nigger Question*.

The 'Occasional Discourse' was derived from a 'mass' of material that Carlyle drafted in the summer of 1849, some of which was developed for publication as 'Latter-Day Pamphlets' in 1850. When explaining why he wrote these pamphlets, Carlyle referred to his desire to dissent publicly from 'philanthropic, emancipatory, constitutional, and other anarchic revolutionary jargon'.[87] These irritants, long wearing at the outer limits of his patience, now seemed to have become utterly intolerable. The *bête noire* of constitutionalism and philanthropy were dealt with in the 'Latter-Day Pamphlets'. In the 'Occasional Discourse' Carlyle set his sights on the 'emancipatory' head of the many-headed hydra of contemporary insincerity and jargon-mongering. This assault, framed by reference to current discussions of British policy towards her West Indian colonies, also took in emancipationist expectations focused on the United States. According to Froude, Carlyle was alarmed by claims that emancipation in the West Indies provided an exemplar for the southern states of the Union.[88] It should be noted, however, that while pro-abolitionist activity may have prompted Carlyle's immediate interest in the issue, the views that he expressed at this time had been aired in private discussions for a number of years.[89] Of at least equal importance was a parallel between the West Indies and Ireland (discussed in more detail below) that was brought to Carlyle's attention by his old friend Thomas Erskine in mid 1848. Erskine claimed that the racial characteristics of the Irish (as deduced by the phrenological analysis of George Combe) made it very likely that Irish self-government would prove to be as disastrous as it had been in 'Hayti', the former slave colony that was a byword for anarchy and economic dissolution in some contemporary literature. Almost a year later, in May 1849, Erskine again pointed a parallel between Ireland and the West Indies. Having read Carlyle's views of Ireland in the *Spectator* and *Examiner*, Erskine encouraged him to extend his analysis to embrace the West Indies.[90]

The concerns lying behind Erskine's remarks need to be considered in the context of a long-running debate (most recently in the House of Commons in February 1848) on the prospects of the British West Indies following the end of slavery in 1833, and the termination in 1838 of the 'apprenticeship' system that was meant to ease planters's adjustment to the new environment.[91] Some of these discussions focused on transactions between the planter-dominated Assembly of Jamaica and the British parliament, and thus raised constitutional and legal issues that Carlyle thought were merely indicative of the paralysis afflicting constitutional jargon-mongering.[92] Others, however, were related more positively to his interests. Foremost among these were questions concerning the availability of labour and the extent to which the end of slavery had deprived planters of the means to cultivate their estates. The fate of these colonies was important in itself, but consideration of this issue was also significant because it fuelled arguments about emancipation in the southern states of the American union.[93]

In contemporary debate on these issues, a major difference of opinion existed between those (usually pro-emancipationists) who remarked favourably on the economic and moral developments that followed the ending of slavery, and a rival lobby (dominated by planters and their supporters) that took a gloomy view of the recent history and future prospects of Britain's West Indian colonies. Members of the anti-emancipation lobby argued that the premature termination of the 'apprenticeship' system deprived the 'free' sugar economies of reasonably priced labour, thereby giving a distinct advantage to the slave economies of Brazil and Cuba and precipitating a sharp decline in the prosperity of Jamaica and other British colonies in the Caribbean. The only hope lay in stimulating the supply of cheap labour by removing restrictions (dating from the termination of the British slave trade) on the importation of labour from Africa.[94] Writers who took a strongly positive view of the results of emancipation rejected these claims. They commended ex-slaves for their industry on their own small holdings and for their willingness to work on plantations at rates that imposed a lower financial burden on planters than the slave system had done. These encouraging economic developments were seen as one aspect of a range of educational, moral and religious advances that had followed the ending of slavery in the British West Indies. While it was acknowledged that some planters had begun to run into financial difficulties in the late 1840s, these were attributed to droughts, absenteeism, shortages of capital, and the deficient enterprise of the planters themselves, rather than the unwillingness of former slaves to work for wages. From this perspective, schemes to enhance the supply of cheap labour through emigration from Africa or India just showed that some planters had not reconciled themselves to the abolition of slavery.[95]

In the 'Occasional Discourse' Carlyle endorsed uncritically many of the claims made by those who presented the West Indian colonies as being well on the way to economic and social disintegration. Throughout this essay he attributed the economic problems facing the planter economies of the West Indies to the racially derived characteristics of former slaves. Blacks were held to be inherently inferior to whites in intellect and moral character – 'what man can doubt' that whites were born wiser than blacks? – and thus in need of perpetual guidance and control by white mentors.[96] At times Carlyle recognised that gross abuses of power were common among slaveholders but this insight did not give rise to any criticism of slavery as such.[97] He saw slavery as a particular application of a general principle – that of hierarchy – that was necessary because of the supposed racially determined inferiority of blacks. The abuses of the power of slave owners were seen as incidental, and while Carlyle wished to see them eliminated, he insisted that the lot of slaves in America and the West Indies compared favourably with that of what he termed the 'white slaves' of Britain and Ireland.

While Carlyle thought that the claim that racial characteristics predisposed blacks to indolence was self-evident, his essay on the West Indies focused on the disastrous impact on this disposition of an environment that made only minimal demands on human industry and ingenuity. Many of the assumptions on which Carlyle relied in discussing these matters corresponded with those found on the anti-emancipation side of contemporary debate. It was claimed that since the termination of the 'apprentice' system in 1838, former slaves declined to undertake wage labour on terms that were compatible with the economic viability of sugar plantations, preferring to lead a life of low yet easy subsistence on small holdings for which it is assumed that little or nothing was paid by way of purchase or rent. For Carlyle, such an existence was an affront to the ethos of labour, one that marked an alarmingly low point of moral depravity. In the 'Occasional Discourse' the image of an idle ex-slave subsisting on 'pumpkins' (watermelons), and the few basic commodities that could be traded for them, exemplified the challenges that Carlyle thought were posed to this ethos by tropical climates and fertile soil. His views on the unnatural and decadent potential of the West Indies were symbolised by references to the 'saccharine' sweet juice of the 'pumpkin', a product that played a role paralleling that of the humble potato in Carlyle's analysis of Ireland's problems. The major difference was that while reliance on the potato was a matter of necessity for the Irish, the watermelon was the West Indian's prelapsian choice. In Carlyle's view, former slaves had exchanged outward bondage for the infinitely more damaging 'soul-tyranny' of idleness and placed themselves beyond the pale of human value. Carlyle's prejudices were not incidental. They rested on a belief in the 'natural' inferiority of blacks; idleness was a product of racially determined characteristics, and these served as key variables explaining the behaviour of ex-slaves and the parlous condition of Britain's West Indian colonies.[98]

Carlyle's characterisation of blacks traded on stereotypes that became increasingly common in English discussions of race over the next decade.[99] In addition to giving the prestige of his name to these ideas, Carlyle endowed them with a distinctive and malign moral leverage by setting them in the context of his 'gospel of labour'. On this account, blacks were deemed incapable of subscribing voluntarily to the gospel of labour, and thus had only a weak affinity with the 'God-like' in humanity. While the doctrine of labour might be construed as lending dignity to a potentially universal form of human agency, these possibilities were not open to those stigmatised by Carlyle's racial views. One practical conclusion of this line of reasoning was that former slaves would only contribute to humanity's earth-forging mission when they were subjected either to the coercive agencies of material necessity, or to forceful direction by their putative superiors. Given the fertility of the West Indies, however, exclusive reliance could not be placed on the invigorating influence of material deprivation; so, while stopping short of proposing the reintroduction of slavery, Carlyle talked vaguely but savagely about the need for West Indian blacks to be subject to coercive discipline. He also insisted that ex-slaves must be prevented from having free access to smallholdings that enabled them to secure an easy subsistence without undertaking paid labour. The rationale for this prohibition – the need to restore the spur of material necessity – smacked of the reliance on mechanical stimuli that Carlyle usually identified with political economy and demonstrated his determination to affirm blacks' inferior moral status. It showed that he thought that unlike the working classes of Britain and Ireland, who could generally be relied upon to avail themselves of opportunities to work, the black labouring classes of the West Indies would only commit to the gospel of labour if compelled to do so.

This account of the implications of the moral status that Carlyle ascribed to blacks played an important role in his reaction to proposals for importing 'free' black labour to the West Indies. While he assumed that local labour was scarce and ruinously priced, he was, nevertheless, highly critical of those who regarded black emigration as an appropriate solution to the supposed crisis in West Indian labour markets. This proposal invoked a market-based solution to problems that were actually caused by an absence of effectively directed human authority, namely a failure of human agency on the part of a putative governing class.[100] Promoters of black emigration (an unholy coalition of philanthropists and political economists) assumed that work should be prompted and regulated mechanically through the laws of supply and demand, and thus ignored the implications of (what Carlyle took to be) incontrovertible truths about the moral character of blacks. In time, Carlyle predicted, the lure of easy subsistence would encourage the growth of an unsustainable labour force reduced to the desperate condition of the virtually landless peasantry of Ireland. Emigration from Africa would thus turn Jamaica into 'Black Ireland' because the population would outstrip the natural means of subsistence without augmenting them with the fruits of concerted human productivity.

A few months before the 'Occasional Discourse' was written, Carlyle had seen examples of this condition in famine-plagued Ireland. Even where starvation was kept at bay, country towns and their rural hinterlands were reduced to the most basic subsistence level, supporting a meagre trade in a few locally produced foodstuffs but unable to sustain any significant 'value added' activities, such as distilling, bacon curing, butter making or milling.[101] So long as the majority of the population were permitted to eschew the gospel of labour and indulge their inherited taste for easy living, this fate awaited the free colonies of the West Indies and would be hastened by stimulating artificially the supply of labour.

The fact that Britain's West Indian colonies were set to reproduce the most disastrous features of the material and moral history of Ireland meant that, in Carlyle's eyes, they represented the antithesis of England's mission: liberty had resulted in idleness rather than a voluntary commitment to the gospel of labour; self-indulgent anarchy had flourished at the cost of chaos-taming striving; and emigration threatened to prepare the ground for moral and economic regression rather than individual and social progression. Carlyle's assessment of the implications of racial characteristics was the key to these paradoxes. He regarded emigration as a distinctly human response to the empirical challenge of the Malthusian dilemma because immigrants who actively subscribed to the gospel of labour boosted the earth's capacity to sustain its population. Carlyle assumed that the English would answer his call because the earlier stages of their mission had demonstrated and confirmed that commitment to this gospel had become second nature to them. The Irish peasantry were in an equivocal position; but, although Carlyle had many harsh things to say about them, he stressed that much of the blame for this unhappy state of affairs should be laid at the door of the Irish upper classes and those in England who supported them. The Irish were the victims of a long train of unjust and unwise government and this pattern could be reversed. Thus when he observed the faces of lower-class Irishmen on a steamer during his visit in 1849, Carlyle discerned 'faculty *misbred*, and gone to waste' rather than congenital incapacity; the whole tenor of his reports on this visit made it clear that he believed that reformation was possible.[102]

In any case, the differences separating the English and the Irish were insignificant in comparison with those that divided whites from blacks. Carlyle had no faith in the potential of black Jamaicans to adopt an appropriate work ethos and, as J. S. Mill noted, he virtually absolved whites of any blame for the parlous condition of the island's economy.[103] In England and Ireland the key problem was a lack of opportunities for labour; colonisation provided a way of escaping from this situation by making England's chaos-taming role a global one. By presenting this mission as a continuation of a long process of development that had confirmed his compatriots' commitment to the gospel of labour, and by stressing its non-materialist basis, Carlyle promoted the idea that the 'English' character was, or at least could be made, proof against the morally and economically deceptive lure of easy subsistence. Edward Gibbon Wakefield's proposals to set the cost of land in settler colonies at a level sufficient to ensure that newly-arrived members of the labouring classes would have to take paid employment for a few years, was one way of guarding against these dangers.[104] But while Carlyle approved of Wakefield's 'systematic' approach to emigration, his faith in the capacity of the English working classes to be inspired by the idea of their mission made the control of land prices (dismissed by a contemporary critic as an 'ingenious attempt at establishing a sort of modified white slavery') unnecessary.[105] The situation was quite otherwise for blacks. Carlyle maintained that the West Indian planters were chronically short of labour because the easiness of subsistence, combined with the blacks' supposed moral flaws, meant that neither the ex-slaves, nor imported 'free' labourers from Africa and Mauritius, could be expected to voluntarily commit themselves to the gospel of labour.

Although he did not offer detailed policy prescriptions to address problems that he claimed to have identified in the West Indies, Carlyle indicated a range of possible approaches to them. His alarmist pessimism at recent developments prompted him to oppose the abolitionist lobby in the United States and Britain, a stance that was supported by wildly inaccurate views of master-slave relationships in the southern states. Throughout the 1850s and well into the 1860s he believed that Southern slaveholders were capable of sustaining benign patriarchal communities in which the true interests of slaves would be reconciled with the requirements of the gospel of labour.

Other conditions required different arrangements. For example, it is likely that Carlyle's essay on Dr Francia, the Dictator of Paraguay, was written with Haiti in mind. In contemporary anti-emancipation literature the free republic of Haiti was portrayed as a dystopia of personal and political emancipation, a bankrupt, corrupt and chaotic state that was disfigured by internal terrorism. Like Cuba, it was exposed to threats to its precarious independence from white free booters eager to take advantage of the situation.[106] Francia's unashamedly authoritarian, but (as Carlyle saw it) righteous regime provided a sharp contrast to the chaotic republic of former slaves. In light of Carlyle's views on the evils facing the British West Indies, it is significant that he counted Francia's draconian measures to ensure that the population laboured effectively – including a gallows to signal the fate that awaits those guilty of poor workmanship – as among his most significant achievements.[107]

Carlyle's later support for Governor Eyre, when he faced legal action in England in 1865 over his responsibility for savage reprisals against rioters and their alleged supporters in Jamaica, was consistent with his approving attitude towards Francia's regime. He claimed that Eyre should be commended for 'saving' the colony; rather than being condemned, he should be empowered to exercise untrammelled authority over it for the next twenty years.[108] In 1853, however, the British colonies in the West Indies seemed more likely to fall victim to economic collapse than to insurrection, a threat that resulted from the absence of effective paternalism. In these circumstances Carlyle scouted the idea that a system of limited but mandatory labour service for those blacks who would not work (like the corveé recently introduced in the Dutch colony of Java) might be the most appropriate solution to the internal problems facing Britain's West Indian colonies.[109] The external challenges posed by other sugar producing economies that still had access to a steady flow of slave labour should be met by withdrawing the Royal Navy from its largely ineffectual blockade of the 'slave coast' of West Africa. The Navy should concentrate its attention, and if necessary its firepower, on the Brazilian and Cuban ports through which slaves were imported.[110]

When he turned his attention to the southern States of the Union in the revised version of the 'Occasional Discourse', Carlyle warned of the dangers and injustice of failing to prevent abuse of slaves by their owners, proposed a system of self-manumission at a fixed, moderate price for American slaves who had acquired property through their own efforts, and insisted that those who remained in a condition of slavery should not be deprived of the right to contract marriages and establish families.[111] These recommendations were designed to strengthen and purify paternalism, not inaugurate general emancipation. This step was precluded by Carlyle's assumptions about the implications of the moral capabilities of blacks for upholding the gospel of labour. Given these assumptions, the positive focus on universal human agency that distinguished Carlyle's gospel of labour gave way to one that emphasised the rights and responsibilities of those who contributed to the ordering of the universe by encouraging, inspiring, and if necessary, coercing others to pay practical homage through labour. Here and elsewhere, Carlyle's casually assumed and unsubstantiated racial views, and his tendency to minimise the rank injustices of slaveholding societies, undercut the humanistic bearing of his critique of political economy: blacks were deemed to be generally incapable of self-fulfilment through conscientious commitment to work and were thus permanently excluded from the condition of moral equality enjoyed by those who subscribed to the gospel of labour.[112]

The close relationship between Carlyle's gospel of labour and his reaction to emancipation in the West Indies was noted by J. S. Mill in a critique of the 'Occasional Discourse' in *Fraser's Magazine*. Mill did not think that his contemporaries' voluntary and involuntary dedication to toil were causes for celebration, he cast doubts on Carlyle's promotion of an ethos of striving, rejected the idea that commitment to labour *per se* should provide the basis for making fundamental moral judgments on the value of individual lives, and called for the development of a 'gospel of leisure' to complement the gospel of labour.[113] Mill's critique of the gospel of labour was part of a more elaborate rebuttal of Carlyle's attempt to justify coercion of former slaves on the grounds that it was necessary to ensure that they contributed to the economic development of Britain's West Indian colonies and hence to England's imperial mission. Mill rejected Carlyle's claims about the natural and inevitable inferiority of blacks, and argued, in terms that he later applied to the status of women, that demonstrations of present incapacity did not warrant assumptions of permanent, 'natural' inferiority, or treatment that perpetuated this state of affairs.[114] The ongoing curtailment of liberty would only be justified on the grounds that it created conditions in which self-development might take place. This requirement was totally at odds with the harsh and authoritarian prescriptions of the 'Occasional Discourse' and with the unwarranted assumptions of permanent and chronic inferiority that underwrote them.

Mill's public attack signaled the end of their once-close relationship, and it has also been seen as representative of a more generally held view that Carlyle had irrevocably taken himself beyond the pale of enlightened and progressive opinion in Britain and in the United States. In fact, the impact of Carlyle's unashamedly racist views was far more ambiguous and complex than this interpretation suggests. The assumption that his statements on the congenital inferiority of blacks, his opposition to emancipation and his hostility to philanthropy made him a pariah, rests on a misreading of racial discourse in mid Victorian Britain.[115] While pro-emancipation sentiment was strong in the late 1820s and 1830s it was not universal. From its inception *Fraser's Magazine* had set its face against this trend and here, as in other circles, invidious comparisons were made between the efforts directed at the welfare of black labourers in the West Indies and the United States and the neglect of the claims of the English working classes.[116] By the late 1840s philanthropists were common targets of satire; there was a widespread waning of pro-emancipation sentiment and a distinct cooling of sympathy for slaves and former slaves. Claims about the natural and permanent inferiority of blacks – advanced in some cases by reference to decline of the British West Indies – were becoming commonplaces, sometimes endorsed by influential figures in anthropology and science.[117] These accounts were contested, but opposition often reflected disagreement over the causes of inferiority, rather than the fact of it. In this context, it was common for slavery to be condemned, but for moves for immediate emancipation to be resisted, especially where former slaves were to be granted political rights.[118] In other cases, support for emancipation did not necessarily indicate an absence of deep-seated racial prejudice. Thus while Ralph Waldo Emerson was staunchly opposed to slavery in the 1830s and early 1840s he continued to see blacks as inherently inferior to whites.[119] All this suggests that, rather than being woefully out of step with prevailing sentiments, Carlyle subscribed to racial views that had a foothold even in progressive opinion and were to become increasingly commonplace over the next two decades.

While the response of Carlyle's literary friends and allies to these ideas was mixed, the stance taken by Mill was by no means representative. People who knew Carlyle well, and even careful readers of his works who did not, can have harboured few illusions concerning the liberal cast of his progressivism. In the past he had made no secret of his views on emancipation and related issues, and his friends had not been slow to register their critical reaction to them. In 1834 John Sterling had been present at a meeting in John Stuart Mill's rooms in the East India House when Carlyle had aired his opinion on the very mixed blessings of emancipation. Two years later in Cheyne Row, Henry Crabb Robinson endured a long, intemperate and aggressively one-sided peroration on blacks' congenital inferiority to whites; this 'fact' was used to justify the retention of slavery in the southern United States.[120] In 1841 Carlyle disappointed an audience of hitherto admiring Americans by asserting that the industrial poor in England were infinitely worse off than American slaves. He laid particular stress on the stable and paternalistic environment of Southern plantations, arguing that the relationship between labourers and their masters was far more important for the moral and spiritual wellbeing of humankind than the presence or absence of abstract personal freedom.[121] Two years later the comparison between white 'freeman' and black slaves resurfaced in *Past and Present*, and in this and other works, Carlyle employed the derogatory term 'quanshee' with obvious relish.[122] Thus while the 'Occasional Discourse' was far more harsh and direct than anything that Carlyle had published previously on slavery and related issues, there is no doubt that the substance of his views on race were known quite widely before this essay appeared.

Given later claims about the damage caused by the 'Occasional Discourse', it should be noted that sharp disagreement with the views advanced there did not necessarily diminish contemporaries' respect for Carlyle's literary achievements. A diverse range of friends – W. E. Forster, Harriet Martineau, the Duke of Argyle and Edward Fitzgerald, for example – dissented strongly from his views on slavery but did not cease to admire him. An American reader, Newton Booth, Governor of California, was originally 'disgusted' by Carlyle's racial views but, on working his way back through Carlyle's corpus to *The French Revolution*, he became a firm convert.[123] Other admirers were careful to make exceptions of Carlyle's views on slavery when praising his works and celebrating his general impact on his readers.[124]

Carlyle's relationship with the Duke of Argyle, the premier aristocrat of Scotland, and Sir Arthur Helps, a senior public servant, illustrate this point in very different ways. When the 'Occasional Discourse' was reissued as a pamphlet in 1853, Argyle, a staunch opponent of slavery, bought up multiple copies, inscribed them 'by Mrs Beecher Stowe', the author *Uncle Tom's Cabin*, and sent them to his friends as a joke.[125] Helps developed a carefully thought out anti-slavery position which relied neither on an unconditional endorsement of personal liberty, nor on incidental data about the treatment of slaves by their masters. Rather, he maintained that when human beings wielded absolute power over others, acts of inhuman cruelty were inevitable; for this reason, slavery was necessarily and unavoidably evil.[126] But while the divergence between Carlyle's views on this issue and those of Helps could hardly be more marked, they remained firm friends. More surprising still, at a time when it seemed that ill health would prevent him from completing the project, Helps considered asking Carlyle to undertake the second volume of *The Conquerors of the New World and Their Bondsmen*, a critical history of the introduction of slavery into the Spanish colonies of South America.[127] These reactions indicate that 'Occasional Discourse' was not a litmus test for the general soundness of Carlyle's intellectual and moral views among his contemporaries.

Mill's fear that Carlyle's essay would lend the credibility of his intellectual and moral influence to pro-slavery interests in the United States proved, however, well founded. Anti-abolitionist reviewers and commentators capitalised on Carlyle's criticisms of emancipation and his favourable view of master-slave relationships in the South in the early 1850s. It seems likely that this interest encouraged the publisher, Thomas Boswell, to think that there would be a market for a reissue of the 'Occasional Discourse' in the wake of the sensation created by the publication of *Uncle Tom's Cabin* in England in 1853.[128] The dilemma that Carlyle's views on slavery presented to American admirers became more pressing as the United States moved towards civil war. Moncure Conway, a staunch advocate of general abolition, complained that he had 'been stirred to the depths, and have had my blood boil at having your name and authority, which I was known to venerate, cast into my face [in the South]'. He claimed that Carlyle's statements in support of Southern slavery were utopian, warning him that his hopes that it could be purged of its abuses were entirely without foundation. The slaveholders were, in fact, 'a wretched and besotted set of despots, stopping at no excess of cruelty, and licentiousness', 'counterfeit' masters whom long experience had shown to be totally unfit to exercise absolute power over others.[129] This remonstrance did not have an immediate discernable effect on Carlyle's published statements, but

Conway claimed he came to accept the force of at least some of his arguments, on one occasion alarming passersby in Hyde Park by the violence of his denunciation of an example of slaveholder infamy that Conway revealed to him. A letter of admonishment from Emerson, and other pleas from American correspondents reinforced these lessons. In September 1863 Carlyle received a long, impassioned, well-reasoned letter from Charlotte Taylor in Washington DC emphasising the iniquities perpetrated by slaveholders in the South and arguing (along the same lines as Helps had done) of the unavoidable tendency for unrestrained power to be abused. Taylor's letter made very skilful use of Carlylean themes – earnestness, truth and sincerity – and chastised him for making light in a dialogue in *Macmillan's Magazine*, 'Illias (Americana) in Nuce', of what she described as her country's 'bitter' 'awful' struggle.[130] Another anti-slavery correspondent, this time from Philadelphia, sent Carlyle a photograph of a black man showing horrific scarring caused by an 'old whipping' administered at Baton Rouge, Louisiana, and a note: 'Sir, Pray observe an instance of "hiring for life". God forgive you for your cruel jest and blindness'.[131]

While these appeals may have influenced Carlyle's views of Southern slaveholders, his public attitude towards emancipation and its racist underpinnings remained unchanged. He reprinted 'Illias (Americana) in Nuce' in all subsequent editions of his collected works, and in 'Shooting Niagara' (1867) expressed regret at the abolition of slavery in the United States, arguing that its abuses could have been easily remedied without removing its undoubted advantages as a mode of organising recalcitrant sections of humanity in the service of the gospel of labour. Six years later he applauded Emerson's daughter's harsh views on blacks, dismissing former slaves as 'nothing but a superfluity and nuisance'.[132]

Intransigence in the face of what Carlyle might privately have seen as valid qualifications of positions expressed in his published works, became increasingly marked in later life. Debate, as opposed to a consideration of other writings as a way of presenting his own views, had never been a feature of Carlyle's literary output. From the late 1840s, however, an unwillingness to even consider, far less bend before, the arguments of others became a matter of grim pride. This stance no doubt owed much to the sense of superiority that had always been one of Carlyle's most overt character traits, but it also reflected the hardening of his views on the merits of his contemporaries. Modern criticism was fatuous or worse, and, as Carlyle wrote in a letter to John Ruskin, the only value to be derived from hostile reviews was the assurance that one's judgments were right; they were signs that the 'physic had began gripping – more power to it'.[133] The course of purging treatment that began with the 'Occasional Discourse' was continued during 1850 with a series of what Carlyle called 'Latter-Day Pamphlets'.

6

Latter-Day Pamphleteer

Between February and August 1850 Carlyle published a series of eight 'Latter-Day Pamphlets' that were then collected in a volume bearing this title.[1] In this form, and with the addition of the revised version of the 'Occasional Discourse', the pamphlets went through many reprints in the various collected and popular editions of his works that were issued in the last two decades of Carlyle's life. They enjoyed a good sale after his death.[2] Carlyle and John Ruskin (who greatly admired the pamphlets) took comfort from the thought that they stood in a minority of two against the concerted and disapproving legions of the world at large. This conceit, combined with Froude's later statements on the overwhelmingly hostile response to the 'Latter-Day Pamphlets', has coloured subsequent accounts of their reception and of their impact on Carlyle's reputation.[3] Although *Punch* joked that the pamphlets showed that Carlyle had finally gone mad, more serious contemporary reviews were mixed. For example, while Carlyle's wholesale condemnation of democratic government was anathema to Helen MacFarlane, the author of a review in a socialist periodical, it was welcomed by the Catholic *Dublin Review*. The latter, however, was deeply hurt by Carlyle's scathing critique of both the modern Papacy and the founder of the Society of Jesus. A writer in the non-conformist *Eclectic Review* applauded Carlyle's exposure of what he took to be the Jesuitical spirit of modern Anglicanism, but rejected his conception of Christianity as a 'formula of vengeance'. Carlyle's condemnation of modern penal theory and practice also received some applause and some censure.[4] Whatever their response to particular positions advanced in the 'Latter-Day Pamphlets', however, Carlyle's contemporaries (and later critics) were struck by the violent language, harsh prescriptions and purulent imagery that burst forth from many passages. James Russell Lowe no doubt had these pamphlets in mind when he noted that Carlyle's tone acquired an increasingly marked hectoring edge as time went on, and that his proposed solutions sometimes carried his taste for exaggeration to cruel extremes.[5]

While the pamphlets canvassed many themes that had already played a prominent role in the 'condition of England' question, their central argument went beyond anything that had been advanced in Carlyle's earlier works.[6] This point emerges quite clearly in a response that Carlyle made to a question posed by his friend Thomas Spedding in May 1850, when the pamphlets were still appearing.

Spedding asked why in Carlyle's account 'God's world' seemed always to be going to the Devil, and also why, if government by the best was such an unreservedly good thing, it had been so rare in human history. Carlyle responded to the first of these queries by saying that while the Devil's ambitions had been only just kept at bay through the painful endeavours of a critical mass of 'ardent souls' – the world was thus always on the verge of *going to* the Devil – the most recent passage in this timeless Manichean struggle was distinguished by dangerous imbalance between the contending parties. One sign of this alarming development was that the reign of truth and virtue, long an unfulfilled but at least fitfully pursued ideal, was being abandoned in favour of its antithesis. It was, Carlyle said, 'as if an age should say to itself, "Sin against God's Laws was always prevalent: Let us give up the notion of anything else but sinning against them".'[7] Folly and falsehood had always been a feature of human life; now, however, it was being touted as wisdom and actively pursued: 'never before did the creature called man believe generally in his heart that lies were the rule in this Earth; that in deliberate long-established lying could there be help or salvation for him, could there be at length other than hindrance and destruction for him'.[8] Carlyle felt so strongly about his contemporaries' mendacity that he was provoked into unlikely sympathy for the Mormons. He privately recorded the view that 'respectable English opinion' compared unfavourably with the earnest, non-hypocritical stance of the Mormons, a sect that, as J. S. Mill's reference to them in *On Liberty* indicates, were often the target of moral panics in the British press.[9]

The 'Latter-Day Pamphlets' confronted this novel and (Carlyle thought) deeply disturbing state of affairs by exposing the underlying spirit of wilful delusion in electoral politics and governmental administration, and in various characteristic cultural, literary and social forms. The way in which these exposés were presented, however, and hence the distinctive and objectionable character of the pamphlets, can only be understood by examining the circumstances in which the project was conceived and Carlyle's intentions in carrying it out.

During the course of 1848 and 1849 Carlyle's state of mind became increasingly, and quite self-consciously, desperate and bitter. Depression of the spirits resulting from personal blows such as the unexpected death of Charles Buller and the inexorable signs of his mother's slow physical decline, was exacerbated by a sense of deep, crushing disenchantment with political and social developments in Europe, Britain and Ireland.[10] One aspect of this disenchantment can be traced in Carlyle's changing view of the revolution in late February 1848 that resulted in Louis-Philippe's abdication and flight from France.

Carlyle responded almost immediately to these events in an article published in the *Examiner*. He described the revolution as 'sternly beautiful, symbolic of immortality and eternity'; it provided a fitting *coup de grâce* to a regime that was a 'huge swindle', the source of the most barefaced and audacious shams imposed upon a mature political community.[11] Unable to grasp what was good in France (and on this occasion Carlyle was uncharacteristically restrained in his comments on the French national character), the Orleanist monarchy concentrated all that was bad to produce a moral and political monstrosity, a 'cunningly devised system of inequity in all its basest shapes'. Carlyle concluded his essay on a note of hope and recruited the revolutionary leader Alphonse Lamartine to help him sound it: "'All fictions are *now* ended", says M. Lamartine at the Hotel de Ville. May the gods grant it. Something other and better, for the French and for us, might then try, were it but afar off, to begin!'[12]

In less than two years these hopes were dashed. Departing royal shams had been replaced by equally dehabilitating democratic ones, with the flight of Louis-Philippe ushering in a period of delirious mob 'rule' across continental Europe. Lamartine, the erstwhile valedictorian of fictions, had become a characteristic unreality, 'the eloquent latest impersonation of Chaos-come-again; able to talk for itself, and declare persuasively that *it* is Cosmos'.[13] Recent developments in Great Britain indicated that the outlook there was equally grim. Prompt and forceful action by government in mid 1848 eliminated any immediate threat from radical Chartists and aborted an Irish uprising. Carlyle did not think that Britain was on the brink of revolution, but, as in 1839, he warned that 'Chartism' would not be 'put down' unless the underlying causes of working-class disaffection were addressed.[14] In any case, since the movement towards democracy seemed to be inexorable, the anarchic tendencies manifest in continental Europe would sooner or later make themselves felt in Britain. In social and economic terms, these tendencies were already clearly apparent. Famine had strengthened its grip upon Ireland, exacerbating the already desperate condition of that country, and pauperism was dangerously prevalent in England. Indeed, while Carlyle was still reflecting on his Irish journey, the moral and material impact of English pauperism was being brought home to a wide audience by Henry Mayhew and provincial correspondents of the *Morning Chronicle*.[15]

These disturbing confirmations of earlier warnings interacted with authorial frustrations and personal depression to produce a state of acute agitation heavily tinged by despair. By November 1849 Carlyle began to fear that his capacity for sympathising with his fellows was atrophying: 'All the old tremulous affection lies in me, but it is frozen'. This sense was 'so marked and scourged, and driven mad by contradictions' that it had 'laid down in a kind of iron sleep'.[16] Carlyle had sought to give vent to some of his public concerns in articles written for the *Examiner* and the *Spectator*, but editorial caution restricted this experiment and blunted its impact. In a search for alternatives, he toyed with the idea of setting up a newspaper and also considered working up a mass of manuscript fragments that he had written over the course of the previous year into a book. The first of these options was quickly abandoned because Carlyle realised that it would expose him to an intolerable amount of uncongenial trouble and considerable risk.[17] The unshaped form of his material made the second option problematic and added fuel to Carlyle's smouldering frustration. As he later recalled, 'in the revolutionary 1848, matters had got to a kind of boiling pitch with me, and I was becoming very wretched from want of voice. Much MS was accumulating on me, with which I did not know what in the world to do'.[18] Carlyle's state of uncertainty, indeed, his apparent helplessness in the face of what he presents as a process beyond his control, persisted until the very end of 1849. In early November the material hovered over the fire, pending a review of clean-copied and edited texts and the result of a trial run of what became the 'Occasional Discourse'. This piece would serve as a 'small pilot engine' or 'proof paper-kite' for 'other masses of bloated stuff'. At Christmas, Carlyle had still not decided whether the material should come out as a book or in a series of pamphlets. Early in the New Year the latter emerged as the favoured option. Towards the close of January 1850 he announced a series of 'reform pamphlets' addressing the 'frightful aspects of human existence ... which, especially since I was in Ireland, have lain like a millstone on me'.[19]

Even allowing for the exaggerated expressions of authorial despair that invariably accompanied Carlyle's writing projects, his account of the material from which the 'Latter-Day Pamphlets' were constructed makes it clear that he had strong reservations about the possibility of forging a coherent work from it. The decision to issue the material in separate parts reflected these reservations. The pamphlets ranged over a number of topics and the authorial voice operated in a cacophony of modes. Carlyle expressed his abhorrence of the ethos of contemporary society, upbraided his readers for their perversity in refusing to understand his earlier addresses to them, and proffered new ideas about the social and political implications of ideas advanced in these works. Even in these pamphlets, however, Carlyle occasionally broke free of the atmosphere of jeremiad to make hopeful appeals to at least some of his contemporaries and to exemplify the dictum that 'The heart that remains true to itself never yet found the big universe finally faithless to it'.[20]

When addressing his contemporaries' shortcomings, Carlyle was particularly prone to adopt violent language and to indulge his penchant for pronouncing harsh judgements and offering absurd, and, in some cases, cruel remedies. Although his role as a censor was well established and seemed to be welcomed by some of his readers, the 'Latter-Day Pamphlets' at times went too far.[21] This point was made in a number of reviews and in private advice tendered by his brother. John Carlyle thought that the violent tone of the 'Occasional Discourse' blunted its impact. He advised his brother to frame the pamphlets in ways that would ensure that they would stand as a 'permanent and unexaggerated protest against various forms of folly that have deep roots in the country'. This advice, and signs of disapproval coming from the shrinking band of callers to the embattled fastness of Cheyne Row, was completely ignored.[22] The tendency to exaggeration that marked the conversational style of his family, colouring both his writing and his parlour talk, was heightened by the need Carlyle felt to 'unburden' himself of frustrations by giving vent to feelings of outrage at the wilful imperviousness of his contemporaries. His private comments also made it clear that he viewed the manuscript material on which the pamphlets were based as a burden that he had to shake off, or even as street sweepings that needed to be cast out.[23] From this perspective, the composition and publication of the pamphlets was an act of catharsis, an inflamed example of a general tendency. As Carlyle later remarked: 'I must *write*; it is my one way of expressing all the imprisoned existence of me, this horrid wrestle I have had ... ever since my poor biography began'.[24]

He was under few illusions about how his efforts would be received, tending if anything to relish the anticipated hostility of readers and reviewers. This was not just a comforting strategy designed to fortify the author against disappointment, and concealing a fervent wish to be proved wrong. Given his views on the degraded state of the public mind, Carlyle could not expect his strictures to be greeted with general enthusiasm. Indeed, in his prevailing frondeurist state of mind, Carlyle saw a hostile reaction as a sign that he had been successful in his attempts to provoke his contemporaries. When the first pamphlet, 'The Present Time' was in the press, he made these provocative intentions quite clear:

> A paper I published in *Fraser's* about *Niggers* has raised no end of clamour: poor scraggy critics of the 'benevolent' school giving vent to their amazement, and uttering their 'Whaf-thaf? Bow-wow!' in a variety of dialects up and down the country ... That will be neither chaff nor sand to what they will hear in these "Latter-Day" Discourses, poor souls!

By launching such an uncompromising assault upon the ideas and actions of his contemporaries, Carlyle sought to demonstrate the distinctive character of his position and finally to shake off those who persisted in trying to recruit him to their cause:

> All the twaddling *sects* of the country from Swedenborgians to Jesuits, have for the last t[en y]ears been laying claim to 'T. Carlyle' each for itself [a]nd now they will all find that said 'T' belongs to a sect of his own, which is worthy of instant damnation. All which is precisely as it must be, as it is, should be. Nay we have considerable amusement over it here; being I suppose, about as well situated for speaking what is our own mind, on occasion as perhaps any 'free King' of these parts, or these times.[25]

Carlyle thought that as far as most of his readers were concerned, the pamphlets were of unappreciated, but highly necessary medicinal value: 'the people read and buy these pamphlets, and violently abuse them, I believe: this means that the people take their physic, and that it is physic to them; what other response could be expected or desired by me?'[26] He hoped that the uncompromisingly combative tone of the 'Latter-Day Pamphlets' would sound a rallying cry to true sympathisers, to those whom Milton had termed the 'fit audience tho' few'.[27] These works were meant to appeal to ardent souls among Carlyle's contemporaries by presenting them with vivid and unmistakable reactions to a range of examples of wilful commitment to vicious folly. He likened the pamphlets to 'red hot cannon balls' that would blast through a screen of delusion and falsity and 'perhaps show the eternal *daylight* thro' it here and there, to good eyes'.[28] These projectiles were aimed at two sets of targets: one shrouded contemporary ideas and practice about the nature, role and conduct of government; the other cloaked a wide range of cultural and social attitudes.

Although Carlyle's earlier claims about the shortcomings of democracy were advanced in more measured tones and with less offensive imagery than he adopted in the 'Latter-Day Pamphlets', few of his readers can have been under any illusions about his views on this issue. *The French Revolution, Chartism, Past and Present* and *Oliver Cromwell* made it quite clear that effective and just government was possible only when power and influence was in the hands of the truly able. The demands for democratisation that had emerged throughout Europe were warning signals rather than precursors of progressive developments. They marked the redundancy of traditional institutions and highlighted the utter inadequacy of elite responses to this promising but also highly risky state of affairs. Carlyle's reservations about democratic representation were shared by many of his contemporaries; indeed, an enthusiastic commitment to democracy was very much a minority taste among nineteenth-century intellectuals and political and social elites.[29] He made it clear, however, that his attack on democracy was merely part of a far broader critique of the British tradition of parliamentary representation. This was a far more radical and contentious line of argument.

The starting point of this critique was 'stump oratory', a term that Carlyle coined to refer to the distinctive ethos of both electoral politics and parliamentary deliberation. Since classical times, anti-democratic thinkers had made much of the baleful influence that unscrupulous demagogues wielded over ignorant, self-interested and collectively unstable lower-class voters. While sharing these reservations, Carlyle also developed a distinctive and fundamental line of criticism (reminiscent of Plato's views on rhetoric in the *Gorgias*) that focused on the intractably problematic relationship between verbal facility and intellectual and moral truth and action. The assumption underlying this line of argument had been aired earlier in comparisons between the depth and moral rectitude of Oliver Cromwell and the insubstantial elegance of Sir Henry Vane the Younger and other English Republicans.[30] In the 'Latter-Day Pamphlets' Cromwell again served as a benchmark, this time, however, in the context of the claim that the credence given to stump oratory in contemporary political culture both reflected and reinforced the wilful inversion of values that distinguished modern society from its predecessors. Carlyle argued that the increasing weight given to spoken and written 'speech' in modern Britain, and particularly the tendency to regard spoken facility as a test of worth, was correlated closely with the rise of an empire of imposture in politics, letters and morals. These developments, traced to the weakening influence of the Protestant spirit since the mid seventeenth century, exemplified the practical unfolding of what Carlyle took to be a particular demonstration of a universal axiom: 'Given a general insincerity of mind for several generations, you will certainly find the Talker established in the place of honour; and the Doer, hidden in the obscure crowd, with activity lamed, or working sorrowfully forward on paths unworthy of him'.[31]

Carlyle's condemnation of the cult of verbalisation incorporated a number of different lines of criticism, all of which revolved around the core idea that 'talk' was a delusive distraction, sustained by illusions of meaningful activity. This was not just a matter of deflecting attention from issues of substance to those of mere form. Rather, he claimed, there was a direct inverse relationship between the plausibility of oratory and a speaker's grasp of significant moral and intellectual truths, resulting from the impossibility of capturing these truths in speech or conveying them through verbal media. The 'best' oratory was removed furthest from the truth since its effectiveness depended upon maintaining the pretence that it gave a full account of what must, by its very nature, remain partly obscure to human beings and beyond the reach of language. Neither the measured periods of the polished parliamentary orator, the self-confident assertions of journalists, nor the tirades of those who harangued the mob from the hustings, bore any positive relationship to the indelible secrets of the universe that 'written in abstruse facts, of endowment, position, desire, opportunity, granted to the man ... interprets itself in presentiments, vague struggles, passionate endeavours; and is only legible in whole when his work is *done*'.[32]

The lack of correspondence between the 'world' and particular expressions of the 'word', might in some cases be attributed to innocent ignorance. Carlyle seems to have taken this view of the English Republicans; they were blind or misguided rather than being vicious.[33] He was far harsher in his judgements on his contemporaries because they had willingly and unblushingly embraced the cause of delusion and outright falsehood. Their speech was proffered in the same way as a counterfeiter's plausible but worthless products. 'True' speech was the banknote 'for an inward capital of culture, of insight and noble human worth' that could be expected to yield benefits to humanity. The forged notes that dominated the exchanges of modern politics stimulated false expectations and rebounded to the ultimate discredit of every one within the field of their circulation. Passing finally into the hands of the poorest classes at the highest possible discount, they produced desperation and revolt.[34]

Carlyle claimed that these exchanges were at the core of modern political culture and that successful engagement in them was a precondition for membership of the political elite of contemporary Britain: 'To wag the tongue with dextrous acceptability, there is for human worth and faculty in our England of the Nineteenth-Century, that one method of emergence and no other ... Vox is the God of this Universe.' Carlyle allowed that people who were prepared to restrict themselves to what he called 'beaverism', the honest but limited and blinkered pursuit of material wealth, might escape from the jealous eye of this deity. However, those who wished to succeed in professions that had the greatest potential for moulding (or debauching) the spirit and intellect of modern society could not adopt this strategy. 'Vox' reigned in the church, in the law and above all, in politics. 'Premiership, woolsack, mitre, and quasi-crown: all is attainable if you can talk with due ability. Everywhere your proof-shot is to be a well-fired volley of talk.'[35] These remarks make it quite clear that while Carlyle focused on the shortcomings of parliamentary government, he set these in the context of a far more general critique of the lack of true meritocracy in literature, the professions and the public service.

Stump oratory was most evident in electoral politics but it was also central to the practice of the representative institutions produced by them. Carlyle predicted that it would become increasingly important as the franchise was widened to embrace a demoralised working class acting under the influence of 'beer' and balderdash', and as the rise of the popular press intruded electioneering on to the floor of the House of Commons. In the 'Latter-Day Pamphlets' he still thought that the fourth estate might play a useful representative role in modern society but by the time he wrote 'Shooting Niagara' in 1867 his position had hardened. The intrusiveness of the press, and MPs' manipulation of it in the hope of ingratiating themselves with the electorate, had turned the House of Commons into a mere 'public debating society' or 'circus'; its proceedings had become 'emptier, ghastlier, more abjectly foolish'.[36]

These developments exacerbated the inherent weakness of parliamentary government: namely, its reliance on oral facility as the basis for judging ability and for assigning offices of power and influence. Carlyle claimed that these practices were totally at odds with the requirement of just and effective government. Just legislative and regulatory enactments corresponded with the requirements of the divine laws that underwrote the universe; they were expressions of ideas that could be grasped only partially by human beings and could not, even in this attenuated form, be conveyed through language. The unavoidable limitations of human understanding and communication meant that even under the most favourable circumstances (far removed from the ethos of the modern world) neither good government, nor good legislation, could be expected to emerge from the deliberative processes of conventional parliamentary government.

> Speak your sincerest, think your wisest, there is still a great gulf between you and the fact. And now, do *not* speak your sincerest, and, what will inevitably follow out of that, do not think your wisest, but think only your plausibilest, your showiest for parliamentary purposes, where will you land with that guidance?[37]

If people of real worth found their way into parliament, surviving the challenges to veracity posed by 'beer' and 'balderdash', they would succeed there only by conforming to the enervating requirements of an environment where speech was king. Substance would be exchanged for show, silent deliberation and action for declaration and inaction.

These considerations led Carlyle to question and then to dismiss any expectation that representative government might be a vehicle of salvation for contemporary society; to the contrary, he argued that the idea of parliamentary *government* was fundamentally incoherent. Carlyle's presentation of this line of argument utilised parallels between the seventeenth and nineteenth centuries that were first developed in his work on Oliver Cromwell. Having enthusiastically endorsed Cromwell's dismissive treatment of the constitutional procrastinations of the Rump Parliament, Carlyle ridiculed modern Whigs' veneration of the 'Commonwealthsmen' and chastised them for heaping abuse on the head of the Lord Protector. 'Constitutional government', as that term was understood by both the Commonwealthsmen and their self-styled successors, was incapable of instituting a new and effective system of order because it relied on rhetoric, encouraged partisanship, and inhibited decisive action.[38]

Carlyle rejected the commonly-held assumption that parliament should be supreme, claiming there was no warrant for this idea either in history, or in common sense. Medieval parliaments functioned effectively because they accepted royal leadership and control, and did not try to play a governing role. Proponents of parliamentary government had ignored these limitations, being misled by the assumption that the Long Parliament was a model that could be imitated and improved on by the present generation. Carlyle argued, however, that while this body had filled admirably the vacuum in leadership caused by the failings of the Stuarts, it did not provide a precedent for parliamentary government as a normal alternative to elite leadership. To the contrary, its success was a consequence of a combination of special circumstances and the unique qualities of its members. The Long Parliament marked the 'cactus-flowerage of the parliamentary tree ... which blossoms only in thousands of years'.[39] The great mistake of all subsequent parliaments, constitutional writers and parliamentary reformers was that they failed to recognise this and insisted on promoting an ideal of government that was dangerously out of line with the underlying realities of politics. As a result, parliaments had assumed a sovereign role – combining both discussion and decision- making – for which they were quite unfitted.

These pretensions were first seen in the Rump and Protectoral parliaments and explained both the futility of these bodies and Cromwell's impatience with them. They later impeded the regeneration of revolutionary France, and destroyed those (most notably the Girondins) who saw constitutional assemblies as the only vehicles of national salvation. In contemporary Britain, the Whigs were the most doctrinaire proponents of parliamentary government, but Carlyle thought that the idea had become a shibboleth of actual or aspiring political actors across the ideological spectrum. The truth of the situation was quite different. British parliaments were mere talking shops whose members were as far removed as it was possible to get from the earnest sincerity of the Puritans of the Long Parliament, and from any grasp of the underlying realities of the human condition. They could not even claim to provide a forum for canvassing issues of popular concern: this role had been assumed by the popular press, the true 'fourth estate' of the modern world. The tragic futility of recent attempts at government was amply demonstrated by Lord John Russell's feeble responses to the challenges that faced contemporary society:

> Does our chief governor calculate that England, with ... Chartism under deck, and such a fire-ship of an Ireland ... chained to her ... can keep the waters on those terms? By her old constitutional methods, of producing small-registration bills, much Parliamentary eloquence, and getting the supplies voted? ... Is it by such alchemy he will front the crisis?[40]

The democratic tendencies of the age dramatically exposed the falsity of parliamentary claims to undertake 'real sovereign work'. Democracy expressed the 'condensed folly' of a morally bankrupt political culture, and its realisation would widen the gap between human legislative enactments and the immutable laws that really governed the universe. It also ignored the overarching necessity for elite leadership in all social conditions. Like John Ruskin, Carlyle found comfort and inspiration in the anti-democratic passages of Plato's *Republic* but he described the impact of democracy on genius in terms that echoed the fulminations of one of his successors, the 'Old Oligarch'. Democracy meant that 'all heavenliest nobleness should be flung out into the muddy streets there to jostle elbows with all thick-skinned denizens of chaos, and get itself ... trampled into the gutters and annihilated.'[41]

The claim that parliaments were incapable of governing in any true sense of the term, was called up repeatedly to support Carlyle's assaults on contemporary moves to reform parliament and extend the franchise. The premise of this argument – that the credence given to electioneering and parliamentary oratory was symptomatic of a wilful disregard for truth – was also utilised in a far broader critique of the ethos of modern Britain. The 'Latter-Day Pamphlets' present three particularly vivid manifestations of the cult of falsehood in contemporary society: the delusions of modern 'philanthropy' as represented in the practice and underlying ideals of 'model prisons'; the 'Jesuitical' basis of the modern spirit; and the choice of icons that best embody this spirit and are thus most worthy of being commemorated by public monuments.

From the early 1830s bold experiments in the design and management of English penal institutions gave rise to a number of 'model prisons' reflecting the impact of a range of ideas on the causes of crime, the nature of criminality and appropriate responses to it. Reform of the prison system was sometimes prompted, as in the case of John Howard's late eighteenth century campaign, by revelations of scandalously inhumane conditions in penal institutions, and high mortality rates among condemned prisoners and those awaiting trial. Direct religious concerns were uppermost in the minds of William Crawford and the Reverend Whitworth Russell, two reformers who had a major impact on the Prison Act of 1839 and continued to exert great influence on the prison inspectorate for most of the next decade. Crawford and Whitworth wished to make prisons sites of moral and religious reformation and strenuously rejected retributive notions of punishment. They sought to tailor penal regimes so that they would promote the spiritual welfare of prisoners, insulating them from corrupting influences and trusting to the transformative effect of heightened religious consciousness.[42] In other cases, including Jeremy Bentham's 'panoptican' regime, changes to prison design and management were a consequence of far-reaching theories of human motivation, behavioural modification and social control. Because 'model prisons' were newly built and carefully planned, they necessarily differed from existing prisons. The buildings that housed these older institutions had served a range of purposes in the past and were marked by piecemeal responses prompted by the implications of rapid population and changes to the penal code during the eighteenth century. From the late 1830s a great deal of reforming energy went into improving prisoners' diet and dress, with the latter being designed to encourage self-respect, rather than serving as a degrading badge.[43]

'Model prisons' were the focus of extensive public comment and there was heated debate between proponents of various regimes. They were also, however, the butt of novelistic satire, most notably, in *David Copperfield* (1850). Carlyle's 'Model Prisons' pamphlet echoed concerns raised in contemporary debate but the purpose of his engagement with it was highly distinctive. Modern views on the treatment of criminals were presented as but one facet of his contemporaries' fatal penchant for falsehood. In this case, the issue hinged on the denial of the idea that the practice of criminal justice should be directly related to a clear and unyielding commitment to the intractable difference between right and wrong.

Carlyle's pamphlet incorporated impressions of the Westminster House of Correction (known as 'Tothill Fields') arising from a visit that he made to this institution in early February 1849.[44] There is a certain irony in this point of reference. Tothill was opened in 1836, four years before Pentonville, the acme of the model prison, and was soon being compared unfavourably with it. The cells were half the size of those at Pentonville and lacked any of its domestic refinements – state-of-the-art plumbing, heating and ventilation.[45] Its exterior was, however, very grand and imposing and this, together with its clean corridors and air of silent tranquillity, was sufficient to prompt Carlyle's scathing attack on the scandalous opulence of prison life. He claimed that model prisons provided levels of comfort, order and quiet that would be a godsend to harassed authors, and were built on a scale that would satisfy the dignity of a duke.[46] He also expressed amazed disgust at society's willingness to privilege felons over hard-pressed members of the honest working classes.

These criticisms were commonplaces that were endorsed by a number of reviewers of 'Model Prisons'. At the same time, however, these reviewers thought that Carlyle's promotion of the idea that criminals should be exposed to the hatred of the community was inhumane and unchristian.[47] In a particularly savage outburst, he castigated inmates of Tothill Fields as

> miserable distorted blockheads, the generality; ape-faces, imp-faces, angry dog-faces, heavy sullen ox-faces; degraded underfoot perverse creatures, sons of *in*docility, greedy mutinous darkness, and in one word, of STUPIDITY, which is the general mother of such.[48]

This characterisation, reflecting Carlyle's belief that those without moral understanding were less than human, provided the rationale for the harsh and at times brutal penalogical prescriptions that are scattered throughout 'Model Prisons'. These details were, however, largely incidental since the contrast between the regime favoured by Carlyle and those attributed to model prisons focused on the morally corrosive ethos of modern society rather than on the character of criminals. Model prisons were characteristic products of 'philanthropy'. Carlyle's critique of philanthropy was not an attack on human compassion, but on what he saw as a powerful force in modern society that privileged human preference over a conception of a moral universe where fundamental values were enshrined in 'natural laws'. These laws were, Carlyle maintained, the source of an intractable distinction between right and wrong that was the keystone of morality, one that all right-thinking individuals were obliged to bring to bear on the choices they made and on their efforts to give effect to them.[49]

Despite appearances, 'Model Prisons' is thus a tract on the intellectual and moral failings of elites, rather than a contribution to penology. That is, it has less to do with prison inmates than with the attitudes towards wrongdoing that underwrote the regimes to which these malefactors were subjected. Carlyle described Pentonville, *the* model prison, as a 'truly villainous incarnation and petrifaction of benevolent Tartuffery', one that drew sharp attention to

> A blind loquacious pruriency of indiscriminate Philanthropism substituting itself, with much self-laudation, for the silent divinely awful sense of Right and Wrong – testifying too clearly that here is no longer a divine sense of Right and Wrong; that, in the smoke of this universal, and alas inevitable and indispensable revolutionary fire, and burning-up of worn-out rags of which the world is full, our life-atmosphere has (for the time) become one vile London fog, and the eternal loadstars are gone out for us![50]

Far from recognising their duty to search out wrong doing and to treat offenders as proper objects of hatred who should be cast out of human society, the devotees of penal philanthropy implied that the immutable laws of the universe, the basis of truth and falsity, were proper subjects of human indulgence. In so doing, they misrepresented the very idea of justice, inverting the relationship between right, as something that should be striven for and accepted, and wrong as something from which human beings should recoil.

Carlyle thought that this inversion was symbolised by the physical conditions in model prisons. While the 'Devil's regiment' benefited from carefully planned physical and dietary regimes, from wonders of modern architectural and technological innovation and environmental serenity and cleanliness, the beleaguered inhabitants of the working-class quarters adjacent to these palatial monuments to vice struggled in the face of incomprehensible economic forces and elite neglect to secure a modicum of the necessities of life. Tothill Fields was blessed with the crowning irony of a governor who possessed a fair range of the qualities of heroic leadership that were so lacking in society at large. Thus while the governing classes would neither care for, nor lead, the working classes, they made lavish provisions for hardened criminals and taxed the poor and still honest to pay for them.[51]

In line with his belief that criminal acts violated fundamental and intractable moral precepts, Carlyle rejected conventional notions of exemplary and deterrent punishment since these approaches reduced it to a strategy in a voluntaristic order. He focused instead on the Old Testament idea that punishment was an act of revenge against those who flouted the laws of the universe. When viewed in this harsh yet just light, the only appropriate personal and collective responses to criminality were private and public demonstrations of loathing for criminals, a 'hatred, a hostility inexorable, unappeasable, which blasts the scoundrel, and all scoundrels ultimately, into black annihilation and disappearance from the sum of things'.[52]

Despite these uncompromising views, Carlyle gave grudging, backhanded praise to reformers such as John Howard who had campaigned to rid prisons of unintended hardships caused by 'prison fever' and other epidemics.[53] He insisted, however, that the desirability of these reforms should not obscure the nature of criminal offending or the intractability of the wrongdoing that it involved. As in other cases where the claims of justice were ignored, the philanthropic disregard of the distinction between truth and falsehood would eventually prompt a distorted, but in some senses an authentic, response from the lower classes: 'Dim oblivion of right and wrong, among the masses of your population will come; doubts as to right and wrong, indistinct notion that right and wrong are not eternal, but accidental, and settled by uncertain votings and talkings will come', and religion will be debased to the self-serving sensualist creed of 'universal love' that Carlyle associated with Balzac, Sue and George Sand.[54]

The leap from Victorian penal practice to the insidiously *louche* moral environment of French sentimentalism is surprising, even by Carlyle's standards. In his mind at least, however, these apparently quite different worlds were brought together by their perverse indifference to the clear and self-evident distinction between right and wrong. Carlyle thought that this distinction formed the irreducible core of religion, marking a point of authentic affinity between different expressions of religious faith and making it possible for him to offer a sympathetic account of the cosmic significance of Islam, and to write with almost unqualified admiration of English Puritanism. Given these views, the way in which he framed his other major assaults on his contemporaries' perverse inversion of truth and falsehood was especially striking.

In 'Jesuitism' Carlyle confronted his contemporaries with a paradox that was meant to strike at the very core of their self-image: although the English prided themselves on their staunch Protestantism, their true patron saint was Ignatius Loyola rather than Martin Luther or John Calvin. Carlyle may have been prompted to represent the prevailing spirit of his contemporaries in these terms because of a recent spate of revisionist accounts of the founder of the Society of Jesus in English publications.[55] He was also aiming a blow at anglo-catholicism, a tendency in the contemporary English Church that was to come in for some harsh treatment in the biography of John Sterling that occupied his attention after he had completed the 'Latter-Day Pamphlets'. Modern Protestants could be tarred with the same brush as the Jesuits because both professed to believe doctrines that they knew to be untrue.[56] On Carlyle's reading, Loyola was 'A bad man ... not good by nature; and by destiny swollen into a very Ahriman of badness'. Jesuitism, the diseased product of a 'prurient-heroic' battle with an ego-fixated consciousness, was a ghastly, fantastic, mirror image of Luther's heroic struggles.[57] It required willing compliance with an intellectual regime that extinguished the 'sacred lamp of intellect' and 'bullied and bowowed' its conscious and unconscious devotees out of their primary loyalty to the 'God of light'.[58] Carlyle regarded these tendencies as characteristic of post-reformation Catholicism. While Abbot Samson and his fellows adhered to a faith that expressed fundamental truths, modern Catholics were devotees of 'popish superstition', a set of ideas and practices that were, as Voltaire recognised, no longer capable of being really believed.[59] In 'Jesuitism' Carlyle claimed that this perverse spirit had infiltrated the souls of almost all of his contemporaries, forming the basis of a widely subscribed to pseudo-religion that was not grounded in truth, and was thus incapable of providing the guidance that humanity required.[60]

The void left by idolatrous self-abnegation to falsehood was filled in part by a working everyday 'faith' that Carlyle dubbed 'Pig Philosophy'. His account of this position took the form of a heavy-handed lampoon on materialistic utilitarianism. Beginning with the proposition that the Universe was an 'immeasurable Swine's trough, consisting of solid and liquid and of other contrasts and kinds; – especially consisting of attainable and unattainable, the latter in immensely greater quantities for most pigs', it concluded with a half coherent denial of the existence of Hell.[61] Carlyle was prepared to concede that at least some of his countrymen gave their allegiance to a potentially more significant deity manifest in literature, poetry and the other fine arts. As practised in the modern world, however, they offered no real hope of redemption. Jesuitism contaminated all aspects of human life and thought: 'All arts, industries and pursuits ... are tainted to the heart with fatal poison; carry not in them the inspiration of God, but (frightful to think of!) that of the Devil calling and thinking himself God; and are smitten with a curse forevermore'.[62] Carlyle singled out for specific condemnation the recently completed Houses of Parliament designed by Augustus Pugin. A building that celebrated parliamentary government was unlikely to have appealed to Carlyle, however satisfying its design. He was, in any case, no admirer of Gothic architecture and found Pugin's evocation of it particularly repellent. Carlyle claimed that the Houses of Parliament were a visual embodiment of the delusions of the modern Catholic spirit and the sight of them filled 'earnest souls' with a compelling urge to seek exorcism.[63] This brief sally against contemporary architectural fashions was followed by a more sustained assault on novelists.

In an exaggerated restatement of his earlier privately stated view that novels presented views of life which were 'untrue' in the sense that they did not discriminate adequately between good and evil, Carlyle now rejected modern fiction out of hand. He claimed that the burgeoning market for novels showed that the reading public was idle and frivolous rather than active and earnest. Writers were 'prating story-tellers' lulling the semi-conscious, post-prandial moments of overfed, torpid voluptuaries. While Carlyle had always been critical of many practitioners of modern letters, he had nevertheless thought a select band of writers would play a role in the future that would parallel that previously undertaken by members of the priesthood. In 'Jesuitism', however, he seemed to hold few hopes for modern literature. It had sunk into a scene of unrelieved moral lassitude and unbuttoned indulgence strongly reminiscent of a harem.

> Wits, story-tellers, ballad-singers, especially dancing-girls who understand their trade, are ... the kind of artists fit for such a stuffed, stupefied Nawaub, in his hours of rumination; upon these his hot heavy-laden eye may rest without abhorrence; if with perceptible momentary satisfaction emerging from his bottomless ennui; – then victory and gold-purses to the artist; be such artist crowned with laurel or with parsley, and declared divine in presence of all men.[64]

Carlyle claimed that the reward system prevailing in contemporary literature demonstrated the perverse self-confidence and celebratory inclinations of a society where falsehood was openly and enthusiastically elevated above truth. This tendency provided the theme of the penultimate pamphlet, 'Hudson's Statute', named after George Hudson, an infamous promoter of railways.[65] Hudson's glittering empire had recently collapsed in a welter of greed, gullibility, misrepresentation and sharp practice. Since this event occurred *after* a subscription had been raised to erect a statute in his honour, but *before* the monument could be commissioned, it seemed perfectly timed to epitomise a career dedicated to inducing the public to part with its money on very risky terms. In his essay, however, Carlyle dwelt on a more fundamental feature of this episode, namely the choice of Hudson as an object of public veneration.[66]

With a bold stroke of irony, Carlyle urged his contemporaries to carry the project to its conclusion on the grounds that Hudson was a true and wholly appropriate icon for the 'new era' they were forging. This point was emphasised by reference to recent calls to raise a statue in honour of Oliver Cromwell, an initiative that Carlyle discouraged on the grounds that the Lord Protector was quite unfit to be endowed with heroic status in the modern world. By contrast, Hudson's ruthless and single-minded pursuit of wealth, his commitment to 'promoterism', and the attachment to falsehood that was integral to that profession, made him an entirely appropriate, if alarming, object of worshipful admiration.[67] As Carlyle had already explained in his lectures on 'hero-worship', human beings were psychologically predisposed to worship; the object they chose reflected the quality of the worshippers and the values of their age.[68] Given the values that were really endorsed by people of the new era, obeisance to conventional deities, or even to those endowed with a shadow of authentic spirituality, must be tainted with intellectual confusion at best, or by base hypocrisy at worst. By contrast, 'The Railway King', as he was known, was a true (false) god for the modern English because his career epitomised the values to which they really subscribed. Hudson had been elected to parliament in 1845, but Carlyle ignored this mark of dubious distinction, focusing instead on what he took to be a far more profound and telling indication of Hudson's hold upon the public imagination. His eminence among his fellow citizen's was established by an exercise of a franchise that was a truer register of their views than might ever be attained through conventional electoral machinery:

> Hudson solicited no vote; his votes were silent voluntary ones, not liable to be false: he *did* a thing which men found, in their articulate hearts, to be worthy of paying money for; and they paid it ... Every vote was the spontaneous product of those men's deepest insights and most practical convictions, about Hudson and themselves and this universe.[69]

The perverse clarity of these popular insights and the strength of the commitment generated by them, lent a note of deep tragedy to Carlyle's statuesque satire. When compared with the tawdry figures who took the leading roles in the complex systems of shams and unrealities that passed for parliamentary government, and who had quickly distanced themselves from him when the scandal broke, the master speculator acquired a certain horrific grandeur. But while he was an entirely appropriate focus for the unqualified approbation of the vast majority of his contemporaries, he could not, of course, be an object of true veneration, or 'hero-worship'. In the 'Latter-Day Pamphlets' the exposure by elevation of George Hudson is counterpoised by a renewal of the search for an authentic hero capable of beginning the process of extricating modern humanity from the stygian quagmire. In the course of this search, Carlyle built on his critique of parliamentary government to propose a radical reform of the political system such that it might serve the cause of truth rather than reflect and reinforce the fascination with falsity that blighted contemporary life.

Despite their super-heated atmospherics, the 'Latter-Day Pamphlets' contain a great deal of cool, lucid and rational analysis of political practice, much of which reflects Carlyle's close attention to current political affairs.[70] The impression of desperate isolation that was cultivated in these pamphlets was a metaphor for Carlyle's perceived lack of impact on his contemporaries rather than a literal account of his degree of engagement with current social and political developments. In fact, his correspondence, personal contacts and wide-ranging reading in periodicals and newspapers meant that he was well informed on day-to-day affairs. In the 'Latter-Day Pamphlets' this knowledge was brought to bear in an analysis that focused on the shortcomings of contemporary British government, and an outline of some of the general principles that needed to be addressed if these were to be overcome. The illiberal tone and bearing of these pamphlets might tend to distract attention from their radicalism, but it should be recalled that Carlyle thought of them as 'reform papers'.[71] While inward reform (reform of the intellect and spirit) was essential, the fact that this would result in an acceptance of the principle and implications of hierarchy led naturally enough to an interest in political machinery. An efficient state both symbolised the society over which it presided, and undertook activities that lay beyond the scope or capacity of social and economic elites. Carlyle made it clear that he regarded reform of government as far more significant than any conceivable reform of parliament. It was equally clear, however, that the changes he proposed would have had profound implications for the role of parliament within the political system.

Carlyle treated administrative (rather than representative) agencies as the key to effective government in the modern world. At present, however, the Colonial, Foreign and Home Offices actively inhibited the adoption of measures promoting the wellbeing of the population at home and England's imperial mission. The energies of the Foreign Office were dissipated in empty diplomatic forms, or misapplied in promoting representative government in areas of the world that were yet free from it. The Colonial Office failed to support governors who had a clear view of the importance of colonies, and favoured those whose who repudiated the Empire and blindly promoted 'responsible government' on doctrinaire *laissez-faire* grounds. The Home Office gave comfort and support to the schemes of philanthropists and turned a blind eye to pauperism. Like other arms of government, it revelled in arcane, time-consuming practices that bore no positive relationship to the interests of the community. In addition to frustrating those with business to transact, these practices demoralised able public servants. Here, as elsewhere, inessential work encouraged idleness and discouraged excellence by inducing an ethos of untruthfulness in work that paralleled that afflicting the arts, morality and religion. In this case, however, the ethos was reinforced by the self-perpetuating perverse vacuity of bureaucratic pride: 'pedant darkness … asserts itself to be *light*'.[72]

Given the role that Carlyle ascribed to government and his view that it provided an important field in which elites should fulfil their obligations to work, the parlous condition of British administration was a matter for especial concern. Carlyle's views on this issue formed an important component of his response to the 'condition of England question' in the 1840s. In the mid 1850s, in the context of the debacles of the Crimean War revealing that British government was a 'mere hulk of chaotic imbecilities', he was equally dismissive of 'Constitutional government, parliamentary debating, potwalloping, freedom of the press, universal palaver *about* government instead of government itself'. Carlyle's expression of this view was distinctive but he was not alone in taking it. To the contrary, his remarks were part of a groundswell of hostile criticism from across the political spectrum.[73] Thus when Thomas Ballantyne, an admirer of Carlyle's who served as deputy editor of the strongly liberal *Manchester Guardian*, published extracts from the 'Latter-Day Pamphlets' in 1855 in a volume titled *Prophecy for 1855*, a reviewer seized on them as part of a campaign to purge government of the ills that had been revealed so painfully in the Crimean campaign. This line was fully in accord with Carlyle's privately stated view that the war was 'proof' of the truth of these pamphlets. Having been swept along the path to war in a torrent of parliamentary and journalistic oratory, the tragically dehabilitating effect of modern ideas was demonstrated in government's conduct of the war.[74]

The welter of confusion that reigned at the heart of contemporary British government was to be replaced by the 'New Downing Street', a focal point for the intellect of the community,

> directing all its energies upon the real and living interests of England, and silently but incessantly, in the alembics of the place, burning-up the extinct imaginary interests of England, that we may see God's sky a little plainer overhead, and have all of us a great accession of 'heroic wisdom' to dispose of.[75]

The departments of state in the New Downing Street would perform a range of functions in relation to pauperism, colonies, popular and elite education that was far wider than that currently assumed by government agencies. They would also refrain from the worthless tasks currently undertaken by 'protocoling establishments' of various kinds, including many of those that required the commitment of resources for military purposes. But while Carlyle indicated likely areas of development and retrenchment, nothing much hung on these details. His primary objective was to establish the need for reform as a matter of principle. Those responsible for the new administrative machinery would assume a general oversight of reviewing, planning and implementation, and could be relied upon to do what was necessary.

Many of Carlyle's comments on the old Downing Street reflected concerns that fuelled Dickensian 'circumlocution office' satire and other critiques of contemporary government. However, the image of government that emerges from Carlyle's account is characteristically radical in its implications. His remarks on self-imposed bureaucratic drudgery are underwritten by the idea that elite expertise and leadership are essential features of good government. He thus insisted that the first and essential step in the reform process was to ensure that a handful of people of real talent exercised direct and effective control over the organs of state. This stress upon leadership went hand-in-hand with an unequivocal promotion of the most thorough going meritocracy, and a demand that ways be found to draw on the hidden talents of the whole community. For this reason, Carlyle thought that recruitment into the Civil Service and promotion in it should reflect merit; he also supported moves to abolish the system of purchasing commissions in the army.[76] Although he placed no reliance on electoral mechanisms – 'I confess I would not exchange the right *attempt* at this, for all the ballot boxes, or want of ballot boxes, in the world' – Carlyle nevertheless insisted that there was a sense in which meritocracy embodied the truth of democracy: 'Not that the noble soul, born poor, should be set to spout in Parliament, but that he should be set to assist in governing men; this is our grand Democratic interest'.[77]

This idea of elite leadership had far-reaching implications for the basis of British government because it meant that the exercise of effective political power would need to be unshackled from a presumptively directive, pseudo-sovereign parliament and made independent of the confused and degrading whims of the electorate. In the 'New Downing Street' Carlyle suggested that ministerial offices and some places in parliament should be filled by appointment, thus creating a class of what might be called 'Queen's' members, as distinct from the 'people's' members who would be elected to the House of Commons in the usual way.[78] These proposals reflected Carlyle's long-held views on the need for active and intelligent government in increasingly complex, modernising societies. If British governments were to respond positively to the challenges of the new era, however, they would need to be directed by a heroic 'chief governor' whose skills and character were appropriate to the requirements of the modern age and who would not be chosen by parliament or answerable to it.

Heroes' situation-specific attributes – their prophetic, military, literary or political merits – were underwritten by a range of common intellectual, moral and spiritual characteristics that produced an unshakeable attachment to sincerity and veracity.[79] Thus while issues of efficiency and expertise played an important role in Carlyle's views on the reform of government, he set these mechanical requirements in a context where dynamic values prevailed. This feature of Carlyle's account of political leadership in 'Latter-Day Pamphlets' was accentuated by the fact that the portrait of 'Chief Governor' of the 'New Downing Street' was not an abstract construct, but was illuminated and vivified by Carlyle's understanding of the merits of the former prime minister, Sir Robert Peel.

Peel was a leading figure in British politics, having held cabinet posts in a number of Tory administrations in the 1820s. He was Prime Minister from 1833–34 and again from 1841–46. In government he pursued a reform agenda in fiscal policy and administration that had been promoted by 'Liberal Tory' elements in the party since the immediate pre-war period. In the case of Peel and his closest associates, this programme was driven by moral imperatives derived from evangelical Christianity rather than by wealth-maximising ideas held by secular reformers such as the philosophical radicals. They argued that government should not seek to interfere with the workings of providence, a stance that outlawed state paternalism towards the poor as well as administrative and financial practices that favoured sectional interests at the expense of the rest of the community.[80] By 1845 Peel was convinced that the protection of a section of the agricultural interest through tariff restrictions on the importation of foreign wheat (the 'Corn Laws') could no longer be justified. This position marked a reversal in Conservative policy and aroused violent opposition within the parliamentary party. When the Corn Laws were repealed with Whig support in 1846, the Conservative Party was split, and in June of that year Peel's Tory opponents took their revenge by defeating his government on a symbolically significant but otherwise minor issue in Anglo-Irish affairs.

Carlyle was originally dismissive of Peel, relishing his discomfort at the strengthening influence of radicals in parliament after 1832 and yoking him with Lord John Russell as representative of the ineffectualness of mainstream parliamentary politics.[81] In 1838 he described Peel as a 'sham', but by late 1841 his hostility had begun to soften. In December of this year he predicted that Peel would repeal the Corn Laws and make a serious attempt to govern the country. In the year following, Peel's reluctance to act to relieve chronic hardship among the working classes in parts of England and Scotland, and his opposition to Lord Ashley's bill to regulate working hours in textile factories, undermined Carlyle's confidence in him.[82] Within a year, however, Peel's conduct on the Corn Law question altered Carlyle's views decisively and permanently. This change, registered in correspondence and in journal entries, was made public in the 'Latter-Day Pamphlets'. Carlyle had long been an opponent of these measures, seeing them as a glaring instance of aristocratic irresponsibility and self-interest. But while Peel's conversion to repeal was crucial in amending Carlyle's view of him, this shift was based on his perception of Peel's personality and of his attitude towards politics rather than on agreement on any particular question of public policy. Carlyle was impressed by the fact that once Peel had formed the view that the Corn Laws were not justifiable, he pressed ahead with their repeal in the face of opposition from his own party and with scant regard for parliamentary or extra-parliamentary debate on this issue. As Carlyle noted after observing the embattled Prime Minister in the House of Commons, Peel made it 'perfectly plain that [he] must prevail'.[83]

This stance testified to Peel's personal courage, a quality that he had demonstrated in 1829 when he supported Roman Catholic emancipation. It also pointed to a view of the relationship between political leaders and their followers that corresponded closely with the requirements of Carlyle's model of heroic statesmanship. As Peel himself put it, 'As heads see and tails are blind, I think heads are the best judges as to the course to be taken.'[84] Peel's dictum reflected his adherence to a political ethos that focused on the national, rather than sectional, interests, and that considered the role of ministers in this light rather than as creatures of the parties to which they belonged. Ministers should provide strong and effective leadership and their party should support their endeavours. A corollary of this attitude towards government was a lofty and detached view of the relationship between a Prime Minister and his party. He 'will not condescend to humiliating submission for mere party purpose; will have neither time nor inclination to be considering how many men will support this public measure, or fly off to gratify some spite or resentment'.[85] Given the realities of the current political environment, this stance made it highly likely that a true statesman would have to be prepared to sacrifice personal ambitions for the sake of principle, as had happened to Peel when he repealed the Corn Laws. In Carlyle's view Peel's willingness to make such a sacrifice confirmed the heightened commitment to renunciation that characterised heroic personalities.[86]

When he identified Peel as a candidate for the role of chief governor, Carlyle did not have to delude himself into thinking that he was a reincarnation of the Lord Protector. Carlyle justified Cromwell's domination of the English Commonwealth on the grounds that only he could give appropriate political and religious form to the spirit of Puritanism. He promoted Peel as a modern hero because he thought he was capable of utilising the potentially progressive forces released by the withering of traditional forms of religious and secular authority and the rise of industrial society. Peel's commitment to administrative reform was seen by Carlyle to reflect his grasp of the need for complex modern societies to be subject to careful, even-handed and intelligent management. Carlyle's assessment of the quality and appropriateness of Peel's style of leadership was reinforced by his evaluation of his character. A capacity for heroic political action showed itself in an individual's physiology, demeanour and behaviour.[87] Carlyle's growing admiration for Peel can thus be charted in his increasingly warm remarks on the former Prime Minister's physical characteristics, in the insights into his character which occurred during their conversations, as well as in his pursuit of lines of action of which Carlyle approved. In Carlyle's judgement, Peel had shown enough in his face, his voice, his mind and his actions to indicate that he possessed the potential for heroic statesmanship.[88] Appreciative remarks on Peel's 'quiet elegance', 'bright eyes' and 'open countenance' contrast sharply with Carlyle's impression of the Whig politician Lord Brougham whom he despised and whose portrait he sought (with Benjamin Disraeli's wry connivance) to exclude from the National Portrait Gallery. Brougham was 'a particularly ignoble looking man; with a … restless dangerous eye; *nothing* but business in his face, no ray of genius, and even a considerable tincture of insincerity. A politician, truly, and *nothing* more'.[89]

'Heroism' was a deeply located psycho-moral attribute that enabled some human beings to grasp the underlying realities of the universe and to see through 'untruths' and 'shams'. While all heroes understood the requirements of their own age and possessed the strength of character to meet these, their special insights and abilities were only appropriate in particular circumstances. Peel lacked the aura of divine, prophetic, priestly, literary or poetic heroism possessed by the figures that Carlyle had celebrated in his lectures *On Heroes, Hero-Worship and The Heroic in History* (1840) and his deeds were of a different order to those of Cromwell or Napoleon. Nevertheless, he seemed, especially when compared with his contemporaries, to possess administrative, moral and political qualities that

Carlyle thought were necessary if the English were to realise the potential of the modern age and avoid its dangers.

Carlyle insisted that heroic leaders must be insulated from the capricious and morally corrosive practices of parliamentary politics; indeed, he saw this form of political leadership as a clear and necessary alternative to parliamentary government. The 'Latter-Day Pamphlets', however, recognised a 'sounding board' role for popularly elected assemblies, provided that they were excluded from legislative or executive functions, or from any role in appointing members of the executive.[90] Heroic leaders would be recognised as such by members of the public at large – a feature of this type of relationship that had been demonstrated by Peel's growing popularity out of doors, and by the shocked public reaction to his unexpected death – but this did not mean they were products of conventional representative systems. Many of Carlyle's contemporaries thought of parliamentarianism as a system of *government*, not as a popularist adjunct of a system of rule in which political power was divorced from successful participation in the representative process and in the assembly that it filled. By contrast, Carlyle's heroic leadership was (as some contemporary reviewers noted) an *alternative* to parliamentary government, not an aspect of it.[91]

The 'Latter-Day Pamphlets' demonstrated Carlyle's ongoing commitment to a radical perspective on the challenges facing British society and its responses to them. James Hannay, an admirer of these works, but one who was not blind to their verbal excesses, applauded Carlyle's capacity to highlight the contrast between the tawdry reality of modern economic, social and political relationships, and the exalted rhetoric adopted by the apologists for an aristocracy and church establishment that played no worthwhile role in the modern world and was wholly reliant on the efforts of others to support its position.[92] The creative role that Carlyle ascribed to heroic statesmen was crucial to the image that he proffered in response to this state of affairs because he thought that effective, inspiring leadership was only possible in a radically reformed political culture.

It has been observed that the interest in heroes in Victorian fiction reflects a widespread judgement that conventional politics was incapable of providing salvation because it merely reflected the general decay of moral meaning in modern society. Hero-worship was a basis for reconstituting the modern state.[93] Contrary to the view that John Stuart Mill ascribed to Carlyle, hero-worship was not a mere worship of power because, like Mill himself, Carlyle stressed the need for both followers and leaders to possess discernment and to display courage. Carlyle believed that heroic leaders would only win endorsement from their contemporaries if heroism was a generalised social force: honest work has ultimate meaning and makes heroes of us all. Seen from this perspective, the quality of leadership depended ultimately on the characteristics of the population as a whole, a point that was implicit in the emphasis that Carlyle placed on the relationship between Cromwell and Puritanism and was made quite explicit in 'Latter-Day Pamphlets': 'Tell me what kind of man governs a People, you tell me, with much exactness, what the net sum-total of social worth in that people has for some time been'.[94] For this reason, Carlyle presented an active, reformed state under the leadership of a heroic figure such as Peel as the focal point of a heroic culture. It would be a '*luminous vitality* permeating with its light all provinces of our affairs', and drawing upon the heroic capacities found within contemporary society.[95] In the 'Latter-Day Pamphlets' Carlyle focused upon the role of government. Elsewhere, however, he made it clear that the principle of heroic leadership should be diffused throughout society. 'Captains of industry' were an important expression of this principle, but Carlyle also thought that at least some of the aristocracy might be encouraged to play their part, indicating in correspondence with the Ashburtons some of the forms that this might take. He urged members of their class to work practically among their dependants, rather than wasting their efforts in speech-making or other conventional good works – 'instituting' and 'dinnering' as Carlyle dismissively put it. Particular stress was laid upon 'teaching', or at least overseeing directly the education of, those for whom they were deemed to be responsible. Lady Ashburton was thus encouraged to set up a 'practical school' on Ashburton's estate. Carlyle thought that her husband should undertake '*exemplary schoolmastership*' and offered to lend a helping hand with this when he had finished *Frederick the Great*.[96]

The distinctive character of a heroic political culture was brought into sharp relief by Carlyle's remarks on 'swarmery' in United States democracy in 'Shooting Niagara'. This term was of German origin ('*schwärmerei*') and had been used by Martin Luther to characterise the Protestant sects that had sprung up in the wake of his break with the Roman Catholic Church. It was applied in the eighteenth century to religious fanaticism, and in the 1790s to mass action in the French Revolution.[97] The term was open to a variety of literal and metaphorical meanings but it is perhaps significant that Carlyle used it to signify a frenzy of verbal concurrence, 'heaping assent on assent', that conveyed his jaundiced judgement of the morally corrupt and intellectually vacuous exchanges between democratic politicians and their constituents. By contrast, a heroic culture eschewed stump oratory in all its forms and rested on an ideal of leadership and recognition that has its source in independent commitment: heroes follow heroes in contrast to the 'swarming' of blind equals. This ideal placed a premium on the moral and intellectual qualities of leaders *and* followers, and, as one of Carlyle's contemporaries noted, it tended to discount the reliance on coercion that was ascribed to Carlyle by some of his critics. A sympathetic reviewer in the *Spectator* observed that a Carlylean society would be held together by a 'metrical unity', made up of a range of harmonics sounded in response to a note struck by the leader. By this means 'the whole inferior body politic should be more or less drawn into the hymn of social duty'. It was noted that this doctrine emphasised 'intensity of purpose, singleness ... wholeness' and depreciated social and political structures and practices that assumed that human interests were diffuse and subdivided.[98]

In 1866 Carlyle reiterated earlier claims that he had given up any hope that conventional parliaments might deal effectively with 'Anarchies, Irish and others'.[99] As a result, he was very reluctant to petition parliament in support of the claims of Edward Eyre, the former Governor of Jamaica.[100] Even at this time, however, he retained some faith in the general population and would have preferred an appeal to it rather than to parliament. As he told Eyre, the defence committee should have taken 'a more courageous, declaratory, and as it were aggressive attitude; virtually that of *appeal to the people of England*'.[101] This comment reinforces the popularist implications of Carlyle's conception of heroism. It also raises interesting issues about his understanding of the purpose of his later writings and their target, suggesting that he wished to reassure the right-minded and to appeal to them to tap the sources of good sense and justice that still slumbered in the general population. At the same time, however, he sought to chastise the corrupt and weak, to undermine their position and discredit their claims to exercise moral leadership in contemporary society.

Carlyle's harsh and unremitting criticisms of 'philanthropy' were central to this programme, but so too was his search for moral and intellectual exemplars. Heroic social and political leadership would make universal heroism possible and thus realise the promise that lay at the heart of Reformation Protestantism and of all genuinely revolutionary and progressive movements:

> It is not to taste sweet things but to do noble and true things, and vindicate himself under God's heaven as a god-made man, that the poorest son of Adam dimly longs. Show him the way of doing that, the dullest daydrudge kindles into a hero.[102]

At present the state was riddled with the falsehoods that were characteristic of the 'new era' and its activities were part of an elaborate, resource-consuming and demoralising piece of theatre. Under the direction of a heroic chief governor it would cease to be a 'dramaturgy' and would be restored as a 'reality'; that is, an authoritative agency whose task was to 'render existence possible, existence desirable and noble' for its subjects.[103] While Carlyle thus promoted a retreat from egalitarian conceptions of politics, he did not abandon his commitment to an ideal of community that sought to give reality to the principle of moral equality.

7

The Voice of the Past

The National Library of Scotland's manuscript catalogue listing of Carlyle as 'essayist and historian' draws attention to the two genres through which he rose to prominence. Essays might gain the attention of the opinion forming classes, but in Carlyle's view they would not enable him to hold it. What was needed was a full-scale, book-length publication that would capitalise on the attention attracted by the essays. A work such as this would cement his reputation as a really significant literary figure who deserved not only to be read and discussed, but also listened to. This ambition was satisfied initially in 1837 by a major historical work, *The French Revolution: A History*. Over the course of the next three decades, five historically focused books played a central role in sustaining his reputation. Two of these were major studies whose scale matched or exceeded that of *The French Revolution: the Letters and Speeches of Oliver Cromwell with Elucidations* (1845), and the *History of Friedrich II of Prussia, Called Frederick the Great* (1858–65). The others, *On Heroes, Hero-Worship and the Heroic in History* (1840), *Past and Present* (1843) and *Early Kings of Norway* (1872), were more limited in scope.

Two philosophical and programmatic statements preceded Carlyle's major forays in history: 'On History' (1830) and 'On History Again' (1833).[1] In these essays Carlyle claimed that historical reflection was inseparable from thought itself, and was central to the spiritual dimensions of human nature and understanding. By treating the present as a condition poised between two 'eternities', past and future, historical reflection acknowledged human infinity and gave a degree of unity to human experience.[2] For these reasons, Carlyle insisted that histories must be underpinned by a coherent account of the 'origins and destiny of mankind'. He was singularly unimpressed by recent contributions to the genre, claiming that neither Sir Walter Scott nor T. B. Macaulay, two of the most popular writers of the period, really had anything to say to their readers.[3] By contrast, Carlyle presented his own historical endeavours as integral to the attempt to shape and reform his contemporaries' understanding of their place in the world and to encourage them to act on the social and political implications of this understanding. In the final analysis, the past had to be understood as a product of humankind's more or less imperfect obedience to divine law. Historical writing was 'a record of God's providence' and in attempting to compile it, the historian constantly grappled with things that could only be explained fully in relation to the totality to which they belonged.[4] The importance that Carlyle ascribed to historical understanding was nicely captured in a critical observation on the followers of Saint Simon. In seeking to establish a new religion, the Saint Simonians ignored the central message of Goethe's thought, namely, that in the modern world the symbolic representation of the divine was recorded in the 'acted *History of Man*'.[5]

By presenting historical writings as *the* vehicle of cultural and cosmic understanding, Carlyle posed a strenuous challenge to historians. Over the course of the next thirty years, his historical productions were prefaced by, interspersed with and forged in the face of what he saw as the almost universal failure of other writers to live up to his understanding of the requirements of the discipline. Whatever the fairness of his criticisms, there is no doubt that Carlyle took these strictures seriously in his own writings. History that was worthy of the name had to fulfil two requirements. First, historians must ensure that their readers were really able to *see* the past, that is, to grasp the significance of historical events and actors in ways that conveyed vivid, instructive and inspirational images that helped them come to terms with the particular manifestations of universal that confronted them. In addition, they must find a way of selecting from the virtually infinite number of past events those that were capable of having 'meaning' for their readers in this sense. These criteria were applied in ways that reflected Carlyle's sense of the character and bearing of his mission.

Carlyle's claim that historical writing should enable readers to see the past gave rise to an interest in historical portraiture. Authentic and accurate portraits provided historians with insights into the characters of leading historical actors, hence Carlyle's habit of having pictures of his subjects close at hand while he wrote on them. Portraits might also stimulate the interest and imagination of readers when they were reproduced as plates in texts.[6] While working on *The French Revolution*, Carlyle was keen to secure copies of pictures of leading figures from late eighteenth-century French history. In his research for *Frederick the Great* he devoted considerable effort to finding reliable contemporary portraits of his subject. After fruitless searches in Germany, Carlyle was delighted to come across a very fine collection of pictures of Frederick and many of his contemporaries in the Queen's collection at Windsor Castle. Towards the end of his life, involvement in a public controversy on the reliability of depictions of John Knox reflected Carlyle's wish to ensure that his contemporaries were presented with images of this admirable and important figure that would enable them to grasp the true significance of his contributions to the reformation of Protestantism in Scotland and England. Carlyle rejected a number of portraits on the grounds that they did not display the character traits that he associated with one who had performed the deeds attributed to Knox.[7]

These concerns extended beyond Carlyle's areas of historical expertise, prompting him to take an interest in gathering and displaying public collections of portraits. When sitting on the selection board of the National Portrait Gallery in London, he found himself in alliance with Benjamin Disraeli in an attempt to exclude Lord Brougham's portrait from the collection. Disraeli's motives for taking this stand are unknown, but Carlyle made his views very clear: Brougham's portrait should not be hung in the gallery while he was alive because the rules of the selection board precluded it. More importantly, however, he did not think that Brougham would ever be worthy of such a distinction. He had done 'nothing worth remembering particularly' and would be quickly forgotten after his death.[8] Partly as a result of his investigations into portraits of John Knox, Carlyle became an advocate for the creation of a collection of nationally significant portraits in Scotland. In a letter in which he explained his views on historical portraiture in some detail, Carlyle wrote that 'Historic Portrait Galleries far transcend in worth all other kinds of National Collections of Pictures whatsoever; and … in fact they ought in every country to exist as the most cherished National Possession'.[9] He claimed that such collections had an important role to play in sustaining morally inspiring national cultures.

But while portraits might assist both readers and historians, the latter could also use their literary skills to bring the past alive. In *The French Revolution* Carlyle employed a highly distinctive and striking narrative technique that made the book seem more like an epic drama than a piece of conventional historical writing.[10] The choice of this form was not merely a matter of structure or presentation; on the contrary, Carlyle thought it appropriate because the subject was of universal significance. The French Revolution was important in relation to the challenges faced by modern European societies and also as a particular manifestation of the inevitable morbidity of social and political institutions and practices. The choice of a dramatic form had significant implications for the character of the historical judgments conveyed by it. While it precluded the conditional and qualified evaluations that feature so often in conventional historical narrative, it meant that the reader could be absorbed in the events themselves, rather than being distracted by references to other historical and contemporary accounts of them.[11] By using the dramatic present tense, speaking in a range of voices representing historical actors, and employing 'narrative glides' (seamless movements from one perspective to another within the space of a single paragraph),[12] Carlyle sought to bridge the gap between readers and action, and thus to overcome as far as possible the central problem of *writing* history:

> It is not in acted, as it is in written history: actual events are nowise so simply related to each other as parent and offspring are; every single event is the offspring not of one, but of all other events, prior or contemporaneous, and will in its turn combine with all others to give birth to new: it is an ever-living, ever-working Chaos of Being, wherein

shape after shape bodies itself forth from innumerable elements ... Narrative is *linear*, Action is *solid*.[13]

In his historical writings, as in *Sartor Resartus*, Carlyle sought to engage the reader in his attempt to grasp the meaning of the past by exhibiting events from a number of perspectives, rather than by setting the historian up as a presiding and omnipotent voice.[14] His approach in this case, however, was conditioned by the complex nature and virtually infinite scope of the subject matter of historical narration. The challenges posed by the 'solidity' of action, the need to locate a particular event in the organic structure to which it necessarily belongs, exacerbate problems of selectivity and compression. These challenges are inseparable from the act of writing since any given author can present only fragments of the range of voices heard: 'In thine own soul is there not as the buzz of ten thousand voices ever sounding, pleading; and thou (even as a loquacious man) reportest only fragments of one voice?'[15] In 'On History Again', Carlyle suggested that of all the events that *might* possibly have survived in the minds of men, those that are 'great and valid', those that have produced 'fruit', were more likely to be recorded and subsequently written about.[16] At various times, however, these events have been interpreted in different ways reflecting the interests of the historian – as, for example, in reflections of Tacitus, Montesquieu and Niebuhr on the events recorded by Titus Livius.[17] World history thus appears as a magic web that is constantly being reshaped by the artistry of the historian and presented to the mind and imagination of a diverse and active readership.

In *Past and Present* Carlyle referred to the 'earnest loving glance' of the historian, a phrase that related to his insistence that historians needed to have sympathy for their subjects and to see them as participating in sets of trans-historical, shared values.[18] This perspective meant that despite his sensitivity to the past and his care in correcting factual errors and misconceptions, Carlyle's historical writings were not exercises in conventional scholarship but were related closely to his literary and social criticism. The test of 'reality' was what had 'meaning' for the present. That was to be determined by reference to the moral and spiritual status of humanity in relation to the particular requirements of a given time and place. Truths were universal, but the distinctive needs of the contemporary audience determined which past expressions of them were most appropriate subjects for the historian to address.[19] Not surprisingly, Carlyle's choice of subjects demonstrated the need for personal authority in modern society. This lesson relied on the identification of a close relationship between heroism and general wellbeing across a vast expanse of time, stretching from the mythical realms of the Norse sagas to the battlefields of modern Europe.

In *On Heroes and Hero-Worship*, heroism appeared in divine, prophetic, poetic, priestly, literary and military-political manifestations, but in Carlyle's major historical studies he focused on the last of these. The exemplary character and conduct of Abbot Samson, the hero of *Past and Present*, Oliver Cromwell, and Frederick the Great, meant that their lives and times were relevant to modern humanity and hence fit subjects of 'living' history. At times, Carlyle seems to suggest that the living past is *the* subject matter of history and the proper focus of historical writing. The historian should give 'voice' to what is living and ignore what is 'dead', allowing it to remain properly silent. In practice, however, he was unable to follow this precept consistently, devoting much attention to the failings of his predecessors, and, as John Morley pointed out, devoting more than half his output to subjects from the reviled eighteenth century.[20] This approach no doubt reflected an increasingly sharp appetite for admonishment, but it was also a consequence of Carlyle's belief that his readers needed to be corrected before they could be instructed. Modern historical literature was pervaded by the influence of 'dilettantism', of antiquarian 'dryasdust' historians, and those who, like the Whig and radical historians of the English Revolution, clung to episodes from the past that were dead and should be left in oblivion. Moreover, as Carlyle made brutally clear in the 'Latter-Day Pamphlets', modern society was pervaded by an ethos of wilful myopia that privileged falsehoods over truth. As long as these influences remained strong, those with a commitment to 'real' history had a duty to expose errors and correct them. They would use the past not just as a source of exemplars, but also of stern warnings, particularly on the implications and effects of large-scale failures in heroism.

Access to primary and secondary works was always a source of difficulty for Carlyle, one that was exacerbated by his aversion to working in public reading rooms. He tried to avoid exposure to the irritating and distracting proximity of other readers by acquiring books himself, borrowing them from friends, or availing himself of loan collections in the London Library. The last of these options was not available when he was working on *The French Revolution*. In securing material for this project, Carlyle relied heavily on the good offices of John Stuart Mill. Mill, who was credited by a French visitor with being exceptionally well informed on the recent history of his native country, shared his knowledge with Carlyle and made his extensive library available to him.[21] During the course of a visit to Paris in the autumn of 1833, Mill gathered material for Carlyle and checked out sources on his behalf.[22] But while Mill's generosity helped Carlyle gain access to printed material, it could not eliminate his misgiving about it. When writing *The French Revolution* he complained in private correspondence about the quality and reliability of these sources, and in notes to the book he offered sharply worded corrections to existing accounts. Even before *The French Revolution* appeared in print, Carlyle publicly chastised those who had gone before him. He was particularly dismissive of the widely acclaimed ten volume study by Adolphe Thiers, dismissing it as superficially orderly, honest and judicial, but inwardly a 'waste, inorganic; no human head that honestly tries can conceive the French Revolution *so*'.[23]

Carlyle's strictures on the need for a new style of historical research and writing that would rescue the past from either total neglect or, what was perhaps worse, the mind-numbing attention of the dryasdust school, came to the fore in his work on Puritanism and the English Revolution. His reading for this project was far more systematic than that undertaken on the French Revolution and his irritation at the state of this material was heightened correspondingly.[24] Late in 1843, when his work on Cromwell was at a critical stage, Carlyle wrote to John Sterling complaining on behalf of himself *and* his subjects: 'The whole stagnancy of the English genius two hundred years thick lies heavy upon me. Dead heroes buried under two centuries of Atheism seem to whimper pitifully "Deliver us! Canst thou not deliver us?"'[25] This plea, part of a far more widespread and vitriolic assault on historical writing on the seventeenth century, reflected Carlyle's frustration at not being able to pursue his long cherished plan to complete a full-scale study of the period. By 1845 he viewed the entire corpus of Civil War literature with loathing. There were he complained 'from thirty to fifty score of unread pamphlets of the Civil War in the British Museum alone: huge piles of mouldering wreck, wherein, at the rate of perhaps one pennyweight per ton, lie things memorable'. Compilations of primary material and the eighteenth-century biographies of Cromwell that Carlyle dismissed with withering scorn, were contemptible because they hindered the articulation of the past by the historian: 'The sound of them is not a *voice*, conveying knowledge or memorial of any earthly or heavenly thing; it is a wide-spread inarticulate slumberous mumblement, issuing as if from the lake of Eternal Sleep'.[26]

Carlyle claimed that *Oliver Cromwell's Letters and Speeches*, an edition 'elucidated' with commentaries and interpolations, rescued its subject from almost two centuries of incomprehension, denigration and neglect. Reviewers were quick to challenge this claim by pointing out that a number of late eighteenth- and early nineteenth-century authors had corrected earlier hostile accounts of the Lord Protector.[27] But when Cromwell had not been abused or neglected, he had, Carlyle thought, been seriously misunderstood. The piles of primary materials could not speak for themselves with out the help of an authentic historian; even apparently sympathetic writers had failed to discern his 'soul' or grasp his essential meaning. Like the Puritan culture that he represented, Cromwell seemed a fantastic figure, one whose sense of himself and his role remained inexplicable to modern historians and readers. Thus while Carlyle gave very qualified approval to William Godwin's *History of the Commonwealth of England* (1824–28), and more generous recognition to the valuable ground clearing operation performed by John Forster in his *Statesmen of the Commonwealth* (1840), he insisted that he alone had grasped the link between Puritanism, Cromwell's character and the significance of the English Revolution for those who had to confront the challenges of the modern world.[28]

Frederick the Great pushed Carlyle's personal commitment to the gospel of labour to the utmost limit of his endurance, making the *French Revolution* and *Oliver Cromwell* seem like light diversions. The sheer bulk of the project, the fact that work on it spanned Carlyle's passage from middle to old age and was doggedly pursued in the face of disillusionment with the topic and the collapse of his wife's physical and psychological condition, exacerbated the usual authorial frustrations. In its earliest stages, grief at his mother's death, the reminder (if one was needed) of human mortality, and the challenges posed by the project, were closely interwoven: 'I am 58 years old; and the tasks I have on hand ... are most ungainly, incongruous with my mood; and the Night cometh; for me too is not distant, what for her has come'.[29] Moreover, although Carlyle felt a deep sympathy with what he took to be the characteristic ethos of the seventeenth century, he was hostile to that of the eighteenth century; it ' did nothing that I can completely approve of and rejoice in, except *cut its own* throat, and so end its dishonest nonsense, in the French Revolution!'[30] The shortcomings of eighteenth-century political and social leadership were such that, by the middle of the century, politics had been reduced to the pursuit of a range of contradictory, unworthy and unreal objectives fuelled by dynastic ambition, cupidity and blind commitment to maintaining ideas and practices that had no place in the modern world, or any positive purchase on the future. Deficiencies in politics signalled a deeper intellectual and spiritual malaise that was epitomised for Carlyle by the near adoration of Voltaire. In the course of *Frederick the Great*, the repugnance that had marked Carlyle's earlier accounts of Voltaire was moderated, but while he was prepared to reappraise this deeply flawed figure in the light of an 'utterly rotten' century, he insisted that the more one learned of Voltaire's life the less heroic he appeared.[31]

The evils of the eighteenth century were reflected in the deplorable state of the primary and contemporary secondary sources on Frederick's life. After a prolonged spell of reading in secondary works, Carlyle complained that he had learned virtually nothing about Frederick: 'the result is still for me a wide-spread inanity; dreary meaningless dimness; what I call a chaotic continent of barren Brandenberg *sand*'.[32] English books on the eighteenth century, almost invariably biased, inaccurate and incomplete, were stamped by the mark of Cain that afflicted virtually all of the products of that most regrettable of epochs. Although German studies were generally earnest and honest, they exhibited Teutonic manifestations of dryasdustism and were even duller than those written in England. If all this was not bad enough, Carlyle's spirits were damped by doubts about Frederick's merits. In mid 1852, at a very early stage in his work on this project, he described Frederick as 'a most brilliant, valiant and invincible human soul', but this level of enthusiasm was not sustained. Within a year, he recorded a lack of 'sufficient *love* for lean Frederick and his heroisms on my part', noting that 'only pain can now *drive* me thro' the subject'.[33] Jane Carlyle regretted that her husband ever began work on the book: 'He has never taken heartily to the subject – ought never to have *tried* to make a silk purse out of a sow's ear – for it needs all possible love for the subject to carry him along thro' such severe labour as he puts into everything he writes'.[34]

One of the major weaknesses of the secondary literature was its obsessive concern with diplomatic manoeuvring. In a sense, however, this focus was understandable since, as Carlyle noted, diplomacy was a major preoccupation of the ruling classes of eighteenth-century Europe. But while going to some trouble to secure access to manuscript material on foreign affairs held in the State Paper Office in London, Carlyle insisted that, like the constitutional and theological debates that absorbed so much attention in the seventeenth century, 'diplomatising' was peripheral to the 'real' history of the eighteenth century. Carlyle's response to military history, the other dominant theme of literature on the eighteenth century, was more complex. He was singularly unimpressed by existing accounts of the military campaigns in which Frederick was engaged, and seemed at times wary of the entire subject. Nevertheless, he went to great lengths to familiarise himself with 'military science', devoting most of the last two-thirds of his history to this subject.[35]

Although *Past and Present* was not written as quickly or fluidly as J. A. Froude thought, its passage into the world was relatively smooth and left few traces of anguish in Carlyle's correspondence.[36] One reason for this was that this project posed less testing evidential challenges than Carlyle's other historical writings. Direct and detailed historical reflections occupied just under a third of a modest single volume work that was, in any case, based primarily on one slight twelfth-century source, Jocelin of Brakelond's *Chronicle of the Abbey of St Edmunds*.[37]

Jocelin's record focuses on the career of Samson, his superior as abbot of the Benedictine community at Bury St Edmunds. *The Chronicle*, published in 1840 from manuscript sources, was exceptional in securing Carlyle's approbation.[38] In stark contrast to most of his other pronouncements on his fellow historians and editors, Carlyle's remarks on the editor of this work were generous and unqualified, reflecting his appreciation of his labours, and perhaps also a more general feeling of gratitude that such an admirable book should have come into his hands.[39] Carlyle saw Jocelin as Samson's 'Boswell', a truly human figure whose testimony provides rare and valuable insights into a past life that has special significance for the present and for the future.[40] While the products of antiquarianism and dilettantism make the past seem like a single 'infinite incredible gray void, without sun, stars, hearth-fires, or candle-light', Jocelin, though 'weak and garrulous' is

> human. Through the thin watery gossip ... we do get some glimpses of that deep-buried Time; discern veritably, though in a fitful intermittent manner, these antique figures and their life-method, face to face! Beautifully, in our earnest loving glance, the old centuries melt from opaque to partially translucent, transparent here and there; and the void black Night, one finds, is but the summing-up of innumerable peopled luminous *Days*.[41]

Past and Present differs from Carlyle's other historical works in that it discusses a relatively stable period in human history, one in which the example of a morally satisfying social and political condition was used to identify the characteristics and requirements of a well-ordered community. While the other histories were also strongly didactic, they focused on periods of rapid, destabilising and, in many ways, bewildering change that presented challenges paralleling those facing Carlyle's contemporaries.

The Early Kings of Norway, Carlyle's last work, celebrated a range of figures – Magnus the Great, Saint Olaf, King Kanut, Olaf the Thickset, and King Sverrir and his successors – who brought order and a degree of prosperity to anarchic Denmark, England and Norway. By modern standards, these men were cruel, rapacious and uncouth, but Carlyle credited them with having laid the basis of all the later achievements of the peoples of north-western Europe, including, of course, the world-forming mission of 'the English'.

> Here, clothed in stormy enough passions and instincts, unconscious of any aim but their own satisfaction, is the blessed beginnings of Human Order, Regulation, and real Government ... Here, at any rate, in this poor Norse theatre, one looks with interest on the first transformation, so mysterious and abstruse, of human Chaos into something of articulate Cosmos; witnesses the wild and strange birth-pangs of Human Society, and reflects that without something similar (little as men expect now), no Cosmos of human society ever was got into existence, nor can ever again be.[42]

The Reformation, the real starting point of *Oliver Cromwell*, marked an epoch across Europe, but, in England at least, its implications were only finally confronted in the seventeenth century. The triumph of Puritanism before 1660 banished the lingering vestiges of a medieval world-view that had long ceased to provide adequate forms in which to clothe the ideas and aspirations of humanity. Carlyle insisted that the significance of Parliament's challenge to the Stuarts and their Laudian allies could only be grasped by those who understood the radical and progressive implications of the Reformation and the Puritan spirit with which it was infused. The Reformation was important in Carlyle's understanding of the significance of historical writing because it exemplified the need for humanity to undergo periodic processes of regeneration.[43] Regeneration required honesty with God and oneself, sincerity, and a search for clarity of feeling and understanding. It relied on inspired insight, rather than on the props of convention and tradition. These qualities were demonstrated in the lives of the English Puritans. They believed in God as a fact, not merely as a figure of speech, and they directed all aspects of their lives by their understanding of the implications of this fact.[44] Puritanism meant 'the heartfelt conformity not to human rubrics but to the Maker's own Laws'. Puritans dedicated their lives to kindling recognition of God dwelling in their own hearts, and to encouraging others to do likewise, by throwing out the challenge: 'Will you serve Christ or Antichrist?'[45]

Although disputes on theological issues and on questions of church government were of great importance to Protestant reformers, Carlyle did not think that these debates were of intrinsic or lasting significance. Rather, they were passing expressions of an ongoing attempt by honest and earnest human beings to grasp at least some of the implications of the system of natural law that underlay the apparent chaos of the human and physical world. In its late sixteenth- and early seventeenth-century context, Puritanism was both a cause and a symptom of the inadequacy of traditional forms of authority, of humanity's need to find a more intellectually convincing and emotionally satisfying framework for its existence than that enshrined in decaying conceptions of medieval kingship and revivalist prelacy. This understanding of Puritanism underwrote Carlyle's account of the background to the English Civil War. It also provided a context for the emergence of Oliver Cromwell as the dominant figure of the period and as a source of instruction and inspiration for both Carlyle and his contemporaries.

In the course of his 'elucidations' to *Oliver Cromwell*, Carlyle made frequent references to what he took to be distinctive and admirable expressions of the Puritan worldview. For example, he noted, with warm approval, an episode on the eve of the Battle of Dunbar in September 1650, when a senior officer interrupted his round of inspection to listen to the preaching of an inspired private soldier. Military justice and high politics were touched with the same spirit. In March 1649, when three renegade officers were sentenced to death for rebellion, the sentences of two of the offenders were commuted in response to what was seen as a divine judgement. Those who were spared had drawn lots on which were written, '*Life given by God*'.[46] A year before this event, the participants in a conference held at Windsor to decide how to deal with the King sought God's guidance on this vexing question, agonising over the possibility that popular suspicion of the army was a sign of divine rebuke for the impurities of its members.[47] Carlyle noted that proceedings such as these made the English Revolution impenetrable to his contemporaries and posed a challenge to historians that only he had thus far been able to meet. 'These are the longest heads and the strongest hearts in England; and this is the thing they are doing; this is the way they, for their part, begin dispatch of business. The reader, if he is an earnest man, may look at it with very many thoughts, for which there is no word at present'.[48]

Carlyle's determination to eulogise a group of historical figures who many of his contemporaries regarded as fanatical revolutionaries demonstrated the radical thrust of his political and cultural criticism.[49] This stance was welcomed by many nonconformists, but it disappointed High Church traditionalists who were originally encouraged by Carlyle's profound distrust of materialism, and heartened by his apparently sympathetic treatment of medieval Christianity in *Past and Present*. As a contemporary reviewer noted, the elucidations and introduction to Carlyle's edition of Cromwell's letters and speeches were 'bitter as wormwood' to modern 'worshippers of kingcraft and priestcraft'.[50] But while Carlyle won applause for standing up for the Protestant cause, some of his liberal contemporaries found it hard to believe that he was seriously proposing a return to the doctrines adhered to by his seventeenth-century heroes.[51] These criticisms miss the point. While he admired the Puritans' attitude to outmoded forms, regarding it as sign that they had grasped an important truth about the character of forms, Carlyle gently criticised them for failing to realise that, except at moments of crisis, thought and action needed to be clothed in appropriate and viable forms. For this reason Puritanism was not a suitable model for contemporary society. It was also at times – in the late 1640s and early 1650s – absorbed with theological issues that were not of lasting significance and could thus be dismissed by the historian. There was, however, a core of Puritanism that Carlyle thought was highly significant for the moral and social wellbeing of his contemporaries and made it eminently worthy of the historian's attention. Puritanism provided an important model of generalised piety, of a concern with realities not chimeras. As such, it was universal, being 'among the great things of the past, which, seen or unseen, never fade away out of the present'.[52]

The diffusion of the Puritan spirit, and its embodiment in the commanding figure of Oliver Cromwell, made it possible for England to part company with the old world without fatally disrupting the fabric of social order. By contrast, the French Revolution destroyed all that was left of the old order, exposing the French people to the full blast of human fanaticism and irrationality.[53] Carlyle likened these forces to geothermal energy released by the earth's crust when it is fractured:

> your 'thin Earth rind' ... once *broken* ... the fountains of the great deep boil forth; fire fountains, enveloping, engulfing. Your 'Earth-rind' is shattered, swallowed up; instead of a green flowery world, there is waste wild-weltering chaos;–which has again, with tumult and struggle, to *make* itself into a world.[54]

The strident and discordant voices of the Parisian press and the National Assembly, the demands of the desperately hungry crowds that poured through the streets of Paris like a teeming cataract, were signs that revolutionary France plumbed a depth of chaos that was beyond the reach of humanity's comprehension, or its powers of description.

> With amazement, not with measurement, men look on the Immeasurable; not knowing its laws; *seeing*, with all different degrees of knowledge, what new phases, and results of events, its laws bring forth. France is a monstrous Galvanic Mass, wherein all sorts of far stranger than chemical galvanic or electric forces and substances are at work; electrifying one another, positive and negative; filling with electricity your Leyden-jars, – Twenty-five millions in number! As the jars get full, there will, from time to time, be on slight hint, an explosion.[55]

In common with his contemporaries, Carlyle was staggered by the cruelty and destructiveness that marked many revolutionary episodes. He insisted, however, that the bestiality displayed in acts such as the annihilation of royalists and clergy in the September Massacres of 1792, explosions of 'powder-mines of bottomless guilt and criminality', were not to be dismissed as inhuman. Rather, they were extreme manifestations of the destructive potentialities of beings that were equally capable of plunging to the depths of hell and soaring to the heights of heaven.[56] Much suffering was inflicted through agencies of insurrection and retribution unleashed by 'sanculottism', but, despite his intense dislike of democracy, Carlyle did not treat its role in the Revolution merely as a warning of the dangers posed by the masses.[57] Advancing an early formulation of a position that played a central role in his 'condition of England' writings, he treated sansculottism as an unconscious reflex of human nature against redundancy and injustice, not (as both Whig and Tory historians suggested) as a product of class interest in the material or political sense.[58] On the contrary, the really significant point about sansculottism was that it was devoid of any stable form. It posed a final, unanswerable challenge to all formulas that had prevailed in French society in the previous epoch, and provided a testing ground for a range of alternatives to them that were thrown up during the course of the Revolution. Seen from this perspective, the sansculottes could not, even in their most savage moments, be seen in a wholly negative light.

> Here … most unexpectedly, comes antique Fanaticism in new and newest vesture; miraculous, as all Fanaticism is … The world of formulas, the *formed* regulated world, which all habitable world is,–must needs hate such Fanaticism like death; and be at deadly variance with it. The world of formulas must conquer it; or failing that, must die execrating it, anathematizing it;–can nevertheless in nowise prevent its being and its having been.[59]

Consistent with this perspective, Carlyle traced the course of the Revolution in a series of increasingly deadly exchanges between redundant formulas and realities.

These exchanges, opening with the meeting of the States General in early May 1789, concluded with the insurrectionary challenge to the National Convention in early October 1795 that was put down by Napoleon Bonaparte's 'whiff of grapeshot'. Since these contests were usually precipitated by the sansculottes, this section of the population might be taken to represent an authentic and productive force of nature that confronted all the moribund formulas of the *ancien régime*, including the very idea of traditional kingship: 'When so much goes grinning and grimacing as a lifeless Formality, and under the stiff buckram no heart can be felt beating, here, once more, if nowhere else, is a Sincerity and Reality'.[60] In a critical passage, Carlyle used the confrontation between Louis XVI and the Parisian mob during the invasion of the Tuileries on 20 June 1792 to epitomise a lack of human connection between the King and his subjects that made reform and reconciliation impossible. While Carlyle's focus on this incident seemed to evoke Edmund Burke's response to an earlier popular intrusion into the private quarters of Marie-Antoinette at Versailles, it did so for very non-Burkean ends. This episode symbolised the unavoidable, indeed long overdue, end of traditional society not the wilful disruption of a sanctified and still viable social order:

> Thus has the Age of Chivalry gone, and that of Hunger come. Thus does all-needing Sansculottism look in the face of its *Roi*, Regulator, King and Able-Man; and find that *he* has nothing to give it. Thus do the two Parties, brought face to face after long centuries, stare stupidly at one another ... and depart, not knowing what to make of it. And yet, Incongruities having recognized themselves to be incongruities, something must be made of it. The Fates know what.[61]

Carlyle's understanding of the significance of the French Revolution had an important bearing on his attitude towards the eighteenth-century context of Frederick the Great. It also goes some way to accounting for his grim determination to carry the project to its conclusion. While he was far from being an admirer of the eighteenth century, and was far less enthusiastic about Frederick than he was about Cromwell or Abbot Samson, Carlyle's interest in his career was sustained by the idea that at least some aspects of the century on which he had left his mark were of enduring importance. Frederick's military skill made it possible for modern Prussia finally to realise an ideal of nationhood that had emerged during the previous two centuries. The impact of this achievement was blunted by the French Revolution, and only begun to seem really significant in the mid 1860s when Carlyle was completing work on his history. In the course of establishing and maintaining the boundaries of the Prussian state, Frederick played a key role in exposing the unequivocal redundancy of the Holy Roman Empire and of the dynastic politics that framed the worldview of the Habsburgs. Moreover, his military success against the French posed a stern challenge to their pretensions to European leadership, raised unanswerable questions about the moral and practical fitness of French elites, and placed strains on the state's financial resources that had fatal consequences for the *ancien régime*. Finally, and despite the general shortcomings of Britain's military and political leadership in the eighteenth century, victories over the French in India and North America in the Seven Years War marked an important stage in the consolidation of its imperial mission, showing that 'England', not France, would shoulder the brunt of responsibility for spreading the gospel of labour in the new epoch.

The idea of heroism – its character, manifestations, presence and absence – was a key theme in all of Carlyle's historical writings. He admired the early Norse kings because they were responsible for establishing the basis of a tradition of social and political order that was being threatened by the myopia and moral weakness of his contemporaries.[62] This tradition was not an abstract one. On the contrary, Carlyle took particular interest in what he saw as the beneficial influence of particular Scandinavian military and political figures on the emergence of England as a coherent moral and political community. The first two Olafs, Tryggveson and St Olaf, were the true heroes of the Norse sagas, playing a role in Carlyle's distillation of this passage of human history that was fulfilled in other times and places by Abbot Samson, Oliver Cromwell and Frederick the Great.

In *Past and Present* Carlyle drew directly on Jocelin's account of Abbot Samson to demonstrate the social and psychological contexts of heroism to his contemporaries.[63] Samson joined the monastic community after experiencing a vision of St Edmund, the martyr-king in whose honour the Abbey was founded. Jocelin emphasises that in so doing he became, quite literally, one of 'St Edmund's men', dedicated to praying for his soul, commemorating his good deeds, and maintaining the temporal privileges (or 'liberties') of his abbey.[64] This double attachment to St Edmund was significant because Carlyle cast the saint himself in a heroic mould, with his beatification confirming rather than creating this status. Edmund's reign was marked by a love of justice, and a practical regard for truth. Samson's devotion to the memory of the Saint – symbolised by his reverential concern for the sanctity of St Edmund's remains, and his equally strong determination to express his devotion by touching the inner wrappings of the Saint's shroud, showed that he possessed heroic potential himself.[65]

But while Carlyle emphasised and celebrated Samson's distinctive strengths and virtues, he also made it clear that in this, as in other cases of authentic hero-worship, heroism should be considered in relation to contemporaries' capacities to respond to it. Samson's fellow monks were inferior to him in all respects, and were thus rightfully subject to his care and control. At the same time as he made this point, however, Carlyle praised the other members of the community for playing their role in the symbiotic relationship that existed between genuine heroes and their followers. In the course of the election that followed the death of

Samson's predecessor, his fellow monks demonstrated their worth by discerning his superior qualities, electing him as the leader of their community, and then cooperating with him as fellow workers in what they saw as their God-ordained labours.

The fact that Samson and his colleagues were religious figures provided Carlyle with the opportunity to show his readers what faith really meant, and how it ought to be expressed in life. Carlyle's celebration of the values underlying medieval society was a standing rebuke to both the Enlightenment thinkers who had scornfully turned their backs on it, and to the dryasdust school whose works obscured rather than illuminated it.[66] The way he portrayed the relationship between life and faith among the community at Bury St Edmunds, however, also served to make an important critical point to his more overtly pious contemporaries. He thus lighted admiringly on the abbot's refreshing reticence on questions of 'personal religion', comparing the monks' serene, instinctive religiosity with the overheated self-conscious obsessions of some of his contemporaries.

> Religion is not a diseased self-introspection, an agonising inquiry: their duties are clear to them, the way of supreme good plain, indisputable, and they are travelling on it. Religion lies over them like an all-embracing heavenly canopy, like an atmosphere and life-element, which is not spoken of, which in all things is presupposed without speech. Is not serene and complete Religion the highest aspect of human nature; as serene Cant, or complete No-religion, is the lowest and miserablest?[67]

Carlyle's account of Samson's attitude towards religion echoed Jocelin's remarks on his abbot's lack of sympathy for non-active, non-social contemplative religiosity. This was shown, for example, in Samson's cool reception of accounts of monks who had withdrawn from the affairs of the world: 'when he chanced to hear of any church leader resigning his pastoral work to become a hermit, he would not utter one word of commendation'.[68]

The limitations of religious formalism were demonstrated in comparisons between Samson and his predecessor, Abbot Hugo. Although a pious man who had scrupulously maintained the 'Rule' of the Order within its cloisters, Hugo left the abbey heavily in debt, its properties in chronic disrepair, and the 'liberties of St Edmund' under threat from the townspeople and other clerical and secular figures.[69] By contrast, Samson focused his energies on material and political responsibilities, beginning with a concerted reform of the domestic economy of the abbey. Far from regarding this as demeaning or materialistic, Carlyle saw Samson as exemplifying the principle that an order based on justice and truth must seek to realise these values in the tasks closest to hand: 'New life enters everywhere, springs up beneficent, the Incubus of Debt once rolled away.'[70] Samson's devotion was intensely *practical*; that is, he believed he would best serve God by fulfilling his duty as head of the abbey and overlord of his barony.

The actions of Samson and other actors – monks, feudal lords, kings, burghers and bishops – in what now seemed a distant, dreamlike world, exemplified the distinction between 'vital' and 'dead' formulae. To the modern Protestant mind the past offered few more fantastic relics than the ideas and rituals that clothed humanity in medieval times. But while Carlyle's background and instincts might have predisposed him to dismiss this world out of hand, he saw it as highly significant both in terms of the history of the nation and in relation to his authorial mission. Samson's intellectual and moral disposition made these formulae vital and real. Consequently, an account of his achievements not only demonstrated the indispensability of formulae as such – 'Monarchism, Feudalism, with a real, King Plantagenet, with real Abbots Samson, and their other living realities, how blessed!' – but also the need for Carlyle's contemporaries to identify formulae that were linked to appropriate measures of human worth.[71] In the infrequently recorded words of Samson, and even more so in his actions, could be seen absolute government without self-interest, just administration without 'owl-eyed pedantry', and worship without self-consciousness of doubt.

Abbot Samson's heroic position in high medieval culture was mirrored by Oliver Cromwell's strongly directive, yet representative, role in relation to Puritanism. Having overcome earlier reservations about Cromwell and his contemporaries, Carlyle emerged from his labourers on the *Letters and Speeches* as the warmest of the Lord Protector's admirers. It is a mistake, however, to see the work solely in terms of Carlyle's tendency to worship 'great', and almost invariably powerful, rulers and warriors.[72] Rather, he uses the figure of Cromwell to explain the distinctive but universally valid features of Puritanism. Heroes like Cromwell focus the heroic qualities of their contemporaries and give effect to them. For these reasons, the recovery of their lives by the historian sheds light upon parts of the past, bringing them alive to readers remote in time and apparently removed from them in interests. Since Cromwell epitomised the spirit of Puritanism, a recovery of his achievements would illuminate a passage in history that was of critical importance for Carlyle and his contemporaries.

Cromwell's military and political achievements were consequences of his greatness of character, rather than being the real grounds for judgements concerning his heroic status. In support of this interpretation, Carlyle highlighted Cromwell's practice of attributing his worldly success to divine dispensation and his adherence to a religiously formulated version of the ethic of renunciation Carlyle championed.[73] Views of this kind were characteristic of Puritanism, but Cromwell was seen as the supreme representative and operative expression of these manifestations of the divine status of humanity. The Lord Protector understood the impulses underlying Puritanism and he possessed the strength of character to give effect to them. Like other heroic figures, he was also able to inspire followers, his dismissal of the Rump being greeted with widespread relief by the ordinary people.[74] This reaction was an inarticulate reflection of the body of beliefs that were common to Cromwell and to considerable sections of the population. In Carlyle's account, the significance of these beliefs is emphasised by his frequent references to the religious professions with which the Lord Protector prefaced his actions. These statements provided an 'indisputable certificate that man once had a soul, that man once walked with God, – his little life a sacred island girdled with eternities and Godhoods'.[75]

Carlyle thought that Cromwell's heroic capacity for decisive action was underwritten by his ability to plumb at least some of the depths of a universe that, because it was fundamentally inscrutable, could not be described in the smooth periods beloved of parliamentary orators. He insisted that the 'painful asseverations, appeals and assurances' of Cromwell's speeches were not (as his detractors claimed) the uneasy productions of a dissembling and hypocritical politician. They in fact represented a sincere man's attempts to express the deep truths and necessary requirements of the human condition, and to grapple with the problems of assuring an orderly transmission to a political structure that corresponded more nearly with the prevailing implications of God's laws. Though Cromwell seemed incapable of speaking effectively in parliament,

> he might *preach*, rhapsodic preaching; above all ... he might be great in extempore prayer. These are the free outpouring utterances of what is in the heart: method is not required in them; warmth, depth, sincerity are all that is required.

These 'outpourings' struck a chord of sympathy, respect, even awe, in those who shared the Puritan experience with Cromwell. They helped forge a sense of common elevated purpose that enabled Cromwell to lead a movement that brought the English back in touch with the realities of human existence and, when recovered by the historian, provided a heroic exemplar for the modern world.[76] The immediate result of Cromwell's heroism was that, for a short time at least, England reaped the benefits of a system of government based on an understanding of the underlying realities of human existence.

In his last major historical work, Carlyle made similar claims about Frederick the Great, but he was unable to present his life and times with anything remotely approaching the enthusiasm that distinguished his treatments of Abbot Samson or Oliver Cromwell. In the early stages of *Frederick the Great*, the putative subject is overshadowed by Friedrich Wilhelm, his father. This approach reflects the reality of Frederick's youth and early manhood, a period during which he suffered grievously at the hands of one whose despotic control of his state appeared benign when compared with the unrelenting and violent tyranny he exercised over his family. Carlyle faithfully recorded the alcohol-fuelled indignities heaped on the young Crown Prince, detailing the physical violence to which he was subjected, his virtual banishment, his attempt to abscond, and the savage penalties inflicted on his accomplices. At the same time, however, he was uncharacteristically reluctant to pass judgement on Friedrich Wilhelm's absurdities and vices, and praised him lavishly for his programmes of internal reform.[77] These aspects of Carlyle's book, which had the effect of making Friedrich Wilhelm the *de facto* hero of the first two volumes of the work, raised questions about his judgement and revived concerns that heroism was largely a matter of will and determination.[78]

Even when Frederick took centre stage, Carlyle's account of his character and achievements lacked the depth, colour and sense of conviction which distinguished his portraits of Samson and Cromwell. He also failed to penetrate the barrier that Frederick had erected to shield himself from his father, and which continued to obscure his personality long after that monstrous shadow had been lifted from his life.[79] Carlyle acknowledged these difficulties, but he nevertheless insisted that he had discerned enough of Frederick's character to convince himself of his marked superiority over his far from heroic contemporaries.

As with Carlyle's other heroic exemplars, the key to this status lay in the interplay between character and engagement with the external world. He thus claimed that once he had passed beyond the reach of parental persecution, Frederick was free of the tendency for self-deception and hypocrisy that was second nature to most of the leading diplomats, sovereigns and statesmen with whom he had to deal. By the lamentable standards of the time, he was honest and straightforward, exhibiting an aversion to duplicity that made him a true ally to those to whom he had given his word.[80] Moreover, Frederick, who was not encumbered by a highly developed self-consciousness or by unhealthy tendencies to introspection, kept his sights firmly set on the realities of his situation, demonstrating that his mind had a strongly practical bent.[81]

Although Carlyle applauded Frederick's intuitive grasp of realities, and discerned a bedrock of true religious feeling beneath layers of scepticism, he was unable to endow these attributes with the cosmic significance that infused the unconscious insights that marked the careers of a Cromwell or a Samson. The 'realities' that confronted Frederick were challenging but mundane. They included the need to come to terms with unreasonable and barbarously pursued crochets of his father, and the economic and military difficulties resulting from his determination to bring the process of state-building to a successful conclusion. In pursuing this objective, Frederick demonstrated great military and strategic skill, admirable determination, and a remarkable capacity to endure in the face of what ordinary men would regard as impossible reverses. These attributes came to the fore in the winter and spring of 1744–45 when the tide of the Second Silesian War seemed to have turned irrevocably against him.[82] They were tested even more severely in the darkest days of the Seven Years War. In the latter case, Carlyle was particularly struck by the fact that Frederick's determination was a deep-seated character trait, not merely a reflection of the passing state of his spirits. His treatment of this theme conveyed echoes of his own experience as an author grappling with a vast, uncongenial task. Frederick's life, like that of his biographer, was 'drenched in misery; but used to his black element, unaffectedly defiant of it, or not at pains to defy it; occupied only to do his very utmost in it, with or without success, till the end come'.[83]

Since Frederick's military achievements had been overshadowed to some degree by Napoleon's, Carlyle was at pains to demonstrate the superiority of his hero's generalship. Although the scale of Napoleon's campaigns dwarfed anything that went before, the balance of forces in Frederick's battles was proportionate to that faced by Napoleon. With the exception of the disastrous Russian campaign, Frederick contended with conditions that were at least as taxing as those faced by Napoleon. Moreover, for most of his career, the French Emperor had large parts of Europe under his control and was able to draw on its resources, while the King of Prussia, a largely isolated figure ruling a relatively small and economically underdeveloped state, was confronted by coalitions embracing most of the significant continental powers. Finally, the superiority of Frederick's achievement was underlined by the economical way in which his battles were fought. In contrast to Napoleon's notorious profligacy with the lives of his troops, Frederick's tactical skill meant that he was able to secure resounding victories while limiting his casualties to a level that could be sustained by a state with a very restricted population. Carlyle acknowledged that on a few occasions (at Olmütz in April 1758, and at Hochkirch in October of the same year) he made costly mistakes.[84] These setbacks were, however, rare exceptions in a record marked by careful preparation, fine judgement, and an admirable capacity for decisive action.

Frederick's military achievements owed much to the way he fostered and developed Friedrich William's legacy. He abandoned the bizarre martinet features of his father's military administration – disbanding, for example, the much-prized 'Potsdam Regiment' of giant guardsmen – but retained its rational aspects, exercising close personal insight over the details of military policy and practice. Attention to detail was also a hallmark of Frederick's domestic governance. Friedrich William had embarked on a series of far reaching administrative, fiscal and economic reforms. In so far as the exigencies of war allowed, these were extended by his son. Frederick the Great thus encouraged efforts to develop the overseas commerce of his subjects, using his political influence to protect them against the highhanded interference of the British and Dutch. He also embarked upon an ambitious building programme in Berlin, brought rural wastelands under cultivation, and promoted the spread of new agricultural techniques that had been developed by English landowners.[85]

When compared with the lengthy and highly detailed accounts of Frederick's military triumphs, Carlyle's treatment of his domestic achievements are slight and cursory. It is quite clear, however, that he relished the fact that these initiatives demonstrated a complete indifference to ideas associated with *laissez-faire*, and scant regard for the sanctity of private property rights. He thus noted with approval that the development of Berlin was undertaken partly at Frederick's expense, and partly at that of the richer inhabitants of the city who were ordered to rebuild their houses in line with his instructions.[86] Frederick's attempts to reform education, public health and the law demonstrated his commitment to a directive, paternalistic and authoritarian conception of personal government that was highly congenial to Carlyle. For example, he welcomed Frederick's approach to law reform on the grounds that it recognised that justice was the basis of positive law not necessarily a product of it.[87] He also applauded Frederick's contempt for the legal profession and his hostility to its obsession with procedures. In this case, as in the related critique of the 'red tape' that tied the hands of British reformers, the antidote was subjection to the firm direction of a benevolent and enlightened political superior.

Carlyle insisted that Frederick's success as a military leader, like that of Cromwell, needed to be considered in relation to a type of character whose distinctive virtues were demonstrated in a range of contexts of political and social leadership. While Frederick's contemporaries at home and abroad were astounded by his military prowess, his standing among his own subjects also reflected their appreciation of his domestic achievements. In Frederick's case, as in that of Carlyle's other heroes, recognition was a significant sign of heroic status and was a necessary condition for effective action. Carlyle made this point clear in a comparison between Frederick and one of his reformist contemporaries in Austria. Austrian government had become so hopelessly conservative and inflexible that, when the Emperor Joseph attempted to imitate Frederick's programme of reform, his efforts were negated by the deadweight of elite hostility from within Austria. These responses confirmed what had already become clearly apparent during the course of Frederick's diplomatic and military campaigns against Austria and its allies. This once mighty power had fallen into a state of blind conservatism amounting, Carlyle thought, to extreme moral cowardice indicative of the fatally moribund condition of the Habsburg dynasty.[88]

Although Frederick (as his patronage of Voltaire made clear) never completely distanced himself from the characteristic delusions of the age, his flaws paled into insignificance when compared with those of his contemporaries, the vast majority of whom are the subjects of a stream of Carlylean ridicule and wry abuse. The Habsburgs, the Electors of the Holy Roman Emperors, and French diplomatic, military and political figures bore the brunt of Carlyle's dismissive ire. He also directed it at George II, his son the Duke of Cumberland, and Britain's ambassadors and statesmen. The personal failings of these individuals quickly made themselves felt. From the conclusion of the War of Spanish succession in 1715, Britain's reliance on subsidies as a major instrument of diplomatic and military policy reflected a mistaken belief that the long purse of a successful commercial society provided an adequate substitute for courageous and well-informed leadership. Carlyle thought that British economic power was only put to appropriate use when William Pitt the Elder made it a handmaiden of effective statesmanship, combining generous subsidies to Frederick with a vigorous military and naval policy.[89]

Admiration for Pitt was heightened by Carlyle's perception that his role in the Seven Years War was critical to the emergence of Britain as an imperial power. Since Cromwell's death, Britain's elite had become divorced from the substantive values associated with Puritanism, preferring those that made Sir Robert Walpole a representative figure of the age. Walpole's exploitation of the materialism of the upper classes so as to secure control of parliament and court, reinforced ideas that debased the moral understanding of the community and destroyed the vestiges of the Puritan spirit that had underwritten Cromwell's military and political achievements.[90] The fact that Pitt at times stood aloof from political intrigues and was determined to take office only on his own terms, suggested to Carlyle that he possessed the character and ability to rise above the morally and practically dehabilitating constraints of the emerging system of parliamentary supremacy.

While Pitt's support for Frederick contributed significantly to the successful completion of his state-building programme, his leadership was also critical in settling the question whether European colonial expansion would bear the stamp of France or Britain. Pitt's foresight in appointing General Wolfe as commander of the British forces in North America paved the way for the critical victory over Montcalm outside Quebec in 1759. This victory put an end to French ambitions in North America and ensured that 'England's mission' would become global, a critical outcome in Carlyle's scheme of things because it meant that imperialism would henceforth be a servant of the gospel of labour, fostering order, development and productive settlement, rather than being attached to a state that was being sacrificed to the morally and practically corrosive impact of a faltering, outmoded, system of absolutism.[91] It also meant that European expansion would not be compromised by reliance on a country whose condition of moral bankruptcy was so advanced that its economic, political and social structure was showing signs of impending collapse.

Carlyle's treatment of the heroic in history was complemented by an array of counter-examples highlighting the dangers posed by prolonged failures to provide social and political leadership. In the *Early Kings of Norway*, for example, Ethelred the Unready's futile attempts to buy off marauding Viking bands foreshadowed the combination of great material wealth and spiritual bankruptcy which Carlyle took to be a distinctive mark of the modern culture.[92] In *Past and*

Present, Abbot Samson's ethic of leadership and its impact on the spiritual and moral condition of his domain were repeatedly contrasted with the dire and potentially fatal condition of contemporary England.

It was typical of the strongly corrective cast of Carlyle's writings, however, that his perspective on the medieval world was radically at variance with that of his contemporaries. By extolling the virtues of medieval Christianity he seemed to be sharing a path with Tractarians, Anglo-Catholics, Puseyites and Young Englanders. Carlyle, however, openly and sharply dissented from what he took to be dilettante history called up in the service of hopeless and delusory nostalgia, dismissing it as a feeble attempt to salvage 'a ruined world by noisy theoretic demonstrations and laudations of *the* Church, instead of some unnoisy, unconscious, but *practical*, total, heart-and-soul demonstration of *a* Church'.[93] By contrast, and despite his deeply ingrained suspicion of Roman Catholicism, *Past and Present* extolled the medieval manifestations of the living spirit of the Catholic faith. Carlyle made it quite clear, however, that this spirit was absent from modern religious practice.

A telling illustration of this point emerged from Carlyle's reflections on the history of the Netherlands during the course of a visit he made there while working on *Past and Present*. Although he was greatly impressed by the inspirational potential of the workmanship apparent in medieval churches in Ghent, this served only to heighten the contrast between an appropriately valued relic of the past and the meaningless sacramental practices of modern Catholicism. 'Things are long-lived, and God above appoints their term; yet when the brains of a thing have been out for three centuries and odd, one does wish that it would be kind enough to die!'[94]

England dispensed with many of the trappings of Catholicism during the course of the sixteenth century, but it had not squarely faced the challenge of completing the Reformation until the mid seventeenth century. In *Oliver Cromwell* and in related work on the history of England in the seventeenth century, Carlyle traced the Civil War to the Stuarts' personal failings and to their incapacity to grasp the significance of Puritanism for ideas of moral, social and political order. James I and Charles I were unable see what Puritanism meant, and were thus incapable of responding appropriately to it. By treating Puritan moves for reformation as challenges to their authority, a thinly concealed rebellion, they alienated the leading members of this movement from the ecclesiastical, legal and political fabric of English society, thereby producing as an *effect* what they took to be a *cause*. When the Puritans questioned the forms of government in church and state by reference to the 'realities' that lay behind all visible forms, James and his son clung stubbornly to the forms themselves. As a result, the Puritans were forced to go beyond Martin Luther's rejection of the 'hollow show of things' to challenge what had become a 'false sovereignty', false because claims to political supremacy were not based on the requirements of divine law.[95] By the end of Charles's third parliament in 1629, the truth of the situation had become clear. While this Puritan-dominated parliament epitomised a nation in search of a leader, Charles showed that he was 'King and Governor, not of them, but of a theoretic England, lying in cloudland, in the brain of his Majesty and some particular men'.[96]

Cromwell emerged from the civil wars as the natural political leader of his country because only he was able to deal effectively with chaos-threatening challenges posed by those who sought to replace bankrupt monarchy with equally dangerous chimeras of parliamentary and republican government. During the 1630s and 1640s, the Long Parliament had given practical effect to the realities of Puritanism and been the focal point of its moral and spiritual energy. When this energy was translated into armed force, it was under the firm control of rank and intellect and was instrumental in carrying through a process of radical change without releasing the forces of chaos on the community.[97] The parliaments of James and Charles symbolised the nation's demand for rule that conformed to the will of God, and when armed conflict broke out the Long Parliament acquired 'a kind of sacredness'.[98] But while Carlyle praised the Long Parliament up to this point, he argued that its role had been misunderstood both by contemporaries and by modern apologists. The keys to this misunderstanding were the faith placed in constitutionalism as the palliative for all weaknesses of social and political order, and the failure to see the need for heroic political leadership. Carlyle did not discount the role that institutions might play in supporting a morally viable society but he strenuously resisted proposals that placed exclusive reliance on them.

As Carlyle's work on the English Revolution progressed, Cromwell came to play an increasingly prominent role in its military and political aspects, over-shadowing, and then eclipsing, leading figures in parliament, particularly the English Republicans, or the 'Commonwealthsmen'. Having become ensnared in the vacuous forms of constitutionalism, the rejectors of empty forms in religion and politics had ironically lost their grip on reality. As attempts to 'settle' the nation dragged on into the 1650s, the position of the Commonwealthsmen in the 'Rump Parliament' became less and less tenable. They became hidebound and, Carlyle thought, probably corrupt as well. These 'hacks in office; a savour of Godliness still on their lips, but seemingly not much deeper with some of them', constituted an 'unreal' parliament in much the same way as the Stuarts were 'unreal' kings. They formed an 'Old Misrepresentative' bogged down by constitutional irrelevancies and lacking the spark of godliness that lay at the heart of the Puritan cause. By 1653 the 'Fag-end of a Parliament ... has failed altogether to realise the high dream of those old Puritan hearts!'[99] This way of looking at the English Republic resulted from Carlyle's judgement on the relative merits of the various actors at the centre of politics, one that provided a way of promoting heroism at the expense of parliamentary government.

Throughout his work, Carlyle emphasised Cromwell's discernment, fortitude and clemency, as well as his ability to use coercion economically and effectively. This combination of capacities was a gift implanted in a few individuals, awaiting unusual political and social developments to call it into play.[100] Non-heroic individuals exhibited contrary characteristics – formalism, a penchant for empty verbalising, and for the creation of intellectual systems that were unintelligible to both their contemporaries and to later generations – that Carlyle thought were typical of the constitutional mind.

These weaknesses were prominent in Carlyle's unflattering portrait of Sir Henry Vane the Younger, a figure who had been painted in heroic colours in William Godwin's *History* and in John Forster's *Statesmen of the Commonwealth of England*.[101] Carlyle gleefully recorded Cromwell's personal abuse of Vane on the occasion of the dismissal of the Rump Parliament, and, while grudgingly acknowledging Vane's intellectual and moral capacities, he emphasised that these did not measure up to the heroic dimension of Cromwell's mind and spirit. 'Grant all manner of purity and elevation; subtle high discourse; much intellectual and practical dexterity: there is an amiable, devoutly zealous, very pretty man;–but not a royal man; alas no! On the whole, rather a thin man' whose 'subtle intellect' has 'wholly vanished … and [is] without meaning to any mortal'.[102] In other words, Vane was part of the dead past, not part of the living and real past in which Cromwell loomed so large. The latter's heroism made him important in the nineteenth century, while Vane's lack of it meant that he was not.

Because Carlyle believed that the realities of the past lived on in the present, his resurrection of Cromwell as a central figure of 'living' history and his incarceration of the Commonwealthsmen among the dead was of more than historiographical significance. Carlyle's rejection of Whig historiography was related closely to his views on the inherent weakness of constitutionalism as an ideology, and parliamentarianism as a system of government. These ideas, already canvassed in Carlyle's earlier works, became, as we have seen, a key theme in the 'Latter-Day Pamphlets'. A disinclination to endorse them did not, however, negate the impact of Carlyle's resuscitation of the Lord Protector. On the contrary, many of those who praised aspects of Carlyle's work commented unfavourably on his indifference to Cromwell's disregard for political liberty and the forms of constitutional government. These responses indicated the differences that separated Carlyle's interpretation from contemporary liberal celebrations of what were seen as the Puritan antecedents of Britain's golden age.[103] For Carlyle, the prevailing condition of British society was a cause for alarm rather than celebration, and its roots lay in the demoralising aftermath of the Cromwellian experiment. Since the 1660s the country had moved further and further away from the spirit of Puritanism with which this experiment was bound up. As time wore on, the already outmoded forms of traditional, monarchical, aristocratic and clerical government that were blindly championed by Charles I and sustained by his successors became precarious adjuncts of a culture dominated by material values. By the middle of the nineteenth century, England was smothered in unrealities and 'phantasms' that were more absorbing and harmful than those that precipitated the conflict between crown and parliament in the first half of the seventeenth century because they reflected a general malaise.

Carlyle's views on Cromwell's reaction to elite failure in England and his attack on delusive solutions to the problems resulting from it were reflected in his accounts of Cromwell's armed incursions into Ireland and Scotland. In seeking to justify Cromwell's conduct in two of the most controversial passages in his career, Carlyle's praise of his hero moved into a new, more exalted register. For example, he claimed that the conditions prevailing in Ireland in the 1640s prevented Cromwell giving effect to the just claims for toleration made by Irish Catholics. He was at pains to show that Cromwell's military conduct was consistent with contemporary views of the rules of war. He also placed great stress on the dire condition of Ireland on the eve of Cromwell's arrival: 'There has been no scene under the sun like Ireland for these eight years. Murder, pillage, conflagration, excommunication; wide-flowing blood, and bluster high as heaven and St Peter'. From this perspective, the atrocities commonly attributed to Cromwell were, in fact, unexceptionable severities that were justified by their intention of bringing a swift conclusion to the anarchy that bedevilled the country in the 1640s and made productive social and economic life impossible.[104] While Carlyle attributed these disasters wholly to the Irish, ignoring the role of maundering English settlers in bringing the country to the brink of desperate anarchy, he laid the blame on clerical and secular elites rather than on the common people.[105]

Elite failures also made it necessary for Cromwell to intervene directly in Scottish affairs on his return from Ireland in 1650. Distancing himself from his wayward compatriots by adopting the voice of the English 'we', Carlyle castigated the leaders of the Presbyterian Assembly and their lay supporters. He credited Cromwell with having saved the Puritan cause in both England and Scotland, thereby returning the boon that John Knox and his followers had conferred on their English neighbours a century before.[106] In many respects, Carlyle's treatment of Scotland was a more fiercely engaged version of his account of Cromwell in Ireland. When dealing with this part of Cromwell's career, his admiration became increasingly free of significant reservations or qualifications. The crucial difference, however, is that while Carlyle assumed that Scotland had the internal resources to take advantage of Cromwell's initiatives, Ireland did not. Irish salvation depended upon the plantation of new elites. This process made some headway in the 1650s, but was effectively abandoned thereafter. Bereft of effective leadership, beset by rapacious landowners, the Irish became the victims of priesthood, unscrupulous faction leaders and the accumulative effect of their own demoralisation.

At various times, Carlyle's commentary on the life and times of Oliver Cromwell drew parallels between the English and French Revolutions, presenting the Diggers and Levellers as prototypical 'sansculottes', and identifying important similarities between the constitution framing of the early 1790s and that of the early 1650s. These parallels served to show how Cromwell's handling of the transformation that took place in the 1640s and 1650s spared England the agonies that the French inflicted on each other in the 1790s. When the French belatedly came to face the fact that the *ancien régime* had become a tissue of unrealities, they did so without the aid of a Cromwell, or the moral fortification of the Puritan spirit.[107]

Although Carlyle's narrative of the 1790s is punctuated by expressions of sympathy for the personal sufferings of the French royal family, his condemnation of the *ancien régime's* corruption, redundancy and stupidity was emphatic and unqualified. By taking this stance, Carlyle set his face against a tradition of apologetics that saw the revolution as an act of pointless sabotage against a regime that showed every sign of possessing both the capacity and the will to fit itself for the modern world. Edmund Burke advanced this line in the closing sections of *Reflections on the Revolution in France*.[108] Carlyle's treatment made it clear that he thought that the hopes of Burke and his disciples were dangerous delusions. He described Louis XV as a 'very Solecism incarnate', an apparently mighty monarch presiding over a regime whose splendid forms could not conceal its lack of substance from its subjects or from itself: 'Belief and loyalty have passed away, and only the cant and false echo of them remains; and all Solemnity has become Pageantry; and the Creed of persons in authority has become one of two things: an Imbecility or a Machiavellism'.[109] With shepherds like these, the flock for which they were responsible was often fleeced but never tended. Even under the more benignly intentioned Louis XVI, concern for the well being of the ordinary people – the rationale of political authority, and of social and economic privilege – was never translated into effective action. Neither the King nor his ministers realised that France was in need of the most radical reform:

> all is wrong, and gone out of joint; the inward spiritual and the outward economical; head or heart, there is no soundness in it … If we pierce through the rosepink vapour of Sentimentalism, Philanthropy, and the Feast of Morals, there lies behind it one of the sorriest spectacles. You might ask, What bonds that ever held a human society happily together, or held it together at all, are in force here? It is an unbelieving people; which has suppositions, hypothesis, and froth-systems of victorious analysis; and for *belief* this mainly, that Pleasure is pleasant. Hunger they have for sweet things; and the law of Hunger; but what other law? Within them, or over them, properly none.[110]

Long a 'despotism tempered by epigram', the government of France was increasingly becoming nothing but epigrams. The honest efforts of reforming statesmen such as Necker and Turgot were unavailing. The real condition of France – one that made revolution unavoidable – was demonstrated by the frenzied outbursts of acclaim that greeted Voltaire on his return to Paris in February 1778 shortly before his death: 'The purport of this man's existence has been to wither up and annihilate all whereupon Majesty and Worship for the present rests'.[111]

The woeful record of royalty, aristocracy and clergy over the course of the eighteenth century meant that, when representatives of the old order fell victim to the ferocious, vengeful appetite of the revolutionaries, attempts to portray them as martyrs failed to carry conviction, and sometimes seemed ridiculous. For example, the provocative displays of dissent in April 1791 by priests who had been expelled from their churches and replaced by elected 'constitutional' clergy, were met not by massacres but by humiliating beatings administered by 'patriot women'. This episode symbolised 'martyrdom without sincerity, with only cant and contumacy'. A few months later, the King allowed himself to be part of the 'sorrowful farce' of the *grande acceptance* of a constitution that stripped him of all real power.[112]

Such humiliating demonstrations of the political impotence of French monarchy and the eclipse of the church to which it was wedded, merely confirmed the impact of the progressive erosion of the socio-cultural underpinnings of France over the previous century or more. This process, a consequence of the moral and spiritual bankruptcy of the social and intellectual elite, was mirrored in the external world by the collapse of royal finances and by a steadily building crisis of confidence in official circles. Belated attempts at financial reform had ramifications for the relationship between the crown and the aristocracy, clergy and third estate that could be addressed only in a meeting of the long uncalled States General. When this body met, the Third Estate pursued a series of constitutional deliberations against a rising tide of popular demonstration and outbreaks of insurrection. As a result, the *grande acceptance* was followed not by a move towards a new order appropriate to the modern world but by a descent into the horror of the Terror.

The immediate precipitating causes of the Terror were the failure of the upper classes to provide the leadership and vision necessary to chart the course to the 'new era' and their wilful preference for falsehood. Seen from this perspective, the Revolution was a standing reminder to the rest of Europe. In the *French Revolution* this warning was framed in terms of a classical motif of retributive 'Furies' that was prominent in Carlyle's later social and political criticism. This motif conferred some meaning on what might otherwise seem senseless outbursts of destruction, and, in so doing, it placed pressure on those who were still deaf to Carlyle's appeals.[113] Carlyle's insistence that only a thin film of civilisation lay between order, beneficial sociability and the fearful chaos of the Terror was reflected in his lurid references to the Revolution's cannibalistic momentum (like Saturn, the Revolution 'devoured its own children'), and more strikingly still, by recalling that at one stage victims' skins were tanned for use in the manufacture of garments. The significance of this repellent trade was heightened by the role that clothes played in Carlyle's presentation of his conception of human life. As he had already explained in *Sartor Resartus*, clothes were the 'formal statement of humanity'.[114]

Although the formulae of the *ancien régime* succumbed quickly to the unforgiving test of reality, other aspects of the revolutionary process were more protracted and uncertain. Its early years were marked by a series of attempts to recreate the French state, beginning with the appointment of the 'National' (subsequently named the 'Constituent') Assembly in August 1789. This body originally represented the reality of the Revolution in the sense that the proclamations and instructions issued by it in the summer of 1789 consigned feudalism to well-merited oblivion. Carlyle applauded the courage and decisive earnestness demonstrated by the Assembly at this stage, but his attitude towards it hardened when it turned its attention to forging a constitution to replace the political and legal forms that it had helped to destroy. The task was a hopeless one because the onset of the Revolution meant that the shared convictions necessary to underwrite constitutional forms, systems of settled law, and habits of beneficial social interaction no longer existed. These prerequisites of social order would need to be re-established before constitution-making could become anything more than a senseless manipulation of empty terms and the body attempting it a 'fatuity and chimera'.[115] The unreality of these proceedings was epitomised in the career of the 'party of the Gironde', a group of constitutionally-minded deputies from the Bordeaux region led by J. P. Brissot. Carlyle described their labours in the first Legislative Assembly in October 1791 as 'shaping only in quicksand', not in marble.[116] By the following year, the real moving force in France was the Jacobin Society. The confrontation between this body and the Girondins came to a head in June 1793, exposing the unreality of the latter's constitution-mongering, displacing the illusion of a middle class 'republic of the virtues' with a 'republic of the strengths' that was committed to liberty, equality and fraternity, and indifferent to property, respectability and moderation.[117]

This interpretation of Girondism was far more radical and dismissive than that of Carlyle's Whig contemporaries. They saw the failure of Brissot and his colleagues as a confirmation of their view that ideas of ancient civic virtue were not viable in modern societies.[118] Carlyle, however, regarded the philosophical radicals and Whigs as the heirs of both the Girondins, and of the constitutional mongering factions of seventeenth-century Puritanism that had been pushed aside by Oliver Cromwell. Like their English predecessors, the

Party of the Gironde was a standing reminder of the lack of heroism inherent in constitutional perspectives on government. It was not that Carlyle thought that members of this party were cowardly, although he noted that the attempts at a *coup* after it left Paris in the summer of 1795 were singularly ineffective. Rather, the Girondins' unshakeable attachment to untrue ideas was taken to mean that they were incapable of heroism and were easy prey for those who embodied, even in passing, some aspects of the realities of a revolutionary situation.

Hero-worship was, in any case, deeply problematic in the French Revolution, and its shortcomings explain why the revolutionary experience remained not just as an unfinished epoch in the history of modern France, but one that had left no figure like Oliver Cromwell to provide inspiration for the future.[119] Carlyle's portrait of Mirabeau has some strong positive elements – admirable coolness in the face of danger, a determination to dispense with redundant formulae, a capacity to mould and where necessary resist the forces of popular insurrection, and general insight and strength of character – but these never amount to anything like an endorsement of heroic status. The verdict on Danton is even more qualified, leaving an overwhelming impression of the destructive features of the revolutionary experience, and of a range of actors who react to the redundancy of formulae rather than having anything to offer in their place. Carlyle acknowledged Robespierre's incorruptibility and earnestness, but he made it clear that the latter was vitiated by being called into the service of destructive fanaticism and the absurd parody of redundant forms represented by the 'cult of reason'.

The establishment of a system of stable and beneficial rule in late twelfth-century Norway by Sverrir, the leader of what Carlyle described as 'a kind of Norse *Jacquerie*: desperate rising of thralls and indigent people, driven mad by their unendurable sufferings and famishings', and Cromwell's achievement in channelling and controlling the fervour of radical Protestantism, showed that chaos may be the harbinger of beneficial order.[120] In the absence of effective leadership, however, the blind energy of the people of France was part of the problem rather than its solution. It fuelled the destructive process and put the spurious alternatives of Girondism and the republican religion of reason to the test; it could not offer a viable way forward. In the last act of Carlyle's drama, the 'whiff of grapeshot' that Napoleon administered to the concerted forces of revivalist royalism and habitual popular insurrection heralded a regime capable of at least bringing the destructive passages of the revolution to a close. In *On Heroes*, however, Carlyle made it clear that Napoleon was not a truly heroic figure. His regime could provide only palliative relief rather than salvation for the French people. Having 'tamed' the French Revolution so that its benefits might be captured by posterity, he lost touch with reality and pursued the very 'semblances' that the Revolution had sought to banish. By assuming the imperial title, allying himself by marriage with the Habsburgs, and coming to an accommodation with the Pope, Napoleon sacrificed truth to a series of self-serving delusions:

> What a paltry patchwork of theatrical paper-mantles, tinsel and mummery, had this man wrapt his own great reality in, thinking to make it more real thereby! ... Like a man that should build upon cloud; his house and he fall down in confused wreck, and depart out of this world.[121]

If heroism was problematic in the context of the French Revolution, it was hardly less so in the century that preceded it. As already noted, Carlyle's treatment of Frederick displayed marked signs of ambivalence about his heroism. These reservations notwithstanding, and to the dismay of some of his readers, he clung tenaciously to his early, largely intuitive, judgment that Frederick was worthy of inclusion in the pantheon of heroic statesmen and soldiers. Even while insisting on Frederick's heroism, however, Carlyle was prepared to allow that both his character and the quality of his achievements were necessarily affected by the moral and spiritual tone of his environment. From this perspective, a study of Frederick's life was salutary because, by bringing home to Carlyle's readers the idea that debased cultures could at best hope for flawed heroes, it affirmed the need for a general reformation of mind, morals and spirit.

Carlyle's historical writings provided large, colourful and inspiring canvasses on which to demonstrate the truth of the diagnoses and prescriptions that he offered his contemporaries in his other writings. The role that these writings played was widely recognised by his readers. They not only debated the literary and historical merits of the works discussed here, but also the plausibility and desirability of the lessons presented in them. There was widespread comment on the ambiguities of Carlyle's treatment of Frederick the Great and scepticism at the claims made on his behalf.[122] But while some reservations were expressed about Cromwell, both he, and Abbot Samson, was received with far more enthusiasm by contemporary critics. This response reflected an appreciation of the merits of these characters but Carlyle's readers also paid tribute to the role that he had played in bringing their virtues alive. As a correspondent put it, some of Carlyle's heroes were 'destined to effect more real good in your pages and through your revivification than when alive in the body.' Carlyle's historical writing 'perpetuates and widens the noblest efforts and achievements of the great men' he had 'given to the world again.'[123]

The idea of elite responsibility was related closely to heroism and played significant celebratory and salutary roles throughout Carlyle's historical writings. Both *The French Revolution* and *Oliver Cromwell* exemplified the ethos of radical reform that underpinned his social and political criticism. At times this prompted censure; at others it was applauded. Thus while James Mozely, an Oxford don associated with the Oxford Movement, disliked the radical tone of Carlyle's work on the French Revolution and the English Civil War, other contemporaries regarded it in a far more positive light.[124] In some cases, as was noted above, this response reflected the concerns of those who identified with modern nonconformity. In others, however, Carlyle's treatment of both Carlyle and the Puritans was seen as part of a far broader, modern and essentially non-sectarian perspective. Thus in reviewing *Oliver Cromwell* John Taylor stressed the universal relevance of Carlyle's (and Cromwell's) commitment to justice, right and truth, claiming that it was in 'harmony with the great social movement that is gathering its energies for decisive action against whatever is at war with the undeniable claim of humanity, all over the world'.[125]

The French Revolution and *Past and Present* were identified particularly closely with Carlyle's views on the failings of modern elites and with his related attempt to promote an active role for government as a way of contending with the challenges facing modern society. While these views accorded with those of a range of contemporary critics and were welcomed by many of Carlyle's readers, they began to seem problematic in some quarters when his promotion of them was accompanied by a barrage of hostile remarks on the constitutional nostrums that Carlyle thought dominated the political thinking of many of his contemporaries and their early modern predecessors.[126] *Frederick the Great* extended significantly the scope for this line of criticism. Despite the large sale of the work, it was not a critical success. The book disappointed some of those who had admired aspects of Carlyle's earlier works, with one such critic commenting that it was not possible to discern in the account of Frederick's life and times any sign of the fruits of what he took to be Carlyle's most admirable literary gift: 'a genuine insight into what is really noble in human action, and exalted in human character'. This writer opined that for those who had always objected to Carlyle's political thinking, *Frederick the Great* provided an almost limitless supply of hostages to fortune: 'he has in this work assaulted morality, the recognised principles of Government, and the British Constitution'.[127] While Carlyle would have been unmoved by this particular line of criticism, he nevertheless shared with many of his critics the view that *Frederick the Great* marked the effective conclusion of his mission.

8

The Sage of Chelsea

Despite more than half a century of indifferent health, Carlyle outlived most of his long-term friends and close family members. John Forster, Charles Dickens and J. S. Mill predeceased him, as did Alick and Jack Carlyle. News of Alick's death in Canada reached Cheyne Row in April 1876. Jack died in 1879, admirably stoic in the face of cancer, taking care not to alarm his ailing elder brother. While Carlyle mournfully observed the impending mortality of family members and friends, others watched over him. Edward Fitzgerald, whose relationship with Carlyle went back more than thirty years, did not visit, or write directly to Carlyle for fear of intruding on him, but he wrote to his niece, Mary Aitken, to enquire after her uncle's health. Younger friends, including Leslie Stephen, John Tyndall, Moncure Conway and W. H. Lecky, visited him. Froude, and William Allingham and his wife Helen, were constant companions.

From 1872 Carlyle's household was managed by Mary Aitken, who was later joined by her husband Alexander Carlyle. For some time Mary continued the close relationship with the second Lady Ashburton that Jane had established. In 1872, however, Carlyle's peace of mind was disturbed by a falling out between the two women that seems to have sprung from Mary's perception that Lady Ashburton had impugned her disinterestedness.[1] Carlyle did not take this view. He was very fond of his niece and her husband, and gently pleased when their son was born. Mary was at his side when her uncle died in the drawing room of his Chelsea home on 5 February 1881. Thomas's last hours were silent but in the days before his death his coherent utterances suggest that he was thinking primarily of his family. He left Mary the lion's share of his not inconsiderable estate, including the lease on the house in Cheyne Row and its furniture.

Thomas was struck down with grief when Jane died and never recovered fully from this blow. The physical toll of old age and the painful memories and regrets prompted by the news of the deaths of his friends exacerbated his melancholic tendencies. His account of his state of mind in May 1870 reflected at least some of the experiences of his later years – 'Gloomy mournful musing, silent looking back on the unalterable and forward on the inevitable and inexpressible' – but it was not all like this. While he was deeply appreciative of those who helped him, he was still capable of deriving amusement from their attempts to promote his welfare. In the summer of 1869, for example, Jack came to stay and took charge of the household's holiday plans. Mary Aitkin (in a letter that would have done her aunt credit) told the second Lady Ashburton that 'Uncle John' has been 'immersed in *Bradshaw*, Time-tables have been brought to bear on all the routes to Norway, Iceland, Shetland, Dundee, Jersey, Guernsey, Bordeaux &c. &c; but as yet nothing has been decided and we are still at Chelsea.' Carlyle enjoyed 'hearing of all the different chances of getting out of London and [is] amused at our ardour to get him started'.[2] In the end, the Carlyles took their holiday at Addiscombe Farm, near Croyden.

The harshness of some of Carlyle's spoken and written judgements on his fellows contrasted with his capacity for friendship and for considerate, indeed generous, treatment of others. The physical and emotional pains of old age did not obliterate these more admirable traits. Thus while he was offended by what he saw as the unjustifiably laudatory tone of obituary notices of John Stuart Mill, Carlyle wrote a soothing letter to Mill's sister to reassure her about her brother's conduct following the destruction of the manuscript of the first volume of *The French Revolution* in March 1835. He told Harriet Mill that Mill's offer of financial compensation to enable him to rewrite the volume was 'conscientiously noble, generous, and friend-like'. He went on to say that the parting of the ways between the two men did not result in any change in his fundamental personal feelings for Mill, or he thought, in Mill's feelings for him.[3]

Earlier on he had gone to considerable trouble to secure a government pension for Leigh Hunt and to organise a subscription for the aged god daughters of Samuel Johnson. When he lived at Craigenputtock Carlyle tried to help an old class mate who was suffering from psychological problems, and he later secured casual employment for one of Hunt's wayward sons. He responded to requests for advice from strangers and wrote letters of introduction for the friends and relatives of acquaintances. As he approached the last decade of his life, Carlyle began to feel some of the unintended consequences of a life-time of thrift and the sustained popularity of his works. 'I find the money saved and strictly economised for many years past has become an embarrassment to me, it being a most difficult matter to decide where and how it is likely to do real good – or the contrary'.[4] As in the past, he was generous in supporting members of his family, dispensing £860 to them in 1870–71 alone. He also provided (by way of the local minister) regular pensions for some old people at Ecclefechan and financial support for the school there.[5] When his printer got into financial difficulties in mid 1870 Carlyle lent him £50.[6]

In old age Carlyle kept up his habit of taking long walks around Chelsea and into the city returning, if necessary, by omnibus. He believed that these excursions aided his digestion and made it easier for him to sleep. They also provided opportunities for a range of contacts with other inhabitants of what he called the 'brick Babylon'. He was well known to bus conductors and their passengers, and gave money to beggars. In an incident recorded by William Allingham, the eighty-year-old Carlyle is shown helping a blind beggar over a wide street crossing.[7] Towards the end of the 1870s Carlyle's declining health and the death of some of his oldest friends reduced the number of visitors to Cheyne Row, but it was not until the closing months of his life that his range of contacts became very limited. Nor was he ignored by the wider world, even if many of the appeals made to him were not taken up.

Any idea that Carlyle would play a substantive role as Rector of the University of Edinburgh ended with his wife's death, a tragedy that followed close on the heels of his triumphant installation in office. From this time on, he usually declined to give public support for causes of which he approved. He was equally unresponsive to appeals on behalf of campaigns against the Game Laws, the purchase of commissions in the army, militarism (an interesting reflection of Carlyle's common, but usually neglected, comments on the futility of war) and the pauperisation of the working classes through neglect of a stern interpretation of the principles enshrined in the Poor Law Amendment Act of 1834.[8] He accepted membership of the Society for the Preservation of Ancient Buildings in 1877, but irritated William Morris, who had issued the invitation, by praising Christopher Wren's London churches, built in a style which Morris disliked.[9] A few years earlier, Carlyle may have been prompted to produce a fragment on stock market speculation by appeals from correspondents, but he never published anything from it.[10]

He was more active on foreign policy issues. In a lengthy letter to the *Times* on the Franco-German War Carlyle upbraided those of his countrymen who sided with France, making her the martyr while ignoring the havoc that the French had wrecked on their continental neighbours in the previous two hundred years. This letter was more about justice than policy since it did not have any implications for the British government's attitude towards Bismark's Germany. Letters on Turkey's treatment of her Balkan subjects were more direct since they promoted an alliance with Russia to end what Carlyle perceived as Turkey's malign influence in the region.

Carlyle's only known attempt to influence the course of domestic public policy in the last decade of his life probably had a personal cause. When he joined with his friend Lady Derby in 1874 (at an official, rather than a public level) to oppose extending drinking hours in London public houses, he might well have been motivated by a wish to limit the nuisances coming from the patrons of a neighbouring gin palace, rather than by principled objections.[11] Although Carlyle shared conventional concerns about the damage done to the working classes by the demon drink and expressed strong views on the inequities of publicans, he was not an open supporter of temperance causes and probably disliked the air of non-conformist philanthropy that pervaded these endeavours.[12] Thomas and

Jane responded to bouts of drunkenness on the part of some of their servants in a remarkably tolerant, or at least fatalistic, manner. His surviving comments on drunkenness among the working classes are tempered by sympathy and free of evangelical censoriousness. While Carlyle complained of being jostled on the street by Christmas drunks in 1855, on another occasion he wryly excused the revelries of the working-class patrons of the neighbouring tavern when he 'remembered that it was the birthday of their Redeemer'. In response to Leslie Stephen's stock objection that the money given to a beggar would be spent on drink, Carlyle replied in terms that would have scandalised many contemporary supporters of temperance: 'no doubt it will be a momentary comfort to the poor fellow'.[13]

Attempts to encourage Carlyle to resume the role of essayist were no more successful than moves to recruit him to public causes. Following the publication of 'Shooting Niagara' in *Macmillan's Magazine* in 1867, he received a letter of congratulation from Alexander Macmillan, one of its proprietors. Carlyle had written the piece to oblige his disciple David Masson, who had recently taken up the editorship of the journal. Macmillan wished to capitalise on this lucky accident to forge an ongoing relationship with someone he regarded as a still valuable asset.[14] John Morley made a similar request in 1869, this time on behalf of his *Fortnightly Review*. Neither these invitations, nor later appeals to write on Burns or Cromwell for the new edition of the *Encyclopaedia Britannica*, were successful.[15]

In 1871 the students of Glasgow University sought in vain to emulate their fellows at Edinburgh by persuading Carlyle to renew a nomination for the rectorship that had first been proposed in 1854. Other demands were harder to shake off. As a proponent of the historical value of portraiture, Carlyle could hardly decline invitations to have his portrait painted. But if one had a duty to make one's face available for the scrutiny of posterity, someone with Carlyle's views on the need to suppress self-consciousness must have felt uncomfortable when striking a pose for the artist. In any case, artists' pretensions were tiresome and the results of their labours were often questionable. When submitting to Whistler's attentions Carlyle sought to mitigate some of these disadvantages by teasing the artist. These sallies were not appreciated by Ruskin's *bête noire*.[16] Carlyle was sceptical about the value of the finished product, complaining that Whistler seemed concerned primarily to capture the fall of his cloak and had neglected the character-conveying role of the artist. Whatever the idiosyncrasies of Carlyle's artistic judgements, he did not fall into the vulgar and morally corrupting error of expecting the portrait painter to flatter him. When Sir John Millais painted his portrait in 1877, Carlyle reported that 'the picture does not please Mary [Aitken], nor in fact myself altogether'. He approved of it, however, because he thought that it was 'surely strikingly like in every feature'. It had been undertaken on the 'fundamental condition' that Millais should paint 'what he himself was able to see there'.[17]

While the attentions of portrait painters were not an unqualified good, they were at least only occasional and relied on Carlyle's acquiescence. Neither of these conditions applied to nuisances that arrived by post. In the late 1860s and 1870s he was plagued by unwanted correspondence from a class of professed admirers who were dismissed as 'beggars and impertinent fools', and from those whose real (and in some cases, declared) object was to secure the autograph of a great man.[18] Other readers sought his guidance on career choices, receiving kindly (but probably unwelcome) advice of the stick to the task nearest at hand variety.

Carlyle was also beset by demonstrations of official and semi-official public esteem. He resisted offers of an honorary doctorate from Edinburgh, but was presented with a *fait accompli* from across the Atlantic. When an elaborate Harvard University degree certificate arrived unannounced at Cheyne Row in November of 1875, Carlyle complained to his brother John that he was unclear how to act. He had never been consulted about the award and would not have accepted it if given the choice.[19] Other honours were bestowed with equally scant regard for his wishes. The American Academy of Arts and Sciences elected him to its most prestigious form of foreign membership in the Political Economy and History Section. The Royal Irish Academy, apparently oblivious of the damage done to his reputation by *The Occasional Discourse on the Nigger Question* and the 'Latter-Day Pamphlets', elected him as one of its thirty honorary members in the Department of Polite Literature. He was repeatedly re-elected as president of the Philosophical Institute of Edinburgh. There is no record of Carlyle's response to these marks of distinction. The lustre of his election to the American Academy may, however, have been tarnished somewhat by the news that he had been chosen to fill a vacancy created by the death of Adophe Thiers, a historian and statesman who Carlyle had condemned in public and private.[20]

Early in 1874 Carlyle accepted induction into the civil class of the Prussian Order of Merit, created, appropriately enough, by Frederick the Great. He deprecated the newspaper fuss generated by the award, commenting privately that a present of 'a quarter of a pound of good tobacco' would have made a greater addition to his happiness.[21] Late in the same year when the Prime Minister, the Earl of Beaconsfield (Benjamin Disraeli) offered him a knighthood and a pension to enable him to live up to the title, it was declined. Carlyle, very far from being an admirer of Disraeli, was nevertheless touched by the delicate and generous way in which the offer had been made. He felt pangs of remorse at the thought of some of his past abuse of Disraeli's character and statesmanship: 'I do ... truly admire the magnanimity of Dizzy in regard to me: he is the only man I almost never spoke of except with contempt and if there is anything in scurrility anywhere chargeable against me, I am sorry to own he is the subject of it.'[22]

Perhaps the most interesting of the public testimonials conferred on Carlyle in the closing years of his life was the address and medal presented to him on his eightieth birthday by a group of his admirers. This memorial, the work of David Masson and James Froude, consciously echoed that sent to Goethe in 1831 on his eighty first birthday. It was unrestrained in its praise, crediting Carlyle with having 'sustained' the rare 'dignity' of 'Hero as Man of Letters'.[23] Some of Carlyle's staunchest admirers – Dean Stanley, William Allingham and W. H. Lecky – registered mild protests at the tone of the address.[24] A sharper response came from Henry Reeve, the editor of the *Edinburgh Review*, who thought it 'needlessly adulatory and overstrained'. Arthur Grote was even more forthright, writing to tell Masson that 'I have a regard and respect for Thomas Carlyle personally, and for *some* of his working it is impossible to withhold a measure of praise. Yet I confess that the almost oriental character of the proposed address, goes far beyond the expression of my admiration, and approaches so near to extravagance in its adulation, that I must decline to become a party to its presentation'.[25] Other diplomatic and practical difficulties had to be overcome. Masson and John Forster scotched a plan (quite inconsistent with Carlyle's disregard for conventional status in the republic of letters), to list the signatories in order of rank. Marian Evans (George Eliot) needed a number of attempts to sign her name properly on a strip of paper that was to be transferred to the letter of presentation.[26] In the event, the exercise was not an unqualified success. Mary Aitken had warned its promoters that her uncle did not like public references to either his age or his 'dead loved ones'.[27] This reticence was reflected in Carlyle's letter of thanks. It was dignified, grateful but very restrained: the 'beautiful transaction ... was altogether gratifying, welcome and honourable to me'.[28] Privately, he viewed the whole business with a degree of ambiguity. While he was touched by his friends' good intentions, he had long believed that fame was not a worthy goal for men of letters and thought that a self-conscious sense of one's importance was incompatible with true heroism.

The impediments to progress reports that Carlyle issued during the course of his labours on *Frederick the Great* often referred to this work as his last major literary task, one he had, perhaps, been unwise to begin. It was, he told his brother John in early 1855, 'the last heavy job I mean to undertake at this time of life. An ill-chosen job, and difficult exceedingly, in this country, in this position and humour.'[29] In the decade of incessant toil that followed, this feeling was reinforced by the demands that the book made on his patience and on the physical and psychological condition of both himself and Jane. When the final set of corrected proofs were dispatched to the printer in early February 1865, Carlyle turned his attention to the outward man, submitting to having a tooth extracted and to less painful ministrations at the hands of his barber.[30] He felt no desire to take up his pen again. To the contrary, as he wrote to his sister Jean later in the year, '"Work" is far, far, from me; all my work seems done; and generally I am well enough content it should be so.'[31]

As with many of Carlyle's personal statements, this reaction to the epic task of trying to present Frederick the Great in a heroic light exaggerated the situation and proved only a partly reliable prophecy. During the remaining sixteen years of his life Carlyle's productivity dropped sharply, but his literary output did not come to a complete stop. From time to time, he worked on the 'Library Edition' of his works and on the various volumes of the 'Popular Edition' that began to appear from 1871. He also completed the series of highly personal memoirs that were published immediately after his death as the *Reminiscences*, gathered material for the *Letters and Memorials of Jane Welsh Carlyle* and wrote 'Shooting Niagara: And After?' This essay was followed by the 'Portraits of John Knox', the letter to the *Times* (18 November 1870) on the Franco-Prussian War, and letters attacking the pro-Turkish Balkan policy of Disraeli's government.[32]

To the burdens of old age were added those resulting from the need to rely on others in the process of composition. During the latter stages of his work on *Frederick the Great*, Carlyle's writing hand began to lose its power and mobility. By the late 1860s his once firm and legible handwriting had become so tremulous and hard to decipher that he was forced to rely on others to commit his views to paper and to deal with his business and personal correspondence. The letters to the *Times* were dictated to his niece, Mary, as was his last book-length work, the *Early Kings of Norway*. Carlyle felt that dependence of this kind was a disincentive to serious literary activity. Despite his reputation as a formidable conversational-ist, he found (perhaps in unconscious recognition of the doctrine of silence) that composition by dictation prevented him expressing himself with the intense care necessary to produce statements that adequately and appropriately conveyed his sense of the truth.

Thus while *Frederick the Great* did not mark the end of Carlyle's literary career, it was a watershed. His later works gave the impression that he felt that his life's work was complete. They either applied previously stated views to current issues, or, as with the *Early Kings*, provided new ways of illustrating themes that had long been central to his mission. Carlyle increasingly felt that he had 'had his say' and that nothing was to be gained by repeating sentiments that had already been rehearsed on a number of occasions and were available in the collected editions of his works. In a substantive sense, his mission had come to an end. He made this clear in 1870 in his reaction to a renewal of Sir George Grey's acquaintance. Formerly Governor-General of South Australia, the Cape Colony and twice of New Zealand, Grey's political career concluded with a term as Prime Minister of New Zealand from 1877–79, heading a government elected on the basis of manhood suffrage. In 1870, however, he was living in

England, hoping to secure election as a Liberal Member of Parliament. One of Grey's interests at this time was the promotion of mass emigration to her colonies by the British Government. On at least two occasions in the summer and early autumn of 1870, he visited Carlyle to seek his active support for a public campaign for imperial emigration. Carlyle thoroughly approved of Grey's views on this topic, introduced him to the Earl of Derby (a former Colonial Secretary and, until the previous year, Foreign Secretary), and lent him written material in support of his campaign. He would not, however, write anything new on the issue or take a public stand, thinking that the time for this level of engagement had passed. As he noted after a visit by Grey to Cheyne Row in September 1870, 'Sir George is a clear, pleasant man, and I thoroughly approve what he is about, but do not retain any vivid interest in it when left to myself; I myself feeling to have *done* with it, and with all similar things.'[33] John Morley made this point in a rather different way when reviewing the library edition of Carlyle's works in the same year. This edition 'may be taken for the final presentation of all that the author has to say to his contemporaries ... The canon is definitely made up. The golden Gospel of Silence is effectively compressed into thirty fine volumes.'[34]

Although Carlyle's active pursuit of his mission came to an end by about 1870 this did not mean that he had ceased to be important in the eyes of many of his contemporaries, or that he had become a great but vague and largely honorific figure on the contemporary intellectual and moral landscape. In 1856 George Gilfillan, once an admirer but now a sharp critic, indulged in a wildly premature celebration of the waning of his influence. Having 'served its generation', the 'gospel of negations' was giving place to what Gilfillan referred to as 'another and nobler evangel'.[35] A quarter of a century after this confident prediction, Carlyle's life and ideas continued to be a source of great interest and inspiration and remained so until long after his death. The sustained interest in his work may seem especially surprising given that Carlyle's mind and opinions were products of the early decades of the nineteenth century. His earliest significant publications appeared in the 1820s and he had established his reputation as an important source of literary and moral guidance before Queen Victoria came to the throne. The crisis of faith presented in semi-fictional form in Sartor Resartus was fuelled by reading Hume, Gibbon and Voltaire, not by nineteenth-century scientific writers.[36] The reference points of his serious public engagements with other literary figures were all pre-Victorian. He commented extensively on German writers active in the late eighteenth and early nineteenth centuries, on Diderot and Voltaire from the generation before, and also (in shorter compass) on Burns, Byron, Coleridge, Johnson and Scott. Although he professed disdain for modern letters, Carlyle read and reread a wide range of contemporary literature up until his death. It is significant, however, that, while expressing emphatic views on the vices and (less often) the virtues of Browning, Charles Darwin, Dickens, G. H. Lewes, Macaulay, John Stuart Mill, Ruskin, Tennyson and Thackeray in his letters and conversation, he did not write or lecture on them, or on any other contemporary writers or poets.

The interest shown in Carlyle's ideas rarely reflected unqualified and unreserved admiration for all aspects of his work. There were uncritical 'Carlylians', but other readers could admire him in spite of what they saw as his totally unacceptable claims on issues such as parliamentary government, democracy, race or the treatment of criminals. These responses relied upon selective readings of Carlyle's works, seizing on what was inspiring and ignoring what was repugnant. They also reflected a common tendency to judge his writings by reference to their general impact, rather than seeing him as a purveyor of particular doctrines. As W. H. Smith put it, in a very mixed view of *Past and Present* in 1843, Carlyle's influence was exercised by 'producing a certain moral tone of thought ... a stern manly, energetic, self-denying character'.[37] A reviewer of the *Letters and Speeches of Oliver Cromwell* made a similar point, seeing Carlyle's treatment of the constitutional and theological disputes of the seventeenth century in relation to a wide-ranging movement that sought to establish human society on the basis of truth, right and justice.[38] John Morley was highly critical of what he saw as Carlyle's reliance on great men and his hostility to systematic, scientific economic and social analysis. He noted, however, that the crisis that Carlyle had identified in the late 1820s was still a pressing issue and had yet to be addressed by his countrymen: 'We are not promoting the objects which the social union subsists to fulfil, nor applying with energetic spirit to the task of preparing a sounder state for our successors.'[39] Reflecting on Carlyle's career after his death, John Tyndall thought that his role was to 'ennoble' and elevate public life, rather than to promote particular measures. He was a dynamic force, not a didactic one; he 'warmed, moved and invigorated', refusing to be 'clipped into precepts'.[40] Alexander Macmillan made a similar point when he told Carlyle that the lesson he had taken from *Sartor* was that 'the opinions and prophecies which do us most good are not those which we swallow whole without question, but those which stimulate us to open our own eyes and minds and hence to think honestly'.[41] Seen from these perspectives, disagreement with Carlyle's views on particular issues was not critical, while even those like Anthony Trollope who were not attracted to Carlyle's ideas or to his style, acknowledged the ongoing impact of his writings.[42]

Even before he became the 'Sage of Chelsea', Carlyle's personality and style of life played an important role in forging his contemporary reputation. This point was noted by Andrew Lang when contrasting Carlyle's career and reputation with that of John Gibson Lockhart. Lockhart, Sir Walter Scott's son-in-law and biographer, was editor of the *Quarterly Review* for nearly thirty years. He was widely recognised as a writer of great talent, and as a knowledgeable and sympathetic critic of contemporary German literature. He also had a sense of mission, seeing the *Quarterly* as a vehicle for pursuing it. Lockhart was as careful as Carlyle to avoid sacrificing popularity for principle, on one occasion warning his publisher of the dangers of relying on the faddish tastes of the 'diners of London' as a gauge of the soundness of the journal's line.[43] Lockhart subscribed to Schiller's dictum on the seriousness of life that Carlyle used as a motto for *Past and Present*, but this did not prevent him consoling Carlyle on the death of his mother-in-law with the waggish remark that Mrs Welsh's demise might at least make him independent of the booksellers.[44] This jest was highly characteristic. While Lockhart saw himself taking a prophetic role in society, his personal style was not of a kind that enabled him to have a lasting moral and spiritual influence on his contemporaries. Carlyle noted this himself. Lockhart was a man of 'considerable faculty', but his talent had 'shaped itself *gigmanically* only'. Lockhart's biographer made a similar point when he observed that the impact of his message to his contemporaries was tempered by the atmosphere of 'toddy and punch, port and claret' that seemed part of Lockhart's way of life. He lacked the 'spirit of martyrdom and renunciation' that was so important a part of Carlyle's appeal to his contemporaries and to later nineteenth-century readers.[45]

In the 1820s and early 1830s a diverse range of people – socialites like the Bullers, world-wise literary and political operators like Francis Jeffrey, battered but buoyant regency men of letters such as Leigh Hunt, and earnest reformers like John Stuart Mill, Ralph Waldo Emerson and other members of the New England intelligentsia – all saw qualities in Carlyle that set him apart from, and elevated him above, the welter of aspirants for literary recognition. By the 1840s he was on friendly terms with a circle that had broadened to include representatives of the working-class literati (Samuel Bamford, Thomas Cooper and Ebenezer Elliot), Charles Gavan Duffy and other 'Young Irelanders', exiled revolutionaries from Europe (Cavaignac, Herzen, Mazzini), and figures from official and political circles in Britain, including Lord Ashburton, Edwin Chadwick, Sir Arthur Helps, Richard Monckton Milnes and Sir Robert Peel.

As Carlyle's career developed, perceptions of his character became inextricably bound up with judgements concerning the importance of his ideas, and the impact that his writings had on those who read them. In one of the earliest full dress reviews of Carlyle's writings from the 1820s and 1830s, J. H. Sterling contrasted Carlyle's evident and uncompromising sincerity and clarity of purpose with what he took to be confused, and in some cases, vacillating and insincere utterances of other consolers and prescribers. Those who set themselves up to proclaim a viable creed for their contemporaries did not merely need 'a new and more ingenious form of words, but a truth to be embraced with the whole heart, and in which the heart shall find as his has found, strength for all combats, and consolation, though stern not festal, under all sorrows'. Carlyle's 'clearness of eye to see what is permanent and substantive, and the fervour and strength of heart to love it, as the sole good of life' marked him out as one entitled 'to the fame of the most generous order of greatness'. Five years later, in 'To Thomas Carlyle', a poem written on his deathbed, Sterling gave character precedence over prophetic wisdom: 'More than the Sage the Man Commend.'[46]

In a volume published in 1844, Carlyle's language, that of a 'gifted painter and poet', was said to present readers with a glimpse of the 'colour' of his soul. When defending Carlyle and the 'Latter-Day Pamphlets' against the barbs of *Blackwood's Edinburgh Magazine* in 1850, James Hannay identified his stance with 'deep and solemn earnestness', 'infinite tenderness', 'enthusiasm' and elevation 'by divine hope'. He claimed that these qualities were only likely to be seen and appreciated by readers who already possessed them to some degree, an echo of Carlyle's views on the symbiotic relationship between members of heroic cultures.[47]

Carlyle's friendship with Sterling was celebrated in the *Life* that he published in 1851. This work aroused resentment among some readers because of its dismissive, impatient treatment of the project (associated particularly with Coleridge) to restore Anglicanism as a source of moral and intellectual guidance. At the same time, however, Carlyle's tender account of his friendship with Sterling furnished more sympathetic readers with important insights into his character and his way of life. As one of his intimates put it, before the publication of the *Life of Sterling*, Carlyle 'had been to the majority of his readers and admirers a mysterious voice vaguely understood to be issuing from somewhere in Chelsea'. This work showed him a 'living, breathing, flesh-and-blood man, consorting freely and socially with his fellows'.[48]

Although Carlyle was sometimes impatient at the unwanted attention of admirers, both he and Jane dealt courteously with a stream of unsolicited requests for advice on literary and even on personal matters. Sometimes these approaches developed into sustained correspondence of a kind that encouraged readers to feel that they shared a sense of common identity with the Carlyles. This happened in the case of Mary Smith, a schoolteacher and poet from a strongly nonconformist background, who corresponded with Jane from 1854. Smith subscribed to a Carlylean ethos of earnest sincerity and salvation through labour, and, like the Carlyles, saw herself as being distinct from, and in some ways, superior to, almost all of those around her. She thus felt entitled, by virtue of her intellectual and moral capabilities, to stand in a relation of equality to kindred souls. Smith's correspondence with Jane confirmed her membership of a charmed and elevated circle: 'I felt I had been recognised as a fellow sufferer with higher and noble souls than myself, and I felt encouraged and strengthened to hope and to hold on my way.'[49] In a phrase that echoed the position that

Carlyle had advanced in some of his early essays on German literary culture, she proclaimed that 'intellect knows no rank'.[50]

Carlyle's popularity was not confined to the conventional middle-class reading public. As with other nineteenth-century authors, the issue of 'cheap' or 'popular' editions made it possible for members of the working-classes to have easy access to their writings.[51] Carlyle complained that Chapman and Hall were slow to take this step, but when they did so in 1870 the decision no doubt reflected an assessment that a demand for his works existed among a wide cross-section of the population, including working-class Carlylians. One such group contacted Carlyle in the mid 1860s, using Thomas Dixon, a cork cutter from Sunderland, as its spokesman. Dixon is known to John Ruskin's readers as the author of letters that provide the starting point to some of the numbers of *Fors Clavigera*, and as the epistolary target of the series of letters published under the title *Time and Tide*. These letters, which focused on labour, contained numerous references to, and allusions drawn from, Carlyle's writings. In December 1866 Dixon wrote to Carlyle on behalf of a group of friends who had clubbed together to send him a portrait of the engraver Thomas Bewick to mark his seventy-first birthday. Since Dixon refers in this letter to a previous gift of Bewick's *A History of British Birds* and provides brief biographical sketches of the donors, it is possible that Carlyle had asked for this information when responding to the earlier gift.[52] Be that as it may, Dixon's letter provides a glimpse of one group of Carlyle's working-class admirers. His colleagues were artisan artists (colourists, portrait painters, wood carvers and a printer-bookseller); all, he noted, from very humble backgrounds. These men were distinguished by their interest in 'Art' and 'Nature', their love of 'good' books, and their thirst for knowledge. Dixon identified the printer-bookseller as a key figure. This man, W. H. Hills, introduced Dixon and his friends to Carlyle's writings and lent books to those who could not afford to buy them. He was, Dixon wrote, 'a man that is at all times willing to aid any young man desirous of knowledge of Art'. This quest seems to have lead Dixon and his friends from Ruskin to Carlyle. Dixon sought practical advice from Carlyle on 'home colonisation' and waste reclamation, key projects in Ruskin's Guild of St George scheme.[53] Judging by the extracts from his letters printed by Ruskin in the appendixes to *Time and Tide*, Dixon was a firm believer in the principle of 'masterhood' and found much to admire in Carlyle's account of Frederick the Great's domestic policy. It was as an exemplar of 'wise teaching on law, government and society'.[54]

J. S. Mill and some of Carlyle's early admirers may have thought mistakenly that his radicalism embraced liberalism and parliamentary reformism, and were thus disappointed when it became apparent that he did not share their views on these matters.[55] Modern readers might sympathise with this perspective and look askance at Carlyle's often savage criticism of democratic government. It must be remembered, however, that democracy was largely untried in nineteenth-century Europe and appreciation of the value of widespread political participation was far from being a general article of faith. For at least some of Carlyle's readers, his promotion of ideas that had far-reaching implications for social and political relations and the ethos that informed them but did not require a commitment to democratic government, was a source of attraction. Although 'Shooting Niagara' gave comfort to some conservative opponents of electoral reform, Carlyle's rejection of democracy could be seen in other, more radical, hues.[56] Dixon and his colleagues were not enamoured of democracy, but they, like John Tyndall, felt that Carlyle's non-democratic radicalism was intellectually and morally refreshing and uplifting. Tyndall recalled that he found in *Past and Present* 'a radicalism so high, reasonable and humane as to make it clear to me that, without truckling to the ape and tiger of the mob, a man might hold the views of a radical'.[57] In Tyndall's case, as in that of a number of important figures associated with the emergence of an ethos of 'scientific naturalism', Carlyle's dismissal of democracy and his demand for elite leadership corresponded with, or at least seemed to provide support for, their view that in modern society cultural leadership would be provided by scientific intellectuals.[58]

Towards the end of Carlyle's life there were attempts to give a loose institutional form to admiration for his ideas. In late 1879 a group of his English admirers formed a 'Carlyle Society' in London. The society, which met at the Bridge House Hotel, London Bridge, aimed to provide a 'centre of union' for his friends and disciples and to 'disseminate his teachings on social, political and religious subjects'.[59] Some time after Carlyle's death, this society was transformed into the 'Society of St Michael', a choice of name that signified its members' determination to wage a vigorous assault on the forces of evil. Another Carlyle Society was set up in Edinburgh where it flourishes to this day.

At a critical stage in his career, Carlyle's spirits had been lifted by financial and moral support from readers in the United States. These supporters, concentrated originally in New England, encouraged Carlyle as he struggled to establish himself. They also provided a market for the first edition of *Sartor Resartus*. Later the United States produced a steady, and at times unwelcome, stream of visitors to Cheyne Row and a flow of letters from American correspondents.[60] After the publication of 'On the Negro Question' in 1849, Carlyle's views on slavery received some endorsement from Southern interests, but rejection of them by other Americans did not necessarily mean that he ceased to be an object of interest and admiration.[61] The response of Newton Booth, the Governor of California, is a case in point. Booth had originally been repelled by Carlyle's racial views but when he discovered his earlier works his position changed radically. *The French Revolution*, particularly the closing appeal to the reader – 'while the Voice of Man speaks with Man, hast thou not the living fountain out of which all sacredness sprang, and will yet spring?' – had a profound effect, converting him into a firm admirer of Carlyle and a proponent of his general approach.[62]

Carlyle's stress on the personal attributes of literary figures and political actors was echoed in frequent references to admirable facets of his own character and way of life. These accounts were significant because they signalled that many of Carlyle's readers regarded him as a teacher and guide rather than being merely another writer. This was why many of his contemporaries seemed indifferent to claims about the vagueness of his doctrines and the extravagance of his prose and speech. It is also why they credited him with a far more profound impact on their lives than other widely read literary figures such as Browning, Dickens, Macaulay, Tennyson and Thackeray.[63] While readers might find instruction or entertainment in these writers' works, they would not receive admonishment, inspiration or a distinctive sense of purpose from them.

The homely and unpretentious ambiance of domestic life in Cheyne Row, Carlyle's sincere lack of regard for material rewards, his personal generosity with money and with his time, and his genuine indifference to both acclaim and hostile criticism, were noted with approval by contemporaries. In some cases, these virtues were seen as saving graces that offset vices of style and opinion. Thus in the early 1870s, Leslie Stephen, who later became a less qualified admirer, re-marked that, although Carlyle's political and philosophical conversation included 'a good deal of arrant and rather pestilent nonsense' he nevertheless provided a fine example of 'manliness' and 'simplicity' for other literary professionals: 'It is a pleasure to see anybody who has the courage to live so little spoilt by the flattery which might have choked him and made him into a windbag.'[64]

Other references to Carlyle's personal qualities identified more positive links between the character of the writer and the social and political implications of his writings. A striking example of this approach appeared in 'An Estimate of Mr Carlyle's Character', an obituary essay published in the St James Gazette in March 1881. In this essay Carlyle was described as the most impressive personality of the period, 'the man who conveyed forcibly to those who approached him that general impression of genius and force of character which it is impossible either to mistake or to define'.[65] These qualities were seen as aspects of a fundamental impartiality that disassociated him from particular classes, creeds or parties. Carlyle's consistency of moral purpose and determination to make this, rather than dignity, fame or wealth, the inspiration of his mission, gave him a distinctive and elevated status as a source of independent judgement.[66] He was, as one critic put it, 'perfectly self-centred', a comment that was meant to applaud his radical independence rather than censor any personal wilfulness.[67] As a result, both the radical and apparently conservative aspects of Carlyle's thought were seen as natural products of the earnest pursuit of truth, rather than being part of a preordained world view purloined from other writers, or merely a reflection of comfortable popular religious, social or political prejudices. This meant that Carlyle's considered critical judgements were not marred by littleness of spirit and sought to concentrate on the larger significance of their subjects. As John Morley so finely put it in an essay marking the appearance of a new 'library edition' of Carlyle's works in 1870,

> he leaves the fulmination to the hack moralist of the pulpit, or the press, with whom words are cheap, easily gotten, and readily thrown forth. To him it seems better worth while, having made sure of some sterling sincerity and rare genuineness of vision and singular human quality, to dwell on, and do justice to that, than to accumulate commonplaces as to the viciousness of vice.[68]

The value that readers placed on these qualities could blunt the impact of significant political differences. Despite Carlyle's deflating response to the political demands of the Chartists, the Chartist poet Thomas Cooper celebrated his willingness to question conventional ideas in a dedicatory poem written in Stafford Gaol in 1845:

> Right noble age-fellow, whose speech and thought
> Proclaim thee other than the supple throng,
> Who glide Life's customed smoothed path along, –
> Prescription's easy slaves – strangers to doubt,
> Because they never think![69]

Cooper's Journal, a short-lived publication from 1850, was a strong advocate of democratic government, but its editor still found it useful to print series of quotations from Carlyle's writings on a range of issues. Cooper drew his readers' attention to Carlyle's ideas on the inevitability of democracy, the need to align legal conceptions of justice with the laws of nature that underwrote all human arrangements, and his insistence that property ownership implied social obligations. He also referred with evident approval to Carlyle's exposure of 'shams' in modern society and to his criticisms of conservatism and aristocracy. Forty years later, George Julian Harney, a veteran Chartist and correspondent of Marx and Engels who had reacted strongly to Carlyle's support for Germany in 1870, appealed to Carlyle's name when he sought to persuade the House of Commons to reconsider the condition of England.[70]

George Jacob Holyoake, whose engagement with radical, freethinking popular politics extended over most of the Victorian period, was a sharp critic of Carlyle's political ideas and objected to the combative tone of much of his work. He described Carlyle as the 'greatest ruffian in literature since the days of Dr Johnson'. Holyoake noted, however, that like the Doctor, Carlyle possessed the 'redeeming virtue' of being an 'honest and heroic' lover of truth.[71] This response reflected a concern with the authenticity of the spirit that Carlyle promoted in his writings and in his private comments on those of others. Thus in 1849 on receiving a copy of *Appel aux honnêtes gens* from the French socialist Louis Blanc who had participated in the 1848 Revolution, he wrote to the author that his work exhibited a 'tone of heart, which powerfully appeals to such. This I believe you to have gained by writing, at present; and this, if nothing else were gained, is a thing to be prized.'[72]

The tendency to incorporate evaluations of Carlyle's character in assessments of the significance of his ideas meant that charges of personal weakness or unworthy conduct assumed a heightened importance. Some of these revelations were published after Carlyle's death in memoirs, lives and letters and diaries. The richest stores had been laid down by Carlyle himself, fuelling the controversy generated by Froude's publication of the *Reminiscences* and by his *Life*. These works have had the effect of obscuring the strong attractions of Carlyle's personality and the eagerness of his contemporaries to seek his company.[73] They prompted censorious commentary on Carlyle's irascibility, his domineering role in private conversations, and the tone of anger, bitterness and exaggeration that punctuated his writings. Some contemporaries treated these outbursts as expressions of egoistic intolerance and impatience that discredited any claim to moral leadership. For example, an obituary reference to Goethe's praise of Carlyle stung Abraham Hayward, a barrister who had published a translation of *Faust*, into writing to the *Times* on 22 February 1881 to propose Mozley's critical review of Carlyle's *Cromwell* an a 'antidote' to 'unduly exalted' judgement on Carlyle's merits as a 'moral guide and reformer'.[74] When the *Reminiscences* were published a few months later, Hayward took advantage of the occasion to continue his assault on Carlyle's intellectual and moral influence and to accuse him of the grossest egotism in all his dealings with others.[75]

Of course, Carlyle left numerous hostages to fortune. His conversational manner had long been a source of intense irritation to some of those who experienced it at first-hand. Francis Galton, the scientist, dismissed him as the 'greatest bore that a man could tolerate ... He raved about the degeneracy of the modern English without any facts in justification'. Goldwin Smith, a liberal politician and journalist who met Carlyle at the Ashburtons' parties, claimed that 'belief in his judgement of men and things could hardly survive a day's intercourse with him'.[76] Herbert Spencer, who had once been attracted to Carlyle's doctrine of renunciation, regarded the prospect of spending time in Carlyle's company with extreme distaste. Having visited Cheyne Row a few times in the early 1850s, he recalled that, when faced with the choice between listening silently to his host's 'absurd dogmas' or getting into a fierce argument with him, he determined to stay away. Spencer was disdainful of Carlyle's counter-philosophical reliance on 'intuitions and dogmatic assertions', and of his preference for passionate exclamation over calm deliberation. He later claimed that those who admired Carlyle were carried away by the alluring attractions of his 'originality and vigour of expression'; this was not a temptation that Spencer's later readers had to resist.[77] Spencer's style of philosophy and his feeling that his life had been blighted by Carlyle's early influence, meant that he was a hostile witness, but even those who were far more favourably disposed to Carlyle expressed some of the same reservations. Charles Darwin thought that Carlyle possessed a strong sense of benevolence and was impressed by his capacity to convey moral truths to his contemporaries. At the same time, however, he was oppressed by Carlyle's despondency and his overbearing conversation. After being subjected to a three hour lecture, Edward Fitzgerald noted that Carlyle was 'very eloquent, looked very handsome; and I was very glad to get away'. John Hunter, an Edinburgh lawyer who claimed to 'love' and 'reverence' Carlyle, nevertheless found his enthusiasm damped by exposure to his conversation and kept away from 'at homes' in Cheyne Row when he visited London in the late 1830s.[78]

In fact, Carlyle's conversational manner varied, showing a tendency to degenerate when he was unwell; it was also affected by the quality of the company and the nature of the subject under discussion. A visitor to Cheyne Row in 1852 noted that, while he was sharply dismissive of an essay on Comte by G. H. Lewes, and fumed over the failings of the short-lived Derby-Disraeli ministry, Carlyle was gentle, charming and good-natured during the rest of the evening. When exposed to the atmosphere of his friend Thomas Erskine's house in Forfarshire, Carlyle's conversation became 'more many-sided, joyous and iridescent'.[79] His sense of humour also helped to transform remarks that might otherwise have seemed unbearably bitter; as Henry Taylor put it after being in Carlyle's company in early 1848: 'the extravagance and the grotesqueness of the attack sheathed the sharpness of it, and the little touch of picturesque ... seemed to give it the character of a vision rather than a vituperation'.[80] Irritation at Carlyle's excesses might be mitigated by the sense that even his less acceptable behavioural traits were related to the moral strengths of his character. Harriet Martineau, for example, attributed Carlyle's occasional outbursts of anger and bitterness to his incapacity to give expression to the highly refined state of his human sympathies: 'He cannot express his love and pity in natural acts, like other people; and it shows itself too often in unnatural speech', gainsaid, Martineau noted, by his demeanour and by the pained sympathy of his eyes and facial expression.[81] Charles Gavan Duffy associated Carlyle's tendency to harangue visitors with his perception of their expectations. This unfortunate by-product of celebrity status was contrasted with the kindness and moderation of Carlyle's private conversational manner with intimates. Duffy found it hard to forgive Carlyle's 'anti-Irish paradoxes and prejudices', but he thought that even when his judgements were severe they were not malicious. They merely reflected the high moral standards that

Carlyle applied to his own conduct as well as that of others. Duffy noted that posterity had pardoned faults in other writers (Wordsworth's overweening sense of superiority; Burke's explosions of passion, and Johnson's harsh judgements) but dwelt at length on Carlyle's.[82]

Like Duffy, the Quaker and statesman W. E. Forster was not blind to the objectionable aspects of some of Carlyle's public displays. He was particularly struck by a blazing row with an Irish clergyman in the dining room of a genteel hotel in the Peak District that left other guests boggling and dumbfounded. Foster nevertheless described Carlyle's general conversational tone as marked by 'a good-natured humorous sarcasm', giving way occasionally to 'a burst of furious indignation or a flash of fiery eloquence'. He was 'a most delightful companion, a rich store of hearty, genial social kindness shining through his assumed veil of misanthropy, and often all the more conspicuous from all his efforts to conceal or disown it, and his eccentric laughter striking out of all manner of everyday trivial occurrences'.[83] Carlyle was at times aware of the impact of his speech but did not seem to regret it. In early 1871 Lord Houghton (Richard Monkton Milnes) and the long-suffering John Forster were exposed to what Carlyle (who had obviously enjoyed himself) described as 'a great deal of contemptuous denunciation, and *Latter-Day Pamphletism* from me; which they took, especially Forster did, with some appearance of real seriousness, and quasi-penitent admission that perhaps it was too true'.[84]

Tolerant reactions to what Goldwin Smith, Dalton and Spencer saw as Carlyle's intolerable verbal dogmatism reflected an appreciation that he placed a premium on independence and sincerity and valued this above mere compliance and agreement for the sake of form or politeness. Although at times this made Carlyle sound rather like John Stuart Mill, his defence of freedom of thought and expression emphasised authenticity and independent judgement rather than individual autonomy. He made this point to Mill in 1833 when the latter nervously expressed disagreement with aspects of Carlyle's treatment of Diderot: 'Every given man, if he be a man at all, looks at the world from a position in several respects his own peculiar one: let him look at it faithfully from thence, note faithfully and believe heartily what he *sees* there.'[85] He reiterated this sentiment in response to a question posed by one of the members of the Royal Commission into the British Museum in 1849, 'everyman should have a sincere opinion, and should be prepared to act on it. ... The Almighty has given him powers of judging, and ... he is responsible for his exercise of the power.'[86] This stance was not necessarily incompatible with Carlyle's conversational style. His talk was sometimes dogmatic and unstoppable but people also noted that Carlyle respected those who held their ground; his vigorous opening thrusts were seen as provocative feints designed to test for a strong reply. He was also quite capable of arguing without rancour and recognising the merits of those with whom he disagreed. Thus when describing his first meeting with John Sterling in February 1835, Carlyle recalled that the two men 'walked westward ... talking on moralities, theological philosophies; arguing copiously, but *except* in opinion not disagreeing.'[87]

Readings of Carlyle that stressed the distinctive and admirable aspects of his character tended to see these qualities exemplified in his works. Contemporaries were particularly struck by his practical commitment to truth and earnestness and by the demonstration of it in his writings, private conversation and public speech. First-hand experience of Carlyle's conversation and public lectures was necessarily very limited, but the impression that he had made on his audiences was broadcast more widely in newspaper reports, and in letters, memoirs and reminiscences. While providing accounts of what Carlyle said, these reports also placed considerable emphasis on the sense of his personality that was conveyed during these performances. For example, a report published in the *Spectator* during his first lecture series in 1837 described Carlyle as a 'man of genius, deeply imbued with his great argument'.[88] Leigh Hunt's notices of the lectures that Carlyle gave on European literature and European revolutions in 1838 and 1839 were published in the *Examiner*. These reviews were not uncritical and irritated Carlyle but they made it clear that his tone and style were original and striking.[89] A later account presented Carlyle's speech in ways that echoed his own remarks on the significance of Oliver Cromwell's language. In Carlyle's case, as in that of the Lord Protector, the absence of conventional oratorical smoothness and control was seen as a positive virtue because it revealed the presence of some far more important qualities:

> His hard, expressive, compound phrases, dragged out with vast energy, from the chamber of his capacious mind, by, as it were, a cable of harsh-sounding broadest-of-broad Scotch, acquired added force from the efforts of their producer ... His eyes glowed as with inspiration, and in the more intricate and emphatic passages, the muscles of his face appeared to quiver with emotion. Evidently he said what he meant, and what he thought.[90]

To many of his contemporaries, Carlyle's life exemplified the commitment to earnestness that played such a central role in his evaluation of others, and in his statements on the way in which life should be approached. His earnestness was particularly appreciated because it was associated with his capacity to provide a clear-sighted, courageous and radical perspective on the problems and prospects of modern British society. Looking back on Carlyle's role in the 1830s and 1840s, Harriet Martineau credited him with being the major single influence on the rise of an ethos of moral and social improvement. He

> infused into the mind of the English nation, a sincerity, earnestness, healthfulness and courage which can be appreciated only by those who are old enough to tell what was our

morbid state when Byron was the representative of our temper, the Clapham Church of
our religion, and the rotten-borough system of our political morality.[91]

Martineau's reference point was the Regency period, but Carlyle's sense of sincerity and earnestness was equally important to later Victorians. Mary Smith, who
was of the next generation, viewed Carlyle's impact in similar terms. Looking
back to the 1850s from the last decade of the nineteenth century, she recalled that
Carlyle's 'universal onslaught on the nothings and appearance of society, gave
strength and life to my vague but true enthusiasm. They proved a new bible of
blessedness to my eager soul, as they did to thousands besides who had become
weary of much of the vapid literature of the time'.[92]

When his essays from the 1820s and early 1830s were issued in collected
editions from 1839 they acquired a lease of life that was independent of their
origins in the periodical press. Carlyle's earliest writings thus retained their
currency until long after his death, playing a key role in establishing and
maintaining his contemporary reputation. As a result, his promotion of German
literature had an ongoing impact on Victorian readers, affecting later estimates of
his contribution to contemporary literary and intellectual culture. More than ten
years after he had ceased to write regularly on the subject, this aspect of his work
was the focus of favourable attention in R. H. Horne's collection exemplifying the
'new spirit of the age'. Like other great men, Carlyle had knocked a window in the
blind walls that surrounded humanity. This window faced to the east, and 'while
some men complain of a certain bleakness in the wind which enters through it', they
should rather 'congratulate themselves and him on the aspect of the new sun beheld
through it ... It has not been his object to discover to us any specific prospect ... but
the sun which renders all these visible'.[93] Carlyle's writings on German literature
were one of the sources of his appeal to undergraduates at Glasgow University in
the 1850s, welcomed, as in the case of Edward Caird, because of their liberating
impact. For Caird, Carlyle pointed 'as through iron bars of a prison-house, the
way out of the narrow and cramping orthodoxies into the broad, generous,
natural-supernatural world outside'.[94] Alexander Ross, a member of an earlier
generation of students at Edinburgh, recalled that it was Carlyle who had 'first
opened before his wonderous eyes new regions not bounded by the Westminster
Confessions'.[95]

The career of *Sartor Resartus* was even more remarkable than that of the
early essays. Having failed to find a publisher, and then suffering the indignity
of a spluttering debut in *Fraser's Magazine*, the work gained a cult following
among the intelligentsia of New England before finally being published in book
form in England in 1838. This edition sold reasonably well and was reprinted in
1841. Thereafter, *Sartor* went through a number of reprints on both sides of the
Atlantic before being incorporated into a succession of uniform and collected

editions. If anything, the demand for the book appears to have increased as time when on. Ironically, given Carlyle's scathing remarks on his contemporaries' penchant for 'puffing', his publisher went to considerable lengths to promote the cheap edition, printing one hundred and fifty thousand advertising flyers for insertion in popular magazines. This strategy paid dividends. Mary Aitkin reported seeing holidaymakers on the Clyde ferries clutching their copies of the easily distinguishable red covered copies of the 'Popular Edition' of *Sartor*. The sales figures for 1871 (20,000 copies) paled into insignificance when compared with the 70,000 copies sold in the year following Carlyle's death.[96]

In his later years, Carlyle was rueful about the sustained popularity of *Sartor Resartus*, going so far as to claim that he had never thought highly of the book. He was exasperated at the failure of some young American admirers to grasp the ironies of the work. More prosaic causes of irritation came from nearer home. In March 1873 Carlyle complained to his brother John of a 'goose' from Durham who asked him to settle a dispute by revealing the 'meaning of *Sartor*'. He flung the offending letter into the fire and confiscated the stamp sent for return postage.[97] These plaudits might have been unwelcome, but the fact that *Sartor* was still generating youthful enthusiasm forty years after it was written supports Francis Espinasse's judgement that it was the '*Pilgrim's Progress* ... of the nineteenth century', pointing the way from 'doubt and despair' to 'blessedness and belief'.[98]

Mary Smith explained the key to this force of attraction in language that echoed Carlyle's treatment of the English puritans. He had shown those with a strong sense of religiosity but weakening faith in conventional understandings of the implications of Christianity, that religion concerned the inward spirit, not the 'outward ordinances' of institutionalised religious observances.[99] The Protestant allusions of this characterisation were particularly significant indicators of the way in which Carlyle's nineteenth-readers viewed him. By vividly and effectively restating the idea that religious affirmations and expressions were separable from the various historical forms in which they had appeared, and by privileging conscience as the abiding home of the spirit of true religion, Carlyle offered invaluable assistance to successive generations of his countrymen. *Sartor*, in particular, became 'as a lighthouse on the rocks to all those who have navigated after him in these tempestuous seas'.[100] Grateful correspondents had made this point directly to Carlyle. In 1847, for example, a reader from Kirkcaldy told Carlyle that he and other seekers of religious truths had been prepared to receive his books when they first came across them in the mid 1840s. These works 'came to me ... like a new revelation', bringing 'a more healthful tone of mind than I had experienced for a third of my life, a kind of harmony is established in my being, which makes everything that happens to me a good ... the soul of god is found in everything'. In 1874, R. M. Spence, a Presbyterian Minister, hailed Carlyle as the 'Professor of God to this generation'.[101] In spite of the strongly Protestant cast of his thinking, and his severe remarks on modern Catholicism, Carlyle's works might also appeal to Catholics. Thus while Thomas Moore, an Irish Catholic living in Derby, did not accept all that Carlyle had written about his countrymen, he saw much to admire in his picture of Cromwell and found in his works generally the 'loving and wise counsel of a beloved and venerated father'.[102]

Proponents of 'scientific naturalism' such as John Tyndall applauded what they saw as Carlyle's pantheism, seeing it as the key to reconciling spirituality with the findings of modern science.[103] For those with more conventional religious views, however, this interpretation of Carlyle was a source of embarrassment and they sought to relieve him of any pantheistic taint so that they might use his ideas as a source of invigorating, non-sectarian reassurance that was compatible with ongoing attachment to Anglicanism, Presbyterianism and even Roman Catholicism.[104] Thus one writer argued that Carlyle's view was that the spirit of God was constantly renewing the universe, a proposition that differed significantly from the pantheistic claim that matter is God.[105] For those who read Carlyle in this way, *Sartor* and other works from the 1820s showed how they might combine a firm commitment to the fundamentally religious basis of human experience with scientifically or philosophically informed scepticism on some aspects of Christian doctrine. Carlyle was credited with having reunited literature and religion after the former had been exorcised from the latter by the devout, and the latter from the former by the sceptical. His quarrel lay not with the true spirit of Christianity but with 'vulgar orthodox sensationalism'.[106] More generally, the notion of 'natural supernaturalism' provided a means through which Carlyle's readers could sustain the importance of a religious impulse, and stress the significance of spirituality, without creeds, dogmas or institutionalised religious faiths.[107]

Here, and in other assessments of Carlyle's importance in providing guidance to those grappling with complexities arising from doubts about conventional religious practices and ideas, attention was focused on the moral implications of his early writings. For example, in an article significantly titled 'Religious Faith and Modern Scepticism' Geraldine Jewsbury credited Carlyle with having left a permanent and elevating mark upon the 'moral tone of the age'.[108] Many readers saw this as part of a process that reformulated and reinvigorated religious ideas. Its attractions might also be appreciated by those who found it refreshing to be able to frame ideals of life that were not encumbered by the legacy of religious traditions and contemporary disputations. Thus in his remarks on Carlyle's appeal to Oxford undergraduates in the 1850s, John Morley noted that one of the attractions of his ideas was that one could be a 'fervent disciple … without adhering to a single article of theological tradition or authority'.[109]

An earlier generation of students at Oxford had expressed a similar degree of enthusiasm only to recoil from it in later years. Matthew Arnold linked Carlyle with John Henry Newman as one of the 'voices' that reached the hearts of him and his contemporaries at Oxford in 1841.[110] Like Arthur Clough, however, Arnold later became highly critical of Carlyle's failure to do more than undermine people's faith in conventional Christianity. He also deprecated the influence that Carlyle's views on the English Puritans had on his contemporaries, noting that he preached earnestness to a people who already had a surfeit of this quality.[111] These judgements were by no means universal since Carlyle was widely praised for the beneficial impact of his writings on those who faced challenges to their religious views. Even in Arnold's case, however, disillusionment with Carlyle's guidance on religious questions, or a dislike of his overwrought preaching style did not necessarily entail the total rejection of his influence. Carlylean ideas continued to play a role in Arnold's mature poetry and prose, and, Puritan earnestness aside, his critical views on his contemporaries' faith in political machinery, on the moral and practical shortcomings of *laissez-faire* and on the injustice of British policy in Ireland, echoed themes from Carlyle's writings.[112]

While Herbert Spencer denounced Carlyle's doctrine of renunciation because it had blighted his life, many of his contemporaries saw it as the centre piece of Carlyle's mission and the most notable and beneficial lesson that they took from *Sartor* and the early essays.[113] When this doctrine was coupled with the gospel of labour, it provided those who were unsettled by challenges to conventional expressions of religious faith and practice with a sense of purpose that was both galvanising and personally assuring. Carlyle's Goethean motto, 'work and despair not', was embraced by many of his contemporaries because it was framed in such a way as to hold out the prospect of salvation without delusion and without feeling the need to fret about ultimate questions. By displacing the concerns of the troubled spirit from the centre of human consciousness and focusing attention on realisation through action, the doctrine of renunciation appealed to those brought up in religious professions that emphasised the need to undergo self-sacrifice while striving after God.

Although some contemporaries were critical of what they saw as the lack of specificity of Carlyle's injunctions, this putative weakness might also be seen as a source of strength. Henry Rose commented that Carlyle's thought was not programmatic. Rather his role was to 'awaken the conscience of the political and social rulers, and to give such a trend to their thoughts as would help them to find the right methods if they honestly sought them'.[114] Moreover, it seems that because the ideas of commitment, duty and action were stated in general terms in Carlyle's writings, they could be taken up by people holding a wide variety of views and occupying a range of social and economic positions. Carlyle's broadly inclusive statements about what counted as 'labour' licensed and encouraged this understanding of the implications of his ideas. They also discouraged the immobilising agonising that *Sartor* had shown to be an understandable, but no longer necessary, response to the inner and outer challenges facing humanity as it tried to come to grips with the modern world.

The sustained popularity of *Sartor Resartus* reflected the persisting attraction of the doctrine of renunciation, and of the closely related gospel of labour, for successive generations of Victorians. Carlyle's identification with this idea was symbolised by the title and subject matter of Ford Maddox Brown's *Work*, a composition dating from the mid 1850s which includes an image of Carlyle. Dante Gabriel Rossetti remarked that this picture 'illustrated all kinds of Carlylianisms'. So too did the murals celebrating commerce and industry that Brown painted on the walls of the Manchester Town Hall.[115] Labour (its demands and its absence) dominated the lives and the consciouness of ordinary Victorians, providing the basis of material life, the focal point of social interaction and the source of identity for the worker.[116] A commitment to work made it possible for individuals to give meaning to their lives by engaging with the realities of human existence. Carlyle's 'Everlasting Yea' was seen as being intensely practical and highly social. It thus provided the means through which modern humanity might liberate itself from cloying shams that were either inherited from the past, or created in response to the dislocating effects of the realisation of the moral and intellectual redundancy of traditional forms and practices.[117] While Carlyle's readers drew a message of 'self-reform' from his writings, the fact that this was to be achieved by the repudiation of self-indulgence and self-interest and commitment to the gospel of labour, meant that his ideas were credited with an important role in forging new social and political ideals. This point was made by John Sterling and David Masson, two admirers of Carlyle who viewed him, as it were, at different stages in his career. From the perspective of the late 1830s and from that of the 1880s the 'Everlasting Yea' was seen in terms of Carlyle's commitment to radical criticism of social and political institutions and practices, and his standing as a disinterested champion of the real interests of the lower classes.[118]

These ideals cut across a range of ideological and class positions. In an article published in April 1881 Julia Wedgwood, an old friend of Carlyle, claimed that he was the first 'poetic thinker' to have presented work as something that was worthy of the attention of those who were not driven to it by economic necessity. Hitherto, labour had been tainted by the servile connotations attached to it in classical culture and by modern ideas that hunger was the spur of economic activity. Carlyle's writings had dispelled these demeaning images and given rise to a conception of work that was consistent with the cultural values of the middle and upper classes and with their social and political roles. Labour gave reality to a spirit of submission and renunciation and to the requirement that social and political privileges ought to be justified practically by the duties that arose from them.[119]

The breadth of Carlyle's definition of 'labour' and his insistence that the obligation to undertake it was universal, both facilitated and encouraged this view of the role of elites in modern society. John Morley saw labour as the key to independence since it was only through a commitment to action that individuals would be encouraged to pursue knowledge and thus free themselves and their fellows from slavery to 'prejudice, unreality, darkness, and error.'[120] Morley thought that the doctrine of labour pointed to the need for statesman to concentrate their attention upon 'one great subject' and to address this before taking up another. He applied this rule in his own political career.[121] Morley was one of the 'university liberals' who rose to prominence in the 1860s. For others associated with this reforming current in mid-Victorian politics, a commitment to renunciation and to the gospel of labour lent support to an emerging ethic of disinterested social service. In the last third of the nineteenth century, this ethic was prominent in the social and political philosophy of 'British Idealism', an intellectual current that looked (as Carlyle had done) to late eighteenth- and early nineteenth- century Germany for inspiration. These philosophers were liberal and democratic in their general political orientation and were not impressed by the authoritarian and hierarchical cast of Carlyle's views on government and representation. Like other readers, however, they were able to make selective use of his ideas. The belief that a sense of fundamental purpose and self-affirmation required active engagement with the concerns of their contemporaries was central to the Idealists' general position, as was their rejection of the view that the moral destiny of humans could be reduced to the arid, self-referential and hedonistic terms of Bentham's utilitarianism. F. H. Bradley, the author of *Ethical Studies* (1876), a work that is usually regarded as the first elaborate published statement of the ethical theory of the British Idealists, was an admiring reader of *Sartor Resartus*. In an undergraduate essay on utilitarianism, Bradley contrasted the 'slavish system' of hedonistic utilitarianism with the 'pure ethic' that was specified by transcendental law and captured by the injunction in *Sartor Resartus* to 'Love not pleasure; love god ... the Everlasting Yea, wherein all contradiction is solved'.[122] In *Ethical Studies* Bradley's claim that self-realisation was pursued through (although not fully achieved in) commitment to one's 'station and its duties' echoed Carlyle's views.

A similar point might be made about the social and political philosophy of T. H. Green, a leading figure in British Idealism. Green may have been among the earnest schoolboy readers of Carlyle at Rugby School, referred to by a witness before the Clarendon Commission that enquired into the great English public schools.[123] He certainly knew Carlyle's work on Cromwell. In a series of lectures on the English Revolution Green expressed reservations about Carlyle's focus on 'great men' but he shared his enthusiasm for the English Puritans. Green's political writings treated the obligations of the middle and upper classes in ways that were similar to the account of Carlyle's position presented by Wedgwood. His claim that the 'State' represented the moral aspirations and agency of the community incorporated the critical stance towards *laissez-faire* that underwrote Carlyle's 'condition of England' writings.[124]

In an essay published in 1892 Caird (a close associate of Green) was critical of Carlyle's contempt for democracy and his lack of feeling for the 'organic unity or *solidarity* of human life' that resulted from the distancing effect of his strong sense of independence. He saw Carlyle's exaggerated reliance on heroic figures as a consequence of his limited appreciation of the forces at work within society. At the same time, however, Caird credited Carlyle with reviving an ethical ideal of the state in nineteenth-century Britain, and with doing more than any other British writer to make moral regeneration a core value in contemporary society.[125]

One of Green's students, Bernard Bosanquet, developed an account of the moral value of personal sacrifice that had strong Carlylian overtones. He also echoed Carlyle's appeal to Goethe's 'here or nowhere is America' in *Sartor Resartus*, encouraging his readers to focus on the duties that confronted them in their day-to-day lives.[126] These duties included those that parents owed to their children, a subset of a more extensive range of obligations through which the actions of individuals sustained the various levels of relationships that made up complex social wholes. Bosanquet thought that state welfare provision would undermine individuals' sense of these obligations, turning them into child-like dependents rather than self-directed, active members of society.[127] He argued for this position in his philosophical works, and gave practical effect to it through his close involvement in the Charity Organisation Society (COS), formed in the 1870s to resist 'indiscriminate' charity by private philanthropists and public agencies.

Carlyle was a (largely nominal) member of the 'Poor Law Reform Association', a body that was a forerunner of the COS.[128] His interest in poor law reform, however, had more to do with his wish to promote opportunities for worthwhile labour than with any great faith in the punitive features of the system of poor relief created by the Poor Law Amendment Act of 1834. Moreover, unlike COS publicists, Carlyle never seems to have reconciled himself to the inevitability of unemployment in market societies. He was, nevertheless, greatly admired by some leading figures in the COS, both because his ideas inspired individuals to make a commitment to the ethic of service that underwrote membership of organisations like the COS, and also because his views on labour and self-sacrifice might make him hostile to state-sponsored poor relief. From this point of view, it is perhaps significant that Sir Baldwyn Leighton, a staunch opponent of outdoor relief on the grounds that it encouraged reliance on charity and discouraged industry and thrift, wrote to Carlyle as an ally on this theme and also on the value of cooperative farms and stores in facilitating independence and self-help among the working classes.[129]

In the late 1840s Carlyle was admired by a number of those associated with the Christian Socialist movement that flourished briefly under the leadership of J. M. Ludlow, Charles Kingsley and F. D. Maurice. Kingsley and Maurice were impressed greatly with *The French Revolution* and *Chartism*, drawing from those works a critique of *laissez-faire* and a conception of the real meaning of Chartism that played a role in framing their response to the turmoil of the 1848 revolutions in Europe and the Chartist challenge to the British state. This version of Christian Socialism incorporated a cataclysmic theory of the consequences of long-sustained injustice to the working classes that echoed Carlyle's views. It proposed alternatives to the recent practices of politics that were strongly anti-egalitarian and anti-democratic.[130] Although Carlyle did not think much of Maurice, and does not seem to have been interested in Christian Socialism, his ideas had an ongoing influence on this movement. When it underwent a revival later in the century his name was evoked in support of its tenets.

In a work published in 1891 Henry Rose presented Carlyle as one of the inspirational precursors of what he called 'the new political economy' that was central to the second wave of the Christian Socialist movement. Rose argued that Carlyle's readers took from his work an unbounded faith in the 'ultimate triumph of the laws and justice and right'. He drew on *Chartism*, *Past and Present*, *Latter-Day Pamphlets* and Carlyle's essays to stress the need for elite leadership and to warn that government 'for the people' did not necessarily require government 'by the people'. He also attacked 'mammon worship' and promoted the organisation of labour and the responsibilities of employers to pay fair wages and to provide stability of employment.[131] Rose saw these themes in Carlyle's writings as supportive of the image of society promoted by Christian Socialists and captured in the Pan-Anglican Synod's definition of socialism as any scheme that 'aims at unifying labour and the instruments of labour (land and capital), whether by means of the State, or the help of the rich, or the voluntary co-operation of the poor'. It placed a premium on unity and order, resisted prevailing tendencies to extreme poverty and widening class divisions, and insisted that society was an organic whole.[132]

Christian Socialism was also of interest to members of the Carlyle Society. A paper on the topic by Howard Paul Campbell was read at one of its meetings and published as a Social Democratic Federation pamphlet in 1884.[133] The federation was a quasi-Marxist organisation led by H. M. Hyndman, an admirer of Carlyle; among its membership at this time was William Morris, who later named Carlyle among the leading intellectual and literary figures of the century. On hearing of his death, Morris remarked to a correspondent that 'Carlyle is off to learn the great secret at last'. Although he was depressed by the 'ferocity' of the gloom that pervaded Carlyle's reminiscences of his wife, he later commented that he found Carlyle's life interesting 'in spite of Froude', and was struck by the evident sincerity of his prose and letters. Carlyle was 'on the right side in spite of all his faults'.[134]

In common with other readers of Carlyle, those who gravitated to socialist organisations in the 1880s and 1890s tended to make selective use of his writings, appealing to his authority when adopting ideas that they found inspiring, and rejecting others that seemed outmoded, or incompatible with their fundamental political values. For example, Frederick Pickles, the Secretary of the Bradford Branch of the Socialist League, decorated handbills with passages from Carlyle's writings. Pickles and his associates were impressed with the image of a new social order that emerged from Carlyle's writings. They saw this as a product of the collective will of the community released through democratic socialism, rather than associating it with hero-worship and elite leadership.[135]

Christian Socialists read *The French Revolution* as a rebuke to a decadent and irresponsible elite and as warning of the consequences that would follow if it did not mend its ways. As with some of the earliest readers of this work, however, it might also be seen in relation to programmes that involved some degree of commitment to the idea that revolutionary action by the working classes might be necessary to free society from the shackles of capitalism. This view was reflected in Edmund Stonelake's response to Carlyle's writings. Stonelake, who was associated with the Social Democratic Federation and other socialist groups in the 1880s, saw *The French Revolution* as a highly compelling, graphic and socially informed account of the causes and conduct of a revolution that still provided a point of reference for some of those on the left wing of British politics.[136]

Robert Blatchford, the founder of the 'Clarion' movement and publisher of the widely circulated *Clarion* newspaper, used Carlyle's writings as a source for his account of socialism as a visionary movement. As a young man, Blatchford was first introduced to Carlyle's writings during his army service when a sergeant gave him a copy of *Heroes and Hero-worship*. He subsequently read *Sartor Resartus* and a range of Carlyle's other works, and was a lifelong admirer of his style, 'the strongest, the most imaginative, the most virile, the most poetical prose writer the world has ever known'.[137] Given Blatchford's support for British imperialism, it is likely that he found Carlyle's statement of 'England's mission' highly congenial. He certainly acknowledged his importance on other topics more closely associated with socialism. Blatchford utilised Carlyle's accounts of mammon-worship and the image of Midas when advancing his own criticisms of the implications of unchecked capitalism on the lives of labourers, and on the quality of human interaction in industrial societies. He also adopted Carlyle's suggestion that state enterprises would provide a means of organising labour and setting a benchmark for the conditions under which it was undertaken. Moreover, in Blatchford's hands, the idea of heroism was applied to ordinary people whose sense of truth and duty sustained human life. He believed that the trust on which socialism relied rested upon the mutual recognition of these heroic values.[138] Like another Independent Labour Party stalwart, James Keir Hardie, Blatchford drew not only on *Sartor Resartus* and *Past and Present*, but also on *Latter-Day Pamphlets*.[139]

These pamphlets had dismayed some of Carlyle's admirers when they were first published in 1850, and have never been a favourite of modern scholars. In the late nineteenth century, however, they enjoyed something of a vogue. By the turn of the century, an anonymous writer with a close connection to Carlyle's publisher reported that they were the most widely read of his works.[140] Blatchford and Hardie's reference to the 'Latter-Day Pamphlets' reflected the fact that, despite their flaws, these writings presented a range of practical policy proposals that were not out of place in debates over the role of the state in the late nineteenth and early twentieth centuries.

The diverse character of the responses to Carlyle's writings points to the ongoing impact of a mission that was conceived more than eighty years before. Carlyle's conception of his role and his congenital tendency for earnest striving and against complacency, meant that although he thought that his mission had come to an end, he was incapable of seeing it as having achieved its end. Responses to his writings seemed to reflect, however, at least some of the qualities of mind and spirit that were the hallmarks of Carlyle's appeal to his contemporaries. They also embraced and celebrated its relentless radical progressivism.

Notes

Notes to Chapter 1: Beginnings

1   Moncure D. Conway, *Thomas Carlyle* (New York, 1881), pp. 147–49; *The Life of Thomas Carlyle* (1881), p. 15.

2   *Times*, 7 February 1881, p. 4. On the following day this newspaper reported death notices appearing in the German press.

3   *Reminiscences*, pp. 9, 4–5, 7–8, 11, 14. Carlyle was the subject of biographical studies before his death but these were overshadowed by J. A. Froude's controversial *Early Life* and *London Life*. David Alec Wilson responded to Froude in a six volume biography published in the 1920s and 1930s. There are modern full scale biographies by Simon Heffer, *Moral Desperado: A Life of Thomas Carlyle* (1995), and Fred Kaplan, *Thomas Carlyle: A Biography* (Ithaca, New York 1983). The married lives of Carlyle and his wife have recently been the subject of a major study by Rosemary Ashton, *Thomas and Jane Carlyle: Portrait of a Marriage* (2002). Ian Campbell's *Thomas Carlyle* (Edinburgh, 1993), a reprint of a book first published in 1974, provides an excellent short introduction to both Carlyle and his writings. A. L. Quesne's *Carlyle* (Oxford, 1982) provides a brief and insightful account of Carlyle's writings.

4   NLS, MS 2884, fol. 175; the phrase appears in the draft of an early chapter of Frederick Martin's 'Autobiography'. Mary Aitken wrote to Martin rebuking him for publishing this work; Carlyle received a written apology from the publisher, Trubner; NLS, MS 2884, fol. 4, 7 June 1877. Although Carlyle was outraged at Martin for retailing what he regarded as tittle-tattle generated by ignorance or spite, he did not reject this particular claim. Indeed, when read in the light of his own recollection of his father's controlled and directed passion, the informant's qualification, that the Carlyle brothers reacted to what they saw as moral transgressions not out of a spirit of bullying or self-interest, makes this account at least plausible.

5   *Reminiscences*, p. 30.

6   *CL*, i, pp. 290–91, 20 December 1820.

7   NLS, MS 2886 H, fos. 73–74. Carlyle did not spare himself from self-criticism; this is apparent in his comments on his own work, and, as Kaplan notes, in his self-recrimination over his treatment of his wife; Kaplan, *Thomas Carlyle*, p. 462.

8   *CL*, v, p. 120. Carlyle does not appear to have been closely attached to a half brother, the offspring of his father's first marriage, perhaps reflecting the central role that Margaret Carlyle played in the family.

9   His losses included those incurred while tenant of the farm on an isolated property called 'Craigenputtock' that was owned by Thomas's mother-in-law, Mrs Welsh; when Alick quit this tenancy his capital had been reduced from £700 to £300; *CL*, v, p. 282. It is ironic that the value of the property to Mrs Welsh was a result of a situation where the demand for farms pushed rents to levels that jeopardized the interests of tenants.

10   NLS, MS 528, fol. 60, 22 April 1876. The correspondence has been collected in Marrs.

11   *CL*, ii, p. 323, 2 April 1823.

12   See below, pp. 41–42.

13   NLS, MS 20752, fol. 43v, 2 December 1868.

14   Michael Flinn et al., *Scottish Population History: From 1700 to the 1930s* (Cambridge, 1977), p. 270.

15   *CL*, vi, p. 161.

16   NLS, MS 528, fol. 71, 9 July 1877.

17   Thomas Murray, *Autobiographical Notes: Also Reminiscences of a Journey to London in 1840*, ed. John A. Fairley (Dumfries, 1911), p. 21.

18   'Inaugural Address at Edinburgh, 2 April 1866, on Being Installed as Rector of the University There', *CME*, vii, pp. 172–73, repeating a claim made in Carlyle's 'Lectures on Literature', delivered in 1838 but not published until after his death; see *LHL*, p. 101.

19   NLS, MS 1763, fol. 24, 5 March 1819.

20   *CL*, viii, pp. 283, 345, 368. Leakage from the keg meant that other parts of this shipment, including books that Carlyle had borrowed from J. S. Mill, were impregnated by the smell of the spirit.

21   Campbell, *Thomas Carlyle*, p. 17.

22   Ibid., p. 29.

23   *Reminiscences*, p. 414; Campbell, *Thomas Carlyle*, p. 23.

24   See Kaplan, *Thomas Carlyle*, pp. 31–32 for insightful comments on Leslie's conception of mathematics and its appeal to Carlyle.

25   Ian Campbell, *Carlyle and Europe: Some Early Contacts* (Edinburgh, 1977), and see below pp. 43–47.

26   NLS, MS 1764, fol. 136.

27   The correspondence (first published by Charles Elliot Norton in 1887) appears in volumes iii–v of *CL*.

28   Murray, *Autobiographical Notes*, p. 15.

29   NLS, MS 1764, fol. 21, 21 June 1814, Thomas Murray to Thomas Carlyle.

30   NLS, MS, 1764, fol. 120, 2 June 1818, James Johnston to Thomas Carlyle; fol. 130v, 20 November 1818, Robert Mitchell to Thomas Carlyle.

31   *Reminiscences*, p. 352.

32   Ibid., p. 220.

33   Ibid., pp. 339–40.

34   *CL*, i, p. 98, 31 March 1817.

35   See Campbell, *Thomas Carlyle*, p. 30.

36   *CL*, i, p. 119, 16 February 1818, and see below p. 34.

37   See Campbell *Thomas Carlyle*, p. 31.

38   *CL*, ii, p. 414, Irving to Jane Welsh, 9 September 1822.

39 See *CL*, i, p. 120, for Carlyle's impressions of Gibbon's work; he thought it impressive, if at times 'obscene'. Masson records Carlyle's later statement on the impact of Gibbon on him; David Masson, *Edinburgh Sketches and Memories* (1892), pp. 263–64.

40 See below, p. 180.

41 See below, pp. 41–43.

42 *CL*, i, p. 282, 19 October 1820, and see below p. 35.

43 *CL*, ii, p. 79, 2 April 1822.

44 *CL*, i, p. 378, 14 August, 1821.

45 NLS, MS 1763, fol. 63, 26 January 1822.

46 As discussed in detail in a later chapter, *Sartor Resartus* presented a poetically powerful, stylized account of the intellectual, moral and spiritual impact of what Carlyle called a 'felt lack of faith'; see below pp. 67–70.

47 *CL*, ii, p. 421, 25 November 1823.

48 T. Wemyss Reid, *Life of the Rt. Hon. W. E. Forster*, 2 vols (1888), i, p. 210.

49 Frederic Harrison, 'Froude's Life of Carlyle'(1885), *The Choice of Books and Other Literary Pieces* (1899), p. 179. Harrison makes the interesting point that Carlyle's account of his relationship with his wife is coloured by the very literary qualities that made him such a powerful writer (p. 186).

50 *SR*, p. 135.

51 *CL*, iii, p. 249, 13 January 1825.

52 *CL*, vii, p. 103 n 5.

53 Ibid., vii, pp. 44, 124. After Carlyle's death William Wylie visited Craigenputtock and provided counter testimony to what he thought were the 'absurd' claims about the 'wild, inhospitable character of the place'; William Howie Wylie, *Thomas Carlyle: The Man and His Books*, ed. William Robertson, second edition (1909), p. 378 n. Wylie's comments do not allow for the psychological impact of prolonged isolation in such a remote spot, nor for the fact that he saw the property half a century after the Carlyles lived there and more than a decade after Carlyle had spent a significant amount of money developing the farm; see above p. 5.

54 *CL*, viii, p. 322, 22 March 1836.

55 *Reminiscences*, p. 142.

56 Anthony Trollope, *An Autobiography*, ed. David Skilton (Harmondsworth, 1996), p. 69.

57 *CL*, xxvii, pp. 330–31, 8 October 1852. In reporting this incident to John Carlyle Jane said she had not told her husband of it 'in case [he] should take it in his head to be uneasy – which is not likely but just possible' (p. 331).

58 *CL*, xxx, pp. 221–22.

59 *CL*, viii, p. 362.

60 Charles and Frances Brookfield, *Mrs Brookfield and Her Circle*, 2 vols (1905), ii, p. 306.

61 See William Allingham, *Diary*, with an introduction by Geoffrey Grigson (1907 repr. Fontwell, 1967), p. 208, for an episode in 1872.

62 *Reminiscences*, p. 155.

63 Charles and Mary Cowden Clarke, *Recollections of Writers* (1878), pp. 85–86. Browning told Ford Maddox Ford that Carlyle saw no merit in Mozart or Beethoven; Virginia Surtees, ed., *The Diary of Ford Maddox Brown* (New Haven, Connecticut, 1981), p. 198.

64 *CL*, xxx, pp. 271–72.

65 NLS, MS 665, 27 October 1841.

66 This essay was written in a state of 'stupefaction' brought on by a cold that left Carlyle deaf in one ear and with his head feeling like a block of wood; *CL*, ix, p. 370.

67 'Sir Walter Scott', *CME*, vi, p. 72.

68 Ibid., pp. 32, 73.

69 *Reminiscences*, p. 145.

70 Robert J. N. Todd, *Caroline Fox: Quaker Blue-Stocking, 1819–1871* (York, 1980), p. 31.

71 NLS, MS 2883, fol. 94, 4 July 1840.

72 *CL*, ii, p. 190; iv, pp. 303–4, 389. Francis Espinasse, *Literary Recollections and Sketches* (1893), pp. 98, 183; see also Fred Kaplan, 'Power and Authority', in Jerry D. James and Rita B. Bottoms, eds., *Lectures on Carlyle and His Era* (Santa Cruz, California, 1985), pp. 3–7.

73 NLS, MS 1767, fos. 173–75, 22 December 1857; fos. 245–46, 21 September 1860.

74 See below, pp. 162–63.

75 *CME*, vi, p. 187.

76 Frederic Harrison, ed., *Carlyle and the London Library: Accounts of its Foundation, Together with Unpublished Letters of Thomas Carlyle to W. D. Christie, CB* (1907), pp. 9–10.

77 Ibid., pp. 62, 83–84, 31.

78 NLS, MS 1775C, fol. 13, 19 November 1865. The question whether the Rector should play a substantive or merely a ceremonial role was discussed in the run-up to the election; see Anna Mill, *Carlyle and Mill: Two University Rectors* (Edinburgh, 1965), p. 6.

79 NLS, MS 1775C, fos. 9–12. For a brief account of the governance of the University and the reform of its faculties see D. B. Horn, *A Short History of the University of Edinburgh, 1556–1889* (Edinburgh, 1967), pp. 154–5, 174–85; Carlyle's old associate Sir David Brewster, now Principal of the University, was among the reformers. In a posthumous account of Carlyle's conversation dating from 1868, he was reported as complaining at the lack of consideration shown to Scottish graduates by the Universities of Oxford and Cambridge. Carlyle favoured Scottish universities because he thought that they were more tolerant than their English counterparts and were free of 'shams'; NLS, MS 1796, fol. 122v.

80 Heffer, *Moral Desperado*, p. 254, writes of the role that Jane's jealousy of Lady Ashburton played in precipitating a nervous breakdown in the summer of 1846. Rosemary Ashton (*Thomas and Jane Carlyle*, pp. 268–73) notes the strains of this period without presenting the outcome in quite such dire terms. She provides a masterly and highly plausible characterisation of the conduct of the parties to this painful drama: 'Carlyle was selfish and acted, for such an honest man, in self-deceiving bad faith. Jane was excessively sensitive and excessively punitive. And Lady Harriet was either surprisingly insensitive or actually malicious', p. 271.

81 NLS, Acc. 11388, no. 25, no date, April 1857?

82 *CL*, vii, pp. 32–33, [9 November 1833].

83 *CL*, xvii, p. 194, 1 December 1843.

84 NLS, Acc. 11388, no. 28, 7 May 1866.

85 Jane Welsh Carlyle, *The Simple Story of My Own First Love*, eds. K. J. Fielding, Ian Campbell and Aileen Christianson (Edinburgh, 2001), pp. 14–15. I am grateful to Professor Campbell for bringing this publication to my attention.

86 Ashton, *Thomas and Jane Carlyle*, pp. 432–34.

87 Frederick L. Mulhauser, ed., *The Correspondence of Arthur Hugh Clough*, 2 vols (Oxford, 1957), ii, pp. 408–9n.

88 Brookfield, *Mrs Brookfield*, ii, p. 438; John Tyndall, *New Fragments* (1892), pp. 369–70. Edith Twisleton told a correspondent in the United States that Jane's taste for acerbic gossip made Becky Sharp seem mild-mannered; Mrs Edward Twisleton, *Letters of the Hon. Mrs Edward Twisleton, Written to Her Family, 1853–1862* (1928), p. 272.

89 Charles Gavan Duffy, *Conversations with Carlyle* (1892), p. 5.

90 *Reminiscences*, p. 140.

91 Ibid., p. 5. See Campbell, *Thomas Carlyle*, p. 61, for a well-balanced comment on the Carlyles's sexual relationship and Ashton, *Portrait of a Marriage*, for far more extensive reflections on this topic. She discusses the miscarriage on pp. 121–22, pointing out that material in support of this reading of some obscure passages in the Carlyles's correspondence and family stories were brought to the forefront by Alexander Carlyle as part of his attempt to rebut hints of impotence in Froude's account.

92 Espinasse, *Literary Recollections*, p. 268; Andrew Symington, *Some Personal Reminiscences of Carlyle* (1886), p. 14; first published in New York in the *Independent* in 1881.

93 *CL*, iv, p. 125, [12 August 1826].

94 See below, pp. 199–200.

Notes to Chapter 2: Literature as Mission

1 Richard Baxter, *A Christian Directory, or Body of Practical Divinity* (1673), sig. A3v.

2 See below, p. 162. Knox's style of admonishment, like that of Carlyle, did not meet with universal approbation; on the former see, for example, the sharp critique in G. Scott-Moncrieff's *Edinburgh* (1947), pp. 21–23.

3 David Masson, *Edinburgh Sketches and Memories* (1893), p. 276, points out that English commentators such as J. A. Froude, whose views were derived from Oxbridge experience, exaggerated the material hardships suffered by Carlyle; while this may be true, the impact of ongoing uncertainty should not be discounted when considering this stage of his career.

4 Carlyle regarded his *Life of Schiller* (1825) as on a par with review work rather than being an original composition; the first attempt at a work which fulfilled this criterion, *Wolfgang Reiner*, was not completed and was never offered to a publisher during Carlyle's lifetime.

5 *SR*, p. 111.

6 *CL*, i, p. 142, 6 November 1818.

7 Ibid., p. 135. Carlyle's aspirations had been encouraged by one of his earliest friends, Thomas Murray, who had first met him in 1810. Murray told Carlyle in 1814 that he expected that his name would be 'inseparably connected with the literary history of the nineteenth century'; Thomas Murray, *Autobiographical Notes: Also Reminiscences of a Journey to London in 1840*, ed. J. A. Fairley (Dumfries, 1911), p. 24.

8 NLS, MS 1764, fol. 120, James Johnston to Thomas Carlyle, 2 June 1818; fol. 130v, Robert Mitchell to Thomas Carlyle, 20 November 1818. Together with Irving and Murray, these

friends from University provided encouragement and support to Carlyle in his early days in Edinburgh.

9   *CL*, i, p. 144, 6 November 1818, p. 159, 15 February 1819, 217n; NLS, MS 1764, Edward Irving to Thomas Carlyle, August 1820, fol. 188.

10 *CL*, i, pp. 261–61, 7 June 1820.

11 See Robert Keith Lapp, *Contest for Cultural Authority: Hazlitt, Coleridge, and the Distresses of the Regency* (Detroit, 1999).

12 *CL*, i, p. 371, 19 July 1821; see also pp. 310–11, 22 January 1822.

13 Ibid., p. 321, 30 January 1821, p. 418, 25 December 1821; ii, p. 70, 23 March 1822, p. 94, 27 April 1822. John Locke's life and the English Commonwealth seemed at times to be promising subjects. Carlyle wrote at length on the latter; unfortunately, given his sharp reaction against 'mechanical philosophy', he never produced a book or even an article on Locke's life or thought. For Masson's comment see David Masson, *Carlyle Personally and in his Writings: Two Edinburgh Lectures* (1885), p. 65.

14 *Two Notebooks*, pp. 276–77.

15 *CL*, iii, p. 147, 2 September 1824.

16 *SR*, p. 119. In 1842 Carlyle urged the young James Hutchinson Stirling against a literary career, advising him to persevere with medicine and to write in his leisure time. It should be noted that these comments refer to literature as a trade – 'the fright fullest, fatalest and too generally despicable of all trades now followed under the sun' – something that Carlyle always disliked; see J. H. Stirling, *Thomas Carlyle's Counsels to a Literary Aspirant* (Edinburgh, 1886), p. 13. By 1850, when he was writing the 'Latter-Day Pamphlets', Carlyle's general attitude towards literature, or at least to contemporary literature, appears to have cooled; see below, pp. 149–50.

17 Cf. Gregory Maertz, 'Carlyle's Mediation of Goethe and its European Context', *Scottish Literary Journal*, 24 (1997), pp. 61–62.

18 *CL*, i, p. 104, 5 July 1817. For an account of Southey's increasingly reactionary view of events such as the Peterloo Massacre see Mark Storey, *Robert Southey: A Life* (Oxford, 1997), pp. 277–79. Carlyle and his old college friends relished Francis Jeffrey's *Edinburgh Review* contribution to the embarrassment caused by the republication of one of Southey's early radical plays; one correspondent described the Poet Laureate as a 'mad poet' and a 'bad political philosopher'; *Reminiscences*, pp. 386–87 and NLS, MS 1764, fol. 90, James Johnston to Thomas Carlyle. Carlyle later formed a far more favourable view of Southey. Having met him for the first time in February 1835, he noted that he and Southey shared a common dislike of democratic government; he even found something honest and sincere in Southey's attachment to the Church of England. Later, he was gratified by Southey's admiration for his *The French Revolution*; see *Reminiscences*, pp. 388–401.

19 *CL*, i, p. 230, 1 March 1820; ii, p. 174, 10 October 1822.

20 Carlyle, 'Edward Irving', *Reminiscences*, p. 247.

21 Lord Macaulay, 'Samuel Johnson' (1831), *Reviews and Essays from "The Edinburgh"* (n.d.), p. 221. Macaulay was highly critical of Croker's inaccuracies, but while he clearly admired Johnson he thought that he would be remembered for his peculiarities rather than for the merits of his writing, or the virtues of his character.

22 'Boswell's Life of Johnson', *CME*, i, pp. 68–71. This essay dates from 1832, but, as noted below, the admiration of Johnston was current among Carlyle's university friends.

23 *CL*, i, p. 60, 22 August 1815.

24 Ibid., p. 273, 15 September 1820.

25 Norma Clarke places this interpretation on discussions that took place in 1825, attributing this, and other displays of concern with his independence, to Carlyle's sense of masculinity; see Norma Clarke, 'Strenuous Idleness: Thomas Carlyle and the Man of Letters as Hero', in Michael Roper and John Tosh, eds., *Manful Assertions: Masculinities in Britain since 1800* (1991), p. 37. This might well be the case, but Carlyle's views on the importance of authorial independence point to a broader agenda.

26 J. M. Sloan observed that Carlyle's talent seems to have given him a privileged position in his family. For example, there is no record of him having been expected to work in the mason's yard or later on the farm; see *The Carlyle Country with a Study of Carlyle's Life* (1904), p. 69. There are occasional references in the letters to Carlyle working in his parents' garden but this (like the gardening that he did at Craigenputtock and Chelsea) seems to have been recreational and therapeutic, not a matter of economic necessity.

27 *CL*, iv, p. 70, 2 April 1826. In his annotations to Froude's *EL* (ii, p. 377) Alexander Carlyle noted that Jane and her mother often quarrelled; NLS, MS 752.

28 See *CL*, i, p. 21, 24 August 1814, and Masson, *Edinburgh Sketches*, pp. 278, 280–81.

29 *Two Reminiscences*, p. 51.

30 NLS, Acc. 10484, Thomas Carlyle to Thomas Murray, August 1824, fol. 53; *CL*, ii, p. 205.

31 'Boswell's Life', pp. 99–100. Years later when commenting on a biography written for the German market, Carlyle was incensed to be described as a 'journalist' (see *Two Reminiscences of Thomas Carlyle*, p. 47). He was unlikely to have been pleased by Herman Merivale's review of the second edition of *The French Revolution*, in which praise for the vigour of Carlyle's style was mixed with references to the impact on it of his early journalism and, most painful of all, the suggestion that Carlyle's 'episodic' structure meant that his firmest adherents were likely to be the 'desultory readers and thinkers of the day'; see 'Carlyle on the French Revolution', *Edinburgh Review*, 71 (July 1840), p. 412.

32 Thomas Carlyle, 'Death of Charles Buller', in *Rescued Essays*, pp. 118–19.

33 Ibid., p. 119.

34 *SR*, p. 50.

35 These matters are dealt with in detail below pp. 147–8, 170–71; on Puritanism see also John Morrow, 'Heroes and Constitutionalists: The Ideological Significance of Thomas Carlyle's Treatment of the English Revolution', *History of Political Thought*, XIV (1993), pp. 205–23, and Clyde de L. Ryals, 'Carlyle and the Law', *CSA*, 14 (1994), pp. 26–27.

36 See James Eli Adams, 'The Hero as Spectacle: Carlyle and the Persistence of Dandyism', in Carol T. Christ and John O. Jordon, eds., *Victorian Literature and the Victorian Visual Imagination* (Berkeley, California, 1995), pp. 213–32.

37 In Frederick Martin's oddly named 'Autobiography', published in the short-lived *Biographical Magazine* in 1877, there is an account (based on information provided by local people) of an exchange between James Carlyle and Sharpe that was witnessed by harvest workers and by Sharpe's visitors. James Carlyle's scorn, sarcasm and whimsy ensured that he got the better of Sharpe, much to the amusement of the latter's companions; NLS, MS

2886H, fos. 72–75. Carlyle reacted angrily to this essay describing it as 'utterly erroneous, false, imaginary and absurd' and abusing the author's local informants; NLS, MS 528, fol. 71, 9 July 1877. It is not clear that these strictures apply to all aspects of the biography; the surviving references to the family's relationship with General Sharpe are certainly contemptuous enough to lend some credence to the account in the biographical essay.

38   Quoted 'Boswell's Life', pp. 102–3.

39   Ibid., p. 101. Carlyle's critical remarks on the *Advice* are recorded in *CL*, i, pp. 77–78.

40   *CL*, vi, p. 270, 2 December 1832.

41   See NLS, MS 1764, fol. 195v, Edward Irving to Thomas Carlyle, December 1820.

42   *CL*, iii, pp. 93–94, 25 June 1824.

43   *Earlier Letters of John Stuart Mill,* ed. Francis E. Mineka, *Collected Works of John Stuart Mill,* (Toronto, 1962–91), pp. 144–45, 9 March 1833; pp. 217, 224, 2 March 1834 and 28 April 1834.

44   See Ian Campbell, 'Carlyle: Sage of Chelsea or Sage of Echelfechan', in Horst W. Drescher ed., *Thomas Carlyle 1981: Papers Given at the International Thomas Carlyle Centenary Symposium* (Frankfurt am Main, 1983), p. 390. One of Carlyle's earliest biographers reported his wife as saying that his idealisation of his countrymen did not survive first-hand exposure to them; see Moncure D. Conway, *Thomas Carlyle* (New York, 1881), p. 129. This remark may reflect Jane's relative lack of interest in returning to Scotland in later life as well as her wry, teasingly deflationary responses to Carlyle's enthusiasms. It is worth bearing in mind, however, that John Carlyle's correspondence with Carlyle on University of Edinburgh affairs in the mid 1860s remarked on the narrow, sectarian views of some of those involved, treating them as an object of shared abhorrence. John referred to the 'narrow, violent and pessimistic sectarians that are peculiar to Edinburgh and would hardly thrive anywhere else' and to a twin obsession with 'money' and the 'defence of Christianity' as a 'curiosity peculiar to Edinburgh'; NLS, MS 1775C, fos. 14, 17, 21 November 1865 and 22 November 1865.

45   See David Amigoni, 'Displacing the Autobiographical Impulse: A Bakhtinian Reading of Thomas Carlyle's Reminiscences', Vincent Newey and Philip Shaw, eds., *Mortal Pages, Literary Lives: Studies in Nineteenth-Century Autobiography* (Aldershot, 1996), pp. 120–39.

46   *Reminiscences,* pp. 139–40.

47   NLS, MS 1764, fol. 52, 10 April 1815, Thomas Murray to Thomas Carlyle.

48   'Burns', *CME*, ii, p. 37; *CL*, iii, pp. 85, 91, 23, 24 June 1824.

49   *CL*, ix, p. 176, 21 March 1837.

50   *CL*, viii, pp. 9–10, 12 January 1835; ix, p. 176.

51   See Leslie Mitchell, *Bulwer Lytton: The Rise and Fall of a Victorian Man and Letters* (2003), pp. 113–14, for an account of Lytton's attitude towards, and reaction to, criticism.

52   *CL*, vi, p. 184, 2 July 1832.

53   John Carlyle's letters on Carlyle's investments and bank accounts (NLS, MS 20752) provide incomplete but interesting insights into this aspect of Carlyle's affairs.

54   David Hodge, *Thomas Carlyle: The Man and Teacher* (Edinburgh and Glasgow, 1873), pp. 50–51, praised Carlyle's simple style of life, noting that while he had become famous he was never rich and famous. Froude, *LL*, i, p. 314; William Aldis Wright, *Letters and Literary*

Remains of Edward Fitzgerald, 3 vols (1889), i, p. 379; Jules Paul Seigel, ed., *Thomas Carlyle: The Critical Heritage* (1971), p. 472.

55 On the issue of editorial discretion over copy see George L. Nesbit, *Benthamite Reviewing: The First Twelve Years of the Westminster Review, 1824–1836* (New York, 1934), p. 131. For Carlyle's transactions with Jeffries see *CL*, v, pp. 195–6; those with Cochrane are in NLS, MS 1766, fol. 1, John Cochrane to Thomas Carlyle, 24 January 1833 and Carlyle's response, *CL*, vi, p. 322, 10 February 1833. On this occasion Carlyle did not follow his earlier suggestion that the best way to deal with Cochrane was 'sharply, almost contemptuously'; ibid., p. 240n. Carlyle did not seem to bear a grudge against Cochrane. In 1841 he supported his candidature as Librarian of the newly established London Library; see Frederic Harrison, ed., *Carlyle and the London Library: An Account of its Foundation, Together with Unpublished Letters of Thomas Carlyle to W. D. Christie, CB* (1907), p. 83.

56 *CL*, v, pp. 195–96, 3 November 1830.

57 Ibid., p. 399, 4 September 1831. It seems clear that Murray only entered into negotiations with Carlyle as a favour to Jeffrey. In common with other London publishers he was very concerned at the slump in the trade and is unlikely to have taken kindly to Carlyle's cavalier remarks on such matters; for an account of Murray's position that draws upon the firm's archives see Thomas C. Richardson, 'John Murray's Reader of *Sartor Resartus*,' *CN*, 6 (1985), p. 40. Carlyle retaliated in the first British edition of this work by appending to it extracts from his correspondence with Murray and the report of his reader, here dubbed the 'Bookseller's Taster'; see *SR*, pp. 211–12.

58 *CL*, vi, pp. 137–38, 5 March 1832.

59 See James Chandler, *England in 1819: The Politics of Literary Culture and the Case of Romantic Historicism* (Chicago, 1998), pp. 267–73. Carlyle did, however, secure close to this sum in 1858 for the first two volumes of *FG*; see Ian Campbell, *Thomas Carlyle*, second edition (Edinburgh, 1993), p. 128.

60 *Two Reminiscences*, p.74

61 See Andrew Elfenbein, *Byron and the Victorians* (Cambridge, 1995), pp. 100–2; J. Don Vann, 'Fraser's Magazine', in Alvin Sullivan, ed., *British Literary Magazines:, The Romantic Age, 1789–1836* (Westport, Connecticut, 1983). *Fraser's* was highly critical of Lytton's aristocratic disdain of the middle classes and of what it took to be the empty vanity of his claim to artistic and intellectual superiority: 'The age of intellect, indeed! – the age of foppery. Not the march of mind, but of fools'. 'Mr Edward Lytton Bulwer's Novels', *Fraser's Magazine*, i (June 1830), p. 516. Lytton Bulwer, who changed his name to Bulwer Lytton, made a virtue out of his dandyism: 'God gave my soul an exterior abode and the very fact there is a soul within the shell, makes me think the shell not to be neglected'; cited Mitchell, *Bulwer Lytton*, p. 87.

62 In Carlyle's cordial correspondence with William Fraser, editor of the *Foreign Review*, one gets a sense of growing pressure resulting from Fraser's willingness to encourage Carlyle to write essays for him and to undertake projects on the history of German and English literature; NLS, MS 1765, William Fraser to Thomas Carlyle, 11? August 1828 and 9 November 1828.

63 John Stuart Mill, 'Diary 1854', *Journals and Debating Speeches*, ed. J. M. Robson, *Collected Works of John Stuart Mill*, (Toronto, 1988), p. 653; this comment dates from December 1854.

64 *Two Notebooks*, p. 275.

65 See Ian Campbell, *Carlyle and Europe: Some Early Contacts* (Edinburgh, 1977), pp. 16-17.

66 *CL*, i, pp. 255, 3 June 1820, 268, 4 August 1820. In a review of William Taylor's *History of German Poetry* Carlyle used an appreciation of Goethe as a yardstick of competence for English Germanists; see J. W. Robberds, ed., *A Memoir of the Life and Writings of the Late William Taylor of Norwich*, 2 vols (London, 1843), ii, pp. 538-51.

67 G. B. Tennyson, *Sartor Called Resartus: The Genesis, Structure, and Style of Thomas Carlyle's First Major Work* (Princeton, 1965), pp. 67, 82n. John Herauld's work indicates that British Germanists prided themselves on being fashionable and important; [John A. Herauld], 'German Poetry, No 1: Mr Taylor's Historic Survey of German Poetry', *Fraser's Magazine*, iv (September 1831), pp. 167-79. The subscription for a presentation medal for Goethe suggests that British admirers of German literature had some common sense of distinct identity.

68 See Chandler, *England in 1819*, pp. 267-73, for an account of this celebratory self image, one that was endorsed even by radical and relatively marginal figures such as Shelley in his 'Defence of Poetry'.

69 NLS, MS 664, fol. 42, 16 September 1827.

70 'Novalis' *CME*, ii, p. 188.

71 'Voltaire', *CME*, ii, p. 145. See Tennyson, *Sartor Called Resartus*, pp. 42-48 for a discussion of the biographical parallels between Carlyle and Schiller.

72 'Jean-Paul Friedrich Richter', *CME*, i, p. 19.

73 'Richter Again', *CME*, iii, pp. 37, 33.

74 'State of German Literature', *CME*, i, p. 34.

75 Carlyle, *Reminiscences*, p. 5.

76 *SR*, p. 77; see Chapter 4 below for a fuller exploration of this theme.

77 'The State of German Literature', p. 32.

78 'Goethe's Helena, *CME*, i, pp. 135-36.

79 'Novalis', pp. 205, 207.

80 Rosemary Ashton has argued that Carlyle's treatment of 'Kantianism' as a form of idealism is quite misguided and tends in its distinction between 'reason' and 'understanding' to rely heavily upon Coleridge's work. Given Carlyle's attitude to Coleridge, made public in his *Life of Sterling*, this dependence is ironic. On these issues see Rosemary Ashton, *The German Idea: Four English Writers and the Reception of German Thought, 1800-1860* (Cambridge, 1980), pp. 97-98. Wolfgang Franke suggests that Irving played an important role with respect to Carlyle's understanding of Coleridge; see 'Carlyle and Edward Irving: The Intellectual Basis of Their Friendship', in Drescher, ed., *Thomas Carlyle in 1981*, pp. 52-53. Ralph Jessop has shown that Carlyle's engagement with German responses to Humean skepticism were mediated through his earlier exposure to Scottish philosophy, particularly to the works of Sir William Hamilton; see 'Carlyle's Scotch Skepticism: Writing from the Scottish Tradition', *CSA*, 16 (1996), pp. 25-35.

81 'State of German Literature', pp. 50-51; *Two Reminiscences*, pp. 46-47.

82 'State of German Literature', p. 58.

83 'Death of Goethe', *CME*, iv, p. 48; 'Goethe' *CME*, i, p. 182.

84 Tennyson, *Sartor Called Resartus*, p. 72. Ashton, *The German Idea*, p. 92, stresses the aesthetic dimensions of Goethe's notion of renunciation and his assumption that duty and inclination would often coincide. Note, however, that Nicholas Boyle has recently argued that a more politically focused conception of renunciation became a stronger theme in Goethe's works after the catastrophe of the French Revolution; see Nicholas Boyle, *Goethe: The Poet and His Age* (Oxford, 2000), ii, pp. 323–26.

85 'Goethe's Helena', *CME*, i, p. 130.

86 'Inaugural Address at Edinburgh, 2 April 1866', *CME*, vii, p. 196.

87 See David R. Sorensen, 'Selective Affinities: Carlyle, Goethe, and the French Revolution', *CSA*, 16 (1996), pp. 1–24.

88 *CL*, viii, p. 39, 3 February 1835; for Emerson's reservations see *CL*, viii, p. 39n.

89 Maertz, 'Carlyle's Mediation of Goethe', pp. 66–67.

90 See Thomas Jeffers, 'Forms of Misprison: The Early- and Mid-Victorian Reception of Goethe's *Bildungsidee*', *University of Toronto Quarterly*, 57 (1988), pp. 501–515.

Notes to Chapter 3: Facing the Modern World

1 William Allingham, *Diary*, ed. Geoffrey Grigson (1907; repr. Fontwell, 1967), p. 205; this remark dates from about 1871.

2 For Macaulay's assault on James Mill see Jack Lively and J. C. Rees, eds., *Utilitarian Logic and Politics: James Mill's 'Essay on Government', Macaulay's Critique and the Ensuing Debate* (Oxford, 1978), pp. 97–130. Carlyle's comment on Dugald Stewart appeared in 'State of German Literature', *CME*, i, p. 67n. Ralph Jessop has shown how Carlyle's knowledge of the intuitionist element in 'Common Sense' philosophy provided him with an alternative to what he (in common with Thomas Reid and Dugald Stewart) took to be the mechanistic accounts of the human mind advanced by John Locke and David Hume; see Ralph Jessop, *Carlyle and Scottish Thought* (1997), pp. 137–38, 142ff.

3 See J. C. D. Clarke, *English Society, 1660–1832* (Cambridge, 1985), pp. 383–92; G. I. T. Machin, *The Catholic Question in English Politics, 1820–1830* (Oxford, 1964), pp. 16–17, and E. R. Norman, *Church and Society in England, 1770–1970* (Oxford, 1976), pp. 41–102.

4 'Moral and Political State of the British Empire', *Quarterly Review*, 44 (1831), p. 300; 'How Will It Work?', *Quarterly Review*, 48 (1832), p. 543. On Carlyle's view of Southey and for an account of the context of 'Signs of the Times' see Wendell V. Harris, 'Interpretative Historicism: "Signs of the Times" and *Culture and Anarchy* in their contexts', *Nineteenth Century Literature*, 44 (1990), pp. 445–49.

5 *CL*, vi, p. 61, 4 December 1831; p. 70, 20 December 1831.

6 See Ian Campbell, *Thomas Carlyle*, second edition, (Edinburgh, 1993), pp. 72–73, for a convincing account of the stimulating effect of the reform crisis of 1831 on Carlyle's political interests.

7 *Two Notebooks*, p. 145.

8 Froude, *EL*, ii, p. 78.

9 William Knighton, 'Conversations with Carlyle', *Contemporary Review*, 39 (1881), p. 917.

10 *LHL*, pp. 62–64. For a very good appreciation of Carlyle's views on religion, one that stresses his insistence on belief, his hostility to the church and its creeds and the difficulties of reconciling his position with Christianity, see Basil Wiley, *Nineteenth-Century Studies* (1949), pp. 105–25.

11 F. R Barton, ed., *Some New Letters of Edward Fitzgerald* (1923), pp. 123–24.

12 See Lawrence Poston, ' Millites and Millenarians: The Context of Carlyle's "Signs of the Times"', *Victorian Studies*, 26 (1983), pp. 395–96.

13 Froude, *EL*, ii, p. 234; *CL*, vi, pp. 14–15, 13 October 1831.

14 *SR*, p. 164.

15 *CL*, vi, p. 37; Froude, *EL*, ii, 234; *CL*, vi, pp. 14–15, 85.

16 See Harris, 'Interpretative Historicism', pp. 451–52.

17 'Characteristics', *CME*, iv, p. 1.

18 *SR*, pp. 12–13; later Teufeldröckh utters a string of 'extraordinary night-thoughts' without expressing the 'slightest feeling in his face' (p. 15).

19 *HHW*, p. 7.

20 *SR*, p. 46.

21 G. B. Tennyson, *Sartor Called Resartus: The Genesis, Structure and Style of Thomas Carlyle's First Major Work* (Princeton 1965), pp. 304–7.

22 'Signs of the Times', *CME*, ii, pp. 240–41, 245–47.

23 *SR*, p. 148.

24 See Poston, 'Millites and Millenarians', pp. 388–91, on which the following sentences rely.

25 James Mill, *Essay on Government*, in Lively and Reece, eds. *Utilitarian Science and Politics*, pp. 93–94.

26 'Signs of the Times', p. 234.

27 In Novalis' case, this critique was directed in part at Frederick the Great, a figure whom Carlyle tried to admire; see 'Faith and Love' in *The Early Political Writings of the German Romantics*, ed. and trans. Frederick C. Beiser (Cambridge, 1996), p. 45 and for Carlyle's account of Frederick's virtues see below pp. 178–80.

28 'Signs of the Times', pp. 234–40.

29 *Two Notebooks*, p. 277.

30 'Signs of the Times', pp. 235–36.

31 'Life of Heyne', *CME*, ii, p. 55.

32 'Signs of the Times, pp. 235–36.

33 *CL*, xii, p. 12, 9 January 1840.

34 'Signs of the Times', p. 249.

35 Ibid., p. 247

36 See Poston, 'Millites and Millenarians', p. 388.

37 *SR*, p. 35.

38 Novalis, 'Christianity and Europe', in Beiser, *The Early Political Writings of the German Romantics*, p. 70. In a letter to Goethe responding to an offer of a copy of his *Theory (or Science) of Colour*, Carlyle recorded his disillusionment with the mechanical treatment of optics in England and France. An oblique reference to Novalis in this letter suggests a stimulus for this formulation; see *CL*, v, pp. 27–28 and note 10, 3 November 1829.

39 'Characteristics', p. 15.

40 Ibid.

41 Ibid., p. 17.

42 See below, pp. 89–90.

43 'Characteristics', pp. 23–24.

44 Ibid., p. 26.

45 Ibid., p. 28.

46 Ibid., p. 36.

47 Ibid., p. 28.

48 'Signs of the Times', p. 251; see Ralph Jessop, 'Metaphor's Prodigious Influence: Carlyle's "Signs of the Times" and *Sartor Resartus*', *Scottish Literary Journal*, 24 (1997), pp. 50–51 for an account of the basis of Carlyle's views on the dangers of applying material metaphors to non-material objects.

49 'Signs of the Times', p. 243.

50 See Ian Campbell, *Carlyle and Europe: Some Early Contacts* (Edinburgh, 1977), pp. 13–17.

51 John Tyndall, 'Personal Recollections of Thomas Carlyle', *New Fragments* (1892), pp. 351, 386–87. Tyndall suggested that Carlyle reacted against presentations of Darwin's ideas only when they seemed to preclude a role for imagination, emotion and 'speculative' action.

52 'Signs of the Times', pp. 244–45.

53 'Sir Walter Scott', *CME*, vi, p. 46.

54 See below chapter 4.

55 See below, pp. 115–19.

56 *SR*, pp. 113–14.

57 Ibid., p. 162.

58 ' Characteristics', p. 25.

59 Allingham, *Diary*, p. 239.

60 'Characteristics', p. 12.

61 *SR*, pp. 39–42.

62 Lee C. R. Baker, 'The Old Clothesman Transformed: Thomas Carlyle's Radical Vision', *Victorian Institute Journal*, 11 (1982–83), p. 49.

63 *SR*, p. 135; *WM*, ii, p. 133.

64 *SR*, p. 114.

65 Ibid., p. 116.

66 Ibid., pp. 126, 130.

67 Ibid., pp. 132–33.

68 *CL*, 6, p.149; *SR*, p. 132. In *Byron and the Victorians*, pp. 106ff, Andrew Elfenbein draws some interesting parallels between Teufelsdröckh's life and George Moore's portrayal of Byron in his contemporary biography. A correspondent later reminded Carlyle that Goethe had admired Byron and included a lament on his death in the second part of Faust; NLS, MS 1767, fol. 162, 25 May 1857.

69 For a full discussion of various fragments deployed by Carlyle see Tennyson, *Sartor Called Resartus*, pp. 226–27.

70 *CL*, vii, p. 81, 21 January 1834; p. 175, 21 May 1834.

71 See Tennyson, *Sartor Called Resartus*, p. 227.

72 See Brian Cowlishaw, 'The Cultural Revolution of *Sartor Resartus*', *CSA*, 16 (1996), pp. 51–52.

73 See Lee C. R. Baker, 'The Open Secret of *Sartor Resartus*: Carlyle's Method of Converting his Reader', *Studies in Philology*, 83 (1986), pp. 231–32.

74 See Gerry H. Brookes, *The Rhetorical Form of Carlyle's Sartor Resartus* (Berkeley, California, 1972), p. 88.

75 See below pp. 140–45.

76 For an account of these advantages of the role of editor see *Past and Present*, pp. 35–36; see also Cowlishaw, 'The Cultural Revolution', pp. 56–58, and, more generally, G. B. Tennyson, 'The Editor Editing, the Reviewer Reviewing', *CSA*, 14 (1994), pp. 43–54.

77 These dimensions of Carlyle's early works will be considered more fully in the next chapter.

78 See Rosemary Ashton, *The German Idea: Four English Writers and the Reception of German Thought, 1800–1860* (Cambridge, 1980), p. 99.

79 Froude, *EL*, ii, p. 211; for an account of this aspects of Carlyle's essay on Boswell's *Life* see David R. Sorensen, 'Carlyle, Boswell's *Life of Johnson* and the "Conversations" of History', *Prose Studies*, 16 (1993), pp. 27–40.

Notes to Chapter 4: The Condition of England

1 'Condition of England' themes play a prominent role in a range of contemporary fiction by Charles Dickens (*Hard Times*), Benjamin Disraeli (*Sybil*), George Eliot (*Felix Holt*), Mary Gaskell (*North and South*) and Charles Kingsley (*Alton Locke* and *Yeast*) and all reflect to some degree their authors's interest in Carlyle's work. For a comparative analysis of important non-literary sources see Michael Levin, *The Condition of England Question: Carlyle, Mill, Engels* (1998) and for a collection of contributions by members of the Conservative Party who were associated with Benjamin Disraeli see John Morrow, ed., *Young England: The New Generation* (1999).

2 *CL*, v, p. 278, 17 May 1831.

3 *CL*, vi, p. 370, 18 April 1831. When he visited Carlyle in this year, Emerson noted that he was preoccupied with pauperism; see Ralph Waldo Emerson, *English Traits* (Boston, 1856), p. 23.

4 See Miriam M. H. Thrall, *Rebellious Fraser's: Nol Yorke's Magazine in the Days of Maginn, Thackeray and Carlyle* (New York, 1934), pp. 122ff; 'The Labourers of England' (1831), 'Letters on the Social Condition of the Operative Classes' (1831–2) and 'The State of the Manufacturing Population' (1838), *The Miscellaneous Works of Thomas Arnold, DD* (1845).

5 'The Chartists and Universal Suffrage', *Blackwood's Edinburgh Magazine*, 46 (1839), p. 289. This periodical took a very similar view of the 'Plug Plot Crisis', part of the context for *Past and Present*, seeing it as the result of combined folly of radicalised members of the working classes and anti-Corn Law interests; see 'Revolt of the Workers', *Blackwood's Edinburgh Magazine*, 52 (1842), pp. 642–53.

6 *CME*, iv, pp. 18–19.

7   *SR*, Bk. III, chs. iv, x.

8   *CL*, vii, pp. 22–23, 28 October 1833.

9   *CL*, ix, p. 69, 9 October 1836; for Carlyle's remarks on Cobbett see Thomas Sadler, ed., *Diary, Reminiscences, and Correspondence of Henry Crabb Robinson*, 3 vols (1868), iii, p. 2, 12 February 1832.

10 *CL*, xi, pp. 60–61, 23 March 1839.

11 See Gareth Stedman Jones, 'The Language of Chartism', in James Epstein and Dorothy Thompson, eds., *The Chartist Experience: Studies in Working-Class Radicalism and Culture, 1830–1860* (1982), pp. 13–14.

12 *CL*, x, p. 117, 27 April 1839. Mill put the matter very differently. While he did not think that the material condition of the working classes had actually worsened, he was happy for Carlyle to make a case for this position; see *The Earlier Letters of John Stuart Mill, 1812–1848*, ed. Francis E. Mineka, *Collected Works of John Stuart Mill*, (Toronto, 1963), p. 414, from early December 1839.

13 See Thomas C. Richardson, 'Carlyle's *Chartism* and the *Quarterly Review*', *CSA*, 10 (1989), pp. 50–55. Given Carlyle's earlier criticism of Croker (see above pp. 00), it is ironic that he should be displaced by him because of Croker's connections with the owner of the periodical. Carlyle had the last word; while his essay is still read widely and reprinted, Croker's has disappeared without trace. It is a very thin and mechanical piece of work devoted to a highly partisan attack on Lord John Russell and the Whigs, with side swipes at the insidious impact of the 1832 reform act and warnings against movements (which Carlyle supported) for a non-sectrarian system of 'national education'; [J. W. Croker], 'Conduct of Ministers: Sketches of Popular Tumults, Illustrative of the Evils of Social Ignorance', *Quarterly Review*, 65 (1839), pp. 283–314. It is hard to imagine that Lockhart would have regarded this tired demonstration of the limitations of official Toryism as a favoured alternative to Carlyle's piece.

14 Froude, *LL*, i, 184; *CL*, xi, p. 221, 5 December 1839.

15 Carlyle commented on the strong early sales of *Chartism* in a letter from 11 January 1840 and again on 25 April of that year; see *CL*, xii, pp. 13–14, 117. On the broadening range of Carlyle's readers see [George S. Venables], '*Chartism*, by Thomas Carlyle', *British and Foreign Quarterly*, 12 (1841), p. 307. Venables, a barrister and a wit, a member of Lady Ashburton's inner circle, to which Carlyle was soon to be admitted, thought that Carlyle's 'high-wrought' 'earnest and ironic' style was not ideally suited to political literature; ibid., p. 308.

16 NLS, MS 1776, fol. 116, 12 May 1843.

17 Frederic Harrison, 'Carlyle's Place in Literature', *Forum*, 17 (1894), pp. 546–47.

18 Frederick Engels, 'The Condition of England: *Past and Present* by Thomas Carlyle' [1844], Karl Marx and Frederick Engels, *Collected Works* (1975), iii, pp. 444–68; Engels, however, thought that Carlyle's hankering after religion would have been swept away if he had been exposed to Ludwig Feuerbach's astringent humanistic critique of religiosity. Ruffini's remark is recorded in *CL*, xvi, p. 306, 22 July 1843.

19 *CL*, xvi, p. 53, 20 February 1843.

20 See Noel Thompson, *The People's Science: The Popular Political Economy of Exploitation and Crisis, 1816–1834* (Cambridge, 1984), chapters 6 and 7.

21 Edward Strachley, 'Some Letters and Conversations of Thomas Carlyle', *Atlantic Monthly*, 73 (1894), pp. 826–27, referring to a conversation that took place on 11 October 1838.

22 *CL*, xi, p. 156, 27 July 1839.

23 *CL*, xiv, pp. 183, 185, 10 May 1842.

24 *Chartism*, *CME*, vi, p. 110.

25 'Corn-Law Rhymes', *CME*, iv, p. 208.

26 *CL*, xi, p. 206, 22 October 1839.

27 *Chartism*, p. 132.

28 Ibid., p. 141.

29 Ibid., p. 140. It is possible that Carlyle adopted the juxtaposition of 'mights' and 'rights' from the subtitle of John Francis Bray's recent work *Labour's Wrongs and Labour's Remedies: Or The Age of Might and the Age of Right* (1839) but he does not address Bray's arguments about economic justice.

30 See Fred Kaplan, 'Power and Authority', in Jerry D. James and Rita B. Bottoms, eds., *Lectures on Carlyle and His Era* (Santa Cruz, California, 1985), pp. 1–4. For a time in the late 1840s Carlyle hoped that Peel might be capable of filling this role (see pp. 154–56).

31 *Two Reminiscences*, pp. 98–99; NLS, MS 527, fol. 80, 4 January 1873.

32 See John Ulrich, 'The Re-Inscription of Labour in Carlyle's *Past and Present*, *Criticism*, 37, (1995), pp. 443–68.

33 *CL*, xxvii, p. 77, 28 March 1852.

34 On the tone of the *Westminster Review* see George L. Nesbit, *Benthamite Reviewing: The First Twelve Years of the Westminster Review, 1824–1836* (New York, 1934), pp. 58–60.

35 Boyd Hilton, *The Age of Atonement: The Influence of Evangelicalism on Social and Economic Thought* (Oxford, 1988), passim; R. K. Webb, *Harriet Martineau: A Victorian Radical* (1965), pp. 100–133. The impact of the Corn Laws on the condition of the working classes was a recurrent theme in annual speeches in favour of repeal given by Charles Villiers, MP for Wolverhampton, including that given in the year in which *Chartism* was written; *The Free Trade Speeches of the Right Hon. Charles Pelham Villiers, M.P.* (1884), pp. 109–114.

36 See Gregory Claeys, *Citizens and Saints: Politics and Anti-politics in Early British Socialism* (Cambridge, 1989), pp. 161–66 and Thompson, *The People's Science*, chapters 6 and 7.

37 For a brief survey see Mark Francis and John Morrow, *English Political Thought in the Nineteenth Century* (1994), pp. 112–18.

38 Saint Simonian statements on the plight of the working classes were endorsed by Carlyle rather than forming the basis of his own views on this issue. Later European initiatives that paralleled English developments to some degree – the emergence of 'social politics' in France during the 1830s and 1840s, and '*Pauperismus*' in Germany – do not appear to have had a discernible impact on Carlyle's response to the condition of England question; see Herman Beck, *The Origins of the Authoritarian Welfare State in Prussia* (Anne Arbor, Michigan, 1995), pp. 1–78; D. Evans, *Social Romanticism in France*, 1830–1848 (Oxford, 1951), passim.

39 NLS, MS 1764, fol. 193, 28 October 1820; Carlyle never owned the translation publicly, probably because he viewed it as being merely a piece of hack -work. A modern reprint of this essay makes a small book of about 45,000 words; see J. C. L. Sismondi de Sismondi, *Political Economy* (New York, 1966). For modern accounts of Sismondi's work see Jean-Jaques

Gislain, 'Sismondi and the Evolution of Economic Institutions', in Gilbert Faccarello, ed., *Studies in the History of French Political Economy* (1998), pp. 229–53; Thomas Sowell, 'Sismondi: A Neglected Pioneer', *History of Political Economy*, 1 (1968), pp. 62–88.

40   J. C. L. S. de Sismondi, *Nouveaux Principles d'Économie Politique* (1819), second edition, 2 vols (Paris, 1827), ii, p. 250; see also Sismondi, *Political Economy*, pp. 1–2.

41   Sismondi, *Political Economy*, p. 64.

42   Sismondi, *Nouveaux Principles*, i, p. 372.

43   *EL*, ii, pp. 79–80, 84–85. The analogy of the 'hodman', a labourer who carries bricks, blocks and mortar in a 'hod', a rectangular box open on three sides, to bricklayers working on elevated scaffolding, came from Fichte (see 'State of German Literature', *CME*, i, p. 50); it probably appealed to Carlyle because of his father's career as a builder.

44   *Chartism*, pp. 112, 116.

45   *CL*, xi, p. 137, 20 June 1839.

46   'At the annunciation of *principles*, of *ideas*, the soul of man awakes '; Samuel Taylor Coleridge, *Lay Sermons*, ed. R. J. White, *The Collected Works of Samuel Taylor Coleridge*, vi (Princeton, 1972), p. 24.

47   'Transactions of the London Statistical Society', *London and Westminster Review*, 38 (April 1839), pp. 45–72. Carlyle praised this article in a conversation with Edward Strachey; see 'Some Letters and Conversation of Thomas Carlyle', p. 823. Given Carlyle's growing animus against the philosophical radicals and the pre-publication history of *Chartism* it is ironic that this piece appeared in Mill's journal and that it was written by John Robertson, its sub-editor.

48   *Chartism*, pp. 118, 130.

49   Ian Campbell, *Carlyle and Europe: Some Early Contacts* (Edinburgh, 1977), p. 17.

50   This line of argument was used by Carlyle to question whether black slaves were worse off then 'free' whites in England and Ireland; the former lacked liberty, but until the mid 1860s, at least, Carlyle thought that they enjoyed the far more significant benefits that resulted from living in well ordered communities; see below chapter 5.

51   See Jules Paul Siegel, ed., *Critical Heritage* (1971), pp. 167–68.

52   See Michael J. Cullen, *The Statistical Movement in Early Victorian Britain: The Foundations of Empirical Social Research* (Hassocks, 1975), pp. 144–45.

53   In an article in the *Edinburgh Review* Chadwick claimed that accurate information would dispel misapprehensions about the causes of pauperism and show that the new poor law administration struck effectively at the root causes of pauperisation, namely, the idleness and moral weakness of the poor themselves; [Edwin Chadwick], 'The New Poor Law', *Edinburgh Review*, 63 (July 1836) pp. 490–91. Early in 1837 Carlyle juxtaposed the desperate and unruly condition of unemployed handloom weavers with Chadwick's and Martineau's celebratory remarks on the 'new' Poor Law'; see *CL*, ix, p. 187. In *Past and Present*, Carlyle referred to Chadwick as 'assiduous, much-abused, and truly useful' (p. 239) but then questioned the narrowly prudential idea of elite responsibility for educating the working classes that he promoted in *Report on the Training of Pauper Children* (1841). For a recent account of Chadwick's assumptions about the causes of pauperism, see Lynn Hollen Lees, *The Solidarities of Strangers: The English Poor Law and the People, 1700–1848* (Cambridge, 1998), pp. 118–19. It is significant that neither the Poor Law Commission nor

its backers saw the need to gather data on seasonal unemployment in urban areas, relying exclusively on calculations showing average annual earnings (ibid., pp. 121–24); both these failings were noted by Carlyle in his critique of statistics. Chartism and anti-poor law agitation often merged, especially in the north of England; see John Knott, *Popular Opposition to the 1834 Poor Law* (1986), pp. 129ff.

54 See David Roberts, 'How Cruel Was the Victorian Poor Law?' *Historical Journal*, 6 (1963), pp. 97–107.

55 *SR*, pp. 158–59.

56 *Chartism*, p. 120.

57 Ibid., p. 121; *CL*, vi, p. 449, 24 September 1833.

58 See Chadwick, 'The New Poor Law', pp. 506–18.

59 *CL*, xiii, p. 275, 11 October 1841.

60 *Past and Present*, pp. 5–6; see Ulrich, 'The Re-Inscription of Labour', p. 446, for an interesting account of the enchantment theme in this work.

61 *Past and Present*, p. 161.

62 See Lawes, *Paternalism and Politics*, pp. 51–57.

63 *Chartism*, p. 124.

64 *CME*, iv, 203–4.

65 *Reminiscences*, p. 35.

66 See below, pp. 204–5.

67 See above, pp. 56–61.

68 *Chartism*, p. 130.

69 For a report by Carlyle of Miss Martineau's views on *laissez-faire* see *CL*, vi, p. 332, dating from 22 February 1833.

70 Mineka, ed., *The Earlier Letters of J. S. Mill*, i, p. 152.

71 *Chartism*, p. 143.

72 Ibid., p. 175.

73 *Past and Present*, p. 18; this slogan is reported in the *Illustrated London News* for August 1843; see Richard Brown and Christopher Daniels, eds., *The Chartists* (London, 1984), pp. 78ff. As in other aspects of Carlyle's analysis, there is significant common ground with Chartist demands, in this case with their view that they were deprived of the just price of their labour; see Stedman Jones, 'The Language of Chartism', pp. 32–33.

74 *Past and Present*, pp. 18–19.

75 Stedman Jones, 'The Language of Chartism', pp. 4–13.

76 *Chartism*, p. 144.

77 *CL*, xiii, pp. 277–78, 12 October 1841. The parallel cut both ways: in 1871 Carlyle described the Paris Commune as a 'tremendous proclamation to the upper classes in all countries'; NLS, MS 527, fol. 51, 29 May 1871.

78 See David Goodway; *London Chartism, 1838–1848* (Cambridge, 1982), pp. 22–23, 31–32, and on parliamentary references to the French Revolution see John B. Lamb, 'Carlyle's "Chartism", the Rhetoric of Revolution and the Dream of Empire', *Victorian Institute Journal*, 23 (1995), pp. 129–50. The language used by Chartist leaders provided the ground for arresting a large number of them for sedition in the latter part of 1839; see Dorothy Thompson, ed., *The Early Chartists* (1971), pp. 19–20.

79   *FR*, i, p. 184.
80   Ibid., pp. 185–86.
81   *CL*, xxiii, p. 23, 26 April 1848.
82   *Past and Present*, p. 4.
83   This visit laid the foundation for Carlyle's later interest in the condition of the Irish working classes. See Charles Gavan Duffy, *Conversations with Carlyle* (1892), p. 5. For Carlyle's appeal to men such as Duffy and John Mitchel see K. J. Fielding, 'Ireland, John Mitchel and his "Sarcastic Friend" Thomas Carlyle', in J. Schwend et al., ed., *Literatur im Kontext: Festscrift für Horst Drescher* (Frankfurt am Main, 1992), pp. 133–35.
84   *Chartism*, p. 126.
85   For recent surveys see Roberto Romani, 'British Views on Irish National Character, 1800–1846', *History of European Ideas*, 23 (1997), pp. 193–219; Roger Swift, 'Thomas Carlyle, *Chartism*, and The Irish in Early Victorian England', *Victorian Literature and Culture*, (2001), pp. 67–83. Popular images reflecting these stereotypes are discussed in L. Perry Curtis Jr., *Apes and Angels: The Irishman in Victorian Caricature*, revised edition (Washington DC, 1997).
86   *Chartism*, p. 125.
87   Ibid., p. 127. More than thirty years later, after reading Froude's work on Ireland, Carlyle remarked that the English made a 'baser figure' as governors of Ireland than even the Irish; NLS, MS 528, fol. 7, 7 March 1874.
88   *CL*, xi, p. 204n, October 1839; *Chartism*, p. 127.
89   *Chartism*, p. 137.
90   *Past and Present*, p. 15. John Plotz's recent suggestion (John Plotz, 'Crowd Power: "Chartism", Carlyle and the Victorian Public Sphere', *Representations*, 20 (2000), pp. 105–6) that Carlyle's claim to articulate the 'real' voice of Chartism, smacked of 'neo-fascist' aspirations to utilize the energy of crowds, ignores Carlyle's views on the behavioral and moral requirements of a heroic culture. His model was the followers of Cromwell, not chronically disoriented sancullottes. He thought that the English working classes become admirable when they started to resemble the former; see below pp. 157–59, 174–77 for a consideration of Carlyle's views of a heroic culture.
91   See Lovett's strictures against the ideas that the working classes needed leaders, whether from the 'respectable' middle classes, or from popularist champions such as Henry Hunt or Feargus O'Connor; William Lovett, *The Life and Struggle of William Lovett* (1875), p. 75.
92   *CL*, xvi, p. 52, 18 February 1843.
93   *Past and Present*, pp. 22, 199.
94   Ibid., p. 24.
95   Ibid., pp. 162, 155.
96   *CL*, xvii, p. 312, 17 March 1844.
97   Hilton, *The Politics of Atonement*, p. 213.
98   See Lawes, *Paternalism and Politics*, pp. 46–54, 114–18.
99   Mill, *Political Economy*, iv, ch. vii, p. 759.
100 *CL*, viii, p. 31, c.3 February 1835. Literature was covered by the same mandate. Carlyle told John Sterling that books were written 'for all men', not just for the rich. He included access to the insights of wise men among the real 'rights of men'; *CL*, xii, p. 263, 19 September

1840. Carlyle remained committed to a liberal and expansive educational ideal and later criticised what he took to be the cramming system of undergraduate teaching at Oxford; see *CL*, xxiii, pp. 80–82, 28 July 1848; 29, p. 47, 13 March 1854. The first of these letters, dealing with Carlyle's support for non-sectarian systems of 'national education', was reprinted in the *Manchester Guardian*.

101   This point was noted by a Benthamite commentator looking back on Carlyle's condition of England writings from the standpoint of the mid 1860s; see 'Mr Carlyle', *Fraser's Magazine*, 72 (1865), p. 791. In an essay that appeared in *Fraser's* when *Sartor Resartus* was serialized in that journal, a case was made for a system of national education that stimulated the growth of intellect and character and differed sharply from mechanical, stifling and narrowly instrumental arrangements currently in place; see 'Present Condition of the People', *Fraser's Magazine*, 9 (1834), pp. 73–74.

102   *Past and Present*, pp. 230–31. Changes made to the first extant draft of *Past and Present* illustrate this point. Carlyle's original speculations on the resources that might be available for governmental initiatives with respect to the organisation of labour did not appear in the published text, partly because of an uncertainty over data but also because this level of operational detail was outside Carlyle's brief. See Grace J. Calder, *The Writing of Past and Present: A Study of Carlyle's Manuscripts* (New Haven, 1949), pp. 116–17.

103   NLS, Acc. 11388.

104   NLS, MS 23167, fos. 40–41.

105   [Arthur Helps], *The Claims of Labour: An Essay on the Duties of the Employers to the Employed* (1844), pp. 43, 45–46. When he reviewed this work for the *Edinburgh Review*, Mill criticised it for encouraging the working classes to rely on the efforts of others; see 'The Claims of Labour', *Essays on Economics and Society*, ed. Lord Robins and J. M. Robson, *Collected Works of John Stuart Mill* (Toronto, 1967–91), pp. 365–89. These concerns did not feature in his very enthusiastic response to *Chartism*; having seen the work in manuscript, Mill told Carlyle that he read the published version of this essay with 'renewed pleasure'; *Additional Letters of John Stuart Mill*, ed. Marion Filipiuk, Michael Laine and J. M. Robson, *Collected Works of John Stuart Mill*, p. 48.

106   Helps, *The Claims of Labour*, p. viii.

107   Ibid., passim.

108   This letter is reprinted in E. A. Helps, ed., *The Correspondence of Sir Arthur Helps, KCB, DCL* (1917), pp. 65–73.

109   Sir Arthur Helps, *Life and Labours of Mr. Brassey* (1872).

110   See Stedman Jones, 'The Language of Chartism', pp. 20–45. The term 'millocracy' was common to both Carlyle and to Chartists, having been used in 1838 in a major Chartist newspaper, the *Northern Star*, ibid, p. 44.

111   *Past and Present*, pp. 148–49.

112   Ibid., pp. 157–58.

113   *Past and Present*, p. 179. Sismondi had earlier suggested that a degree of free trade might be usefully reconciled with a more interventionist role for the state; see *Political Economy*, p. 73.

114   Lord John Manners and his Young England colleagues were highly impressed with a tightly regimented, strongly paternalistic enterprise that they visited in 1842; see Morrow, ed.,

Young England, p. 14. This was, no doubt, an unusual example, but Anthony Howe notes that from the 1830s there was a growing emphasis on philanthropy – particularly support for 'rational amusements', religious and educational institutions – among northern cotton masters, motivated in some cases by a wish to forge a distinctive social identity; see A. Howe, *The Cotton Masters, 1830–1860* (Oxford, 1984), p. 273. For a more general account of 'employer paternalism' with some specifically Carlylean reference points, see G. R. Searle, *Morality and the Market in Victorian Britain* (Oxford, 1998), pp. 270–71. Brian Lewis, *The Middlemost and the Milltowns: Bourgeois Culture and Politics in Early Industrial England* (Stanford, California, 2001), pp. 289–96, relates the rise of systematic 'factory paternalism' to condition of England literature of the 1830s and 1840s.

115   NLS, MS 527, fol. 88, 20 March 1873.

116   *Past and Present*, p. 76.

117   Ibid., p. 74.

118   Ibid., pp. 239–42.

Notes to Chapter 5: Work, Race and Empire

1   Extracts on the 'gospel of labour' figured prominently in Thomas Ballantyne's *Passages Selected from the Writings of Thomas Carlyle with a Biographical Memoir* (1855).

2   'Carlyle and Neuberg', *Macmillan's Magazine*, 50 (1884), p. 284.

3   *CL*, iii, p. 431; iv, p. 102.

4   See Ian Campbell, 'Carlyle's Religion: The Scottish Background', in John Clubbe, ed., *Carlyle and his Contemporaries: Essays in Honor of Charles Richard Sanders* (Durham, North Carolina, 1976), pp. 18–20; J. M. Sloan, *The Carlyle Country With a Study of Carlyle's Life* (1904), p. 70.

5   *Past and Present*, pp. 172, 169.

6   *Past and Present*, p. 177.

7   Friedrich Schiller, *Letters on the Aesthetic Education of Man*, cited in *Schiller*, p. 177. See also Tom Lloyd, 'Society and Chaos: Schiller's Impact on Carlyle's Ideas about Revolution', *Clio*, 17 (1987), pp. 51–64.

8   *Past and Present*, p. 136.

9   Ibid., p. 170.

10   Frances Espinasse, *Literary Recollections and Sketches* (1893), p. 60, quoting a letter from 28 August 1841.

11   NLS, MS 516, fol. 15, 5 September 1855.

12   Carlyle was so dismissive of Mill's *On Liberty* that he abandoned an attempt to write a systematic critique of it; the surviving text is published in full in D. J. Trela, 'A New (Old) Review of Mill's *On Liberty*: A Note on Carlyle's and Mill's Friendship', *CN*, 6 (1984), pp. 23–27. For Carlyle's views on 'free labour' see William Allingham, *Diary*, ed. Geoffrey Grigson (1907; repr. Fontwell, 1967), p. 209; Andrew James Symington, *Some Personal Reminiscences of Carlyle* (Paisley, 1886), p. 25. Since these qualifications remained unpublished during his lifetime, Carlyle was exposed to criticism for his supposedly 'abstract' view of labour by J. S. Mill (see below p. 130) and by pro-Chartist figures such as Joseph

Barker, author of *The People: Their Rights and Liberties, their Duties and their Interests*, second series, i (1851), p. 153.

13   *Past and Present*, p. 215; Allingham, *Diary*, p. 209.

14   *CL*, xxvii, pp. 29–30, 5 February 1852. This letter was written to the Secretary of the Poor Law Reform Association, a group to which both Carlyle and J. S. Mill belonged.

15   Symington, *Some Personal Reminiscences*, p. 41.

16   *CL*, xxv, p. 157, 10 August 1850.

17   Ibid., xxix, p. 24, 18 January 1854. Later, in *FG*, Carlyle described wasteful work as inhuman; iii, p. 199.

18   See A. M. C. Waterman, 'The Ideological Alliance of Political Economy and Christian Theology', *Journal of Ecclesiastical History*, 34 (1983), pp. 231–44.

19   *Past and Present*, pp. 134–35.

20   Ibid., p. 116.

21   Ibid., pp. 173–74.

22   *Reminiscences*, p. 5; *CL*, iv, p. 27; this comment was made later on a letter dating from 1826.

23   *Past and Present*, p. 114

24   Thomas Carlyle, 'Notes of a Three Day Tour to the Netherlands, August, 1842', *Cornhill Magazine*, new series, 53 (1922), pp. 506–7. For Coleridge's remark see Samuel Taylor Coleridge, *Table Talk*, ed. Carl Woodring, *The Collected Works of Samuel Taylor Coleridge* (Princeton, 1990), ii, p. 81, 4 May 1830. This reference suggests that Carlyle continued to read Coleridge despite the dim view he had taken of him.

25   *Chartism* and *Past and Present* predated T. B. Macaulay's hugely successful *History of England from the Accession of James the Second*, the first two volumes of which appeared in 1848, but not his numerous essays on historical topics, or earlier Whig accounts with a strong constitutional focus such as Lord John Russell's *An Essay on the History of the English Government and Constitution* (1821), Henry Hallam's *History* (1827) and Sir James Mackintosh's *History of England* (1831). It should be recalled that when *Past and Present* was being written Carlyle was deeply immersed in reading English history as part of his Cromwell project, so it is plausible to see him offering a conscious alternative to the prevailing historiography. From another perspective, Carlyle's claims about the 'English' assumption of moral and industrial leadership might be seen to imply a rejection of Saint-Simonian claims of French superiority; see Georg Iggers, *The Cult of Authority: The Political Philosophy of the Saint-Simonians* (The Hague, 1957), p. 122.

26   *Past and Present*, pp. 135–38.

27   Ibid., p. 138.

28   Ibid., p. 145.

29   Ibid., p. 139; *Chartism*, p. 160.

30   NLS, MS 527, 12 April 1873.

31   NLS, Acc. 11388, TC to Lord Ashburton, 15 November 1857. A little earlier Carlyle had condemned the British military administration in India, blaming it for creating the climate that made mutiny likely; NLS, MS 23167, fos. 124–25, 5 October 1859.

32   K. J. Fielding, 'Unpublished Manuscripts – 1: Carlyle Among the Cannibals', *CN*, 1 (1979), p. 25. Carlyle was reviewing Augustus Earle's *Narrative of a Residence in New Zealand* (1832).

33 In commenting on likely developments in New Zealand, Buller predicted a 'fusion' of Maori and settlers, a process that would be greatly to the advantage of the former; see Miles Taylor, '*Imperium et Libertas?* Rethinking the Radical Critique of Imperialism during the Nineteenth Century', *Journal of Imperial and Commonwealth History*, 19 (1991), p. 6. This view was a commonplace but, given their friendship, Buller's references to it may be of some significance with respect to assumptions underlying Carlyle's position.

34 See above, p. 102.

35 For a critical account of this tradition see Donald Winch, *Riches and Poverty: An Intellectual History of Political Economy in Britain, 1750–1834* (Cambridge, 1996), pp. 288–322.

36 *Chartism*, p. 185.

37 In early life, Carlyle had not seen emigration as an attractive prospect, describing it to one correspondent as a 'fearful destiny' (*CL*, i, p. 156; see ibid, ii, p. 30 for a similar statement). At various times in the 1830s, however, he toyed with the idea of emigrating to Canada, South Australia or New Zealand, sometimes as a way of escaping the drawbacks of life in Britain, sometimes inspired by the prospect of the role that he might play in a newly forming society; see Fielding, 'Unpublished Manuscripts 1'. These were flashes of passing interest, rather than settled or consistently pursued plans.

38 *Chartism*, pp. 185–86.

39 NLS, MS 518, fol. 5 and 527, fos. 7, 9, 11; 1770, fos. 147–48; 1769, fos. 204–5; 528, fol. 47; 1771, fol. 147.

40 James Milne, *The Romance of a Pro-Consul: Being the Personal Life and Memoirs of the Right Honourable Sir George Grey, KCB* (1899), pp. 185–87. Carlyle arranged for his niece to copy extracts on emigration from his writings for Grey to use in his campaign; see Edmund Bohan, *To Be a Hero: Sir George Grey, 1812–189* (Auckland, 1998), pp. 243–44. On Carlyle's support for the working men's association initiative, see C. C. Eldridge, *England's Mission: The Imperial Idea in the Age of Gladstone and Disraeli* (Chapel Hill, North Carolina, 1973), p. 111.

41 'Colonisation – The Only Cure for National Distress – Mr Buller's Speech', *Fraser's Magazine*, 27 (1843), p. 739.

42 William Knighton, 'Conversations with Carlyle', *Contemporary Review*, 39 (1881), p. 913. Thomas Holt's suggestion that Carlyle's position complimented that of official thinking obscures the distinctive basis of his position on colonies as sites of labour; Thomas C. Holt, *The Problem of Freedom: Race, Labor and Politics in Jamaica and Britain, 1832–1932* (Baltimore, 1992), p. 248. For accounts of expectations concerning the economic benefits of empire see P. J. Cain, 'Economics: The Metropolitan Context', in *The Oxford History of the British Empire*, iii, *The Nineteenth Century*, ed. Andrew Porter (Oxford, 1999), pp. 31–52, and for the role of technology in the imperial context see Robert Kubicek, 'British Expansion, Empire, and Technological Change', ibid., pp. 247–69.

43 Bernard Semmel, *The Rise of Free Trade Imperialism: Classical Political Economy, the Empire of Free Trade and Imperialism* (Cambridge, 1970), pp. 147–48.

44 *CL*, xxvii, pp. 130–31, 30 June 1852; xxviii, p. 133, 12 May 1853.

45 A witness presenting evidence to the Parliamentary Committee on Aborigines in 1836 claimed that Britain had been 'invested with wealth and power, with arts and knowledge, with the sway of distant lands, and the mastery of restless waters, for some great and

important purpose in the government of the world.' *Reports from Committees*, ii (1837), p. 75. In his review of Earle's account of New Zealand, Carlyle spoke disparagingly of the missionaries, suggesting that the Māori were wiser than they; see Fielding, 'Unpublished Manuscripts – I', p. 26. This judgement may have been influenced by the opposition of some missionaries to settler colonies.

46   Cf. Jude V. Nixon, 'Racialism and the Politics of Emancipation in Carlyle's "Occasional Discourse on the Nigger Question"', *CSA*, 16 (1996), pp. 92–93.

47   *CL*, xxiii, p. 222n.

48   *SR*, pp. 119–21.

49   See below, pp. 177–81, 181–86, 188–90.

50   *LDP*, pp. 123–25.

51   See ibid., pp. 75–76 for Carlyle's views on the 'Don Pacifico Affair', and Moncure D. Conway, *Thomas Carlyle* (New York, 1881), p. 107 for a record of Carlyle's hostile comments on late nineteenth century imperialism. In July 1850 Carlyle responded positively to a request for a supportive comment on a peace congress that was called to coincide with the opening of the Great Exhibition at the Crystal Palace: 'the *less* war and cutting of throats among us … The better for us all'; quoted R. H. Sheperd, *Thomas Carlyle*, 2 vols (1881), ii, 107. A letter expressing his regret at not attending was read out at the congress held in London in July 1851; *Times*, 24 July 1851, p. 5. Carlyle was appalled by the reckless slaughter of the Crimean War, a consequence of poor generalship and the atmosphere of hysteria whipped up by newspaper opinion; *CL* xxix, pp. 178–79, 26 October 1854. Anti-war campaigners appealed again for Carlyle's support in early 1871(after his pro-German comments in the context of the Franco-German War); NLS, MS 1770, fos. 5–6, 13 January 1871. Although he refused to give public support for this initiative, this was not because he opposed the scheme. By this stage (as discussed below, pp. 195–96) Carlyle generally declined to be drawn on a range of issues (emigration, pauperism) because he felt he had already had his 'say' on them.

52   See Grace J. Calder, *The Writing of Past and Present: A Study of Carlyle's Manuscripts* (New Haven, 1949), p. 171.

53   Carlyle, 'Irish Regiments (Of the New Era)', *Spectator*, 13 May 1848, Sheperd, *Thomas Carlyle*, ii, p. 401. Cf. John B. Lamb, 'Carlyle's "Chartism", the Rhetoric of Revolution and the Dreams of Empire', *Victorian Institutes Journal*, 23 (1995), pp. 138–42, who treats Carlyle as a proponent of imperialistic conquest.

54   NLS, MS 527, fol. 11.

55   *LDP*, p. 129.

56   See Majory Harper, 'British Migration and the Peopling of Empire', in Porter, ed., *Oxford History*, iii, p. 76. In urging the state to take an active role in emigration, Carlyle was promoting a position that corresponded with the recommendation of a parliamentary Select Committee that reported in 1841. This recommendation, framed by particular reference to the plight of Highlanders, was ignored by the government; ibid., p. 81.

57   *CL*, vi, p. 373; vii, p. 60; ix, p. 97. On Froude's position see Peter Cain, ed., *Empire and Imperialism: The Debate of the 1870s* (Bristol, 1999), pp. 7–8. Buller took this view too: see 'Colonisation – The Only Cure for National distress – Mr Charles Buller's Speech', p. 744. For a more wide-ranging account of Carlyle's attitude towards the United States see

K. J. Fielding, 'Carlyle and the Americans: "Eighteen Million Bores"', *CSA*, 15 (1995), pp. 55–64.

58   These rationales were canvassed by C. A. Bodelsen in his classic work, *Studies in Victorian Imperialism* (1924; repr. 1960), p. 23.

59   See John Ulrich, 'The Re-Inscription of Labor in Carlyle's *Past and Present*', *Criticism*, 27 (1995), pp. 443–68.

60   Thomas Richards notes that huge models of consumer goods were common sights on the streets of London in the 1840s; see *The Commodity Culture of Victorian England: Advertising and Spectacle, 1851–1914* (Stanford, California, 1990), pp. 48–49.

61   *On Trades Unions, Promoterism and the Signs of the Times*, in D. J. Trela, 'Thomas Carlyle *On Trades Unions* ... An Unknown and Nearly Unpublished Manuscript', *Victorian Institute Journal*, 25 (1997) p. 239; the context of these comments is discussed in Trela's introduction, pp. 233–34.

62   NLS, Acc. 10484, fol 34. In his personal dealings with local tradesmen Carlyle seemed resigned to suffer at their hands: a cheque stub in the NLS records a payment of £1/3/4 for 'painting a door – very ill'; NLS, MS 20753, 21 September 1868.

63   In 1865 Carlyle described the question of master and workman relationships as the most important facing the country; NLS, Acc. 11439, Thomas Carlyle to Lady Lothian, 2 December 1865.

64   Carlyle received presentation copies of Ruskin's works from the mid 1850s, reading them with care, and often with great admiration. He was particularly impressed with Ruskin's critique of John Stuart Mill's political economy in *Unto this Last* (1860) and was delighted with the fifth letter of *Fors Clavigera* (1871) in which Ruskin criticised mechanistic views of science and raised important environmental issues; see George Allan Cate, ed., *The Correspondence of Thomas Carlyle and John Ruskin* (Stanford, California, 1982), pp. 89, 159.

65   See John R. Reed, 'A Friend to Mammon: Speculation in Victorian Fiction', *Victorian Studies*, 27 (1984), pp. 179–202.

66   *Command 11: Report from the Select Committee on Loans to Foreign States; House of Commons, 29 July 1875.*

67   'Carlyle, *On Trades Unions, Promoterism*', pp. 243–44. Although this work remained unpublished during his lifetime, Carlyle's hostility to the practices that were dealt with in it was noted by his contemporaries, two of whom, Alexander Hadfield, the editor of the *Daily Telegraph*, and Sir Charles Russell MP, a member of the Select Committee, encouraged him to lend public support to their campaign against them; NLS, MS 1771, fos. 215–18, 28 May 1875; 230, 8 August 1875. As with other appeals made to Carlyle in the 1870s, these fell on deaf ears.

68   See above pp. 87–88.

69   Carlyle wrote two essays (now lost) for the *Examiner* on this theme. His friend John Forster, the editor, declined to publish them on the grounds that they were too far in advance of public opinion in England. Carlyle later agreed with this verdict, saying that the subject really needed to be addressed in a measured book-length study not in a 'sermon' delivered to a 'bewildered' populace; *CL*, xxiii, pp. 86–87, 130.

70   *CL*, xxv, pp. 7–8, 20 January 1850.

71   Ibid., xxiv, pp. 58, 103n.

72   Ibid., p. 261.

73   Ibid., p. 101n.

74   Ibid., p. 173.

75   Ibid., p. 118.

76   [Carlyle], 'Trees of Liberty', *The Nation*, 1 December 1849, in Sheperd, *Thomas Carlyle*, ii, p. 405.

77   *CL*, xxiv, p. 150.

78   Ibid., p. 173.

79   Thomas Carlyle, *Reminiscences of My Irish Journey in 1849* (1882), p. 57.

80   *CL*, xxiv, p. 254.

81   Carlyle's sharply critical views on 'landlordism' and absentee owners had been aired in the press more than a year before his visit in 1849 and may explain Clarendon's nervousness about it; see Carlyle, 'Legislation for Ireland', *Examiner*, 13 May 1848, in Sheperd, *Thomas Carlyle*, ii, pp. 385–87.

82   NLS, MS 1773, fol. 235v; this letter is not dated but the opening salutation inquiring after the health of Jane Carlyle makes it clear that it was written just after Carlyle's departure from Ireland and before Duffy had heard from him.

83   *CL*, xxiv, p. 256.

84   See 'Irish Regiments (Of the New Era)', *Spectator*, 13 May 1848, in Sheperd, *Thomas Carlyle*, ii, pp. 398–404.

85   See *CL*, xxiii, pp. 86–88, 112, 162–63, for remarks dating from the closing months of 1848; *FG*, iv, p. 7.

86   NLS, MS 1776, fos. 243v, 258v; Duffy, *Conversations*, pp. 120, 130, 135–37, 156–57. Carlyle's views on the possibility of improvement in Ireland suggest that Amy Martin's attempt to push the metaphor of contagion to produce a racial (as opposed to a moral) account of Anglo-Irish relationships is misplaced; see Amy E. Martin 'Blood Transfusions: Constructions of Irish Racial Difference, The English Working Class, and Revolutionary Possibility in the Work of Carlyle and Engels', *Victorian Literature and Culture*, 32 (2004), pp. 83–102. It is perhaps significant that Martin focuses on *Chartism* and does not consider Carlyle's other statements on Ireland. Towards the end of his life Carlyle was highly sceptical of the impact of Gladstone's attempts to reform Irish landholding. He claimed that the immediate task facing those who sought to govern Ireland effectively was to deal with 'that astonishing supreme Court of Irish Justice, Court consisting of 5 or 6 truculent ragamuffins sitting in their skibbeen house over whiskey and blunderbuss'; Carlyle to Fitzjames Stephens, 3 June 1870, The Norman and Charlotte Strouse Collection of Thomas Carlyle MS, University of California, Santa Cruz, #93, NLS microfilm.

87   *LL*, ii, p. 24.

88   Ibid., p. 25.

89   In a letter to J. S. Mill from March 1833 Carlyle remarked that those who were horrified at the condition of slaves in British colonies should perhaps focus their attentions closer to home and concern themselves with the plight of the English working classes (*CL*, vi, p. 351). For a recent discussion of labour issues in the West Indies in relation to conditions in England see Seymour Drescher, 'Free Labor *v.* Slave Labor: The British and Caribbean

Cases', in Stanley L. Engerman, ed., *Terms of Labor: Slavery, Serfdom, and Free Labor* (Stanford, California, 1999). Ian Campbell has pointed out that Carlyle may have been influenced by a series of letters by 'Presbyter' that appeared in the *Dumfries and Galloway Courier* in December and January 1829–30; see Ian Campbell 'Carlyle and the Negro Question Again', *Criticism*, 13 (1971), pp. 286–287.

90 NLS, MS 1766, fos. 210–211, 1 June 1848; 240v, 1 May 1849.

91 See E. M. Palmegiano, *The British Empire in the Victorian Press, 1832–1867* (New York, 1987), p. 45.

92 For example 'The Jamaica Question', *Edinburgh Review*, 69 (July 1839), pp. 537–56.

93 Aileen Christianson, 'On the Writing of the Occasional Discourse on the Negro Question', *CN*, 2 (1980), pp. 15–17, refers to Charles Lyell's *Travels in North America* (1845) and to an article in the *Times* on 25 September 1849.

94 See [W. E. Aytoun], 'Our West Indian Colonies', *Blackwood's Edinburgh Magazine*, 63 (1848), pp. 219–38.

95 The *Eclectic Review*, a periodical with strong evangelical affiliations (its profits were gifted to the British and Foreign Bible Society), was a stalwart of this view of the benefits of emancipation; see 'The West Indies: Results of Emancipation', *Eclectic Review*, new series, 16 (1841), pp. 471–85 and 'Results of Emancipation', *Eclectic Review*, new series, 23 (1848), pp. 197–220. The second of these articles attacked changes to emigration regulations applying to West Africa, recently promulgated by Lord Grey, the Colonial Secretary.

96 'Occasional Discourse on the Negro Question', *CME*, vii, p. 106.

97 See David Theo Goldberg, 'Liberalism's Limits: Carlyle and Mill on "The Negro Question"', *Nineteenth –Century Contexts*, 22 (2000), pp. 206–7.

98 As Jude Nixon points out, these aspects of Carlyle's account mean that racism was central to his argument rather than being merely accidental; see 'Racialism and the Politics of Emancipation', p. 95. But while Carlyle's views on blacks and Jews – in February 1854, for example, he described a visitor to Cheyne Row as a 'Jew of the deepest type, *black* hooknosed Jew, with the mouth of a shark; coarse, savage, infidel, hungry ...with considerable *strength* of heart, head and *jaw*'; *CL*, 29, p. 29, 10 February 1854 – signaled an endorsement of prejudices that were common among his contemporaries, the basis of his position on race is far from clear. T. Peter Park has suggested that the racial prejudices expressed in Carlyle's writings were not biologically grounded since this approach was too mechanical for his tastes; see T. Peter Park, 'Thomas Carlyle and the Jews', *Journal of European Studies*, 20 (1990), pp. 16–17. It is possible that Carlyle's views had a cultural or historical basis, although some blacks (for example Dr Francia, the dictator of Paraguay – see below pp. nnn–nnn) seemed immune from these influences.

99 See Douglas A. Lorimer, *Colour, Class and the Victorians: English Attitudes to the Negro in the Mid-Nineteenth Century* (1978) pp. 122–23, and Seymour Drescher, *From Slavery to Freedom: Comparative Studies in the Rise and Fall of Atlantic Slavery* (New York, 1999), pp. 300–1. Carlyle's relationship to these developments is discussed in Catharine Hall, 'Imperial Man: Edward Eyre in Australasia and the West Indies, 1833–66', in Bill Schwarz, ed., *The Expansion of England: Race, Ethnicity and Cultural History* (1996), pp. 148–49.

100 'Occasional Discourse', pp. 83–84.

101 Carlyle, *Irish Journey*, pp. 126–27.

102   Ibid., p. 17.

103   [J. S. Mill], 'The Negro Question', *Fraser's Magazine*, 45 (1850), p. 27.

104   In the year in which the 'Occasional Discourse' appeared Wakefield (an ally of Charles Buller's on Canadian affairs in the early 1830s) published a sustained defense of his scheme in *A View of the Art of Colonisation* (1849); his theory had first been expounded in a series of letters in the *Morning Chronicle* in 1829 collected under the title *A Letter to Sydney, the Principal Town of Australasia* (1829). There is surviving correspondence between Carlyle and Wakefield.

105   The political economist G. Poulett Scrope in 1836, cited by Semmel, *The Rise of Free Trade Imperialism*. p.117.

106   'Occasional Discourse', p. 104. Christianson ('On the Writing', pp. 15–16), refers to two articles on the threat to Cuba in the *Examiner* on 22 and 29 September 1849; this paper was well known to Carlyle, being edited by his friend John Forster.

107   Carlyle, 'Dr Francia', *CME*, vii, pp. 47–49.

108   Froude, *LL*, ii, pp. 351–53 and NLS, MS 1796, fos. 107–108, 3 September 1866: Eyre had acted with 'promptitude, sagacity and intrepidity to trample out … fire in the *powder room*'.

109   In a fragment relating to the 'Negro Question' Carlyle suggested that a scheme of this kind might also be applied to work-shy whites; NLS, Acc. 7359.

110   'Occasional Discourse', pp. 108–110. The first part of this proposal met with approval in 'African Coast Blockade', *Westminster and Foreign Quarterly Review*, 51 (1850), p. 529.

111   'Occasional Discourse', pp. 98–100.

112   Contrary to David Levy's claim, it is Carlyle's gratuitous racism rather than his hostility to political economy which underwrites his views on slavery; cf. David M. Levy, '150 Years and Still Dismal', *Ideas on Liberty*, 50 (March 2000), p. 8.

113   [Mill], 'The Negro Question', pp. 27–28.

114   Ibid., p. 30.

115   Ironically, Mill himself used 'philanthropy' as a term of disapprobation. In his case, however, he associated this unwelcome tendency with dangerous paternalism towards the poor: 'English benevolence can no longer be accused of confining itself to niggers and other distant folk; on the contrary everybody is all agog to do something for the poor'; *Earlier Letters of John Stuart Mill, 1812–1848*, ed. Francis E. Mineka (Toronto, 1963), *Collected Works of John Stuart Mill*, p. 640, 8 November 1844.

116   See, for example, 'The Anti-Slavery Society', *Fraser's Magazine*, 1 (1830), pp. 610–23; 'The Colonist *versus* the Anti-Slavery Society', *Fraser's Magazine*, 2 (1830), pp. 334–41.

117   See Drescher, *From Slavery to Freedom*, pp. 300–1; Andrew Porter, 'Trusteeship, Anti-Slavery and Humanitarianism', in Porter, ed., *The Oxford History*, pp. 213–14.

118   Lorimer, *Colour, Class*, pp. 138–41; Christine Bolt, *Victorian Attitudes to Race* (1971), p. 36. Catharine Hall includes a treatment of Carlyle in her discussion of the decline of abolitionist sentiment in the 1840s and 1850s in *Civilising Subjects: Metropole and Colony in the English Imagination, 1830–1867* (Cambridge, 2002), pp. 338–79. She suggests his concerns at blacks's lack of commitment to labour were shared by some abolitionists in this period; see pp. 360–61.

119   See Peter S. Field, *Ralph Waldo Emerson: The Making of a Democratic Intellectual* (Lanham,

Maryland, 2002), pp. 167–81. Even when Emerson abandoned this view of blacks he continued to believe that the triumph of American freedom was a distinctly Anglo-Saxon achievement; ibid. p. 198.

120 William Howie Wylie, *Thomas Carlyle: The Man and His Books* (1909), p. 342. Thomas Carlyle, *Life of Sterling*, pp. 92–93; for Henry Crabb Robinson's response see *CL*, ix, p. 368 note. There was an echo of the earlier discussion in Carlyle's marginal annotations to Mill's *Political Economy* where he objected to anti-slavery passages; see Murray Baumgarten, 'In the Margins: Carlyle's Markings and Annotations in his Gift Copy of Mill's *Principles of Political Economy*' (Santa Cruz, California 1980), pp. 66–106.

121 *CL*, xii, p. 254; xii, p. 275.

122 *Past and Present*, pp. 182–83, 238.

123 NLS, MS 1771, fos. 131–33, 10 September 1874.

124 This position appears in a range of contemporary evaluations of Carlyle's writings; see Robert Steele Coffey, *Thomas Carlyle and Some of the Lessons of His Career* (Bradford,1881); [James Hannay], *Blackwood v. Carlyle: A Vindication By a Carlylian* (1850), pp. 38–39; David Hodge, *Thomas Carlyle: The Man and The Teacher* (Edinburgh and Glasgow, 1873), pp. 30–31; Symington, *Some Personal Reminiscences*, pp. 121–23; William Howie Wylie, *Thomas Carlyle: The Man and His Books*, second edition (1909), p. 344, published originally in 1881.

125 *CL*, xxviii, p. 195, 9 July 1853. Carlyle greatly appreciated this jest; see Dowager Duchess of Argyll, *George Douglas, Eighth Duke of Argyll: Autobiography and Memoirs*, 2 vols, (1906), i, p. 412, ii, p. 189.

126 [Arthur Helps], *Friends in Court. Book II* (1849), pp. 329–41. This point was reiterated by another of Carlyle's pro-emancipation friends, W. E. Forster in 'American Slavery, and Emancipation by the Free States', *Westminster Review*, new series, 3 (1853), p. 139. Significantly, while Carlyle was not openly hostile to Helps' pro-emancipationist response to *Uncle Tom's Cabin*, he was very irritated by what he saw as the public mania prompted by the work; *CL*, xxvii, p. 185, 27 July 1852, p. 382, 29 December 1852.

127 *Correspondence*, pp. 391–92. Helps told Carlyle that people thought the first volume of this work was very Carlylean; Carlyle, for his part, wrote a warm letter of appreciation when he received a copy of the second volume of Helps's book; *CL*, xxvii, p. 142, 8 June 1852.

128 *CL*, xxviii, p. 138, 13 May 1853. It seems clear from this letter that the initiative came from the publisher rather than from Carlyle; the opportunity was seized with alacrity.

129 NLS, MS 1773, fol. 207, undated; Conway, *Carlyle*, pp. 93–94; NLS, MS 1773, fol. 206. Conway later noted that like many of his compatriots, Carlyle was opposed to emancipation rather than in favour of confederacy; he had little respect for the confederate leadership, rather admired Lincoln, and was saddened by his assassination – see Moncure D. Conway, *Autobiography*, 2 vols (1904), i, pp. 363–65. An earlier critic saw Carlyle as a dupe of misinformation from the South; see [Elizur Wright], *Perforations in the Latter-Day Pamphlets by one of the 'Eighteen Millions of Bores'* (Boston, 1850), p. 35.

130 'Ilias (Americana) in Nuce', *Macmillan's Magazine*, 8 (May 1863), p. 301, a heavy-handed five-line dialogue reducing the conflict between the northern and southern states to the issue of whether servants should be 'hired for life'. Froude notes that while Carlyle had second thoughts about the war, he allowed this piece to appear in post-war editions of

his works (*LL*, ii, p. 266 where it is reprinted). Not surprisingly given the carnage of the American Civil War, Carlyle's cavalier treatment of its causes gave rise to a great deal of sharp criticism in the American press.

131 NLS, Acc. 11388 no. 30, 27 August 1863; 29 August 1863. The close dating of these letters and the fact that the photograph looks as if it is mass-produced, suggests that Carlyle may have been the target of a campaign.

132 Carlyle, 'Shooting Niagara', pp. 204–5; NLS, MS 527, fol. 93, 7 May, 1873. Gillian Workman's claim that Carlyle's support for Edward Eyre – demonstrated by his active role on the Governor Eyre Defense Committee between 1866–69 – was not determined by his views on race is consistent with the surviving evidence; see Gillian Workman, 'Thomas Carlyle and the Governor Eyre Controversy: an Account with Some New Material', *Victorian Studies*, 18 (1974–75), p. 81. In private correspondence Carlyle's abuse is even handed – 'Blockheads black, and ditto white' (NLS, MS 617, 11 April 1866) – and a parliamentary petition that he drafted called for swift repressive action to be taken against 'seditious Incendiaries, of black-savage type or white-savage type'. Like Matthew Arnold, Carlyle was worried about anarchic tendencies among elements of the British working classes, as well among former slaves in the colonies. However, Workman's claim that Carlyle's violent language was merely part of a rhetorical strategy and did not indicate racial hatred, needs to be qualified. If Carlyle did not hate blacks, he did at least rely on derogatory stereotypes to condemn their moral standing and had no faith in their moral potential.

133 Cate, ed. *Correspondence*, p. 76.

Notes to Chapter 6: Latter-Day Pamphleteer

1 *Carlyle's Latter-Day Pamphlets*, ed. M. K. Goldberg and J. P. Seigel (Ottawa, 1983) provides a facsimile of the original text, textual notes and a valuable introductory essay. Jules Seigel provides a very good account of the genesis of these pamphlets in Jules P. Seigel, 'Latter-Day Pamphlets: The Near Failure of Form and Vision' in K. J. Fielding and Rodger L. Tarr. Eds., *Carlyle Past and Present: A Collection of New Essays* (1976), pp. 155–61.

2 See below, p. 221.

3 Froude, *LL*, ii, pp. 27–40. Froude suggested (p. 40) that the outcry against the pamphlets damaged their sale but there is no evidence of this; the passage to which he refers concerns Carlyle's financial returns, a matter on which he wrangled with Chapman; see *CL*, xxv, pp. 68, 75–76, 80–81 and note 19 below. Fred Kaplan's suggestion that the 'Latter-Day Pamphlets' played a pivotal role in how Carlyle's audience saw him does not give sufficient weight to the mixed response to these writings. It is probably true, however, that the extravagance of these works made him more vulnerable to the criticisms of those who were in any case hostile to his views and the way in which he stated them; see Fred Kaplan, *Thomas Carlyle* (Ithaca, New York, 1977), p. 356.

4 Helen MacFarlane, 'Democracy: Remarks on the Times, Appros of Certain Passages in No. 1 of Thomas Carlyle's Latter-Day Pamphlets', *Democratic Review of British and Foreign Politics, History & Literature* April 1850, pp. 423–35, May 1850, pp. 449–53; 'Carlyle's Works', *Dublin Review*, 29 (1850), pp. 182–83, 200–3; 'Latter-Day Pamphlets', *Eclectic*

Review, new series 28 (1850), pp. 397, 406–7; 'Charles Dickens and David Copperfield', *Fraser's Magazine*, 42 (1850), pp. 707–10.

5   James Russell Lowe, *My Study Windows* (1887), pp. 173–74.

6   Cf. Fred Kaplan, 'Power and Authority', in Jerry D. James and Rita B. Bottoms, eds., *Lectures on Carlyle and His Era* (Santa Cruz, 1985), p. 7.

7   *CL*, xxv, p. 89, 31 May 1850.

8   *LDP*, p. 12.

9   See Clyde de L. Ryals, 'Thomas Carlyle on the Mormons: An Unpublished Essay', *CSA*, 15 (1995), pp. 49–54. Ryals notes that Carlyle also applauded the Mormons' strict hierarchy. A prescient reviewer of *Oliver Cromwell* had noted that Carlyle's strictures on belief might apply to Mormonism as well as to Puritanism; see 'Thomas Carlyle – *Letters and Speeches of Oliver Cromwell*', *North British Review*, 4 (1846), p. 521.

10 Marrs, p. 668.

11 Thomas Carlyle, 'Louis-Philippe', *Examiner*, 4 March 1848, reprinted in R. H. Sheperd, *Memoirs of the Life and Writings of Thomas Carlyle*, 2 vols (1881), ii, p. 365.

12 Ibid., pp. 366–67, 369. Carlyle's response to the termination of the Orleanist regime reflected a view that was common in liberal and progressive circles in Britain. A highly critical treatment of the tone, principles and practices of the regime was published under the title, *France: Her Governmental, Administrative and Social Organisation, Exposed and Considered in Its Principles, in Its Working, and in Its Results* in 1844, with a second edition in 1847. I owe this reference to the kindness of Professor J. A. W Gunn who is working on British public opinion and the Orleanist monarchy.

13 *LDP*, p. 6.

14 *CL*, xxiii, p. 23, 26 April 1848.

15 *CL*, xxiv, pp. 298–99, 28 November 1849; see also *LDP*, p. 23. For an account of the reports and their impact see E. P. Thompson, 'Mayhew and the *Morning Chronicle*', in E. P. Thompson and Eileen Yeo, eds., *The Unknown Mayhew: Selections from the Morning Chronicle, 1849–1850* (1971), pp. 11–50.

16 *LL*, ii, p. 23.

17 *CL*, xxiii, p. 274 (22 March 1848); p. 86 (4 August 1848); pp. 35–36 (26 May 1848).

18 *CL*, xxiii, pp. 35–36, 26 May 1848; xxiv, p. 88n.

19 *CL*, xxiv, pp. 286, 10 November 1849, 313, 23 December 1849; xxv, p. 9, 25 January 1850. The fact that Carlyle and Chapman and Hall did not begin to discuss terms until the series was well underway is indicative of the haste surrounding its launch and the lack of certainty about the scope and duration of the venture. Edward Chapman's complaints at the unusually high cost of corrections to the proofs suggests that Carlyle did not finalise the texts of each pamphlet until the last minute. *CL*, xxv, p. 51n. The cost of corrections to numbers 1–4 were one and a half times the composition costs; Chapman told Carlyle that one half was the norm. Chapman managed to get his own way over the mode of payment (a royalty based on sales not copies printed as Carlyle optimistically suggested) and over maximum length; Carlyle later complained that he was penalised financially 'for doing too much' (*CL*, xxv, p. 210, 13 September 1850).

20 Recorded in Francis Espinasse, *Literary Recollections and Sketches* (1893), p. 131. The discordant but comprehensive range of strategies adopted in the 'Latter-Day Pamphlets'

explain why Henry Larkin, a contemporary admirer, saw them as the 'epitome' of Carlyle, conveying his aspiration and his radicalism but also his despair and his shortcomings; they were, Larkin thought, the 'truest and sincerest utterance of his deepest convictions.' See Henry Larkin, *Carlyle and the Open Secret of His Life* (1886), p. 209.

21 See for example 'A Pilgrimage to Utopia; or the Autobiography of a Visionary (2)' *Electic Review*, new series, 27 (1850), p. 477 and 'Latter-Day Pamphlets', *Electic Review*, new series, 28 (1850), pp. 387–88.

22 *CL*, xxv, p. 11, 26 January 1850; NLS, MS 1775B, John Carlyle to Thomas Carlyle, 14 January 1850. In the last pamphlet Carlyle openly owned their 'offensive' and 'alarming' character, warning his readers that he had one last shock in store for them, *LDP*, p. 251. This passage also includes references to the 'grouse ramadham' observed by the English upper classes, an ungracious allusion to a Highland shooting party hosted by Lord Ashburton that took place in the autumn of 1849. For an account of the reception facing visitors at this time see Espinasse, pp. 179–80. Given the willful extremism of the 'Latter-Day Pamphlets' there is a certain irony in Carlyle's contemporaneous criticism of the tendencies to exaggeration that he saw in Charles Kingsley's *Alton Locke* and his advice to the author to avoid these in his future works; see *CL*, xxv, pp. 208, 210, 12 September 1850; p. 267, 31 October 1850.

23 *CL*, xxiv, p. 306, 7 December 1849.

24 *CL*, xxv, p. 255, 12 November 1850.

25 Ibid., p. 11, 26 January 1850.

26 Ibid., p. 114.

27 *CL*, xxix, p. 165, 8 October 1854.

28 *CL*, xxv, p. 29, 18 February 1850.

29 See for example, Michael Levin, *The Spectre of Democracy: The Rise of Modern Democracy As Seen By Its Critics* (New York, 1992).

30 See below, pp. 183–84.

31 *LDP*, p. 149.

32 Ibid., p. 166.

33 See below pp. 183–84.

34 *LPD*, pp. 152–53.

35 Ibid., pp. 163, 157–58, 159. Carlyle's criticism of the culture of talk identified a nineteenth-century development that has been a source of interest in modern scholarship; see J. S. Meisel, *Public Speech and the Culture of Public life in the Age of Gladstone* (New York, 2001) and Matthew Bevis, 'Volumes of Noise', *Victorian Literature and Culture* (2003), pp. 577–91.

36 NLS, MS 1798, fos. 19–20; rejected draft material dated 7 August 1867.

37 *LDP*, p. 172.

38 See below, pp. 183–85.

39 *LDP*, p. 186.

40 [Thomas Carlyle] 'Ireland and the British Chief Governor', *Spectator*, 22, (13 May 1848), p. 464.

41 *CL*, xxviii, pp. 136–37, 13 May 1853.

42 See Christopher Harding et al., *Imprisonment in England and Wales: A Concise History* (Beckenham, 1985), pp. 147–54.

43   See John Pratt, *Punishment and Civilization* (2003), pp. 35–80 for an account of these developments and critical reactions to them.

44   *CL*, xxiii, p. 224, 5? February 1849.

45   Henry Mayhew and John Binny, *The Criminal Prisons of London and the Science of Prison Life* (1862, repr. 1972), pp. 363–70.

46   *LDP*, pp. 45–46. Carlyle refers here to a 'Chartist poet' who benefited from these opportunities: 'walking rapidly to and fro in his private court, a clean, high-walled place; the world and its cares quite excluded, for some months to come: master of his own time and spiritual resources to, as I supposed, a really enviable extent.' The subject of this comment was Ernest Jones who served a 2 year term in Tothill; see Miles Taylor, *Ernest Jones, Chartism, and the Romance of Politics, 1819–1869* (Oxford, 2003), pp. 121–36. In a notice written after his release advertising poems written in prison with his own blood, Jones reacted sharply to Carlyle's gibe; 'Ernest Jones to the People', *Red Republican*, 10 August 1850, p. 64. In 1859, after having been declared bankrupt, Jones appealed to Carlyle for financial support referring to the need to keep his household intact so that he might look after his children whose mother had died. Carlyle duly dispatched a cheque for £5, marking the stub 'For Jones the Chartist'; NLS, MS 1767, fos. 228–29.

47   See, for example, 'Carlyle's Latter Day Pamphlets', *Chambers' Edinburgh Journal*, new series, 14 (1850), pp. 27–28; 'Charles Dickens and David Copperfield', pp. 707–10; 'A Pilgrimage to Utopia; or the Autobiography of a Visionary (2)', p. 145.

48   *LDP*, p. 47.

49   See above p. 95.

50   *LDP*, p. 43.

51   Ibid., pp. 48–49.

52   Ibid., p. 65.

53   Ibid., p. 53. A reviewer of 'Model Prisons' defended Howard on the grounds that he had really been a model Carlylean hero: bold, disinterested, intrepid and effective; 'Thomas Carlyle and John Howard', *Fraser's Magazine*, 41 (1850), p. 410.

54   *LDP*, p. 68. Carlyle wrote, but did not publish, an even more extreme statement of this view; see Fred Kaplan, '"Phallus-Worship" (1848): Unpublished Manuscripts III – A Response to the Revolution of 1848', *CN*, 2 (1980), pp. 19–23.

55   See, for example, 'The Jesuits', *Oxford and Cambridge Review*, 1 (1845), pp. 225–48.

56   This suggestion was made by a reviewer; see 'Latter-Day Pamphlets', *Eclectic Review*, new series, 28 (1850), pp. 406–7.

57   *LDP*, p. 255.

58   Ibid., p. 262.

59   *FG*, ix, p. 247.

60   *LDP*, p. 266–67.

61   Ibid., pp. 268–70.

62   Ibid., p. 271.

63   Ibid., p. 273. It is perhaps significant that Pugin was a convert to Catholicism.

64   Ibid., p. 278.

65   Carlyle may have chosen Hudson as his subject following a prompt from Thomas Erskine. At the beginning of May 1849 Erskine asked Carlyle for his view of Hudson, describing him

as an 'ominous' sign 'of the times'; NLS, MS 1766, fol. 240v, Thomas Erskine to Thomas Carlyle, 1 May 1849.

66 Hudson courted publicity, marking his election as MP for Sunderland in August 1845 with a large and elaborate civic dinner attended by peers and members of the cathedral chapter at Durham, one of whom spoke in praise of him. Hudson's public fall began in February 1849 with the revelation that he had sold shares to one of his companies at highly inflated prices. By the time that Carlyle's pamphlet appeared in July 1850, other scandals, including cases of straightforward embezzlement, had come to light and Hudson's fall was complete; he continued, however, to attend the House of Commons. See A. J. Arnold and S. McCartney, *George Hudson: The Rise and Fall of The Railway King* (2004), pp. 141–43, 173–83.

67 See above p. 118.

68 *HHW*, pp. 13–14.

69 *LDP*, p. 225.

70 Jules Seigel, 'Carlyle and Peel: The Prophet's Search for a Heroic Politician and An Unpublished Fragment', *Victorian Studies*, 26 (1983), pp. 181–83.

71 Goldberg and Seigel, 'Introduction', *Latter Day Pamphlets*, pp. xxxvii, xl.

72 *LDP*, p. 83.

73 NLS, MS 516, fol. 22, Thomas Carlyle to John Carlyle, 15 December 1855; MS 1798, fol. 6, 23 March 1855. Olive Anderson has shown that the Crimean War brought into sharp focus a body of criticism of administrative machinery and the constitution; see *A Liberal State at War* (1967), parts 1 and 2.

74 'The Decline of Party Government', *Westminster and Foreign Quarterly Review*, new series, 8 (1855), pp. 125–50; for Carlyle's statement see *CL*, xxix, p. 249, 8 February 1855.

75 *LDP*, pp. 115–16.

76 *CL*, xxix, pp. 34–35, 1 March 1854; NLS, MS 527, fol. 41, Thomas Carlyle to John Carlyle, 10 February 1871.

77 *CL*, xxix, p. 35, 1 March 1854; *LDP*, pp. 99–100, 102.

78 Thomas Hare, a pioneer of proportional representation, tried later to recruit Carlyle to his cause on the grounds that elections organised on this principle would ensure that 'intelligence is enabled to select intelligence', thus providing a solution to the problems that Carlyle had identified in the 'Latter-Day Pamphlets'; NLS, Acc. 11388, no. 30, Thomas Hare to Thomas Carlyle, 26 April 1860. There is no indication that Carlyle endorsed this view; indeed, a remark in one of the pamphlets may in fact signal his rejection of proportional representation: 'All classes, if they happen not to be wise, heroic classes,– how, by the cunningest jumbling of them together, will you ever get a wisdom or a heroism out of them?' (*LDP*, p. 233). His ongoing and unqualified hostility to electoral politics was demonstrated amply in his last published writing on the issue, 'Shooting Niagara' (1867).

79 *HHW*, p. 107.

80 Boyd Hilton, *The Age of Atonement: The Influence of Evangelicalism on Social and Economic Thought, 1795–1855* (Oxford, 1988), pp. 220–26.

81 *CL*, viii, p. 117, 12 May 1835.

82 *CL*, xiii, p. 311, 2 December 1841; xiv, p. 209, 26 June 1842; xvii, pp. 324–25, 30 March 1844.

83   Marrs, p. 631.

84   C. S. Parker, ed., *Sir Robert Peel from his Private Papers*, 3 vols (1899), iii, p. 474.

85   Cited Paul Adelman, *Peel and the Tory Party* (1989), p. 29; Peel vowed that he would never again 'burn my fingers by organising a party', cited ibid., p. 76. For other accounts of Peel's view of party see Norman Gash, *Sir Robert Peel* (1972), pp. 708–10; Ian D. C. Newbold, 'Sir Robert Peel and the Conservative Party', *English Historical Review*, 158 (1983), pp. 529–57. Cf. Seigel, 'Carlyle and Peel', p. 182 where Peel is described as a 'staunch party man'. For a re-examination of Carlyle's perception of Peel see John Morrow, 'The Paradox of Peel as Carlylean Hero', *Historical Journal*, 40 (1997), pp. 97–110.

86   *HHW*, pp. 52–53 where Carlyle illustrates this by reference to a core value of Islam: it 'means in its way denial of self, annihilation of self.'

87   These signs of heroism are apparent throughout Carlyle's writings on Cromwell and they also play a prominent role in his reports of meetings with Peel; see Froude, *LL*, i, pp. 465–66. For discussions of the idea of political heroism in Carlyle's writings see Thomas Calviner, 'Heroes and Hero-worship: Not so Simple in The French Revolution', *Victorian Institute Journal*, 13 (1985), pp. 83–96; Philip Rosenberg, *The Seventh Hero* (Cambridge, Massachusetts, 1974), pp. 176–204; Chris Vandem Bossche, *Carlyle and the Search for Authority* (Columbus, Ohio, 1991), pp. 97–102.

88   Work on Peel's reputation among his close colleagues suggests that the insights that Carlyle gained during the course of his brief acquaintance with the former prime minister were not at variance with at least some contemporary judgements; see Boyd Hilton, 'Peel: A Reappraissal', *Historical Journal*, 22 (1979), pp. 613–14.

89   *CL*, v, p. 397, 4 September 1831.

90   Later, in *Frederick the Great*, Carlyle attributed these functions to 'Tobacco Parliaments', attended by the King and his intimates after dinner. These fora were not elected bodies and in the reign of Frederick's father they hampered good government; *FG*, ii, pp.114–31. Jules Seigel seems mistaken when he writes that Carlyle's enthusiasm for Peel restored his faith in parliament ('Peel and Carlyle', p. 191); rather, the 'Chief Governor' was to preside over a series of reforms that would remove the House of Commons from an authoritative position in the machinery of government.

91   For contemporary remarks on the radically unconstitutional implications of the 'Latter-Day Pamphlets' see the reviews by Aytoun and Masson in Jules Paul Seigel, ed., *Carlyle: The Critical Heritage* (1971), pp. 325, 327, 359–61.

92   [James Hannay], *Blackwood v. Carlyle: A Vindication By a Carlylian* (1850), pp. 28–29, 41.

93   Catharine Gallagher, *The Industrial Reformation of English Fiction, 1832–1867* (Chicago, 1985), pp. 195–200. In contrasting his position with that of Carlyle, Mill wrote that the 'honour and glory of the average man is that he is capable of following the initiative of a leading individual: that he can respond internally to wise and noble things, and be led to them with his eyes open'; *On Liberty, Essays on Politics and Society*, ed. J. M. Robson and Alexander Brady, *Collected Works of John Stuart Mill* (Toronto, 1967–1991), p. 269. In Mill's case this ideal was often seen as a distant objective so Carlyle's position was more demanding and impatient.

94   *LDP*, pp. 106–7; this point is also stressed in the fragment published in Seigel, 'Carlyle

and Peel' pp. 193–95. In 'The Near Failure' Seigel seems to endorse the judgement about the overwhelmingly negative caste of the pamphlets that marked some contemporary responses to them; see pp. 172–73. There is a good account of the social context of heroism in Rosenberg's *The Seventh Hero*, pp. 188–93 but his view that none of Carlyle's work after *Past and Present* is worth discussing means that he has not considered the role of heroism in the 'Latter-Day Pamphlets'.

95 *LDP*, p. 8; italics added.

96 NLS, Acc. 11388, Thomas Carlyle to Lord Ashburton, 29 November 1855 and 15 September 1857; Thomas Carlyle to Lady Ashburton, 7 April 1857. Carlyle's ideas on these issues were reflected in Lady Ashburton's charitable practice. She avoided involvement in charitable organizations – 'philanthropic machines' in Carlyle's terms – preferring to work closely in superintending the domestic lives of labourers' families on her husband's estates; see K. D. Reynolds, *Aristocratic Women and Political Society in Victorian Britain* (Oxford, 1998), p. 103.

97 See Anthony La Vopa, 'The Philosopher and the *Schwärmer*: On the Career of a German Epithet from Luther to Kant', in Lawrence E. Klein and Anthony J. La Vopa, ed., *Enthusiasm and Enlightenment in Europe, 1650–1850* (San Marino, California, 1998), pp. 85–115.

98 'Mr Carlyle's Singing Peers', *Spectator*, 12 October 1867, p. 1140.

99 *Two Reminiscences*, p. 105.

100 See Gillian Workman, 'Thomas Carlyle and the Governor Eyre Controversy: An Account with Some New Material', *Victorian Studies*, 18 (1974–75), p. 89.

101 Quoted ibid., p. 101.

102 *HHW*, pp. 64–65.

103 *LDP*, p. 139.

Notes to Chapter 7: The Voice of the Past

1 These essays appeared originally in *Fraser's Magazine*, the first as 'Thoughts on History' and the second as '*Quae Cogitavit*'; they are referred to here by the titles used in *CME*. Carlyle's letters give few clues on the genesis of these pieces, but the fact that both were offered to Fraser to 'print if he wished,' suggests that they were written entirely at Carlyle's initiative; see *CL*, v, p. 127, 6 August 1830 and *CL*, vi, p. 339, March 1833.

2 Carlyle, 'On History', *CME*, ii, p. 253.

3 Carlyle, 'Scott' *CME*, vi, p. 50; *Two Notebooks*, pp. 276–77. J. S. Mill shared Carlyle's views on this matter, noting in his journal that objects of widespread popular admiration should not be the measure of an age: 'Otherwise one might say that the present age will be known and estimated by posterity as the age which thought Macaulay a great writer'; 'Diary 1854', in *Journals and Debate Speeches*, ed. J. M. Robson, *Collected Works of John Stuart Mill*, (Toronto, 1988), p. 653. Carlyle's lack of respect for Macaulay was reciprocated. Macaulay ridiculed him in private, on one occasion entertaining his listeners with a peroration on the forthcoming opening of parliament that parodied the style of the French Revolution; see Ellen Twistelton's *Letters*, pp. 255–56, 16 December 1854. This parody may have focused on Carlyle's imaginative account of the proces-

sion preceding the opening of the Estates General in the summer of 1789; see *FR*, i, pp. 115–31.

4   Hedva Ben-Israel, *English Historians on the French Revolution* (Cambridge, 1968), p. 130. Ben-Israel's chapter on Carlyle's *French Revolution* is among the best treatments of this work. For a more recent account of history as totality and historical writing as a wide-ranging search for symbols of meaning, see Anne Rigney, 'The Untenanted Places of the Past: Thomas Carlyle and the Varieties of Historical Ignorance', *History and Theory*, 35 (1996), p. 343. The most detailed analysis of the conception and reception of Carlyle's work on Cromwell is D. J. Trela's *A History of Carlyle's 'Oliver Cromwell's Letters and Speeches* (New York, 1992); on Carlyle's Cromwell in its nineteenth century context see Timothy Lang, *The Victorians and the Stuart Heritage: Interpretations of a Discordant Past* (Cambridge 1995), pp. 122–38 and Blair Worden, *Roundhead Reputations: The English Civil Wars and the Passions of Posterity* (2001), pp. 264–95. For an account of the conception of history informing Calyle's study of Frederick the Great see Morse Peckham, 'Frederick the Great', in K. J. Fielding and Rodger L. Tarr, eds., *Carlyle Past and Present: A Collection of New Essays* (1976), pp. 198–215.

5   *CL*, v, p. 278, 17 April 1831.

6   Jesus Christ seems to have been a notable and interesting exception to this general rule. After viewing Holman Hunt's *Life of Christ*, Carlyle commented that he disliked 'all pictures of Christ: you will find that men never thought of painting Christ till they began to lose the impression of him in their hearts'; *The Life of Thomas Carlyle* (1881), p. 15.

7   See *CL*, xxix, pp. 194–95, 9 November 1854, for an account of his visit to Windsor, during which he met Prince Albert and had a very agreeable conversation on German history.

8   William Allingham, *Diary*, introduction by Geoffrey Grigson (1907, repr; Fontwell, 1967), p. 80.

9   *CL*, xxix, p. 77, 2 May 1854.

10   John D. Rosenberg, *Carlyle and the Burden of History* (Oxford, 1985), p. 77. It is ironic that while these works were greatly admired by contemporary readers, and aspects of Carlyle's technique were adopted by Victorian novelists, it was not taken up by historians.

11   See Ben-Israel, *English Historians*, pp. 143–46, who notes that Carlyle's extensive reliance on memoirs facilitated this approach, but inhibited more conventional historical analysis.

12   Rosenberg, *Carlyle and the Burden of History*, p. 77.

13   'On History', pp. 257–58. Contemporary reviewers were generally appreciative of Carlyle's capacity to make actors and actions 'come alive', comparing his treatment of the English Civil War most favourably with that of William Godwin on this score; 'Oliver Cromwell's Letters and Speeches', *Shilling Magazine*, 3 (1846), p. 183. See also *Knights Penny Magazine*, 15 (1846), p. 82; *North British Review*, p. 527; 'Oliver Cromwell's *Letters and Speeches*', *Examiner* (13 December 1845), p. 787. This judgment was endorsed by Herman Merivale in a review for the *Edinburgh Review*, but he thought that the advantages of Carlyle's presentation of the French Revolution had been purchased at some scholarly cost since he relied on a narrow range of contemporary accounts without making allowance for the perspective of the reporter: 'Truth, that is, accuracy of detail, is hardly to be looked for ... Verisimilitude his recitals frequently have; and it is surprising to perceive the life-like reality which is communicated to stories so familiar as those of the chief events of the Revolution,

by the mere art of the word-painter'; 'Carlyle on the French Revolution', *Edinburgh Review*, 71 (1840), pp. 415–16, 419, 433.

14 See Rosemary Jann, *The Art and Science of Victorian History* (Columbus, Ohio, 1985), pp. 50–52.

15 K. J. Fielding, 'Unpublished Manuscripts – II: Carlyle's Scenario for *Cromwell*', *CN*, 2 (1980), p. 8. Carlyle later noted that there were five accounts of the Battle of Hohenfriedberg (1745), 'all modestly written, each true looking from its own place'; *FG*, vi, p. 62.

16 'On History Again', *CME*, iv, p. 218.

17 Ibid., p. 219.

18 *Past and Present*, p. 43 and see below p. 169.

19 See Joseph W. Childer's 'Carlyle's *Past and Present*, History and a Question of Hermeneutics', *Clio*, 13 (1984), p. 257.

20 John Morley, 'Carlyle' in John Morley, *Critical Miscellanies*, 3 vols (1886), i, p. 158.

21 Barrie M. Radcliffe and W. H. Chaloner, trans. and ed., *A French Sociologist Looks at Britain: Gustave d'Eichthal and British Society in 1828* (Manchester, 1977), p. 61. Eichthal, a follower of Saint Simon, was later friendly with Carlyle, but this visit to England predated the Saint Simonian's interest in Carlyle's ideas; he first attracted their attention as author of 'Signs of the Times' and 'Characteristics'. See Ben-Israel, *English Historians*, pp. 133–35, 140–41, for a succinct account of the role Mill played in assisting Carlyle's research for *The French Revolution*.

22 Francis E. Mineka, ed. *The Earlier Letters of John Stuart Mill, 1812–1848*, in *Collected Works of John Stuart Mill* (Toronto, 1963), pp. 138–40, 146–47, 149–50, 190–91, 203.

23 'Parliamentary History of the French Revolution' (1837), *CME*, vi, p. 3. Privately, Carlyle was even more scathing, drawing attention to what he saw as the tawdry moral tone of Thiers's work: 'every hero of his turns out to be perfectly justified in doing whatsoever – he has succeeded in doing'; Mineka, *Earlier Letters.*, p. 139n. It is ironic that this comment (reported by Mill) reflects a view of 'great men' that was later attributed to Carlyle and for which he was roundly criticised. Mill's postscript, in which he declines to follow Carlyle in thinking that Napoleon's 'one excellence, strength of will' outweighs the 'entire want of an virtuous purpose, and the willingness to employ any even the most paltry means' (ibid., p. 141) was prescient. While highly critical of Theirs, Carlyle was, however, appreciative of the efforts of two other French scholars, P. J. B. Buchez and P. C. Roux, who produced a multi-volume compilation of newspaper material, debates and pamphlets published as *Histoire Parlementaire de la Révolution Française* (1833–36); 'Parliamentary History', pp. 7–9. Buchez and Roux's collection was Carlyle's main source of primary material, supplemented by bound volumes of the *Moniteur*; see Ben-Israel, *English Historians*, p. 141.

24 Ben-Israel, *English Historians*, pp. 141–42, notes that although Carlyle's reading on the French Revolution was extensive, it tended to be haphazard, and did not involve systematic firsthand work with primary sources. Carlyle made heavy use of memoirs, but his only way of guarding against their inaccuracy and partiality was to check them against each other.

25 *CL*, iv, 4 December 1843.

26 *OC*, i, pp. 2, 3. In his lectures on heroes and hero-worship, Carlyle had been more guarded in claiming novelty for his rescue of Cromwell: 'Here, this day, who knows if it is not rash

in me to be among the first that ever ventured to pronounce him not a knave and a liar, but a genuinely honest man?'; *HHW*, p. 217.

27 See *North British Review*, p. 525; *Tait's Edinburgh Magazine*, 13 (1846), pp. 38, 40–41.

28 *CL*, xii, p. 361; *OC*, i, p. 16. On Godwin's *History* see John Morrow, 'Introduction', William Godwin, *History of the Commonwealth of England. From Its Commencement to the Restoration of Charles the Second* [1824–8], 4 vols in 8 (Bristol, 2003), i, pp. v–xxxiv, and on Forster's work see Lang, *The Victorians and the Stuart Heritage*, pp. 103–108.

29 *CL*, xxix, pp. 8–9, Journal, 8 January 1854. For an account of the writings of *FG* see Arthur A. and Venna H. Adrian, 'Frederick the Great: "The Unutterable Horror of a Prussian book"', in Fielding and Tarr. eds., *Carlyle Past and Present*, pp. 180–87.

30 Ibid., p. 165, 8 October 1854.

31 Ibid., p. 247, 8 February 1855.

32 NLS, MS 551, fol. 161v, 8 October 1854; *CL*, xxix, pp. 16–17n.

33 *CL*, xxvii, p. 139, 6 June 1852; xxviii, p. 152, 20 May 1853.

34 NLS, MS 1763, fol. 281, 16 January 1859.

35 Reviewers, including those who were otherwise hostile to the project, applauded these aspects of Carlyle's study warmly.

36 See Grace Calder, *The Writing of Past and Present: A Study of Carlyle's Manuscripts* (New Haven, 1949), passim.

37 References to this work are from the modern translation by Diana Greenway and Jane Sayers (Oxford, 1989).

38 Calder, *The Writing of Past and Present*, pp. 25–27. The *Chronicle* was one of a number of the Camden Society's contributions to a rising demand for original texts for the study of English history. Some of these publications were typical dryasdust productions that provoked Carlyle's ire – see D. J. Trela, 'The Writing of "An Election to the Long Parliament": Carlyle's Primary Research and the Book Clubs', *CSA*, 14 (1994), pp. 71–82. Carlyle's response to the *Chronicle* and his annoyance that certain 'living' texts had not yet been published, strongly suggests that he welcomed these developments when they recovered aspects of what he took to be the 'living' past. The movement to publish manuscript material was assisted on an official level by initiatives such as the reorganisation of the Record Commission chaired by Carlyle's old friend and pupil Charles Buller MP.

39 Linda Georgiana, 'Carlyle and Jocelin of Brakelond: A Chronicle Rechronicled', *Browning Institute Studies*, 8 (1980), pp. 103–27, argues that Carlyle's use of this source was very 'loose', but while this may be true on textual grounds, the themes that Carlyle extracts from this work seem to come quite naturally from it. Even the textual point may be overstated: the translations of passages from the *Chronicle* that Carlyle reproduces in his text are virtually identical with those in the modern translation; see note 37.

40 *Past and Present*, p. 36.

41 Ibid., pp. 41, 43.

42 *Early Kings of Norway*, p. 96.

43 See Eugene Goodheart, 'English Social Criticism and the Spirit of Reformation', *Clio*, 5 (1975), p. 77.

44 *OC*, i, p. 50.

45 Thomas Carlyle, *Historical Sketches of Notable Persons and Events in the Reigns of James*

I and Charles I, ed. Alexander Carlyle (1902), pp. 42, 225. This volume collected previously unpublished materials from Carlyle's project on the seventeenth century. See *CL*, vi, pp. 260–61, 19 November 1832, p. 303, 12 January 1833, and *HHW*, pp. 132–37 for earlier references to Puritanism; Carlyle regarded Scotland as the source of Puritanism in England and New England.

46 *OC*, ii, p. 106.

47 Ibid., i, p. 288.

48 Ibid, p. 286.

49 The radical implications of Carlyle's accounts were noted by a range of reviewers. See, for example, *Blackwood's Edinburgh Magazine*, 61 (1847), p. 415; *The Christian Remembrancer*, 11 (1846), pp. 243–44, 253; *North British Review*, 4 (1846), p. 506; *Prospective Review*, 2 (1846), p. 125; *Tait's Edinburgh Magazine*, 13 (1846), p. 50; *Westminster Review*, 46 (1847), p. 433.

50 *North British Review*, 4 (1846), p. 526. William Sewell, the Oxford High Churchmen, expressed reservations about the pantheistic implications of Carlyle's religious views, but went on to offer a generally favourable account of his ideas, applauding his attack on the 'spirit of the age' and parliamentary government, and attributing his shortcomings to the Church's failure to enlighten an essentially 'good and elevated mind'; see 'Carlyle's Works', *Quarterly Review*, 66 (1840), pp. 446–503. Kathleen Tillotson has suggested that Carlyle might have had some sympathy for the Puseyites in the 1830s because he thought they undermined the Church of England; see Kathleen Tillotson, 'Matthew Arnold and Thomas Carlyle', *Proceedings of the British Academy*, 42 (1956), p. 138. See Worden, *Roundhead Reputations*, pp. 283–85 for a recent consideration of nonconformist responses to Carlyle's treatment of Cromwell and the Puritans.

51 See, for example, the reviews from *Blackwood's* (pp. 393, 402, 423), *Christian Remembrancer* (p. 260), and the *North British Review* (p. 516), cited in note 49.

52 Froude, *LL*, i, p. 211. For Carlyle's reservations about the adequacy of Puritanism, see *HHW*, p. 189, and *OC*, v, pp. 134–35.

53 *OC*, i, p. 156.

54 *FR*, p. 34.

55 Ibid., ii, p. 95.

56 Ibid., iii, p. 22.

57 Ben-Israel, *English Historians*, pp. 145–46. Carlyle might have adopted the term 'sansculottism' from German sources. It appears as 'Sanskulottismus' in Friedrich Schlegel's 'The Concept of Republicanism' (1796) and had general currency in the 1790s; see Frederick C. Beiser, ed., *The Early Political Writings of the German Romantics* (Cambridge, 1996), p. 105 and note.

58 Biancamaria Fontana, *Rethinking the Politics of Commercial Society: The Edinburgh Review, 1802–1832* (Cambridge, 1985), pp. 18, 22.

59 *FR*, i, p. 185.

60 Ibid., p. 218.

61 Ibid., ii, p. 222.

62 *Early Kings of Norway*, p. 96.

63 The details of Carlyle's characterisation of Samson's heroism, and his treatment of the

implications of medieval religion, spirituality and 'forms', suggest that Culler's verdict that Samson is merely a 'pre-incarnation of Cromwell', rather than a medieval figure, is mistaken; see Culler, *The Victorian Mirror of History*, p. 69. This interpretation did not occur to Carlyle's contemporary critics, and it ignores his general strategy of seeing heroes as exemplifying universal characteristics in forms appropriate to particular historical circumstances.

64 Jocelin, *Chronicle*, pp. xvi, 46–47.

65 *Past and Present*, pp. 102–8. Carlyle highlighted the attitude towards heroes in the medieval and modern periods by contrasting the reverence accorded to St Edmund's remains when his tomb was opened during the course of building work, with the disrespectful pillaging of John Hampden's grave in 1828: 'certain dignitaries of us … raised him also up, under cloud of night, cut off his arm with penknifes, pulled the scalp off his head,–and otherwise worshipped our Hero Saint in the most amazing manner!', ibid., p. 103.

66 See Rosemary Jann, 'The Condition of England Past and Present: Thomas Carlyle and the Middle Ages', *Studies in Medievalism*, 1 (1979), pp. 16–17.

67 *Past and Present*, p. 52.

68 Jocelin, *Chronicle*, p. 37. An example of the integration of the apparently profane and the sacred occurs in Carlyle's sketch scenario for a drama on Cromwell. Jenny Geddes, whose courage and discernment in flinging a stool at the head of a preaching Episcopalian divine symbolized the rejection of this mode of church government in post-Reformation Scotland, is depicted as 'talking of her household cookeries and business, of religion withal'; Fielding, ed., 'Unpublished Manuscripts – II', p. 8.

69 Ibid., pp. 3–7.

70 *Past and Present*, p. 80.

71 Ibid., p. 111.

72 Cf. Worden, *Roundhead Reputations*, pp. 271–72.

73 See, for example, the annotations to Cromwell's statements in *OC*, i, pp. 88–89; ii, pp. 136 and n., 255 n. iv, p. 35.

74 *OC*, iii, p. 196.

75 Ibid., i, p. 89.

76 *HHW*, p. 201. Cromwell's lasting significance contrasted with what Carlyle took to be the short-lived fame of Napoleon. Napoleon's military prowess was not sufficient to make him a hero; see ibid. pp. 221–22.

77 *FG*, i, pp. 286–91.

78 See below, p. 190.

79 *FG*, iv, p. 28.

80 *FG*, v, pp. 15, 273.

81 Frederick's character frustrated his poetic aspirations, but this was not a cause for regret on Carlyle's part. To the contrary, he claimed that the weakness of Frederick's poetry confirmed that he was really suited to silent and determined action rather than to the pursuit of literary fame.

82 *FG*, vi, p. 3.

83 Ibid., viii, p. 280.

84 Ibid., pp. 19, 80–81. In correspondence, Carlyle compared Frederick's skill and economy

with the costly blunders that marked the recent British campaign in the Crimea; *CL*, xxix, p. 175, 20 October, 1854.

85   *FG*, iii, pp. 48–50, 271; iv, pp. 7–9; vi, pp. 222–27.

86   Ibid., iii, pp. 48–50.

87   Ibid, x, pp. 135–46; iv, pp. 244–46.

88   Ibid., vi, pp. 244–45; x, pp. 178–79.

89   Ibid., vii, pp. 14, 26.

90   Ibid., viii, pp. 136–37.

91   Ibid., pp. 15–16, 217–20.

92   *Early Kings of Norway*, p. 43.

93   *Past and Present*, p. 101.

94   Thomas Carlyle, 'Notes of a Three-Day's Tour to the Netherlands, August 1842, I & II', *Cornhill Magazine*, new series, 53 (1922), pp. 632, 510; see also Michael Cotsell, 'Carlyle, Travel and the Enlargements of History', in Michael Cotsell, ed., *English Literature and the Wider World, 1830–1876* (1990), pp. 83–97.

95   *HHW*, p. 114; Carlyle, *Historical Sketches*, p. 221.

96   Carlyle, *Historical Sketches*, p. 221.

97   Ibid., p. 233.

98   *OC*, i, p. 246, and see above pp. 143–44.

99   Ibid., iii, pp. 183, 186, 184.

100 Hence Carlyle's fascination with the signs of the paranormal in Cromwell's early life; see *OC*, i, 42–43.

101 John Forster, *The Statesmen of the Commonwealth of England*, 5 vols. (1840), v; Godwin, *History of the Commonwealth*, iii, pp. 118–119.

102 *OC*, iii, p. 168.

103 Lang, *The Stuart Inheritance*, pp. 136–37.

104 *OC*, ii, p. 143. In an unpublished sketch his verdict was expressed in even harsher language: prior to Cromwell's arrival, Ireland was like a 'black subterranean kennel, tearing dead horses and one another'; Fielding, 'Unpublished Manuscripts II', p. 10. Aspects of Carlyle's defence of Cromwell in Ireland touch on issues that have been the focus of recent revisionist historical scholarship; for a review of this work and an assessment of the campaign, see J. C. Davis, *Oliver Cromwell* (London, 2001), pp. 107–11.

105 See 'Carlyle's Cromwell', *Dublin University Magazine*, 27 (1846), p. 245.

106 The Portraits of John Knox', *CME*, viii, pp. 134, 145–46.

107 Richard Cronin, *Romantic Victorians: English Literature 1824–1840*, (Basingstoke, 2002), pp. 46–47, 52–53, contrasts Carlyle's stance with the complacent programme of Macaulay's *History of England*.

108 In so doing he was advancing a position that was gaining widespread acceptance across party lines from the 1820s; see Ben Israel, *English Historians on the French Revolution*, pp. 53–56.

109 *FR*, i, pp. 19, 9–10.

110 Ibid., p. 32.

111 Ibid., p. 37.

112 Ibid, ii, pp. 127, 165–66.

113 See Jann, *The Art and Science of Victorian History*, p. 40. As noted above (pp. 95–96), the retribution theme is particularly important in Carlyle's treatment of the Irish dimensions of the 'condition of England question'.

114 *FR*, iii, pp. 209–10.

115 Ibid., i, p. 188.

116 Ibid., ii, p. 174.

117 Ibid., pp. 205–6; iii, pp. 138–39.

118 Fontana, *Rethinking the Politics*, p. 33.

119 See Thomas Culviner, 'Heroes and Hero-Worship: Not So Simple in the French Revolution', *Victorian Institute Journal*, 13 (1985), pp. 83–96.

120 *Early Kings of Norway*, p. 92.

121 *HHW*, pp. 221–22.

122 See 'Carlyle's Frederick the Great', *British Quarterly Review*, 29 (1859), pp. 239–81; 'Carlyle's Frederick the Great', *Blackwood's Edinburgh Magazine*, 98 (1867), pp. 38–56.

123 NLS, MS 1773, fos. 82v–83, 13 June 1879.

124 'Oliver Cromwell's Letters and Speeches', *Christian Remembrancer*, 11 (April 1846), pp. 252–54.

125 'Oliver Cromwell's Letters and Speeches', *Prospective Review*, 11 (1846), p. 125.

126 See, for example, 'The French Revolution', *Edinburgh Review*, 71 (1840), pp. 417, 425; 'Politics and Faith', *National Review*, 12 (1861), pp. 450–51.

127 'Frederick the Great', *North British Review*, 43 (1865), pp. 79, 125.

Notes to Chapter 8: The Sage of Chelsea

1 NLS, Acc. 11388, no. 29, 24 November 1877.

2 NLS, MS 527, fol. 16, 26 May 1870; Acc 11388, no. 29, 23 August 1869.

3 NLS, MS 1778, fos. 1v, 3, 17 May 1873. Carlyle's irritated remark on obituaries of Mill is in NLS, MS 527, fol. 94, 10 May 1873.

4 NLS, MS 1775D, 1 May 1870, fol. 190v.

5 NLS, Acc. 7988, 22 January 1866; NLS, MS 1775E, 23 April 1871, 4 December 1871.

6 NLS, MS 20753, fol. 17, 24 August 1870; this loan was 'to be repaid in the middle of October'. The sums need to be multiplied by more than fifty to give any conception of their scale in modern terms.

7 William Allingham, *Diary*, ed. Geoffrey Grigson (first publ. 1907; repr Fontwell, 1967), p. 244.

8 NLS, MS 1769, fos. 165–67, 27 January 1870 (Game Laws); MS 1769, fos. 257–59, 20 September 1870 (army commissions); 1770, fos. 5–6, 13 January 1871 (peace campaign); MS 1770, fos. 262–63, 13 July 1873, MS 1771, fos. 215–18, 28 May 1875, MS 1771, fos. 229–30, 8 August 1875 (stock market swindles); MS 1770, fol. 127, February 1872 (poor law reform).

9 Norman Kelvin, ed., *The Collected Letters of William Morris*, 2 vols (Princeton, 1984–87), i, p. 361. Carlyle disliked the gothic architecture that Morris admired, much preferring St Paul's Cathedral to Westminster Abbey; see Allingham's *Diary*, p. 233.

10　See above pp. 118–19.

11　NLS, MS 1771, fos. 70–71, 21 June 1874.

12　He read a violent sermon on this topic to the politician Joseph Chamberlain when he visited with John Morley; see John Viscount Morley, *Recollections*, 2 vols (1918), i, pp. 153–54.

13　Moncure Conway, *Autobiography: Memories and Experiences of Moncure Daniel Conway*, 2 vols (1904), i, p. 360. Over the Christmas of 1855–56 the streets were full of 'all manner of mechanics and poor people fitted out with beer; stumbling *against* one; threatening to quarrel occasionally'; *CL*, xxix, p. 232, 6 January 1856.

14　NLS, MS 1768, September 1867, fol. 283.

15　NLS, MS 1769, fol. 117, 17 April 1869; MS 1771, fos. 203–4, 5 May 1875. A year later Morley published a finely nuanced evaluation of Carlyle's writings and of his impact in the *Fortnightly Review*. This essay, later republished in Morley's collected essays, ('Carlyle', John Morley, *Critical Miscellanies*, 3 vols (1886), i, p. 135–201), exhibited the mixture of general admiration and strong dissent from some of Carlyle's views that characterised nineteenth century responses to his ideas and influence.

16　See Allingham 29 July 1873; Carlyle complained that Whistler had asked originally for two or three sittings but took a great deal more and only brought them to an end when he 'rebelled'. Michael Goldberg's treatment of these exchanges is remarkable for its failure to credit Carlyle with any humorous intent; Michael Goldberg, 'Gigantic Philistines: Carlyle, Dickens and the Visual Arts', in Jerry D. Adams and Rita B. Bottoms, eds. *Lectures on Carlyle and His Era* (Santa Cruz, California, 1985), pp. 17–43.

17　NLS, MS 528, fol. 72; 16 July 1877.

18　NLS, MS 528, fol. 36; 1 September 1875.

19　NLS, MS 528, fol. 44, 20 November 1875. Carlyle declined an LLD offered by the University of Edinburgh in 1866; NLS, MS 1768, fol. 146, 17 March 1866.

20　NLS, MS 1773, fol. 47, 9 October 1878 (American honour); MS 1772, fos. 40–44, 20 March 1876 (Royal Irish Academy); MS 1772, fos. 47–48, 29 March 1876 (Philosophical Institute). For Carlyle's criticism of Thiers in the 1830s see above p. 166.

21　NLS, MS 528, fol. 5, 14 February 1874.

22　NLS, MS 528, fol. 24; 1 January 1875. Carlyle's attitude to the two great parliamentary figures of the 1860s and 1870s was even-handed. Scathing comments on Disraeli were matched by those on his great rival Gladstone.

23　NLS, MS 1778, fol. 110v.

24　NLS, MS 1778, fos. 58, 107; superficial changes were made to the draft but they were not of a kind that accommodated even the moderate objections to the tone of the memorial.

25　NLS, MS 1778, fol. 80, 25 November 1875.

26　NLS, MS 1778, fos. 87–88, 27 November 1875.

27　NLS, MS 1778, fol. 107, 30 November 1875.

28　NLS, MS 1778, fol. 122.

29　NLS, MS 525, fol. 1, 6 January 1855.

30　NLS, MS 526, fol. 23, 6 February 1865.

31　NLS, MS 518, fol. 9, 27 September 1865.

32　The letter on the Franco-Prussian War may have been prompted by John Carlyle. He wrote to his brother on 23 October urging him to say something publicly about the war in response to the ill-informed support for France and to draw on his expertise on the history of Franco-German relations that was acquired during his work on *Frederick the Great*; NLS, MS 1775D, fol. 246.

33 NLS, MS 527, fol. 11, 13 April 1870.

34 Morley, 'Carlyle', p. 135.

35 George Gilfillan, 'Carlyle and Sterling', *Galleries of Literary Portraits*, 2 vols (Edinburgh, 1856–57), i p. 176.

36 David Daiches, *Carlyle and the Victorian Dilemma* (Edinburgh, 1963), pp. 6–7.

37 [W. H. Smith], 'Past and Present by Carlyle', *Blackwood's Edinburgh Magazine*, 54 (July 1843), p. 123. The burgeoning sales of Carlyle's works in the closing decade of his life makes it hard to credit claims about his waning influence. As examples cited above suggest, those who disagreed with Carlyle on some issues might be impressed by other ideas and by the force of his personality. Cf. Michael Timko, 'God's of the Lower World: Romantic Egoists and Carlylean Heroes', *Browning Institute Studies*, 14 (1986), p. 129.

38 'Oliver Cromwell's Letters and Speeches', *Prospective Review*, 11 (1846), pp. 124–25.

39 Morley, 'Carlyle', p. 137.

40 John Tyndall, *New Fragments* (1892), p. 394.

41 NLS, MS 1768, fol. 282.

42 Anthony Trollope, *An Autobiography*, ed. David Skilton (Harmondsworth, 1996), pp. 72, 160, 224.

43 Thomas C. Richardson, 'Carlyle's *Chartism* and the *Quarterly Review*', *CN*, 10 (1982), p. 52.

44 Andrew Lang, *The Life and Letters of John Gibson Lockhart*, 2 vols (1897), ii, pp. 234–35.

45 Ibid., i, p. 220.

46 [John Sterling], 'Carlyle's Works; *Sartor Resartus*', *London and Westminster Review*, 33 (1839), pp. 3, 11; NLS, MS 1766, fol. 147.

47 R. H. Horne, ed., *A New Spirit of the Age*, 2 vols (1844), ii, p. 269; [James Hannay], *Blackwood v. Carlyle: A Vindication. By a Carlylian* (1850), pp. 37, 40; the ascription of this work to Hannay follows the Bodleian Library Catalogue.

48 Francis Espinasse, *Literary Recollections and Sketches* (1893), p. 188.

49 Mary Smith, *The Autobiography of Mary Smith, School Mistress and Nonconformist* (1892), p. 247.

50 See above, pp. 44–45.

51 Richard D. Altick, *The English Common Reader: A Social History of the Mass Reading Public, 1800–1900* (Chicago, 1957), pp. 259–60. The first collected edition began to appear in 1856; see *CL*, xxxi, p. 109 which records the conclusion of the negotiations between Carlyle and Chapman and Hall.

52 Dixon seems to have been an avid reader of Bewick's works, citing his *Memoir* (1862) in a letter reprinted by Ruskin in *Time and Tide by Weare and Tyne: Twenty Five letters to a Working Man of Sunderland on the Laws of Work* (1867, repr. 1908), p. 233. These letters included a reference to a statement on the London mob that was attributed to Carlyle. His public disavowal of this statement produced a painful but short-lived breach between the two men; see Fred Kaplan, *Thomas Carlyle* (Ithaca, 1977), pp. 496–97. Bewick came from

a social background that was similar to Carlyle's but was located on the English side of the border. Of a strongly religious bent, he was opposed to egalitarianism and to parliamentary government.

53 NLS, MS 1768, fos. 195–96E, 3 December 1866; MS 1769, fol. 8, 14 February 1868. Carlyle may have met Dixon in the Spring of 1873; on 27 April Lord Leighton, the painter, invited him to lunch to meet Dixon, 'a highly intelligent and unassuming man', who was too diffident to call on Carlyle; NLS, MS 1770, fos. 241–42.

54 Ruskin, *Time and Tide*, p. 223

55 This suggestion was offered by Moncure Conway, *Autobiography*, ii, p. 103.

56 'Dangers of Democracy', *Westminster Quarterly Foreign Review*, 33 (1868), pp. 1–37.

57 A. S. Eve and C. H. Cressey, *Life and Work of John Tyndall* (1945), p. 17.

58 Frank M. Turner, 'Victorian Scientific Naturalism and Thomas Carlyle', in Frank M. Turner, *Contesting Cultural Authority: Studies in Victorian Intellectual Life* (Cambridge, 1993), p. 137. Ruth Barton has stressed the depth and enthusiasm of Tyndall's Carlylean scientific naturalism; see Ruth Barton, 'John Tyndall, Pantheist: A Rereading of the Belfast Address', *Osiris*, second series, 3 (1987), pp. 111–34.

59 NLS, MS 1773, fos. 107–8, 21 October 1879; a year later this group was meeting in the Bridge House Hotel, London Bridge; NLS, MS 1773, fol. 64, 4 December 1880.

60 NLS, MS 1773, fos. 51–52, 31 December 1878, 104, 12 October 1879, and see below p. 213.

61 See, for example, comments by James DeBow and George Fitzhugh in Jules Paul Seigel, ed., *Thomas Carlyle: The Critical Heritage* (1971), pp. 310, 369–74.

62 NLS, MS 1771, fos. 131–33, 10 September 1874; MS 666, 2 February 1881; *FR*, iii, p. 274. Newton Booth (1825–1892) subsequently served a term in the United States Senate. The *Dictionary of American Biography* notes that he was widely recognised as a 'man of exceptional ability and unquestioned integrity.'

63 J. H. Stirling, *Thomas Carlyle's Counsel to a Literary Aspirant* (Edinburgh, 1886), p. 27.

64 F. W. Maitland, *The Life and Letters of Leslie Stephen* (1906 repr. Bristol, 1991), pp. 231, 288.

65 'An Estimate of Mr Carlyle's Character', *St James Gazette*; NLS, MS Acc. 10484.

66 This view of Carlyle emerged from reviews of *Chartism* in the *Spectator* shortly after its publication: 'The Topic of Topics', *Spectator*, 4 January 1840, pp. 6–10 and 'The Curse of Party', *Spectator*, 11 January 1840, pp. 35–36. See 'Carlyle: Mirage Philosophy', *Blackwood's Edinburgh Magazine*, 85 (1859), pp. 138, 154; 'Thomas Carlyle on Modern Sociology', *Eclectic Review*, 114 (1861), p. 340; 'Mr Carlyle', *Fraser's Magazine*, 72 (1865), p. 784.

67 See Alexander H. Japp, *Three Great Teachers of Our Own Time: Being an Attempt to Deduce the Spirit and Purpose Animating Carlyle, Tennyson and Ruskin* (1865), pp. 20–21, and David Hodge, *Thomas Carlyle: The Man and Teacher* (Edinburgh and Glasgow, 1873), pp. 23–26, 50–51. Hodge's pamphlet began life as an address to an undergraduate society in Edinburgh, thus lending credence to Pringle-Pattison's recollection of the strength of interest in Carlyle's writings in Scottish universities in the 1870s; see A. Seth Pringle-Pattison, 'Introduction', *Selected Essays of Thomas Carlyle* (1909), p. viii.

68 Morley, 'Carlyle', pp. 184–85.

69 Thomas Cooper, *The Chartist, the Purgatory of Suicides: A Prison-Rhyme* (1845).

70 *Cooper's Journal*, 1, 16 February 1850, p. 103; 23 February 1850, p. 119; A. R. Schoyen, *The Chartist Challenge: A Portrait of George Julian Harney* (1958), pp. 271, 280.

71 George Jacob Holyoake, *Sixty Years of an Agitator's Life*, third edition, 2 vols (1893), i, p. 193.

72 *CL*, xxiii, pp. 261, 105.

73 Masson noted that while Carlyle did tend to see things through a 'veil of crepe' after Jane's death, Froude's editorial interventions were unremittingly and unfairly gloomy: 'his mood is too uniformly like that of a man driving a hearse'; Masson, *Carlyle Personally*, pp. 35, 17.

74 Henry E. Carlisle, ed., *A Selection from the Correspondence of Abraham Hayward QC, from 1834 to 1884*, 2 vols (1886), ii, p. 10. James Bowling Mozley, a Fellow of Magdalen College, Oxford and a member of the Oxford Movement, was highly critical of Carlyle's tone, of what he saw as his focus on power and the absence of any independent moral standard in his evaluation of Cromwell's career; 'Carlyle's Cromwell', *Christian Remembrancer*, 11 (April 1846), pp. 243–315.

75 [Abraham Hayward], 'Thomas Carlyle and his Reminiscences', *Quarterly Review*, 151 (1881), pp. 385–428. Anne Procter wrote to Hayward endorsing the views expressed in his letter and review. The widow of 'Barry Cornwall' was outraged by what she regarded as patronising and unkind comments on her late husband and father; see Carlisle, *A Selection*, ii, p. 318.

76 Francis Galton, *Memoirs of My Life* (1908), pp. 169–70; Arnold Haultain, ed., *A Selection from Godwin Smith's Correspondence* (n.d.), pp. 161–62.

77 Herbert Spencer, *An Autobiography*, 2 vols (New York, 1904), i, pp. 440–41. The reference to Spencer's reaction against his early endorsement of Carlyle's idea of renunciation relies upon Mark Francis's interpretation which will appear in his forthcoming study, *The Intelligent Philistine*.

78 Francis Darwin, ed., *The Life and Letters of Charles Darwin*, 3 vols (1887), i, pp. 77–78; F. R. Barton, ed., *Some New Letters of Edward Fitzgerald* (1923), p. 165; Helen Watt, *John Hunter: The Forgotten Tenant of Craigcrook* (Edinburgh, 1972), p. 50.

79 Thomas S. Baynes, 'An Evening with Carlyle', *Athenaeum*, 2 April 1887, pp. 449–50; William Knights, *Retrospects*, first series (1904), p. 2.

80 Henry Taylor, *Autobiography*, 2 vols (1885), i, p. 332.

81 Harriet Martineau, *Autobiography*, 3 vols (1877), i, p. 382; these remarks were written in 1857.

82 Charles Gavan Duffy, *Conversations with Carlyle* (1892), pp. 181, 50–51. Duffy was prepared to give Carlyle the benefit of the doubt but deeply resented Froude's hostile remarks on his countrymen: he thought the 'mimicking' of Carlyle's views by Froude was 'past human patience'; NLS, MS 1770, fol. 234, 22 March 1873.

83 T. Wemyss Reid, *Life of the Right Honourable William Edward Forster*, 2 vols (1888), i, pp. 207, 208–9, 211; these impressions were recorded in 1847. Ian Campbell's transcription of, and commentary on, passages in Monckton Milnes diaries convey a vivid impression of Carlyle's conversation; see Ian Campbell, 'Conversations with Carlyle: the Monkton Milnes' Diaries', *Prose Studies*, 8 (1985), pp. 48–57 and its sequel, 'More Conversations with Carlyle', *Prose Studies*, 9 (1986), pp. 22–29.

84 NLS, MS, 527, fol. 41, 10 February 1870.

85 *CL*, vi, pp. 400–1, 13 June 1833. Carlyle told Duffy that while Mill had a genius for clarity of expression, his narrowly logical approach prevented him from seeing many valuable things; Duffy, *Conversations with Carlyle*, p. 166. A later comment to Allingham that Mill had 'wasted away his soul' (Allingham, *Diary*, p. 239) implied that Carlyle thought he had had the capacity to see more but had not capitalised on it; Carlyle's ongoing respect for Mill suggests that he saw this as a tragic outcome of aspects of Mill's character, rather than a matter of honesty or application.

86 *Minutes of Evidence taken before the Commissioners to inquire into the Constitution and Management &c, of the British Museum, 8 February 1849*, pp. 284, 285.

87 Conway, *Autobiography*, p. 123; Carlyle, *Sterling*, p. 93, italics in original.

88 R. H. Shepard, ed., *Memoirs of the Life and Writings of Thomas Carlyle*, 2 vols (1881), i, p. 170

89 See Charles Richard Sanders, 'Carlyle and Leigh Hunt', in Charles Richard Sanders, *Carlyle's Friendships and Other Studies* (Durham, North Carolina, 1977), pp. 151–60.

90 [John Dix], *Lions: Living and Dead; or Personal Recollections of 'The Great and Gifted'* (1852), p. 193. James Grant also noted the earnestness of Carlyle's public speech; *Portraits of Public Characters*, 2 vols (1841), ii, p. 159. Although the inclusion of Carlyle in Grant's gallery says something of the notice he had gained by this time, the inaccuracies of his account must have been very irritating. Grant says that Carlyle was resident in Germany from his early years (p. 144), now lived in a small cottage in Brampton and enjoyed a private income (p. 161).

91 Martineau, *Autobiography*, i, p. 387.

92 Smith, *Autobiography*, p. 133.

93 Horne, *A New Spirit of the Age*, ii, pp. 256–57. The same point was made by the author of an unsigned review published in 1846. Carlyle had redeemed 'Germans, and the admirers of the German mind from the coarse stigmas which had for too long been affixed to their names'; 'Thomas Carlyle', *Albion*, 23 (23 May 1846), p. 246.

94 Sir Henry Jones and John Henry Muirhead, *The Life and Philosophy of Edward Caird* (Glasgow, 1921), p. 23.

95 Alexander Ross, *Memoirs of Alexander J. Ross* (1888), p. 7; admiration was not mutual. Carlyle and his wife met Ross in the mid 1850s and disliked him heartily; see *CL*, xxx, p. 234 n.

96 See Altick, *The English Common Reader*, p. 243; NLS, MS 527, fol. 39, 21 January 1871, fol. 49, 15 May 1871; NLS, Acc. 9775, 14 December 1872.

97 K. J. Fielding, 'Carlyle and the Americans: "Eighteen Million Bores"', *CSA*, 15 (1995), pp. 61–62; Allingham, *Diary*, p. 230; NLS, MS 527, fol. 89, 22 March 1873.

98 Francis Espinasse, *Literary Recollections and Sketches* (1893), p. 57.

99 Smith, *Autobiography*, pp. 66–67.

100 Alfred Francison, *Natural Lessons from the Life and Work of Carlyle* (1886), pp. 15, 20.

101 NLS, MS 1773, fos.178–79, 1 August 1847; NLS, MS 1771, fol. 163, 10 December 1874. In illustrating Carlyle's importance for the upcoming generation, the first of these correspondents enclosed a printed copy of an extract from *Sartor* that had been produced on a hand press by his daughters, one of a series of 'striking passages' that they printed for private circulation.

102 NLS, MS 1773, fol. 240v, undated; MS 1773, fol. 78, 13 June 1879.

103 See Barton, 'John Tyndall, Pantheist', passim.

104 NLS, MS 1773, James Dunn to Thomas Carlyle, undated, fol. 240v; Dunn was a friend of John Sterling; MS 1773, Thomas Moore to Thomas Carlyle, fos. 78–80, 13 June 1879.

105 See Peter Bayne, *Lessons from My Masters, Carlyle, Tennyson, and Ruskin* (1879), p. 23 and Robert Steele Coffey, *Thomas Carlyle and Some of the Lessons of His Career* (Bradford, 1881), p. 15.

106 'Thomas Carlyle' *Albion*, 23 (1846), p. 246; 'Thomas Carlyle and His Critics', *Eclectic Review*, 114, (1861), p. 31.

107 See Turner, 'Victorian Scientific Naturalism', p. 141.

108 'Religious Faith and Modern Scepticism', *Westminster and Foreign Quarterly Review*, 52, no. 11 (1850), p. 397.

109 Morley, *Recollections*, i, pp. 16.

110 This account relies heavily on Kathleen Tillotson's brilliant Warton Lecture on English Poetry for 1956: 'Matthew Arnold and Carlyle', *Proceedings of the British Academy*, 92 (1956), pp. 133–54.

111 G. W. Russell, ed., *The Letters of Matthew Arnold, 1848–1888*, 2 vols (1901), ii, p. 222.

112 These themes may be seen in *Culture and Anarchy* and in some of Arnold's late essays, including 'The Nadir of Liberalism' (1886), 'The Zenith of Conservatism' (1887) and 'The Incompatibles' (1887).

113 NLS, MS 1771, fol. 159, 3 December 1874.

114 Henry Rose, *The New Political Economy: The Social Teaching of Thomas Carlyle, John Ruskin and Henry George* (1891), p. 70.

115 George Birbeck Hill, *Letters of Dante Gabriel Rossetti to William Allingham, 1854–1870* (1897), p. 190, 18 December 1856. For a study of the Town Hall murals see Julie F. Codell, 'Ford Madox Brown, Carlyle, Macaulay, Bakhtin: The Pratfalls and Penultimates of History', *Art History*, 21 (1998), pp. 324–66.

116 For examples drawn from the rural working classes see Barry Reay, *Rural Englands* (2004), pp. 132–33.

117 Smith, *Autobiography*, p. 133.

118 [John Sterling] 'Carlyle's Works; *Sartor Resartus*', pp. 8–9, 58–59; David Masson, *Edinburgh Sketches*, pp. 297–99.

119 [Julia Wedgwood], 'A Study of Carlyle', *Contemporary Review*, 39 (1881), p. 595.

120 Morley, 'Carlyle', p. 180. As was the case with other contemporaries, Morley's high regard for some of Carlyle's leading ideas went hand in hand with the sharp rejection of others, including his worship of great men.

121 See D. A. Hamer, *John Morley: Liberal Intellectual in Politics* (Oxford, 1968), pp. 88–89.

122 F. H. Bradley, 'Utility as (1) an End or (2) Standard of Morality' (c1867–69), *Collected Works of F. H. Bradley*, 12 vols, edited by W. L. Mander and Carol A. Keene (Bristol, 1999), i, p. 56. I am grateful to Professor Keene for bringing this reference to my attention. In Bradley's later philosophy this realm was identified with 'the Absolute'.

123 Altick, *The English Common Reader*, pp. 181–82. Unfortunately, the commissioners did not press the witness, H. L. Warner, on which of Carlyle's works appealed to his school fellows.

124 T. H. Green, *Lectures on the Principles of Political Obligation and Other Writings*, ed. Paul Harris and John Morrow (Cambridge, 1986), pp. 213, 89–106, 194–212.

125 Edward Caird, *Essays on Literature and Philosophy* (Glasgow, 1892), pp. 24–41, 264, 266.

126 *SR*, p. 135; *Wilhelm Meister*, ii, p. 133; Bosanquet quoted this phrase in the preface to the first edition of his major political work, *The Philosophical Theory of the State* (1899), p. xi.

127 See John Morrow 'Community and Class in Bosanquet's New State', *History of Political Thought*, 21 (2000), pp. 485–99.

128 See above pp. 21, 244–14.

129 NLS, MS 1770, fol. 127, February 1872; NLS, MS 1773, fos. 278–81 (1873?). In a pamphlet published in 1875 Leighton characterised outdoor relief as a mechanical response to destitution and looked instead to prevent it by '*enforcing provident habits*'; Sir Baldwyn Leighton, Bart., *Depauperisation: Being a Letter Addressed to Lord Lyttelton* (1875), p. 16. In February 1880 C. S. Loch, a founding member and long-time Secretary of the COS, wrote Carlyle a letter of warm appreciation: 'I am more indebted to you than to any other person for showing me the truth of life and what the test of right and wrong should be'; NLS, MS 1773, fol. 139, 8 February 1880.

130 See Edward Norman, *The Victorian Christian Socialists* (Cambridge, 1987), pp. 11, 42, and Charles E. Raven *Christian Socialism, 1848–1854* (1920), pp. 53–54.

131 Rose, *The New Political Economy*, pp. 37, 45–64.

132 Ibid., pp. 15, 21.

133 W. Howard Paul Campbell, *The Robbery of the Poor* (1884); see Peter d' A. Jones, *The Christian Socialist Revival, 1877–1914* (Princeton, 1968), p. 313.

134 Kelvin, *The Collected Letters of William Morris*, ii, pp. 14, 121.

135 See Fenner Brockway, *Socialism over Sixty Years: The Life of Jowett of Bradford, 1864–1944* (1946), pp. 28–30.

136 Edmund Stonelake, *The Autobiography of Edmund Stonelake*, ed. Anthony Mor-O'Brien (Glamorgan, 1981), pp. 57–58.

137 Robert Blatchford, *My Eighty Years* (1931), p. 169; Robert Blatchford, *My Favourite Books* (n.d.), p. 127.

138 Robert Blatchford, *The Nunquam Papers* (1895), pp. 148–52.

139 Jonathan Mendilow, 'Carlyle, Marx and the ILP: Alternative Routes to Socialism', *Polity*, 17 (1984), pp. 244–46.

140 *Thomas Carlyle: A Brief Account of his Life and Writings* (1902), pp. 35–36. This pamphlet, published by Chapman and Hall, lists the various editions of Carlyle's works available from that house. It gives the impression of being a promotional exercise, in which case the author might be expected to have access to accurate sales figures for Carlyle's writings.

Bibliography

Unless indicated otherwise the place of publication is London.

WORKS BY THOMAS CARLYLE

Carlyle's Latter-Day Pamphlets, ed. M. K. Goldberg and J. P. Seigel (Ottawa, 1983).

Collected Letters of Thomas and Jane Welsh Carlyle, ed. Charles Richard Sanders, et. al., 31 vols (Durham, North Carolina, 1970–2004).

'Death of Charles Buller', in Percy Newberry, ed., *Rescued Essays of Thomas Carlyle* (1892).

Historical Sketches of Notable Persons and Events in the Reigns of James I and Charles I, ed., Alexander Carlyle (1902).

'Ireland and the British Chief Governor', *Spectator*, 13 May 1848.

'Irish Regiments (of the New Era)', *Spectator*, 13 May 1848.

'Legislation for Ireland', *Examiner*, 13 May 1848.

Lectures on the History of Literature, second edition (1892).

'Louis-Philippe', *Examiner*, 4 March 1848.

'Notes of a Three-Day's Tour to the Netherlands, August 1842, I and II, *Cornhill Magazine*, new series, 53 (1922), pp. 493–512, 626–40.

On Heroes, Hero-worship, and the Heroic in History, ed. Joel Brattan, Mark Engel and Michael Goldberg (Berkeley, California, 1993).

On Trades Unions, Promoterism and the Signs of the Times, in D. J. Trela, 'Thomas Carlyle On Trades Unions, Promoterism and the Signs of the Times: An Unknown and Nearly Unpublished Manuscript', *Victorian Institute Journal*, 25 (1997), pp. 230–50.

Reminiscences, ed. K. J. Fielding and Ian Campbell (Oxford, 1997).

Reminiscences of My Irish Journey in 1849 (1882).

Sartor Resartus: The Life and Opinions of Herr Teufelsdröckh in Three Books, ed. Mark Engel and Rodger L. Tarr (Berkeley, California, 2000).

Selected Essays of Thomas Carlyle, ed. A. Seth-Pringle-Pattison (1909).

The Correspondence of Thomas Carlyle and John Ruskin, ed. George Allan Cate (Stanford, California, 1982).

The Letters of Thomas Carlyle to his Brother Alexander with Related Family Letters, ed. Edwin W. Marrs, Jr. (Cambridge, Massachusetts, 1968).

'Trees of Liberty', *The Nation*, 1 December, 1848.

Two Notebooks of Thomas Carlyle, ed. Charles E. Norton (1898).

Two Reminiscences of Thomas Carlyle, ed. John Clubbe (Durham, North Carolina, 1974).

Works of Thomas Carlyle, half crown edition, 20 vols (1893–94).

OTHER PRIMARY WORKS

'African Coast Blockade', *Westminster and Foreign Quarterly Review*, 52 (1850), pp. 500–41.

Arnold, Thomas, *Miscellaneous Works of Thomas Arnold DD* (1845).

Barker, Joseph, *The People: Their Rights and Liberties, Their Duties and Their Interests*, second series (1851).

Baxter, Richard, *A Christian Directory, or Body of Practical Divinity* (1673).

Blatchford, Robert, *The Nunquam Papers* (1895).

Bosanquet, Bernard, *The Philosophical Theory of the State* (1899).

Bradley, F. H., *Collected Works of F. H. Bradley*, 12 vols, ed. W. L. Mander and Carol A. Keene (Bristol, 1999).

Bray, Francis, *Labour's Wrongs and Labour's Remedies: or The Age of Might and the Age of Right* (1839).

Cain, Peter, ed., *Empire and Imperialism: The Debate of the 1870s* (Bristol, 1999).

Caird, Edward, *Essays on Literature and Philosophy* (Glasgow, 1892).

Campbell, W. Howard Paul, *The Robbery of the Poor* (1884).

Carlyle, Jane Welsh, *The Simple Story of My Own First Love*, ed. K. J. Fielding, Ian Campbell and Aileen Christianson (Edinburgh, 2001).

[Chadwick, Edwin], 'The New Poor Law', *Edinburgh Review*, 63 (1836), pp. 487–537.

Coleridge, Samuel Taylor, *Lay Sermons*, ed. R. J. White, *Collected Works of Samuel Taylor Coleridge* (Princeton, 1972).

——, *Table Talk*, ed. Carl Woodring, *Collected Works of Samuel Taylor Coleridge*, 2 vols (Princeton, 1990).

'Colonisation – The Only Cure for National Distress – Mr Buller's Speech', *Fraser's Magazine*, 27 (1843), pp. 735–50.

Command 11: Report from the Select Committee on Loans to Foreign States; House of Commons, 29 July 1875.

Cooper, Thomas, *The Chartist, the Purgatory of Suicides: A Prison–Rhyme* (1845).

[Croker, J. W.], 'Conduct of Ministers: Sketches of Popular Tumults, Illustrative of the Evils of Social Ignorance', *Quarterly Review*, 65 (December 1839), pp. 283–314.

Emerson, Ralph Waldo, *English Traits* (Boston, 1856).

Engels, Frederick, 'The Condition of England: *Past and Present* by Thomas Carlyle'(1844), Karl Marx and Frederick Engels, *Collected Works* (1975), 3, pp. 444–68.

'Extinction of Slavery', *Westminster and Foreign Quarterly Review*, 52 (1848–49), pp. 202–205.

[Forster, W. H.], 'American Slavery and Emancipation by the Free States', *Westminster Review*, new series, 3 (1853), pp. 125–67.

Gilfillan, George, *Galleries of Literary Portraits*, 2 vols (Edinburgh, 1856–57).

Green, T. H., *Lectures on the Principles of Political Obligation and Other Writings*, ed. Paul Harris and John Morrow (Cambridge, 1986).

[Hannay, James], *Blackwood v. Carlyle: A Vindication. By a Carlylian* (1850).

[Helps, Arthur], *The Claims of Labour: An Essay on the Duties of the Employers to the Employed* (1844).

——, *Life and Labours of Mr Brassey* (1872).

Jocelin of Brakelond, *Chronicle of the Abbey of St. Edmunds*, trans. Diana Greenway and Jane Sayers (Oxford, 1989).

Leighton, Sir Baldwyn, Bart, *Pauperisation: Being a Letter Addressed to Lord Lyttelton* (1875).

Lively, Jack and Rees, J. C., eds. *Utilitarian Logic and Politics: James Mill's 'Essay on Government', Macaulay's Critique and the Ensuing Debate* (Oxford, 1978).

Macaulay, Lord, 'Samuel Johnson' (1831), *Reviews and Essays from "The Edinburgh"* (n.d.), pp. 206–38.

Mill, John Stuart, *Essays on Economics and Society*, ed. Lord Robbins and J. M. Robson, *Collected Works of John Stuart Mill* (Toronto, 1967–1991).

——, *Journals and Debating Speeches*, ed. J. M. Robson, *Collected Works of John Stuart Mill* (Toronto, 1967–1991).

——, *On Liberty, Essays on Politics and Society*, ed. J. M. Robson and Alexander Brady, *Collected Works of John Stuart Mill* (Toronto, 1967–1991).

——, *Principles of Political Economy: With Some of their Applications to Social Philosophy*, ed. V. W. Bladen and J. M. Robson, *Collected Works of John Stuart Mill*, 2 vols (Toronto, 1967–1991).

——, 'The Negro Question', *Fraser's Magazine*, 45 (1850), pp. 25–31.

Minutes of Evidence taken before the Commissioners to inquire into the Constitution and Management &c, of the British Museum, 8 February 1849.

Morrow, John, ed., *Young England: The New Generation* (1999).

'Mr Edward Lytton Bulwer's Novels', *Fraser's Magazine*, 1 (June 1830), pp. 509–32.

Novalis, 'Christianity and Europe: A Fragment', in Frederick Beiser, ed. and trans., *The Early Political Writings of the German Romantics* (Cambridge, 1996), pp. 59–80.

'Our West Indian Colonies', *Blackwood's Edinburgh Magazine*, 63 (1848), pp. 219–38.

Parker, C. S. ed., *Sir Robert Peel from his Private Papers*, 3 vols (1899).

'Present Condition of the People', *Fraser's Magazine*, 9 (January 1834), pp. 72–87.

'Revolt of the Workers', *Blackwood's Edinburgh Magazine*, 52 (1842), pp. 642–53.

'Results of Emancipation', *Eclectic Review*, new series, 23 (1848), pp. 197–220.

Rose, Henry, *The New Political Economy: The Social Teaching of Thomas Carlyle, John Ruskin and Henry George* (1891).

Schlegel, Friedrich, 'Essay on The Concept of Republicanism ...', in Frederick C. Beiser, ed. and trans., *The Early Political Writings of the German Romantics* (Cambridge, 1996), pp. 93–112.

Sismondi, J. C. L. S., *Nouveaux Principles d'Économie Politque* (1819), second edition, 2 vols (Paris, 1827).

——, *Political Economy* (1824, rpr. New York, 1966).

'The Anti-Slavery Society', *Fraser's Magazine*, 1 (October 1830), pp. 610–23.

'The Chartists and Universal Suffrage', *Blackwood's Edinburgh Magazine*, 46 (1839), pp. 289–303.

'The Colonist *versus* the Anti-Slavery Society', *Fraser's Magazine*, 2 (October 1830), pp. 334–41.

'The Decline of Party Government', *Westminster and Foreign Quarterly Review*, new series, 8 (July 1855), pp. 125–50.

'The Jamaica Question', *Edinburgh Review*, 69 (1839), pp. 537–56.

'The West Indies: Results of Emancipation', *Eclectic Review*, new series, 9 (1841), pp. 471–85.

'Transactions of the London Statistical Society', *London and Westminster Review*, 29 (April 1838), pp. 45–72.

Wakefield, Edward Gibbon, *A Letter from Sydney, the Principal Town of Australasia* (1829).

——, *A View of the Art of Colonisation* (1849).

CONTEMPORARY COMMENTARIES, LETTERS, MEMOIRS AND REMINISCENCES

Additional Letters of John Stuart Mill, ed. Marion Filpiuk, Michael Laine and J. M. Robson, *Collected Works of John Stuart Mill* (Toronto, 1962–1991).

Allingham, William, *Diary*, with an introduction by Geoffrey Grigson (1907 repr. Fontwell, 1967).

'An Estimate of Mr Carlyle's Character', *St James Gazette* (1881).

Argyll, Dowager Duchess of, *George Douglas, Eighth Duke of Argyll: Autobiography and Memoirs*, 2 vols (1906).

Ballantyne, Thomas, *Selected Passages from the Writings of Thomas Carlyle with a Biographical Memoir* (London, 1855).

Blatchford, Robert, *My Eighty Years* (1931).

Barton, F. R., ed., *Some New Letters of Edward Fitzgerald* (1923).

Bayne, Peter, *Lessons from My Masters: Carlyle, Tennyson, and Ruskin* (1879).

Baynes, Thomas, S., 'An Evening with Carlyle', *Athenaeum*, 2 April (1887), pp. 449–450.

Brockway, Fenner, *Socialism Over Sixty Years: The Life of Jowett of Bradford, 1864–1944* (1946).

Brookfield, Charles and Frances, *Mrs Brookfield and Her Circle*, 2 vols (1905).

Carlisle, Henry E., ed., *A Selection from the Correspondence of Abraham Hayward QC, from 1834 to 1884*, 2 vols (1886).

'Carlyle and Neuberg', *Macmillan's Magazine*, 50 (1884), pp. 280–97.

Coffey, Robert Steele, *Thomas Carlyle and Some of the Lessons of His Career* (Bradford, 1881).

Conway, Moncure D., *Autobiography*, 2 vols (1904).

——, *Thomas Carlyle* (New York, 1881).

Darwin, Frances, ed., *The Life and Letters of Charles Darwin*, 3 vols (1887).

[Dix, John], *Lions: Living and Dead; or, Personal Recollections of 'The Great and the Gifted'* (1852).

Duffy, Charles Gavan, *Conversations with Carlyle* (1892).

Earlier Letters of John Stuart Mill, Francis E. Mineka, ed., *Collected Works of John Stuart Mill* (Toronto, 1962–1991).

Espinasse, Francis, *Literary Recollections and Sketches* (London, 1893).

Eve, A. S. and Cressey, C. H., *Life and Work of John Tyndall* (1945).

Francison, Alfred, *Natural Lessons from the Life and Work of Carlyle* (1886).

Froude, James Anthony, *Thomas Carlyle: A History of the First Forty Years of His Life, 1795–1835*, new edition, 2 vols (1896).

——, *Thomas Carlyle: A History of His Life in London, 1834–1881*, new edition, 2 vols (1897).

Galton, Francis, *Memoirs of My Life* (1908).

Grant, James, *Portraits of Public Characters*, 2 vols (1841).

Harrison, Frederic, ed., *Carlyle and the London Library: Accounts of Its Foundation, Together with Unpublished Letters of Thomas Carlyle to W. D. Christie, CB* (1907).

Haultain, Arnold, ed., *A Selection from Godwin Smith's Correspondence* (n.d.).

Helps, E. A., ed., *The Correspondence of Sir Arthur Helps, KCB, DCL* (1917).

Hill, George Birbeck, *Letters of Dante Gabriel Rossetti to William Allingham, 1854–1870* (1897).

Hodge, David, *Thomas Carlyle: The Man and the Teacher* (Edinburgh and Glasgow, 1873).

Holyoake, George Jacob, *Sixty Years of an Agitator's Life*, third edition, 2 vols (1893).

Horner, R. H., ed., *A New Spirit of the Age*, 2 vols (1844).

Japp, Alexander, H., *Three Great Teachers of Our Own Time: Being An Attempt to Deduce the Spirit and Purpose Animating Carlyle, Tennyson and Ruskin* (1865).

Jones, Sir Henry and Muirhead, J. H., *The Life and Philosophy of Edward Caird* (Glasgow, 1921).

Kelvin, Norman, ed., *The Collected Letters of William Morris*, 2 vols (Princeton, 1984–87).

Knighton, William, 'Conversations with Carlyle', *Contemporary Review*, 39 (1881), pp. 904–20.

Knights, William, *Retrospects*, first series (1904).

Lang, Andrew, *The Life and Letters of John Gibson Lockhart*, 2 vols (1897).

Larkin, Henry, *Carlyle and the Open Secret of His Life* (1886).

Lovett, William, *The Life and Struggle of William Lovett* (1875).

Lowe, James Russell, *My Study Windows* (1887).

Martin, Frederick, 'Thomas Carlyle: An Autobiography', *Biographical Magazine* i, (1887), pp. 1–22.

Martineau, Harriet, *Autobiography* (1877).

Masson, David, *Edinburgh Sketches and Memories* (1893).

——, *Carlyle Personally and in His Writing: Two Edinburgh Lectures* (1885).

Maitland, F. W., *The Life and Letters of Leslie Stephen* (1906, repr. Bristol, 1991).

Morley, Viscount John, *Recollections*, 2 vols (1918).

Mulhauser, Frederick L. ed, *The Correspondence of Arthur Hugh Clough*, 2 vols (Oxford, 1957).

Murray, Thomas, *Autobiographical Notes: Also Reminiscences of a Journey to London in 1840*, ed. J. A. Fairley (Dumfries, 1911).

Ratcliffe, Barrie M. and Chaloner, W. H., eds. and trans., *A French Sociologist Looks at Britain: Gustave d'Eichthal and British Society in 1828* (Manchester, 1977).

Reid, Wemyss, T., *Life of the Right Honourable William Edward Forster*, 2 vols, (1888).

Robberds, J. W., ed., *A Memoir of the Life and Writings of the Late William Taylor of Norwich*, 2 vols (1843).

Ross, Alexander, *Memoirs of Alexander J. Ross* (1888).

Russell, G. W., ed. *The Letters of Matthew Arnold, 1848–1888*, 2 vols (1901).

Sadler, Thomas, *Diary, Reminiscences, and Correspondence of Henry Crabb Robinson*, 3 vols (1868).

Shepard, R. H., *Memoirs of the Life and Writings of Thomas Carlyle*, 2 vols (1881).

Smith, Mary, *The Autobiography of Mary Smith, School Mistress and Nonconformist* (1892).

Spencer, Herbert, *An Autobiography*, 2 vols (New York, 1904).

Stirling J. H., *Thomas Carlyle's Counsels to a Literary Aspirant* (Edinburgh, 1886).

Strachley, Edward, 'Some Letters and Conversations of Thomas Carlyle', *Atlantic Monthly*, 73 (June 1894), pp. 822–34.

Stonelake, Edmund, *The Autobiography of Edmund Stonelake*, ed. Anthony Mor-O'Brien (Glamorgan, 1981).

Surtees, Virgina, ed., *The Diary of Ford Maddox Brown* (New Haven, Connecticut, 1981).

Taylor, Henry, *Autobiography*, 2 vols (1885).

Twistelton, Mrs Edward, *Letters of the Hon. Mrs Edward Twistelton, Written to Her Family, 1853–56* (1928).

Tyndall, John, *New Fragments* (1892).

Symington, Andrew James, *Some Personal Reminiscences of Carlyle* (Paisley, 1886).

The Life of Thomas Carlyle (1881).

Thomas Carlyle: A Brief Account of his Life and Writings (1902).

[Wright, Elizur], *Perforations in the Latter-Day Pamphlets by one of the 'Eighteen Millions of Bores'* (Boston, 1850).

Wright, William Aldis, *Letters and Literary Remains of Edward Fitzgerald*, 3 vols (1889).

Wylie, William Howe, *Thomas Carlyle: The Man and His Books*, second edition (1909).

CONTEMPORARY REVIEWS

'A Pilgrimage to Utopia; or, The Autobiography of a Visionary I', *Eclectic Review*, new series, 27 (1850), pp. 358–62.

'A Pilgrimage to Utopia; or, The Autobiography of a Visionary 2', *Eclectic Review*, new series, 27 (1850), pp. 470–77.

[Bain, Alexander], 'Cromwell's Letters and Speeches', *Westminster Review*, 46 (1847), pp. 432–473.

'Carlyle Against Downing Street', *Leader*, 30 March 1850, pp. 14–15.

'Carlyle: Mirage Philosophy', *Blackwood's Edinburgh Magazine*, 85 (1859), pp. 127–54.

'Carlyle's Cromwell', *Dublin University Magazine*, 27 (1846), pp. 228–45.

'Carlyle's Frederick the Great', *Blackwood's Edinburgh Magazine*, 98 (1865), pp. 38–56.

'Carlyle's Latter-Day Pamphlets', *Atheneum*, 2 February 1850, pp. 126–27, 2
     March 1850, pp. 227–28, 6 July 1850, pp. 704–705, 24 August 1850,
     pp. 894–95.
'Carlyle's Latter-Day Pamphlets', *Chambers' Edinburgh Journal*, new series, 14
     (July 1850), pp. 147–54.
'Carlyle's Letters and Speeches of Oliver Cromwell', *Metropolitan Magazine*, 46
     (April 1846), pp. 293–311.
'Carlyle's Oliver Cromwell', *Knight's Penny Magazine*, 15 (1846), pp. 81–96.
'Carlyle's Works', *Dublin Review*, 29 (1850), pp. 169–206.
'Carlylism', *Rambler*, 1 (1850), pp. 354–66.
'Charles Dickens and David Copperfield', *Fraser's Magazine*, 42 (1850),
     pp. 707–10.
'Chartism', *Monthly Chronicle*, 5 (February 1840), pp. 97–107.
'Chartism and the Labouring Classes', *Christian Examiner*, 29 (1840),
     pp. 110–24.
'Cromwell', *Blackwood's Edinburgh Magazine*, 61(1847), pp. 393–423.
Harrison, Frederic, 'Carlyle's Place in Literature', *Forum*, 17 (1894), pp. 537–50.
——, 'Froude's Life of Carlyle' (1885), Frederic Harrison, *The Choice of Books
     and Other Literary Pieces* (1899), pp. 175–202.
[Hayward, Abraham], 'Thomas Carlyle and his Reminiscences', *Quarterly
     Review*, 151 (1881), pp. 385–428.
'History of Frederick the II', *British Quarterly Review*, 29 (1859), pp. 238–82.
'History of Frederick the Great', *North British Review*, 43 (1865), pp. 79–126.
'History of Frederick the Second' *Athenaeum*, 18 September 1859, pp. 351–54.
'History of Frederick the Second', *Athenaeum*, 25 September 1865, pp. 388–90.
[Jewsbury, Geraldine], 'Religious Faith and Modern Skepticism', *Westminster
     and Foreign Quarterly Review*, 52 (1850), pp. 379–402.
'Latter-Day Pamphlets', *The Critic*, new series, 9 (1850), pp. 96–97.
'Latter-Day Pamphlet No. II', *The Critic*, new series, 9 (1850), p. 145.
'Latter-Day Pamphlets', *Eclectic Review*, new series, 28 (1850), pp. 385–409.
'Latter-Day Pamphlets', *English Review*, 16 October 1851, pp. 331–51.
'Latter-Day Pamphlets', *The Examiner*, 2 February, 1850, pp. 68–69; 2 March
     1850, pp. 132–34; 29 June, 1850, pp. 404–6.
'Latter-Day Pamphlets', *Prospective Review*, 6 (1850), pp. 212–29.
MacFarlane, Helen, 'Democracy: Remarks on the Times, Apropos of Certain
     Passages in no. 1 of Thomas Carlyle's Latter-Day Pamphlets', *Democratic
     Review of British and Foreign Politics, History & Literature*, April 1850, pp.
     423–25, May 1850, pp. 449–53.
[Merivale, Herman], 'Carlyle on the French Revolution', *Edinburgh Review*, 71
     (1840), pp. 411–45.
Morley, John, 'Carlyle', *Critical Miscellanies*, 3 vols (1886), i, pp. 135–201.

[Mozley, James Bowling] 'Carlyle's Cromwell', *The Christian Remembrancer*, 11 (1846), pp. 243–315.

'Mr Carlyle', *Fraser's Magazine*, 72 (1865), pp. 778–810.

'Mr. Carlyle's Oliver Cromwell's Letters and Speeches', *Tait's Edinburgh Magazine*, 13 (1846), pp. 38–50.

'Oliver Cromwell's Letters and Speeches', *Athenaeum*, nos. 945–7 (1845), pp. 1165–67, 1193–95, 1218–19.

'Oliver Cromwell's Letters and Speeches', *The Examiner*, 13 December 1845, pp. 787–89.

'Oliver Cromwell's Letters and Speeches', *The Critic*, new series, 2 (1845), pp. 653–56, 694–95.

'Oliver Cromwell's Letters and Speeches', *The Examiner*, 13 December 1845, pp. 787–89.

'Oliver Cromwell's Letters and Speeches', *Shilling Magazine*, 3 (1846), pp. 182–84.

'Oliver Cromwell's Letters and Speeches', *Prospective Review*, 11 (1846), pp. 119–58.

'Oliver Cromwell – Puritanism', *Christian Examiner*, 40 (1846), pp. 440–59.

'Oliver Cromwell Vindicated by Thomas Carlyle', *Chamber's Edinburgh Journal*, new series, 5 (1846), pp. 8–11, 23–26, 131–33.

'Past and Present, by Carlyle', *Blackwood's Edinburgh Magazine*, 54 (1843), pp. 121–38.

'Politics and Faith', *National Review*, 12 (1861), pp. 432–57.

'Sartor Resartus', *Christian Examiner*, 21 (1836), pp. 74–84.

Seigel, Jules Paul, ed., *Thomas Carlyle: The Critical Heritage* (1971).

[Smith, W. H.], 'Past and Present by Carlyle', *Blackwood's Edinburgh Magazine* (1843), pp. 121–38.

[Sterling, J. H.], 'Carlyle's Works', *The London and Westminster Review*, 33 (1839), pp. 1–68.

[Sewell, William], 'Carlyle's Works', *Quarterly Review*, 66 (1840), pp. 446–503.

'The Curse of Party', *Spectator*, 11 January 1840, pp. 35–36.

'The Topic of Topics', *Spectator*, 4 January 1840, pp. 6–10.

'The Works of Thomas Carlyle', *British and Foreign Review*, 16 (1844), pp. 262–93.

'Thomas Carlyle', *Albion*, 23 (1846), pp. 246–48.

'Thomas Carlyle and His Critics', *Eclectic Review*, 114 (1861), pp. 25–57.

'Thomas Carlyle on Modern Sociology', *Eclectic Review*, 114 (1861), pp. 316–51.

'Thomas Carlyle – *Letters and Speeches of Oliver Cromwell*', *North British Review*, 4 (1846), pp. 505–36.

[Venables, George S.], '*Chartism,* by Thomas Carlyle', *British and Foreign Quarterly,* 12 (1841), pp. 303–35.

[Wedgwood, Julia], 'A Study of Carlyle', *Contemporary Review,* 39 (1881), pp. 584–609.

SECONDARY WORKS

BOOKS

Adelman, Paul, *Peel and the Tory Party* (1989).

Altick, Richard D., *The English Common Reader: A Social History of the Mass Reading Public, 1800–1900* (Chicago, 1957).

Anderson, Olive, *A Liberal State at War* (1967).

Arnold, A. J. and McCartney, S., *George Hudson: The Rise and Fall of the Railway King* (2004).

Ashton, Rosemary, *The German Idea: Four English Writers and the Reception of German Thought, 1800–1860* (Cambridge, 1980).

——, *Thomas and Jane Welsh Carlyle: Portrait of a Marriage* (2002).

Beck, Herman, *The Origins of the Authoritarian Welfare State in Prussia* (Anne Arbor, Michigan, 1995).

Ben-Israel, Hedva, *English Historians on the French Revolution* (Cambridge, 1968).

Boham, Edmund, *To Be a Hero: Sir George Grey, 1812–1898* (Auckland, 1998).

Bodelsen, C. A., *Studies in Victorian Imperialism* (1924; repr. 1960).

Bolt, Christine, *Victorian Attitudes to Race* (1971).

Bossche, Chris Vandem, *Carlyle and the Search for Authority* (Columbus, Ohio, 1991).

Boyle, Nicholas, *Goethe: The Poet and His Age,* 2 vols (Oxford, 1999, 2000).

Brookes, Gerry H., *The Rhetorical Form of Carlyle's Sartor Resartus* (Berkeley, California, 1972).

Brown, Richard and Daniels, Christopher, eds., *The Chartists* (1984).

Calder, Grace, J., *The Writing of Past and Present: A Study of Carlyle's Manuscripts* (New Haven, 1949).

Campbell, Ian, *Carlyle and Europe: Some Early Contacts* (Edinburgh, 1977).

——, *Thomas Carlyle,* second edition (Edinburgh, 1993).

Chandler, James, *England in 1819: The Politics of Literary Culture and the Case of Romantic Historicism* (Chicago, 1998).

Claeys, Gregory, *Citizens and Saints: Politics and Anti-politics in Early British Socialism* (Cambridge, 1989).

Clarke, J. C. D., *English Society, 1660–1832* (Cambridge, 1985).

Cronin, Richard, *Romantic Victorians: English Literature, 1824–1840* (Basingstoke, 2002).

Cullen, Michael, *The Statistical Movement in Early Victorian Britain: The Foundations of Empirical Social Research* (Hassocks, 1975).

Culler, Dwight A., *The Victorian Mirror of History* (New Haven, Connecticut, 1985).

Curtis, L. Perry Jr., *Apes and Angels: The Irishman in Victorian Caricature*, revised edition (Washington, 1997).

Daiches, David, *Carlyle and the Victorian Dilemma* (Edinburgh, 1963).

Davis, J. C., *Oliver Cromwell* (2001).

Drescher, Seymour, *From Slavery to Freedom: Comparative Studies in the Rise and Fall of Atlantic Slavery* (New York, 1999).

Eldridge, C. C., *England's Mission: The Imperial Idea in the Age of Gladstone and Disraeli* (Chapel Hill, North Carolina 1973).

Elfenbein, Andrew, *Byron and the Victorians* (Cambridge, 1995).

Evans, D., *Social Romanticism in France, 1830–1848* (Oxford, 1951).

Field, Peter S., *Ralph Waldo Emerson: The Making of a Democratic Intellectual* (Lanham, Maryland, 2002).

Flinn, Michael, et al., *Scottish Population History: From 1700 to the 1930s* (Cambridge, 1977).

Fontana, Biancamaria, *Rethinking the Politics of Commercial Society: The Edinburgh Review, 1802–1832* (Cambridge, 1985).

Francis, Mark and Morrow, John, *A History of English Political Thought in the Nineteenth Century* (1994).

Gallagher, Catharine, *The Industrial Reformation of English Fiction, 1832–1867* (Chicago, 1985).

Gash, Norman, *Sir Robert Peel* (1972).

Hall, Catherine, *Civilising Subjects: Metropole and Colony in the English Imagination, 1830–1867* (Cambridge, 2002).

Hamer, D. A., *John Morley: Liberal Intellectual in Politics* (Oxford, 1968).

Harding Christopher et al., *Imprisonment in England and Wales: A Concise History* (Beckenham, 1978).

Heffer, Simon, *Moral Desparado: A Life of Thomas Carlyle* (1996).

Holt, Thomas C., *The Problem of Freedom: Race, Labor, and Politics in Jamaica and Britain, 1832–1932* (Baltimore, 1992).

Howe, Anthony, *The Cotton Masters, 1830–1860* (Oxford, 1984).

Jann, Rosemary, *The Art and Science of Victorian History* (Columbus, Ohio, 1985).

Jessop, Ralph, *Carlyle and Scottish Thought* (1997).

Kaplan, Fred, *Thomas Carlyle* (Ithaca, New York, 1977).

Knott, John, *Popular Opposition to the 1834 Poor Law* (1986).

Lang, Timothy, *The Victorians and the Stuart Heritage: Interpretations of a Discordant Past* (Cambridge, 1995).

Lawes, Kim, *Paternalism and Politics: The Revival of Paternalism in Early Nineteenth-century Britain* (Basingstoke, 2000).

Lees, Lynn Hollen, *The Solidarities of Strangers: The English Poor Law and the People, 1700–1848* (Cambridge, 1998).

Lepp, Robert Keith, *Contest for Cultural Authority: Hazlitt, Coleridge and the Distresses of the Regency* (Detroit, 1999).

Levin, Michael, *The Condition of England Question: Carlyle, Mill, Engels* (1998).

——, *The Spectre of Democracy: The Rise of Modern Democracy as Seen by its Critics* (New York, 1992).

Lewis, Brian, *The Middlemost and the Milltowns: Bourgeois Culture and Politics in Early Industrial England* (Stanford, 2001).

Lorimer, Douglas A., *Colour, Class and the Victorians: English Attitudes to the Negro in the Mid-Nineteenth Century* (1978).

Machin, G. I. T., *The Catholic Question in English Politics* (Oxford, 1964).

Meisel, Joseph S., *Public Speech and the Culture of Public Life in the Age of Gladstone* (New York, 2001).

Mill, Anna, *Carlyle and Mill: Two Edinburgh Rectors* (Edinburgh, 1968).

Milne, James, *The Romance of a Pro-Consul: Being the Personal Life and Memoirs of the Right Honourable Sir George Grey, KCB* (1899).

Mitchell, Leslie, *Bulwer Lytton: The Rise and Fall of a Victorian Man of Letters* (2003).

Nesbit, George, L., *Benthamite Reviewing: The First Twelve Years of The Westminster Review, 1824–1836* (New York, 1934).

Norman, E. R., *The Victorian Christian Socialists* (Cambridge, 1987).

——, *Church and Society in England* (Oxford, 1976).

Palmegiano, E. M., *The British Empire in the Victorian Press, 1832–1867* (New York, 1987).

Pratt, John, *Punishment and Civilization* (2003).

Quesne Le, A. L., *Carlyle* (Oxford, 1982).

Reynolds, K. D., *Aristocratic Women and Political Society in Victorian Britain* (Oxford, 1998).

Richards, Thomas, *The Commodity Culture of Victorian England: Advertising and Spectacle, 1851–1914* (Stanford, California, 1990).

Rosenberg, John D., *Carlyle and the Burden of History* (Oxford, 1985).

Rosenberg, Philip, *The Seventh Hero: Thomas Carlyle and the Theory of Radical Activism* (Cambridge, Massachusetts, 1974).

Schoyen, A. R., *The Chartist: A Portrait of George Julian Harney* (1958).

Searle, G. R., *Morality and the Market in Victorian Britain* (Oxford, 1998).

Semmel, Bernard, *The Rise of Free Trade Imperialism: Classical Political Economy, the Empire of Free Trade and Imperialism* (Cambridge, 1970).

Sloan, J. M., *The Carlyle Country with a Study of Carlyle's Life* (1904).

Storey, Mark, *Robert Southey: A Life* (Oxford, 1997).

Taylor, Miles, *Ernest Jones, Chartism and the Romance of Politics, 1819–1869* (Oxford, 2003).

Tennyson, G. B., *Carlyle and the Modern World* (Edinburgh, 1971).

——, *Sartor Called Resartus: The Genesis, Structure and Style of Thomas Carlyle's First Major Work* (Princeton, 1965).

Thompson, Noel, *The People's Science: The Popular Political Economy of Exploitation and Crisis, 1816–1834* (Cambridge, 1984).

Thrall, Miriam, M. H., *Rebellious Fraser's: Nol Yorke's Magazine in the Days of Maginn, Thackeray and Carlyle* (New York, 1934).

Todd, Robert, J. N., *Caroline Fox: Quaker Blue-Stocking, 1819–1871* (York, 1980).

Trela, D. J. *A History of Carlyle's Oliver Cromwell's Letters and Speeches* (New York, 1992).

Ulrich, John, *Signs of Their Times: History, Labor, and the Body in Cobbett, Carlyle, and Disraeli* (Athens, Ohio, 2002).

Watt, Helen, *John Hunter: The Forgotten Tenant of Craigcrook* (Edinburgh, 1972).

Webb, R. K., *Harriet Martineau: A Victorian Radical* (1965).

Wiley, Basil, *Nineteenth-Century Studies* (1949).

Winch, Donald, *Riches and Poverty: An Intellectual History of Political Economy in Britain, 1750–1834* (Cambridge, 1996).

Worden, Blair, *Roundhead Reputations: The English Civil Wars and the Passions of Posterity* (2001).

ARTICLES AND CHAPTERS

Abbot, W.C., 'The Fame of Cromwell', *Yale Review*, new series, 2 (1913), pp. 315–49.

Adams, James Eli, 'The Hero as Spectacle: Carlyle and the Persistence of Dandyism', in Carol T. Christ and John O. Jordon eds., *Victorian Literature and the Victorian Visual Imagination* (Berkeley, California, 1995), pp. 213–32.

Amigoni, David, 'Displacing the Autobiographical Impulse: A Bakhtinian Reading of Thomas Carlyle's Reminiscences', in Vincent Newey and Philip Shaw, eds., *Mortal Pages, Literary Lives: Studies in Nineteenth-Century Autobiography* (Aldershot, 1996), pp. 120-39.

ApRoberts, Ruth, 'A Latter-Day French Carlylean', *CSA*, 16 (1996), pp. 109–116.

Baker, Lee, C. R., 'The Old Clothesman Transformed: Thomas Carlyle's Radical Vision', *Victorian Institute Journal*, 11 (1982–3), pp. 45–60.

——, 'The Open Secret of *Sartor Resartus*: Carlyle's Method of Converting his Readers', *Studies in Philology*, 83 (1986), pp. 218–35.

Barton, Ruth, ' John Tyndall, Pantheist: A Rereading of the Belfast Address',
    Osirisi, second series, 3 (1987), pp. 111–34.
Baumgarten, Murray, 'In the Margins: Carlyle's markings and annotations in
    his gift copy of Mill's *Principles of Political Economy*', in *Carlyle: Books and
    Margins* (Santa Cruz, California, 1980), pp. 66–106.
Beavis, Matthew, 'Volumes of Noise', *Victorian Literature and Culture*, 23
    (2003), pp. 577–91.
Block, Edward, Jr., 'Carlyle, Lockhart and the Germanic Connection: The
    Periodical Context of Carlyle's Early Criticism', *Victorian Periodicals Review*,
    16 (1983), pp. 20–27.
Cain, P. J., 'Economics: The Metropolitan Context', in *The Oxford History of
    the British Empire*, iii, *The Nineteenth Century*, ed., Andrew Porter (Oxford,
    1999), pp. 31–52.
Campbell, Ian, 'Carlyle and the Negro Question Again', *Criticism*, 13 (1971),
    pp. 279–90.
——, 'Carlyle in the 1830s', *Notes and Queries*, new series, 21 (1974),
    pp. 336–39.
——, 'Carlyle's Religion: The Scottish Background', in John Clubbe, ed.,
    Carlyle and his Contemporaries: Essays in Honour of Charles Richard Sanders
    (Durham, North Carolina, 1976), pp. 3–20.
——, 'Carlyle: Sage of Chelsea or Sage of Echelfechan', in Horst W. Drescher
    ed., *Thomas Carlyle 1981* (Frankfurt am Main, 1983), p. 385–403.
——, 'Carlyle: Sense and Style', *CSA*, 14 (1994), pp. 13–24.
——, 'Conversations with Carlyle: The Monckton Milnes Diaries', *Prose
    Studies*, 8 (1985), pp. 48–57.
——, 'More Conversations with Carlyle: The Monckton Milnes Diaries: Part 2',
    Prose Studies, 9 (1986), pp. 22–29.
Childers, Joseph, W., 'Carlyle's *Past and Present*, History and a Question of
    Hermeneutics', *Clio*, 13 (1984), pp. 247–58.
Christensen, Aileen, 'On the Writing of the Occasional Discourse on the Negro
    Question', *CN*, 2 (1980), pp. 13–21.
Clarke, Norma, 'Strenuous Idleness: Thomas Carlyle and the Man of Letters as
    Hero', in Michael Roper and John Tosh, eds., *Manful Assertions: Masculinities
    in Britain Since 1800* (1991), pp. 25–43.
Codell, Julie, F., 'Ford Maddox Brown, Carlyle, Macaulay, Bakhtin: The Pratfalls
    and Penultimates of History', *Art History*, 21 (1998), pp. 324–66.
Cotsell, Michael, 'Carlyle, Travel, and the Enlargements of History', in Michael
    Cotsell, ed., *English Literature and the Wider World: Volume 3, 1830–1876*
    (1990), pp. 83–97.
Cowlishaw, Brian, 'The Cultural Revolution of *Sartus Resartus*', *CSA*, 16 (1996),
    pp. 51–60.

Culviner, Thomas, 'Heroes and Hero-worship: Not So Simple in *The French Revolution*', *Victorian Institute Journal*, 13 (1985), pp. 83–96.

——, 'Thomas Carlyle and Sir Arthur Helps: II', *Bulletin of the John Rylands University Library*, 64 (1982) pp. 407–32.

Drescher, Seymour, 'Free Labor v. Slave Labor: The British and Caribbean Cases', in Stanley L. Engerman, ed., *Terms of Labor: Slavery, Serfdom, and Free Labor* (Stanford, California, 1999), pp. 50–86.

Fielding, K. J., 'Carlyle and the Americans: "Eighteen Million Boors"', *CSA*, 15 (1995), pp. 55–64.

——, 'Ireland, John Mitchel and his "Sarcastic Friend" Thomas Carlyle', in J. Schwend et al., eds. *Literatur im Kontext: Festscrift für Horst Drescher* (Frankfurt am Main, 1992), pp. 131–44.

——, 'Unpublished Manuscripts – 1: Carlyle Among the Cannibals', *CN*, 1 (1979), pp. 22–28.

——, 'Unpublished Manuscripts – II: Carlyle's Scenario for *Cromwell*', *CN*, 2 (1980), pp. 6–13.

Franke, Wolfgang, 'Carlyle and Edward Irving: The Intellectual Basis of their Friendship', in Hans Drescher, ed. *Thomas Carlyle 1981* (Frankfurt am Main, 1983), pp. 47–69.

Georgiana, Linda, 'Carlyle and Jocelin of Brakelond: A Chronicle Rechronicled', *Browning Institute Studies*, 8 (1980), pp. 103–27.

Gislain, Jean-Jacques, 'Sismondi and the Evolution of Economic Institutions', in Gilbert Faccarello, ed., *Studies in the History of French Political Thought* (1998), pp. 229–53.

Goldberg, David Theo, 'Liberalism's Limits: Carlyle and Mill on "The Negro Question"', *Nineteenth-Century Contexts*, 22 (2000), pp. 203–16.

Goldberg, Michael, 'Gigantic Philistines: Carlyle, Dickens, and the Visual Arts', in Jerry D. Adams and Rita B. Bottoms, eds., *Lectures on Carlyle and his Era* (Santa Cruz, California, 1985), pp. 17–43.

Goodheart, Eugene, 'English Social Criticism and the Spirit of Reformation', *Clio*, 5 (1975), pp. 73–96.

Hall, Catharine, 'Imperial Man: Edward Eyre in Australasia and the West Indies, 1833–66', in Bill Schwarz, ed., *The Expansion of England: Race Ethnicity and Cultural History* (1996), pp. 130–70.

Harding, Anthony, J., 'Sterling, Carlyle, and the German Higher Criticism: A Reassessment', *Victorian Studies*, 26 (1983), pp. 269–85.

Harper, Marjory, 'British Migration and the Peopling of Empire', in *The Oxford History of the British Empire*, iii, *The Nineteenth Century*, ed. Andrew Porter (Oxford, 1999), pp. 75–87.

Harris, Wendell V., 'Interpretive Historicism: "Signs of the Times" and *Culture and Anarchy* in Their Contexts', *Nineteenth-Century Literature*, 44 (1990), pp. 441–64.

Hilton, Boyd, 'Peel: A Reappraisal', *Historical Journal*, 22 (1979), pp. 585–614.

Hirsch, Gordon, 'History Writing in Carlyle's *Past and Present*', *Prose Studies*, 7 (1984), pp. 225–31.

Jackson, Leon, 'The Reader Retailored: Thomas Carlyle, his American Audiences, and the Politics of Evidence', *Book History*, 2 (1999), pp. 146–72.

Jann, Rosemary, 'The Condition of England Past and Present: Thomas Carlyle and the Middle Ages', *Studies in Medievalism*, 1 (1979), pp. 15–31.

Jeffers, Thomas, 'Forms of Misprision: The Early- and Mid-Victorian Reception of Goethe's *Bildungslidee*', *University of Toronto Quarterly*, 57 (1988), pp. 501–15.

Jessop, Ralph, 'Carlyle's Scotch Scepticism: Writing from the Scottish Tradition', *CSA*, 16 (1996), pp. 25–36.

——, ' Metaphor's Prodigious Influence: Carlyle's "Signs of the Times" and *Sartor Resartus*', *Scottish Literary Journal*, 24 (1997), pp. 46–58.

Jones, Gareth Steadman, 'The Language of Chartism', in James Epstein and Dorothy Thompson, eds., *The Chartist Experience: Studies in Working-Class Radicalism and Culture, 1830–1860* (1982), pp. 3–58.

Kaplan, Fred, '"Phallus-Worship" (1848): Unpublished Manuscripts III – A Response to the Revolution of 1848', *CN*, 2 (1980), pp. 19–23.

——, 'Power and Authority', in Jerry D. Adams and Rita B. Bottoms, eds., *Lectures on Carlyle and His Era* (Santa Cruz, California, 1985), pp. 1–15.

Kubicek, Robert, 'British Expansion, Empire, and Technological Change', in *The Oxford History of the British Empire*, iii, *The Nineteenth Century*, ed., Andrew Porter (Oxford, 1999), pp. 247–69.

La Vopa, Anthony, 'The Philosopher and the *Schwärmer*: On the Career of a German Epithet from Luther to Kant', in Lawrence E. Klein and Anthony J. La Vopa, eds., *Enthusiasm and Enlightenment in Europe, 1650–1850* (San Merino, California, 1998), pp. 85–115.

Lamb, John B., 'Carlyle's "Chartism," the Rhetoric of Revolution, and the Dream of Empire', *Victorian Institute Journal*, 23 (1995), pp. 129–150.

Levy, David M., '150 Years and Still Dismal', *Ideas on Liberty*, 50 (March 2000), pp. 1–8.

Lloyd, Tom, 'Society and Chaos: Schiller's Impact on Carlyle's Ideas About Revolution', *Clio*, 17 (1987), pp. 51–64.

Maertz, Gregory, 'Carlyle's Mediation of Goethe and its European Context', *Scottish Literary Journal*, 24 (1997), pp. 59–78.

Martin, Amy E., 'Blood Transfusions: Constructions of Irish Racial Differences, the English Working Class, and Revolutionary Possibility in the Work of Carlyle and Engels', *Victorian Literature and Culture*, 24 (2004), pp. 83–102.

Mendilow, Jonathan, 'Carlyle, Marx and the ILP: Alternative Routes to Socialism", *Polity*, 17 (1984), pp. 225–47.

Morrow, John, 'Community and Class in Bosanquet's New State', *History of Political Thought*, 21 (2000), pp. 485–499.

——, 'Heroes and Constitutionalists: The Ideological Significance of Thomas Carlyle's Treatment of the English Revolution', *History of Political Thought*, 14 (1993), pp. 205–223.

——, 'Introduction', William Godwin, *History of the Commonwealth of England: From Its Commencement to the Restoration of Charles the Second* (1824–28, repr. Bristol, 2003), i, pp. v–xxxiv.

——, 'The Paradox of Peel As Carlylean Hero', *Historical Journal*, 40 (1997), pp. 97–110.

Newbold, D. C., 'Sir Robert Peel and the Conservative Party', *English Historical Review*, 158 (1983), pp. 529–57.

Nixon, Jude V., 'Radicalism and the Politics of Emancipation in Carlyle's "Occasional Discourse on the Nigger Question"', *CSA*, 16 (1996), pp. 89–108.

Park, Peter T., 'Thomas Carlyle and the Jews', *Journal of European Studies*, 20 (1990), pp. 1–21.

Plotz, John, 'Crowd Power: "Chartism", Carlyle and the Victorian Public Sphere', *Representations*, 20 (2000), pp. 87–114.

Porter, Andrew, 'Trusteeship, Anti-Slavery and Humanitarianism', in *The Oxford History of the British Empire*, iii, *The Nineteenth Century*, Andrew Porter, ed., (Oxford, 1999), pp. 198–221

Poston, Lawrence, 'Millites and Millenarians: The Context of Carlyle's "Signs of the Times"', *Victorian Studies*, 26 (1983), pp. 381–406.

Reed, John R., 'A Friend of Mammon: Speculation in Victorian Fiction', *Victorian Studies*, 27 (1994), pp. 179–202.

Richardson, Thomas C., 'Carlyle's *Chartism* and the *Quarterly Review*', *CSA*, 10 (1989), pp. 50–55.

——, 'John Murray's Reader of *Sartor Resartus*', *CN*, 6 (1985), pp. 38–41.

Rigney, Anne, 'The Untenanted Places of the Past: Thomas Carlyle and the Varieties of Historical Ignorance', *History and Theory*, 35 (1996), pp. 338–57.

Roberts, David, 'How Cruel was the Victorian Poor Law?' *Historical Journal*, 6 (1963), pp. 97–107.

Romani, Roberto, 'British Views on Irish National Character, 1800–1846', *History of European Ideas*, 23 (1997), pp. 193–219.

Ryals, de L Clyde, 'Carlyle and the Law', *CSA*, 14 (1994), pp. 25–32.

——, 'Thomas Carlyle and the Mormons: An Unpublished Essay', *CSA*, 15 (1995), pp. 49–54.

Sanders, Charles Richard, 'Carlyle and Leigh Hunt', in Charles Richard Sanders, *Carlyle's Friendships and Other Studies* (Durham, North Carolina, 1977), pp. 151–60.

Seigel, Jules Paul, 'Carlyle and Peel: The Prophet's Search for a Heroic Politician and an Unpublished Fragment', *Victorian Studies*, 26 (1983), pp. 181–95.

Schor, Hilary, M., 'The Stupidest Novel in London: Thomas Carlyle and the Sickness of Victorian Fiction', *CSA*, 16 (1996), pp. 117–132.

Sorensen, David, R., 'Selective Affinities: Carlyle, Goethe, and the French Revolution', *CSA*, 16 (1996), pp. 61–74.

Sowell, Thomas, 'Sismondi: A Neglected Pioneer', *History of Political Economy*, 1 (1968), pp. 62–88.

Swift, Roger, 'Thomas Carlyle, *Chartism*, and the Irish in Early Victorian England', *Victorian Literature and Culture*, 21 (2001), pp. 67–83.

Taylor, Miles, '*Imperium et Libertas?* Rethinking the Radical Critique of Imperialism during the Nineteenth Century', *Journal of Imperial and Commonwealth History*, 19 (1991), pp. 1–23.

Tennyson, G.B., 'The Editor Editing, The Reviewer Reviewing', *CSA*, 14 (1994), pp. 43–54.

Thompson, Dorothy, 'Ireland and the Irish in English Radicalism before 1850', in James Epstein and D. Thompson, eds., *The Chartist Experience: Studies in Working Class Radicalism and Culture, 1830–1860* (1982), pp. 120–49.

Thompson, E. P. 'Mayhew and the *Morning Chronicle*', in E. P. Thompson and Eileen Yeo, eds., *The Unknown Mayhew: Selections from the* Morning Chronicle (1971), pp. 11–50.

Tillotson, Kathleen, 'Matthew Arnold and Carlyle', *Proceedings of the British Academy*, 42 (1956), pp. 133–54.

Timko, Michael, 'Gods of the Lower World: Romantic Egoists and Carlylean Heroes', *Browning Institute Studies*, 14 (1986), pp. 125–40.

——, 'Thomas Carlyle: Chaotic Man, Inarticulate Hero', *CSA*, 14 (1994), pp. 55–68.

Trela, D. J., 'Carlyle, Bulwer, and the *New Monthly Magazine*', *Victorian Periodicals Review*, 22 (1989), pp. 157–62.

——, 'Carlyle and the Periodical Press: Unused Manuscripts for the Revision of *Shooting Niagara: And After?*' *Studies in Scottish Literature*, 27 (1992), pp. 167–74.

——, 'Carlyle's *Shooting Niagara*: The Writing and Revising of an Article and Pamphlet', *Victorian Periodicals Review*, 25 (1992), pp. 3–34.

——, 'A New (old) Review of Mill's *Liberty*: A Note on Carlyle and Mill's Friendship', *CN*, 6 (1984), pp. 23–27.

——, 'The Writing of "An Election to the Long Parliament": Carlyle, Primary Research and the Book Clubs', *CSA*, 14 (1994), pp. 71–82.

Turner, Frank, M., 'Victorian Scientific Naturalism and Thomas Carlyle' in Frank M. Turner, *Contesting Cultural Authority: Essays in Victorian Intellectual Life* (Cambridge, 1993), pp. 131–150.

Ulrich, John, '"A Labor of Death and a Labor Against Death": Translating the Corpse of History in Carlyle's *Past and Present*', *CSA*, 15 (1995), pp. 33–48.

——, 'The Re-inscription of Labor in Carlyle's *Past and Present*', *Criticism*, 37 (1995), pp. 443–68.

Waterman, A. M. C., 'The Ideological Alliance of Political Economy and Christian Theology', *Journal of Ecclesiastical History*, 34 (1983), pp. 231–44.

Workman, Gillian, 'Thomas Carlyle and the Governor Eyre Controversy: An Account with Some New Material', *Victorian Studies*, 18 (1974–75), pp. 77–102.

Index